NEVER ENOUGH

The Story of The Cure

NEVER ENOUGH

The Story of The Cure

Jeff Apter

OMNIBUS PRESS

London • New York • Paris • Sydney • Copenhagen • Berlin • Madrid • Tokyo

Exclusive Distributors
Music Sales Limited,
14-15 Berners Street,
London W1T 3LJ, UK.

Music Sales Corporation,
257 Park Avenue South,
New York, NY 10010, USA.

Macmillan Distribution Services,
53 Park West Drive,
Derrimut, Vic 3030,
Australia.

To the Music Trade only
Music Sales Limited,
14-15 Berners Street,
London W1T 3LJ, UK.

Every effort has been made to trace the copyright holders of the photographs in this book but one or two were unreachable. We would be grateful if the photographers concerned would contact us.

Cover photograph by Kevin Estrada/Retna
Typeset by Galleon Photosetting, Ipswich.
Printed in the United States of America.
A catalog record for this book is available from the British Library.

Visit Omnibus Press on the web at www.omnibuspress.com

For my brimful of Asha

Contents

Prologue

Los Angeles Forum
July 27, 1986

Jonathan Moreland did not belong here. Surrounded by teens and 20-somethings, their faces painted ghostly white, their lipstick applied haphazardly in a cosmetic tribute to Robert Smith, their new Anglo pop hero, Moreland – decked out in cowboy boots and matching hat – was a living, breathing anachronism. It seemed as though he'd taken a wrong turn at Nashville and never quite found his way back home. The Cure definitely didn't seem like his kind of band.

But music was the last thing on Moreland's mind as he shouldered his way through the crowd, finding his seat inside the LA Forum, which was filled to its 18,000 capacity. The Forum definitely wasn't a Jonathan Moreland kind of place, either. A hideous beige in colour and shaped like an upturned bowl, this venue had played host to most of the world's biggest rock'n'roll acts, especially in the heady Seventies. You could see such stars as Led Zeppelin, Neil Young, The Faces and The Rolling Stones, often for less than 10 bucks, with a contact high guaranteed as part of the admission price – the pot smoke that hung in the air was almost thick enough to carve. ("If you're from LA," one knowledgeable local informed me about the Forum, "it's part of your rock'n'roll heritage.") It was also a venue where shows generated a huge amount of bootlegs in the pre-download world – they usually came with the guarantee: "Bore 'Em in the Forum".

Rock'n'roll history, however, wasn't on Jonathan Moreland's mind as he found his seat. He was in an even darker mood than some of The Cure's funereal dirges. Rejected by a woman called Andrea, whom he thought was the love of his life, he'd arrived at the last date of the current Cure tour, their final US show for almost 12 months, with one goal: to make a lasting impression. To (literally) drive home his point, he'd managed to smuggle a seven-inch hunting knife past the venue's security guards. While The Cure's hairdryers cooled backstage, and the band added a final flourish to their industrial strength hair gel and make-up, Moreland reached for his knife as the house lights dimmed.

The Cure may have threatened to implode almost every day of the past eight years, but 1986 had actually been a very good year. The signs were all positive: the British quintet, led by Robert Smith, mope pop's very own Charlie Chaplin, had finally settled on a line-up that didn't feel the need to throttle each other after each show. That wasn't the case four years earlier, during the seemingly endless tour in support of their fourth album, the terminally bleak *Pornography*. During those shows, Smith and bassist Simon Gallup had even turned on the faithful, sometimes jumping headfirst into the crowd to silence those who'd made clear their objections to The Cure's new musical direction (and obsessions). Strange days, indeed.

But it was now 1986 and Smith seemed as content as his contrite, restless nature would allow. He'd even eased up on his boozing, while his Olympian drug-taking had now been modified to more acceptable recreational standards. At its peak, he and buddy Steve Severin, of Siouxsie & The Banshees, had once recorded an indulgence piece called *Blue Sunshine* while gobbling acid tabs as if they were boiled lollies. Then they'd retire to Severin's London flat for all-night binges, while taking in his seemingly endless stash of gory horror videos. This became known as Smith's "chemical vacation". Around the same time, Smith was also working on new Cure material and a new Banshees album, which, not surprisingly, led to the worst of his many emotionally unstable periods. But that was now in Smith's past.

And having worked their way through several US labels, in a seemingly futile effort to replicate their slowly building UK success, it seemed as though The Cure's fourth and latest American home, Elektra, actually had the band's best interests at heart. Robert Smith, like so many others before and after him, had learned early on that music is a business where losing control (both creative and commercial) can be disastrous. He'd allowed the artwork of their debut album, 1979's *Three Imaginary Boys*, to represent the trio as a lampshade, a refrigerator and a vacuum cleaner and had been living it down ever since. But even before then, when the then Easy Cure was signed by German label Ariola/Hansa in 1977 (when the trio were still teenagers), they'd been instructed to record an assortment of rock chestnuts and greatest hits, rather than their own material, which led to one of the quickest terminations of contract this side of a Britney Spears marriage vow. Robert Smith truly had learned by experience. Now their first best-of collection, *Standing On A Beach: The Singles*, was on the fast track to US chart success. And MTV had taken to the eccentric Tim Pope-directed clip for 'Inbetween Days', which featured dancing fluoro socks, like some long-lost sibling.

Their biggest-ever Stateside tour had opened three weeks earlier, when the good ship Cure docked at the Great Woods Center for the Performing Arts in Mansfield, Massachusetts. OK, it wasn't Madison Square Garden, but the cult of The Cure – which would soon reach frantic, sometimes frightening levels of adoration – was clearly building. Fans rushed the stage when the band appeared, even trying to work their way past security for a personal audience with Smith, their new pop idol. This concert – and those that followed – wasn't so much a rock show as a gathering, a fact that wasn't lost on the *Maiden Evening News*. The local rag observed the serious devotion that Cure lovers felt towards their object of desire, noting how "teenie-bopper girls dressed in black and white with punky hairdos risked their lives trying to get past a group of gruff security monsters to give Smith a kiss".

Over the ensuing weeks, such high-profile rags as *Rolling Stone* turned their spotlight on The Cure and, in particular, their seductively odd frontman. Smith was christened "the male Kate Bush", "the thinking teen's pin-up", "the security blanket of the bedsit set" – even "a dark version of Boy George" – while The Cure caravan rolled on through New York, Philadelphia, Detroit, Chicago, Dallas and San Francisco, playing to increasingly larger and ever more fervent crowds. It wasn't Beatlemania, sure, but it was a clear sign that The Cure were destined for bigger things than their stop-start success so far suggested. Hell, they might even make it home without beating the stuffing out of each other.

By the night of July 27, as the band (and bandwagon) rolled into Los Angeles for their farewell headliner at the Forum, Smith – who'd just hacked off most of his trademark bird's-nest of hair, simply for shock value – was warming to both the tour and his bandmates. This was a significant development for a man who'd threatened to kill off The Cure virtually every time they took a forward step. In fact, he'd almost brought his contrary plan to fruition in 1982. After the punishing, depressing *Pornography* tour, he'd shelved the band for months and hidden away in his bedroom at his parents' home in Crawley, Sussex. He'd then turned his back on The Cure, defecting to the Banshees camp, craving the near-anonymity of being just another guy in the band, rather than life as the creative force and focal point of The Cure.

Smith had to be persuaded back to Cureworld by long-time manager Chris Parry, and even then only under the proviso that he could release the seemingly throwaway 'Let's Go To Bed'. It was a song that was actually designed by Smith to either kill off the band forever or at least alienate every young mopeful who'd likened The Cure's gloomy moodscapes to those of Joy Division and the doomed Ian Curtis. Much to Smith's bewilderment, the very unCure-like 'Let's Go To Bed' became an accidental hit, while its sequel, the equally disposable – at least to Smith's ears – 'The Lovecats', went even larger, becoming their biggest UK single. What was a confused 23-year-old Robert Smith to do? When he realised that The Cure were the band that refused to die, he chose simply to let it be. Now here he was in America receiving the full star treatment.

Cure co-founder (and occasional whipping boy) Laurence "Lol" Tolhurst took the time to sum up neatly the buoyant mood inside Camp Cure. "I think this is The Cure that you'll see until it stops being The Cure," he told a reporter. "I can't see anybody else coming into the band. It's really always been a band made up of friends more than anything else. But I don't think we have any friends left who can play anything." Robert Smith agreed. He told the *Aquarian Weekly* that this version of The Cure was built to last – maybe. "Unless something really drastic happens on the American tour, like if someone flips out completely, I know that this line-up will make the next record." Smith didn't realise the tragic prescience of his comments.

Back inside the LA Forum, The Cure's crew checked their watches, as Smith prepared to lead the 1986 version of the band – Smith, old friends Tolhurst, Simon Gallup and Porl Thompson, plus the recently recruited Boris Williams – out of the backstage darkness and onto the stage. It was then that Jonathan Moreland made his move, at the exact moment when the crowd's Cure-fever was almost tangible. Leaping out of his seat, Moreland removed his hunting knife and began to stab himself furiously in the chest and stomach, splattering blood over anyone unfortunate enough to be seated near him. Just before the onset of shock, or the realisation of just how deep and dangerous his wounds were, Moreland stood on his chair, stripped off his shirt and continued to plunge the blade into his tattooed chest. The crowd around him were both bloody and confused. Thinking that this must be part of the performance of a band renowned for their obsession with dark music and even darker themes, some of the crowd cheered Moreland on as his blood loss increased to a dangerous level. But when police and security enveloped Moreland, the truth sank in: this was no act, this was a real suicide attempt. As word leaked backstage of Moreland's grisly self-mutilation, Robert Smith started to wonder whether The Cure was cursed: for every bit of forward momentum, there was another bizarre incident, or walkout, or breakdown.

Perry Bamonte, then Cure roadie and later a member of the band, was on stage when the stabbing took place. "I saw the commotion," he told me in 2005, "and heard screaming and the crowd clearing as the guy jumped onto his seat and began plunging a knife into his gut. It was surreal and disturbing. [Then] a cop fired a tazer [stun gun] at him and he went down."

Stunned, the local police sergeant, Norman Brewer, spoke with Moreland as he was being hauled away to an ambulance. Moreland had told him that The Cure faithful encouraged him in his bloodlust. "As the crowd grew louder," Brewer stated, "he stabbed himself deeper and harder." As he was rushed to hospital, the critically injured Moreland moaned a confession. "I did it because I won't ever be able to have the woman I love." He died soon after.

Somehow, the show went on and The Cure reached the end of both their set and the tour. But Smith's uncharacteristically upbeat mood had soured considerably. By the time they returned to London, a spokesman for Fiction Records – the label headed by Chris Parry, a man who'd taken a chance in 1978 on a four-track Easy Cure cassette that had been lobbed into his postbox – issued a statement. "They could not believe anyone would do that at one of their gigs," the statement read. "It was a bitter ending for them because it happened on the last night of what has been a successful US tour."

But the Forum disaster was yet another bump in the road for The Cure. Even by 1986, their career had run an incredibly haphazard course – sometimes caused by the band, other times by forces outside of their control – ever since Smith and Tolhurst had started fumbling with guitar and drums at the Notre Dame Middle School in 1972. For every high such as 'Boys Don't Cry' or a headlining show, there was another spate of band infighting, a new Smith meltdown or a sacking – or something as perverse as Moreland's suicide. For the erstwhile Three Imaginary Boys, it was a reminder of how unpredictable – and sometimes downright dangerous – the pop life could be.

Chapter One

"Crawley is grey and uninspiring with an undercurrent of violence. It's like a pimple on the side of Croydon."

– Robert Smith

IT may be located halfway between London – 35 miles away to the north – and Brighton on the south coast, but Crawley is hardly the kind of town where the seeds of musical revolution are grown. According to one writer, Crawley was "the doormat you wipe your feet on before leaving the countryside for London". When the Smith family relocated there from Blackpool in 1966, the clubs of London – such as The Marquee, where in the mid-Sixties The Who promised (and delivered) "Maximum R&B", and The Bag O'Nails, where Jimi Hendrix began his supernova rise – might as well have been located on another planet. It was not very likely that you'd see Carnaby Street's dedicated followers of fashion strolling like peacocks up and down the High Street. Mind you, in the late 20th century, Crawley would house some unusual residents, including Robin Goodridge, the drummer for Nirvana clones Bush, and Adam Carr, a man whose claim to fame was being voted Homosexual Author of the Year by *The Gay Times* (twice, no less).

But in the main, middle-class Crawley in Sussex was sensible, solid and unchanging. As Robert Smith once observed of his home, some 30-odd years and 30 million record sales since he and band co-founder Laurence "Lol" Tolhurst first exchanged glances on a school bus on the way to primary school in 1964: "Crawley is grey and uninspiring with an undercurrent of violence. It's right on the edge of a green belt, next to Gatwick Airport. It's a dreadful place. There's nothing there. My dad work[ed] for Upjohns pharmaceutical company. He had to move down to Sussex for his job. They're based in Croydon. All my school-ing took place around Crawley. It's like a pimple on the side of Croydon."

Driving Smith's point home just that little bit further, a recent examination of all things Crawley noted: "There is loads to do in Crawley provided you only want to get drunk or fit, both at considerable expense." Today, at least 14 pubs line the High Street, which keep well-known tippler Robert Smith pleasantly occupied on the occasions when he returns from his home in Bognor to check in on his parents, Alex and Rita, who still call Crawley home.

Mind you, Crawley was a town with a plan. It was officially designated a "New Town" on January 9, 1947, not long after the end of the Second World War, with a design capacity built into the planned infrastructure for 50,000 residents. (Today, around 85,000 live in Crawley.) During its post-war growth spurt, the small local villages of Ifield to the west, Worth to the east, Pease Pottage to the south and Lowfield Heath to the north were gradually engulfed by this "New Town". It was expanding quickly.

As characterless as this town of offices and engineering firms appears, the recorded history of this "New Town" – though hardly the stuff of famous battles or daring discovery – does date back over 1,000 years. In fact, the first development in the area is thought to have occurred as far back in time as 500 BC. Some 400 years later, the first simple furnaces began to be used in the area. The roots of a long-held tradition in the Sussex area were thus sown, as documented by the name of one of Crawley's neighbourhoods, the rhapsodically titled Furnace Green. By AD 100, those utilitarian Romans had settled in the area and begun to extend and improve the furnaces. By the ninth century, Worth Church was erected; it's now situated in the west of the New Town area and is thought to be one of the oldest buildings of its kind in the UK. It's believed that the fleeing armies of King Harold may have taken refuge there, after being defeated at Hastings in 1066. But in keeping with the area's uninspiring history, they were just passing through on their way elsewhere.

And so the relatively mundane development of the town (and this travelogue) progressed through the ages. Twenty years after King Harold took that fateful arrow in his eye at Hastings, the Doomsday Records failed to mention the hamlet (although nearby Ifield and Worth rated an entry, being valued by King William's recorders at a princely 20 shillings apiece). Then, in 1203, the Manor of Crawley was awarded a licence to hold a weekly market in the High Street; one Michael de Poyninges is recorded as having given King John a Norwegian goshawk there during the very same year. Less than 50 years later, the Church of St Margaret was established in Ifield; it still stands in the Ifield Village Conservation Area. It was only in 1316 that records first showed Crawley under its Saxon-derived current name. It was formerly known as Crawleah and Crauleia. And the etymology? "Craw" meaning "crow" and "leah" meaning pasture. Not so glamorous.

By 1450, the George Hotel was established in the High Street, offering stables and room for carriages to allow horsemen and their passengers an overnight stay on the way to somewhere more exciting. (Several centuries later, the George would be used by infamous Crawley local, John George Haigh, the so-called "Acid Bath Murderer", to pick up at least one of his victims.) Crawley was still very much a transit point, little more than a village in a forest clearing. The horse-drawn carriages, when not stopping overnight at the George Hotel, were charged a toll to travel along the road – the original Toll House once stood in the north of the town. Some of the old timber-framed coaching houses from the period can still be found in the High Street (albeit in a renovated state, occupied by thoroughly modern businesses).

The importance of iron works in the area increased dramatically during the 17th century, but it wasn't until the extension of the railway line from London to Brighton, in 1848, that some life was breathed into this town and the population duly increased. But for many, Crawley was still a name seen on a sign from the window of a passing train, as you hurtled towards London or rattled down to the coast at Brighton. The town's population did continue to increase, though, especially when nearby Gatwick Aerodrome was opened in 1938. During World War II, Crawley suffered some damage, much like any town of its size, when 24 homes were destroyed by aerial bombing. Once the rubble had been cleared and England started to regain its post-war bearings, MP Lewis Silkin announced that the area around Crawley, Three Bridges and Ifield had been chosen as one of the afore-mentioned New Towns.

Fifteen years later, Robert Smith and his family – his father James Alexander Smith, mother Rita Mary (née Emmott) and siblings Richard, Margaret and baby Janet – moved from Smith's birthplace of Blackpool, Lancashire, to this green and uninspiring town. They settled first in Horley in December 1962, at a house in Vicarage Lane where their next-door neighbour was the grandmother of Robert's future Cure partner Lol Tolhurst (who at the time lived two streets away, in Southlands Avenue). They then shifted to Crawley in March 1966, so that Alex Smith could be closer to the base of his employer, Upjohns. By then, the population of the area was around 50,000, a rapid increase from the 9,000 who had lived there at the turn of the century. In the same year that the Smiths had come south, 1962, the additional neighbourhood of Furnace Green had been added to this so-called "New Town". It was a rich irony that Alex Smith worked for pharmaceutical firm Upjohns, given his son's Olympian drug consumption in the Eighties. Earlier, he'd served in the RAF, completing his training in Canada.

Born on April 21, 1959, Robert James Smith was the third Smith offspring, preceded by his sister Margaret, who was born on February 27, 1950, and his brother Richard, who was born on July 12, 1946. Smith's second sister, Janet, was born some 18 months after Robert, establishing a hefty gap in ages between the two elder and two younger Smith children. Smith insists that he was an unplanned child and that Janet was conceived primarily for his company. "My mum wasn't supposed to have me," he said in 1989. "That's why there's such a big age gap between us. And once they got me, they didn't like the idea of having an only child, so they had my sister. Which is great, because I would have hated not having a younger sister." Smith took full advantage of his new-found role as older brother, even discouraging Janet from speaking so he could act as interpreter. "I would say, 'Oh, she wants ice cream,' when in fact she was desperate to go to the toilet."

Speaking in 2000, Smith admits that while he only lived in the north for three years, it took him some time to shake off his Blackpool brogue, which led to the usual winding-up in the playground – sometimes worse. "I was born in Blackpool," he recalled, "and the first few years of my life were spent up there. When I came down south, I actually had a broad northern accent and the piss was taken out of me mercilessly at school. That probably didn't help me integrate."

In another, even earlier discussion of his childhood, Smith recalled that both his parents had held onto their northern intonation. "I used to have a northern accent because my mum and dad used to talk like that at home," he said. "It always stuck out at school, which I never realised at the time. I thought everyone was saying 'grass' incorrectly. But I toned it down on purpose when I got into my teens. By then I think it might have been a bit pretentious to have affected a northern accent."

Smith clung to some strong memories of his time in Blackpool, which he felt explained his lifelong attraction for the seaside. "I'm sure that spending the first few years of your life by the sea means that you harbour a great love for the sea," he once said. "Every time I have a holiday I always go to the sea." Smith and his wife Mary, the first and only true love of his life, now reside in Bognor, which fulfils his long-held dream of living by the water. Smith figures his seaside life is simply an extension of his very early childhood in coastal Blackpool. "I wanted to wake up and hear the sea," he admitted. "It's bound to my childhood, to pure happiness, to innocence. I love the music and the perfume of the sea."

Smith's recollections of Blackpool are so powerfully connected to the innocence of his childhood that he's since found it almost imposs-ible to return. He just doesn't want the illusion shattered. "I have such strong memories of it: the promenade, the beach, the smell, it's a magical memory, that evocative time of innocence and wonder. My earliest memories are sitting on the beach at Blackpool and I know if I went back, it would be horrible. I know what Blackpool's like – it's nothing like I imagined it as a child."

Smith's father Alex owned a Super-8 camera and even before the Smiths went south, he would film his family, especially baby Robert, fooling about on the beach. In a 2001 interview, Smith would reveal to Placebo singer (and major Cure fan) Brian Molko another of his earliest memories. "There are a lot of films where I can be seen running like a crazy man, with some donkeys in the background. I remember seeing my sister eat worms – and to be honest, I dug them up and she ate them. I was about three and she was two. And my mother punished me. It must be one of the few times I was hit. I also remember the smell of the donkeys."

Invention, myth-making and straight-out piss-taking on the part of Robert Smith – often due to the repetitive nature of endless interviews – has resulted in a particularly murky rendering of his pre-Cure life story. He has variously referred to there being a history of drunkenness in the Smith family, a trait he's done his best to uphold over the past 30 years. Smith has even partly blamed the up-all-night approach of his parents – who still occasionally tour with the band and are usually the last pair standing – for his well-documented fondness of a toxic lifestyle. He's often referred to an Uncle Robert (one of the inspirations for The Cure's 1989 hit, 'Lullaby'), who appeared to have all the dirty-old-man qualities of Uncle Ernie, so creepily portrayed by Keith Moon in Ken Russell's film *Tommy*.

Smith was raised in a staunchly Roman Catholic environment, which resulted in his questioning of God and existence in 1981's intensely dour *Faith* album. Smith insists that he and his mother once took a trek to the Vatican City, where he met the Pope: "Not the present one, about three Popes ago," he said. "I was in St Peter's and there was a Mass and he was carried in on a chair and I grabbed hold of his hand." As recently as 2003, he told a French television audience that being raised in a Catholic family "is a good recipe for being turned into furniture the rest of your life". However, Smith continued to attend Sunday services in the Friary, in Crawley, with his partner Mary, as late as 1980 and possibly beyond – only the blue ribbons in his spiked hair separating him from the other worshippers. (This, of course, he would deny, insisting that "the last time I was taken to church was when I was about eight".)

In keeping with their faith, Sunday was regarded as a special day in the Smith home and it's a tradition he has continued to maintain, more out of habit than devotion to all things Catholic. "The sense of Sunday being a special day, and the tradition of having the family around, has always remained with me," he said in 2004. But Smith's recollections of the Sundays of his youth are, he admits, "quite . . . dismal". "There was certain music on the radio, the same dinner, a huge argument between my brother, who was intensely communist, and my father, who had just been bumped up into the hierarchy [of the firm Upjohns] . . ."

The Smith household might have been lively but it wasn't violent: according to Smith, his father only once raised a hand in anger in his direction. "At the age of 12, I told my parents I wouldn't be having any kids," Smith revealed. "That was the only time my father slapped me." Interestingly, Smith has stuck to his 1971 vow of no children, despite having been married since 1988.

Generally, life at home for Robert Smith was as good if not better than most of his Crawley peers and pals. His parents were relatively lenient; his brother Richard (aka 'The Guru') smoked pot and his sisters loved rock'n'roll: what more could he want? "I was always treated as an equal by my family," Smith once said. "I had a really good family life. School almost seemed to be the opposite. I couldn't understand how the rigidity of school is designed to put you off reading and wanting to know anything. So I got very bitter in my teens."

Smith maintained this cynicism and uncertainty about life's real meaning, which has permeated much of the darker side of The Cure's music. Again, at times, he has indirectly blamed parts of his upbringing – especially his Catholic school education – for his questioning, restless nature. "I do not have faith in anything except for what I can see with my own eyes and lay my fingers on," he has said. "But I know that some people have a very strong faith and I envy them. In the back of my mind I would love to have such faith. But then I wonder if they aren't just fooling themselves?

"I got into quite a lot of trouble [at school] through wanting to change things. I was on this crusade. And I got frequently suspended [only once, actually], which I thought was ludicrous. I would always conduct my arguments in a very civilised manner and the recourse teachers saw was to put me on suspension."

At the age of 11, Smith had taken an entrance exam to a public boys' school, but threatened to run away from home if his parents forced him to attend. "My dad thought it would be good for my education, but my mum appreciated that I actually wanted to mix with girls. She thought that growing up in a house where I've got two sisters, it would be abnormal to suddenly send me to an all-male environment."

What is known of Smith and his pre-Cure obsessions – many being the typical domain of any middle-class English child growing up in the Sixties – would help explain many of his later musical and creative themes, hang-ups and obsessions.

As depicted so graphically by director Tim Pope in the band's 1989 video for 'Lullaby', spiders are not Robert Smith's favourite insects. They've been freaking him out since he was a child. "Spiders are one of the phobias I've not been able to overcome," he confessed years down the line. "When I was young, I was really scared of spiders – and they always used to be in my bed. They weren't actually there, but I imagined they were. Fat spiders with thin, long legs that look like they're going to burst make me go really weird."

Smith spent much of his childhood in a home that was "not exactly tastefully decorated". The house was adorned with what he would remember as "weird-patterned wallpaper and weird-patterned carpet that didn't match". Smith would stare intensely at these patterns, inducing an almost hallucinatory state of mind. "I'd always see faces coming out of the patterns," he once said, "like ghosts emerging from the carpet and wallpaper." A very young Smith would go to bed with a dim light nearby; as he tried to drift off to sleep, he'd imagine shapes and images. "Things would come out of the wall. Some of them were friendly shapes but sometimes I'd see a light at the corner of the ward-robe and I was sure there was something behind it. Except once. There was a funny-looking man in a mackintosh whispering in Polish. That might have been a dream, come to think of it."

In 1964, aged five, Smith's out-of-control imagination led him to believe that the family home had an unwelcome visitor who was visible only to him. He was convinced there was someone living in the house in a secret room. "I knew they were there, but I also knew I wouldn't be able to see them, even if I found the room. I'd hear creaking and think it was a person on the stairs. I'd rush out of the bedroom to catch them and there would be no one there. They were too fast for me."

Even before then, aged three in 1962, Smith's illusions of Santa Claus were forever shattered when he spotted Saint Nick rolling down the street on the back of a lorry. "I was crushed. There was no way Father Christmas would be sitting in that stupid fucking lorry. I never recovered from that." Smith, instead, would mark Christmas by watch-ing *Mary Poppins*, a tradition he maintained into adulthood. He would always be reduced to a blubbery mess by film's end. "I remember being taken to see it by my mum and I came out thinking it was completely real. I was thinking, 'Fucking hell, why haven't I met anyone like Mary Poppins? Why can't my mum slide up banisters?'" Smith's mother eventually had to break the news to him that it was a fantasy, which, Smith says, crushed him almost as much as the sight of Santa on a lorry.

Robert Smith immersed himself in the type of early heroes and hero-ines who were the stuff of standard childhood reading. His cartoon heroes included Dennis the Menace, "obviously a huge influence on me". Smith had been reading the *Beano* comics and books since he was three years old. (Even today, his mother continues to buy Smith *The Beano Book* every year.) The attraction of someone billed as "The World's Wildest Boy" obviously had an irresistible pull for someone like Smith with trouble in mind. He admitted to envying the Menace for having his pet cat Gnasher because, as a child, Smith was never fortunate enough to own a cat or dog "that was blindly devoted to me". Smith once attended a fancy-dress party as Dennis the Menace, decked out in a red- and black-striped jumper knitted by his mother Rita. "I found this cat on the way," he recalled, "and I walked in with the cat, pretending it was Gnasher.* Nobody believed me. In fact, everyone thought I was fucking stupid." Smith responded by throwing the cat out of a nearby window. The startled animal landed on its back, thereby ruining Smith's belief "that cats land on their feet all the time".

Such characters as Noddy were big favourites with a very young Robert Smith. Noddy "fuzzy-felts" hung above the head of his bed, alongside pictures of Catwoman and Queens Park Rangers' Stan Bowles.† "I sort of liked Noddy," Smith said. "He seemed to have a brilliant life. He would jump in his stupid red motorcar with his friend, Big Ears, and something weird would always happen. The ideal life, in a way," said Smith, a man also not averse to running away from his problems, especially in the early days of The Cure.

Andy Pandy was another of Smith's childhood pals. His favourite of the Andy Pandy stories was *Watch With Mother*. Smith was impressed that nothing could really go wrong in this vivid make-believe world. "Andy Pandy was always going to go to sleep in his basket with Teddy and the world was a happy place." While Smith thought Andy Pandy's companion Teddy to be "godlike", he wasn't so sure about rag doll Looby Loo. "She never did anything. Weird."

A more direct childhood influence on Smith's later songwriting, strange as it may seem, was Peter Pan, the kid who refused to grow up. Before Smith developed a serious thing for Betty Boop – "the perfect woman" – he was deeply enamoured of the fairy Tinker Bell. "I kept wishing Tinker Bell would come alive and rescue me," he said. But more importantly, Smith was smitten with Never-Never Land, a permanent escape from the real world. "The idea of Never-Never Land is awful because it's the best idea in the world," he said in 1989. "At least half the songs I've written are about Never-Never Land."

---

* Gnasher was actually a dog!
† Smith has remained a serious QPR fan throughout his life and was a well-regarded school footballer.

Years after this childhood obsession, Smith remained so fond of the story that he considered playing 'You Can Fly' at the end of concerts, as he and the band wandered off backstage.

Another youthful obsession was Lewis Carroll's timeless *Alice In Wonderland*, a story tailor-made for a man who spent much of his working life tapping into his incredibly colourful (and sometimes deeply morbid) imagination. "I love the idea of a little girl having these strange adventures in the realms of the imagination." Smith – who would go on to describe his role in The Cure as that of a "benign dictator" – was also drawn to *Alice In Wonderland*'s Queen of Hearts, mainly because she was so powerful. "The power to have someone's head chopped off is brilliant," he has admitted.

Smith's father Alex had dreams of his youngest son becoming a writer. There was little or no television-watching in the Smith house; Smith has said that his principal entertainment while growing up was "reading and records". When Robert was three, his father insisted that he read the newspaper and become acquainted with the world. Smith, however, preferred to lose himself in such books as C.S. Lewis' *Narnia Chronicles* – hugely popular in the United Kingdom – a seven-volume series with deeply allegorical allusions to the Bible and the life of Jesus Christ that his father would read to him as bedtime stories.

"I adored running away in those tales," said Smith, "it was my only reassuring moment. I was just discovering the incredible power of literature: it provided consolation and evasion."

Another childhood moment that Smith would revisit regularly as The Cure's worth increased was a strangely eerie occurrence in the Smith family hallway when he was six years old, not long after the family moved into their home at Crawley. There was an old, "really horrible" (Smith's words) mirror located in the hallway, which Smith did his best to avoid. He was convinced that he'd caught an unfamiliar reflection in the mirror. "I used to hate that mirror. Every time I came downstairs I used to avoid looking at it." (Even later in his life, Smith's home was noticeably short on mirrors. Some things stayed with him, clearly.)

Smith insists that his nickname at school – he first attended St Francis Primary School, then St Francis Junior School, where he was enrolled between 1966 and 1969 – was Sooty, "because I never spoke". But before football and then music grabbed his attention, Smith displayed a notable theatrical flair, taking the role of Nanki-Poo in a junior school production of Gilbert & Sullivan's *Mikado* that is still remembered by senior staff at St Francis almost 40 years on.

While Robert Smith and his schoolmates were coming to grips with the delicate nuances of wailing "we are gentlemen from Japan" in a Crawley assembly hall, a different kind of musical revolution was happening elsewhere in England. In 1968, the first Isle of Wight Festival was held. This was a bare-bones type of festival: the stage was perched precariously on the back of two lorries, the stars were San Franciscans The Jefferson Airplane, and the crowd numbered around 10,000. In 1969, however, the festival grew substantially when Bob Dylan, emerging from self-imposed seclusion, agreed to close the show. Decked out in preacher-man white and helped along by his mid-Sixties backing combo, The Band (themselves reluctant stars), the so-called "British Woodstock" pulled an estimated 150,000 punters. The following year, Robert Smith's brother, Richard, then 24, insisted that his 11-year-old sibling accompany him to the next Isle of Wight Festival, which ran between August 26 and 30.

While the opening few days showcased local acts, soloists and second-division hopefuls, including Procol Harum, Supertramp and Tony Joe White, the festival's final two days (and nights) blazed brightly, thanks to stellar performances from pyro-progs, Emerson, Lake & Palmer (making their debut, the supergroup very nearly succeeded in burning down the stage – 30-odd years later, Keith Emerson is a Santa Monican neighbour of Lol Tolhurst), along with Woodstock survivors John Sebastian, Ten Years After, The Who and Sly & The Family Stone. Electric gypsy Jimi Hendrix, the man whom the 11-year-old Robert Smith and much of the bumper crowd had come to see, shared the Sunday bill with an eclectic bunch: cosmic folkie Donovan, raggedy-voiced poet Leonard Cohen, Richie Havens, space ritualists Hawkwind, The Moody Blues, Brit folkies Pentangle, Ralph McTell, protest queen Joan Baez and soon to be prog superstars Jethro Tull.

As the organisers had discovered the previous year, art and commerce were uncomfortable bedfellows at the 1970 festival. A small community of ticketless hippies took over a nearby hill and the inevitable occurrence of fucking and various other bodily functions, frequently in full and shocking view, scared the hell out of the conservative locals. One of the event's organisers, Ron "Turner" Smith, had to call the Health Department to have the hillside area – 'Desolation Row' –

disinfected because of the stench of human waste. A resident, meanwhile, reported that "a stark naked man jumped out and danced" in front of her car, while there were numerous reports of nude bathing at nearby Compton Beach.

Robert Smith's number one guitar hero, Jimi Hendrix, eventually took the stage on the Sunday night, August 30, working his way through a set that included Dylan's 'All Along The Watchtower', The Beatles' 'Sgt Pepper's Lonely Hearts Club Band', his own 'Machine Gun' and, as a tip of his Fender to the British crowd – and a twist on his standard psychedelic reworking of 'The Star-Spangled Banner' – he tore through 'God Save The Queen'. But as the final soaring strains of 'In From The Storm' rained over the crowd, young Robert Smith was nowhere to be seen. When Richard Smith had gotten lucky with a female festival-goer, he zipped Robert into their shared tent, thereby denying him the chance to check out what was to be Hendrix's final UK performance. Eighteen days later Hendrix was found dead in a London flat, having choked on his vomit in his sleep.

"My brother took me," Smith said in 2004, "but I wouldn't say that I was aware that I was at a concert. I was 11 at the time. Jimi Hendrix played and I stayed in the tent. I just remember two days of orange tent and dope smoke." Smith would be a tad more forthright in an interview with a Spanish newspaper, when he spoke of his Isle of Wight experience. "My brother left me locked in the tent while he left to fuck or get stoned. I have not forgiven him since." (As compensation, his brother took Robert to see Kubrick's *2001: A Space Odyssey*. Smith was hooked, seeing the film 11 times in a fortnight. "That gave me a bit of brain damage as well.")

Robert Smith still has a faded photo of himself at the Isle of Wight Festival, standing outside his orange tent, "with a glazed expression on my face".

Smith's youthful interest in Hendrix was more than just a passing fascination: Hendrix's image and music represented a completely different way of life for the kid from comfortable, predictable Crawley. To Smith, Hendrix was an alien. "They'd not live like us, speak like us, eat like us. Hendrix was the first person I had come across who seemed completely free, and when you're nine or 10 your life is entirely dominated by adults," Smith admitted. Understandably, Hendrix made Smith believe that there may be more to life than a stint as centre forward for QPR. "Hendrix was the first person who made me think it might be good to be a singer and a guitarist – before that I wanted to be a footballer."

The first Hendrix song to which Smith was exposed was 'Purple Haze'; his brother Richard had played it to him when Robert was eight, in 1967. His response was both swift and immediate – he simply wouldn't stop playing the record until he'd worn a completely new groove in the vinyl. "I was just awestruck by it," Smith said. "I must have played it 20 times a day; I drove everyone in the house mad." Smith went as far as to memorise the song, but not with a plan of emulating Hendrix's peerless guitar moves. Instead he learned the song inside out by singing it. "I learned to sing all the drum parts, the bass, the guitar solo – I was just obsessed by it."

It was Smith's brother Richard – a hippie who'd backpacked through Asia, returning from India with, as Smith would relate, "lots of pictures of women with eight arms to stick on my bedroom wall" – who'd have a big impact on his impressionable sibling, as well as his schoolyard buddy Lol Tolhurst. Smith's rebellious brother would smoke pot in the family house, in full view of his parents. But his elder sister Margaret also introduced Smith to a key musical influence: The Beatles. When Smith was six, the melodic chime of The Beatles album *Help!* – a plea for help from John Lennon, as it turned out – would blare, repeatedly, from the other side of Margaret's bedroom door. She was also a serious Stones fan. Smith was hooked. "I would sit on the stairs, listening through the door," he recalled almost 40 years later. "It made me realise there was another world going on beyond my immediate environment. The melodies on these tunes are so fantastic and the imagination that goes into these songs is just unreal." While the very young Smith was moved to tears by the music, it would continue to have the same effect on him as a 44-year-old. "It's so perfect it makes me weep," he said in 2003. "I listen to *Help!* and I'm filled with hope that the world could be a better place."

In the mid-Sixties, there was no avoiding The Beatles or the Stones, so the youthful Smith chose to dive straight in. "My older sister and older brother had all their records and instead of listening to childish little things, I was listening to rock," said Smith. By the time he was seven, Smith insisted that he knew the complete repertoire of Jagger & Richards and Lennon & McCartney.

It was also during the formative years of his life that Smith first heard the mysterious, ill-fated singer/songwriter Nick Drake, whose downbeat moodscapes would have a significant and quite tangible impact on Smith's early work with The Cure. Smith was 10 when he first listened to Drake's 1969 album *Five Leaves Left*, courtesy, again, of his brother Richard. Just like Hendrix and 'Purple Haze', Smith's conversion was quick and absolute, although Smith realised that Drake was "on the other side of the coin to Jimi Hendrix – he was very quiet and withdrawn". As his musical career advanced, Smith would aspire to emulate Drake's understated songwriting and singing. But at the age of 10, it was more Drake's heartfelt style that swayed Robert Smith. To Smith, Drake's depth of feeling felt convincingly real. "[He] wasn't worried about what people thought of him. He wasn't worried about being famous. I think also that because he had an untimely death like Jimi Hendrix, he was never able to compromise his early work. It's a morbid romanticism [something Smith and The Cure could definitely relate to] but there is something attractive about it."

Smith's parents, both of whom were musically inclined (his father sang, his mother played the piano), had no objections to their son's love of rock – in fact, they encouraged it, while at the same time gently steering young Robert in a more formal musical direction. While all the time encouraging their children to discuss their favourite records – Smith would remember "staggering talks about Slade and Gary Glitter" – Alex and Rita Smith also introduced them to classical music, in an attempt to, in Smith's words, "enable me to have a larger vision of rock".

Another of Smith's early music heroes was David Bowie. He and his lifelong partner, Mary Poole, would share their first dance to the accompaniment of Bowie's 'Life On Mars'. Smith first laid eyes on the man who fell to earth on *Top Of The Pops* on July 6, 1972. Bowie was decked out in his jumpsuit of many colours and crooning 'Starman' while draped suggestively over his sidekick and guitar man Mick Ronson. Bowie's grandstanding performance introduced what would soon become known as glam rock to the mainstream. It was a pivotal moment in pop history in the UK – and was as far removed from the previous week's *Top Of The Pops*, when urchin piano man Gilbert O'Sullivan crooned 'Ohh-Wakka-Doo-Wakka-Day', as was humanly possible. A generational change had happened, all in the space of seven days.

Smith insisted that everyone his age remembered the event. "It's like Kennedy being shot, [but] for another generation. You just remember that night watching David Bowie on TV. It was really a formative, seminal experience." And Smith wasn't alone – another onlooker was Echo & The Bunnymen's Ian McCulloch. "As soon as I heard 'Starman' and saw him on *Top Of The Pops* I was hooked," McCulloch would state. "In 1972, I'd get girls on the bus saying to me, 'Eh la, have you got lippy on?' or 'Are you a boy or a girl?' Until he turned up it was a nightmare. All my other mates at school would say, 'Did you see that bloke on *Top Of The Pops*? He's a right faggot, him!' And I remember thinking, 'You pillocks,' as they'd all be buying their Elton John albums, and *Yessongs* and all that crap. It made me feel cooler."

Gary Kemp, future songwriter for Spandau Ballet, also looked and learned. "I watched it at a friend's council flat," he recalled. "My reality was so far removed from this guy's place, that my journey from that moment on was to get there, and I think the same applies to most of my generation."

Robert Smith's love of all things glam was swift and absolute. He would boast of his affection for Sweet, Slade, Marc Bolan and T. Rex ("who I secretly loved because my brother considered that to be music for women"). Roxy Music was another Smith favourite; he'd first seen them perform 'Pajamarama' on TV at around the same time as witnessing Bowie camp up 'Starman'. The attraction was as physical as it was musical: Smith was a big fan of Ferry's quiff and his pink leopard jacket.

But Bowie was the deepest kick of all for Robert Smith. By this time Bowie had been through more makeovers than Joan Collins; pop crooner, earnest folkie, spaced oddity, Ziggy Stardust – he was exactly the kind of pop chameleon that appealed to the lateral-thinking Robert Smith. Within weeks of his star turn on *Top Of The Pops*, Bowie had made his second assault on the UK Top 20; along with fellow glamsters T. Rex and Mott The Hoople (riding high on their Bowie-penned 'All The Young Dudes', no less), he was sharing chart space with such peculiar bedfellows as Cliff Richard, David Cassidy and Donny Osmond. And Bowie's thing for reinvention wasn't lost on Robert Smith: over The Cure's four decades, Smith wouldn't just reinvent the band musically, but his public image was in a constant state of evolution, from the serious young insect of *Faith* and *Pornography* to the lipstick-smudged Lovecat and beyond.

Smith would ponder the fine art of reinvention during a 1989 interview, where he freely admitted that the idea of disappearing for a time and then returning in a new skin had its appeal. "In fact, it appeals to me so much, I do it every couple of years. I think I enjoy The Cure because I do come back as a different person every time.*

"I felt that his records had been made with me in mind," recalled Smith. In fact, Smith was so inspired by Bowie's *Top Of The Pops* performance that he counted his pocket money and bought Bowie's epochal *The Rise And Fall Of Ziggy Stardust And The Spiders From Mars*, which had been released a month earlier. It was Smith's first – and most prized – LP purchase. "He was blatantly different," said Smith.

Bowie's androgynous appeal and uncertain sexual persuasion would lead to a division amongst the students at St Wilfrid's Catholic Comprehensive School (as it would at thousands of other schools across the UK): Smith willingly stood on the side of the cross-dressing Starman. Smith recalled how the school was divided "between those who thought he was a queer and those who thought he was a genius.

"Immediately, I thought: this is it. This is the man I've been waiting for. He showed that you could do things on your own terms; that you could define your own genre and not worry about what anyone else is doing, which I think is the definition of a true artist."

While Hendrix and Bowie seemed natural-born heroes for a musically curious kid such as Robert Smith, Alex Harvey was a much less obvious choice as a musical role model. Born in Scotland, Harvey was a rock'n'roll journeyman who'd worked his way through the UK skiffle boom of the Fifties, eventually forming The Alex Harvey Big Soul Band in 1959. Just like The Beatles, Harvey crossed the Channel to Hamburg, Germany, in the early Sixties; it was there that he cut his first album, 1963's *Alex Harvey And His Soul Band*, which, perversely, didn't actually feature his band. Unlike the Fab Four, however, Hamburg wasn't the start of a supernova career for Harvey – quite the opposite. He dissolved the Big Soul Band in 1965, heading home for a period

---

* Years later, Smith would help Bowie, the master of reinvention, celebrate his 50th birthday in front of a full house at New York's Madison Square Garden, fulfilling his teenage dream of singing alongside the Thin White Duke.

until he moved to London, where he fell under the spell of psychedelia, forming the short-lived Giant Moth. But neither a spell in the pit band of a production of *Hair*, or a solo album (1969's *Roman Wall Blues*) did much for Harvey's profile. It wasn't until the early Seventies, when he recruited the Scottish band Tear Gas – guitarist Zal Cleminson (a particular favourite of Smith's), Chris Glen, Hugh McKenna, and Ted McKenna – and renamed them The Sensational Alex Harvey Band, that Harvey finally worked his way out of the musical ghetto, if only briefly. The band's third album, 1974's *Impossible Dream*, became Harvey's first UK chart record; it even briefly dented the US charts in March of the following year. Commercial success ensued with his spring 1975 release, *Tomorrow Belongs To Me*; both the album and his flamboyant take on Tom Jones' 'Delilah' reached the UK Top 10. On the back of this, Harvey's 1973 album, *Next*, returned to the hit parade, while in September 1975, the obligatory live set also reached the UK Top 20 and the US Top 100.

By this time, 16-year-old Robert Smith, who'd first seen Harvey play two years earlier in 1973, was a true believer. Smith and girlfriend Mary Poole followed Harvey to virtually all of his shows in the south of England. "People talk about Iggy Pop as the original punk," Smith said in 1993, "but certainly in Britain the forerunner of the punk movement was Alex Harvey. His whole stage show, with the graffiti-covered brick walls – it was like very aggressive Glaswegian street theatre."

It was Harvey's every-bloke appeal that had Smith spellbound. He was the anti-David Bowie; a far more tangible – and attainable – ideal than the enigmatic Ziggy. Smith explained that Harvey was "the physical manifestation of what I thought I could be. He never really got anywhere, even though he had something so magic when he performed – he had the persona of a victim and you just sided with him against all that was going wrong. I would have died to have had Alex Harvey as an uncle. Alex Harvey was the closest I ever came to idolising anyone." Smith proudly wore a striped black-and-white shirt wherever he went – a Harvey signature – which he'd compare to a gang uniform. "People look a certain way so if they see someone else dressed that way they can talk to them." The only thing about Harvey that Smith didn't consider worth emulating was his looks: he found the guy "much too old and ugly".

For two years, Smith was as committed an Alex Harvey fan as you were likely to find. Harvey offered a musical respite from some of the seriously questionable outfits being played to death at the time. As Smith realised, "Without him I'd have been into Supertramp, those sort of horrible groups. If I thought we [The Cure] had the same impact on people as The Sensational Alex Harvey Band had on me, I'd be . . ." – here Smith found himself lost for words – "he was the only person who made me think, it must be fucking brilliant to be Alex Harvey. It was like believing in a creature, a myth that was presented to you on stage."

Harvey's time in the spotlight was relatively short: although 1976 was another banner year for him and his Sensational Band, as 'Boston Tea Party' made the singles chart and *Penthouse Tapes* became a Top 20 hit, the inevitable slide set in and the band dissolved. *Rock Drill* was their swansong. Harvey died on tour in Belgium in 1982, from a heart attack brought on by heavy boozing, just before reaching his 47th birthday, while Smith and The Cure were readying possibly the most disturbing – and disturbed – album of their lives, *Pornography*. Twenty years later, however, Smith and The Cure would perform a very public eulogy for Harvey, covering 'The Faith Healer' at a huge Hyde Park show.

While his idols outside of rock'n'roll – Spike Milligan, Tommy Cooper, footballer Rodney Marsh – were more typical, mainstream obsessions, Smith's youthful heroes, such as Bowie, Hendrix and Alex Harvey, were all fringe-dwellers. Bowie was an alien beamed in from another planet; Hendrix was an African-American who brought the psychedelic blues to English audiences; Harvey was a regular bloke shouting to be heard above the lipstick and bell-bottoms of glam rock. And they all helped to contribute to the outsider status that Smith would embrace so willingly during his teens in Crawley and in the nascent stages of The Cure's career. Nevertheless, Smith did have other, more mainstream enthusiasms, such as twin-guitar fanciers Thin Lizzy – "They were fabulous, I saw them probably 10 times in two years; the actual sound of them live was just so overpowering, it was better than drinking" – and Irish axeslinger Rory Gallagher – "I thought his guitar playing was fabulous."

By the time he was 14, in 1973, Smith was talking up his (non) ambitions: he intended never to be a slave to a regular job; his life goal was to "sit on top of a mountain and just die". He did, however, have at least one job outside of The Cure. "He was a postman one Christmas; they'd always hire extra," Lol Tolhurst said to me. "That lasted about a week or two until he ditched his mailsack in a river somewhere and told them he wasn't coming back and that was it. I don't remember him having any other full-time job." The Cure's first bassist, Michael Dempsey, does recall that Smith also held down a gardening job – but only for a few weeks.

So The Cure was born out of indolence, apparently, not burning ambition. When The Cure had become one of planet pop's most unlikely superstars in the late Eighties, Smith still insisted that he didn't form The Cure for either sex or drugs. Instead, it was "just the best way to avoid getting up in the morning".

In his own way, Lol Tolhurst agreed with Smith. "We didn't have a master plan; we didn't really have one until the mid-Eighties," he replied when I asked him about the evolution of The Cure. "We were pretty young; we didn't have any idea of what was going to happen. In some ways that was our saving grace. Some bands today do it as a career move; to us it was just something we felt like doing.

"Some of the early shows were just an excuse to have a party; we'd book a local church hall, charge a small amount to come in, we'd buy some beer and have a party. It was more for the sake of something to do than anything else."

"None of us had a really strong vision of being superstars," figured Michael Dempsey.

Both Smith and Tolhurst had older brothers – schoolmates, as it turned out – who'd taken the everyday route of school, higher education and a "normal" life of wife and children and a house in the suburbs. Smith and Tolhurst weren't so thrilled by what they saw. "Both of our brothers had taken that path, but we thought, 'Here's what life could be, comfortable but ultimately tedious, or we could do something different,'" said Tolhurst. "That's what drove us."

Much later in his life, Smith would agree that his rebellious outlook was pretty standard teenage moodiness, even if it meant life and death to him at the time. In 2003, he came clean. "It's normal, as a teenager, to love this idea of being a victim – the whole world is against me, no one understands me."

Yet Smith would build much of The Cure's early career on this cult of the outsider. His morbid fascination with both death and the French existentialists, notably Jean-Paul Sartre and Albert Camus, seemed a natural progression from his typically dour, normal-life-sucks teenage hang-ups.

But Smith's education was not all doom, gloom and heated play-ground debate about that "poofter" David Bowie. Between 1970 and 1972 he attended Notre Dame Middle School, which was experiment-ing with open-plan classrooms and in the process actually encouraging freethinking in its pupils.* So liberal was Notre Dame, Smith would insist, that he turned up for classes in 1970, at the age of 11, wearing a modified black velvet dress. "I really don't know why," he pondered. "I thought I looked good. My teachers were so liberal they tried hard not to notice." Smith survived the day at school, but as he walked home he was jumped and beaten up by a pack of four not-so-open-minded fellow Notre Damians.

Lol Tolhurst was there, looking on. "Robert went to a jumble sale and got a black velvet dress, really long and tight fitting," he told me. "His mother cut it down the middle and made it into a pair of trousers. Which was fine until you saw him on the playground with his legs together, so it looked like he was wearing a dress." As Tolhurst read it, this was simply an attempt on Smith's part to see how flexible the school's few rules really were. "Our thing was to operate just within the letter of the law. Some of the teachers knew what we were up to and tried to pin something on us."

Smith agreed, saying that he wore the dress "for a dare", as a way of testing how far he could push his teachers' casual approach to authority. "I'd worn it all day because the teachers just thought, 'Oh, it's a phase he's going through, he's got some kind of personality crisis, let's help him through it.'"

On another occasion, Smith decided to experiment with his sister's cosmetics before attending school. "I locked myself in the bathroom and went to school wearing make-up." This time around, however, Smith's teachers weren't as tolerant. "I got sent back home immedi-ately," he said. And the response of Smith's parents? "They were quite patient with me," Smith said. "They hoped I would simply stop it one day."

---

* It didn't last: Notre Dame's original site is now a housing development.

Every bit the storyteller, more than once Smith has said that his first experiment with make-up coincided with his first attempt at cross-dressing. Either way, he was beaten up on the way home from school, which he didn't consider "a very fair reward" for his efforts. Not that it put him off, of course.

As for Notre Dame, its so-called "middle school" experiment had been introduced into some British schools in the early Seventies; it was designed to "bridge the gap" and soften the transition between junior and senior school. "It was supposed to be very liberal," Smith stated in 1989. "You had 'open class'; if you had a class you didn't like, you could move to another. You'd address the teachers by their Christian names – that sort of set-up."

Lol Tolhurst, one of Smith's Notre Dame classmates and future Cure co-founder, was equally surprised by Notre Dame's freewheeling approach to education. "Looking back, it was strange. I now send my [teenage] son [Gray] to a similar school," Tolhurst said to me. "But that was the Seventies. At one point I remember we didn't have any set lessons; we were given projects to do and asked to report back at the end of the week to tell what we had done with them. We weren't really supervised."

Speaking in *Ten Imaginary Years*, the band's first official biography, published in 1988, Smith admitted to embracing the "revolutionary" teaching methods. He also discovered that it was an easy system to abuse. "If you were crafty enough," he said, "you could convince the teachers you were special: I did nothing for virtually three years. But it was at heart a Catholic school, so there was still a certain amount of religious education."

Smith sleepwalked through his studies, only putting in the effort required to achieve a pass mark. English was the one subject that managed to maintain his interest and enthusiasm. When asked, Smith recalled that his school reports stated: "Something in the order of, I was doing less than I could. That was pretty accurate because at the time I was consciously trying to do as little as possible."

Another positive aspect of Smith's "middle school years" – especially for a youth whose goal was to avoid the nine-to-five grind that he witnessed every day of the working week in Crawley – was that he met Laurence "Lol" Tolhurst and Michael Dempsey.

Born and raised in Horley, Surrey, on February 3, 1959, Tolhurst, like Smith, had siblings with vast age differences. One of six children, his oldest sibling, his brother Roger, had been born in 1942 (followed by Nigel in 1946, who died two months later; John, who was born in 1947 and Jane, who was born in 1951). And again like Smith, Tolhurst had a sister, Barbara, who was born in 1960. Tolhurst's father William had served in the Navy for 15 years; 10 years in China prior to World War II and then another five in Europe and the Middle East during the war. Both Smith and Tolhurst had attended St Francis Primary and Junior Schools; Smith recalled meeting Tolhurst on the school bus on his first day of primary school.

"He lived in the next street and we went to school on the same coach," Smith said. "But he made no impression on me whatsoever. He remembers me, though not very favourably."

The Tolhursts were a strongly musical family: Lol's father William played the piano, while his younger sister Barbara would eventually opt for a career as a music teacher. And his mother Daphne was incredibly supportive when one of her sons showed a certain musical aptitude. "My mother was always very interested in music and arts," Tolhurst said, when we spoke in early 2005. "She gave me my love of all those things. It's only in hindsight that I realise that not a lot of parents do that. She was always encouraging me in those areas. When we started the band, she was very supportive. I went from having a secure job to this very unsecure [sic] thing and about half the money I formerly had. I was still living at home and she didn't bat an eyelid."

Michael Dempsey, the future Cure bassist, was born on November 29, 1958, in what was then known as Salisbury, Rhodesia (now Harare, Zimbabwe). One of four Dempsey children, Michael and his family had shifted to Salfords in Surrey in 1961. Before enrolling at Notre Dame in 1970, which Dempsey now remembers as requiring a "horrible train commute" from Salfords, Dempsey had attended Salfords County School. Dempsey insists that his family were "emphatically not musical", although his mother Nancy played piano and sang in the local Catholic church choir. Just like Smith (and Tolhurst), Dempsey acquired a handy musical education from a sibling, his sister Anne, who was five years his senior. "Anne had the record collection," Dempsey told me in early 2005. "It was a weird assortment: the soundtrack to *Lawrence Of Arabia*, [prog rockers] Gong, early T. Rex, when they were Tyrannosaurus Rex. It was an eclectic mix." And just like

Smith, Dempsey was inspired by Bowie's star turn on *Top Of The Pops*. "It was rare to see anything extreme," he said. "And it was also cool to like the thing that shocked your parents most."

While Notre Dame's more *laissez faire* approach to learning had been too tempting for Smith not to abuse, it did imbue him with a certain "anything goes" attitude. This would be the perfect manifesto for a band such as The Obelisk (as The Cure were first known), and the many other hopefuls who emerged in the post-punk period. But Smith, Tolhurst and Dempsey first had some chops to learn.

Unlike another of his childhood favourites, Pinocchio, Smith admits that he had no problem with attending school – "I actually enjoyed it while I was there" – but that his questioning outlook towards religion led to him being deemed "unsuitable". He was eventually suspended from St Wilfrid's Comprehensive School, which he attended between 1972 and 1977. "I was suspended from school," he recalled, "when I was supposed to be doing exams because my attitude towards religion was considered wrong. I thought that was incredible."

Describing itself as a "thriving and caring Catholic comprehensive school", St Wilfrid's was established in 1953. Their mission statement – "we pride ourselves on being committed to the whole person and the whole community; we are conscious each child has been created in the 'image and likeness of God' and pursue not only academic excellence but also spiritual growth based on Gospel values" – was inevitably going to cause some unrest for those pupils acclimatised to Notre Dame's more easy-going approach. But Smith wasn't alone; Lol Tolhurst was also feeling the pain, especially at the hands of one particular teacher.

"He was a wizened old man, a chain-smoker," Tolhurst told me, "who'd written all these books. He lectured us on all kinds of things. On the first day he grabbed me and said, 'Tolhurst, I know your brother: what are you going to be – a first-class student or a bee in my bonnet?' It was a lot different to Notre Dame."

Smith described St Wilfrid's as "the most fascist school I'd ever been to. You couldn't do anything. They'd re-introduced school uniforms, the whole thing – it was an entire process of clamping down. And that bred a lot of resentment amongst people of my age. We felt like we were used as guinea pigs."

Tolhurst was also shocked by the difference between Notre Dame and St Wilfrid's. It took him all of one day to discover the difference in approach. "I remember feeling very anxious about going there, because I had long hair," Tolhurst admitted. "I wondered what they were going to say about that. There was one teacher who was feared by all, a Mrs Slater, who grabbed me on my first day there and picked on me about something. Many years later I was sitting in a club in Sydney [Australia] and this voice said, 'Mrs Slater wants to see you in her office, boy.' It was her son. It was very strange. It still put the fear of God in me."

Michael Dempsey, however, actually preferred St Wilfrid's to Notre Dame, although he wasn't thrilled by either school. "I've seen Robert say that Notre Dame was radical," he said to me, "but I don't think it was that alternative. It was just a mix of the religious and more secular schooling. But they were outside the mainstream."

What St Wilfrid's did instil in Robert Smith, and Lol Tolhurst, was a realisation that their daydream about not having a regular job should be pursued with extreme prejudice. Which led them, inevitably, to music.

Smith and Tolhurst had been tinkering with musical instruments when they were students at Notre Dame; their bond had strengthened when they discovered that they were both members of the British league of the Jimi Hendrix fan club. (Smith's relationship with Dempsey began when they realised that they both owned electric guitars.) But even earlier, Smith had been taking piano lessons, in part to keep up with the musical progress of his piano-playing sister, Janet, whom Smith would insist was the family's "musical genius". But frustrated by his lack of progress (and prowess) and determined to find an instrument that Janet couldn't master, Smith started playing guitar, "because her hands were too small to get around the guitar neck and I thought, 'She can't beat me at this.'" Smith figured he was "six or seven" when he first fondled a six-string, "[but] I wasn't very good." Smith remembered his one and only guitar teacher as "the gayest bloke I ever met . . . He was horrified by my playing."

So instead, Smith's brother Richard talked him through a few basic chords, while he also learned by ear, mimicking the playing he heard in his brother's top-shelf record collection.

It was Christmas 1972 when Smith received his first "proper" guitar, a present from his parents. The guitar was a Woolworth's cheapie, christened the "Top 20". As basic as it was, it would remain Smith's number one axe for some time, much to the horror of his bandmates, record producers and Fiction Records boss Chris Parry.* In 1973, Smith formed his first band with Janet, his "hippie" brother Richard and some friends. They named themselves, for reasons that remain unclear to this day, The Crawley Goat Band.

Next was a group named The Group, mainly because it was the only school band in existence, "so we didn't need a name".

Lol Tolhurst, just like Smith, had his older brother to thank for his nascent musical career. When Lol was 13, Roger Tolhurst told his family that he was relocating to Tasmania, Australia. Before departing to the other side of the planet, he asked his much younger brother if he'd like some kind of farewell gift: Tolhurst asked for some drumsticks and a "how-to" book on drumming. He was on his way.

Smith's initial musical education had taken place at home in Crawley, where he learned the good book according to Jagger & Richards and Lennon & McCartney, and then saw the light when Bowie shocked the *Top Of The Pops* audience. But his more practical education began in the music room at Notre Dame Middle School. While skipping lessons, Smith, Tolhurst, Dempsey and several others started tinkering with whatever instruments they could lay their hands on. A new sound was born.

"We'd go to the music room and pull out their instruments and bash out songs on them," Tolhurst told me. "I remember some of the first songs we played: we got some sheet music from the local music store and played 'Whiter Shade Of Pale' – which is very strange because it's a keyboard song and all we had was guitar and drums – 'Heart Of Gold' by Neil Young, and some Paul Simon song. It was a question of us trying to learn something. They were very strange choices but that was the only sheet music they had from the last century in the store."

Tolhurst was also a dab hand with the wheels of steel; he'd spent most of his time at Notre Dame spinning discs at lunchtime discos. "I

---

* Even when he could afford better gear, Smith had the pick-ups from his Top 20 axe fitted to his brand new Fender Jazzmaster, "to the amazement of everybody", according to Tolhurst.

was the DJ. I remember playing all these Black Sabbath records and the nuns would be nodding away."

Dempsey, every bit the pragmatist, was drawn to the music room for other reasons. "It was warm," he told me.

Soon after, in April 1973, Smith, Dempsey and Tolhurst were ready to make their public debut. According to Smith, they played a piece to the class, featuring Smith on piano, Tolhurst on drums, Dempsey and Marc Ceccagno playing guitars and Alan Hill on bass. "We called ourselves The Obelisk and the whole thing was horrible! But still much better than studying." Given Smith's response to their one-off performance, it's possibly a good thing that no one can quite recall what song they massacred. Lol Tolhurst still has no idea. "It was a complete nightmare but quite interesting," he recalled in 2005.

Dempsey still has strong memories of Ceccagno, the only black pupil at St Wilfrid's. "He was quite mysterious, very sharp, very funny. He was also quite influential – he was possibly the first nihilist amongst us." His nihilistic outlook clearly rubbed off on both Smith and Dempsey, if not the more easy-going Tolhurst, particularly when combined with their sixth-form reading list: Albert Camus' *The Outsider*, Shakespeare's *Othello*, Milton's *Paradise Lost*. "We were good readers – and it helped reinforce your sense of isolation," Dempsey figured, reasonably enough. Another book he and Smith both savoured was Evelyn Waugh's *A Handful Of Dust* – they'd even thought about calling the band Brat's Club, as a nod to the book.

It was around the same time as Obelisk's indifferent debut that Smith would lose his virginity with Mary Poole, "the nicest girl in school", whom he'd first encountered in Drama Class at St Wilfrid's. "I went out with her because everyone else wanted to," Smith admitted. Typically, their first sexual encounter wasn't quite Mills & Boon-worthy. "We were at someone's party, a fancy dress party," he recalled. "I went as a surgeon. I remember because I poured all this tomato ketchup down me. At the time I thought it was a really good idea, but after an hour it really began to stink. Every time I moved I was completely overpowered by the sweet sickly smell of tomato ketchup."

While Smith's ideas about lovemaking and romance hadn't developed in quite the way he'd hoped, music was becoming an increasingly useful outlet for him, especially now that he was making the difficult transition from the more relaxed Notre Dame Middle School to the "fascist" St Wilfrid's Comprehensive.

As The Obelisk morphed into a band called Malice, it seemed as though Robert Smith – the teenager who was hell-bent on doing everything he could in order to do nothing at all – might just have found his calling.

Chapter Two

"We don't like your songs. Not even people in prison would like this."
                                    – Hansa exec to The Easy Cure, 1977

IN many ways punk rock was the revolution that never quite happened. Even in June 1977, when a snarling, spitting Johnny Rotten helped the barnstorming Sex Pistols gatecrash the UK Top 10 with their anti-anthem 'God Save The Queen', the green-toothed former John Lydon was still sharing chart space with such relentlessly mainstream acts as Rod Stewart (moaning 'I Don't Want To Talk About It'), Barbra Streisand (crooning 'Evergreen' from her 10-tissue weepie *A Star Is Born*) and The Jacksons. Even the unbearably cute Muppets were in the same Top 10 as The Sex Pistols. And during the heyday of punk, it wasn't as though the airwaves and charts were completely laid waste as the purveyors of all things punk had planned: in the wake of the Pistols, regular chart-toppers still included such lightweight easy-listeners as Brotherhood Of Man, Showaddywaddy, Hot Chocolate and Olivia Newton-John. But as a young and impressionable Robert Smith was soon to understand, the concept of punk was flawless – you didn't have to be a note-perfect singer or a master craftsman to play, as so many prog rock posers of the time would have you believe. A fuck-you attitude, a certain indefinable sense of alienation, a fine line in bondage trousers and some strategically placed safety pins were all you needed to form a punk band. And thousands of disenfranchised youngsters (mixed with the usual bandwagon-jumpers, of course) heeded the call to arms.

Robert Smith remembers punk from a slightly different perspective to most people. He was no Joe Strummer, out to kick the establishment in the arse. For Smith, punk wasn't so much a social movement as a chance for him and his mates "to go out and get drunk and jump about". To Smith, 1977 was the peak of punk. "It was just good fun. The summer of 1977 was like this pinnacle. Everyone says, 'Oh, 1975.' It wasn't at all. In 1977, The Sex Pistols were number one. And in the charts there was like The Stranglers, The Buzzcocks. It was brilliant. You thought, 'Ah, things are changing.'"

Lol Tolhurst had a similar punk-inspired awakening. "It was the end of the Seventies; to a lot of people who started at that time, the idea of being in a band and making records was kind of like a pipe dream," he said. "To us, we thought you had to be really, really good to do that and it seemed out of our reach. But then all the punk stuff started happening and we realised, 'Hey, we can do this.' We'd flick through the *Melody Maker* and go and see The Stranglers and realise we're not tremendously different to that. Up until that point, it all seemed too mysterious to us, too complex."

As with many of the best revolutions, there were a couple of possible locations for the epicentre of punk. Radicals on the English side of the Atlantic would swear on a stack of *Sniffin' Glue* mags that punk came to be in Sex, the Chelsea boutique owned and operated by Vivienne Westwood and her partner, Malcolm McLaren, the same man who'd been savvy enough to manage The New York Dolls, briefly, in 1975, before turning his attention to The Sex Pistols. Americans, however, insist that the revolution officially began in 1974 when New Yorker Hilly Kristal threw open the doors of CBGBs (as in "country bluegrass blues", the type of music he'd actually intended to put on display in his club). The shoebox-sized sweatbox, located in bum's paradise The Bowery, would soon welcome such acts as The Ramones and Johnny Thunder & The Heartbreakers through its doors, as the punk outbreak spread on both sides of the Atlantic.

While cultural historians still debate its origins some three decades later, what is known to be fact is this: by the second half of the Seventies, some truly pioneering acts – The Ramones, The Sex Pistols, The Clash, Blondie, The Damned, Australian outcasts The Saints – had at the very least embraced the do-it-yourself attitude of punk, if not the back-to-basics, three-chords-one-too-many aggression that typified punk rock's sound. In LA, such clubs as The Fleetwood and The Masque dared to put The Weirdos and Black Flag on their bills, while at the same time Rodney Bingenheimer, the self-styled Mayor of Sunset Strip, flogged the music of The Ramones, the Pistols and The Clash on his *Rodney On The ROQ* radio show. Meanwhile, in the UK, these very same reprobates were glaring from the pages of *New Musical Express*, *Melody Maker* and elsewhere. *Slash* celebrated the scene in the

USA. The mainstream media, naturally, feared punk like the plague, especially when The Sex Pistols made their infamous appearance on Thames TV's *Today* show in December 1976, Steve Jones daring to drop the word "fucker" on live television. After a reporter witnessed the male-bonding ritual that was slam dancing, the *LA Times* ran a paranoid banner headline that screamed: THE SLAM. Punk's lure to the youth of many nations was irresistible.

Suburban Crawley was several light years away from the dingy clubs of London, New York and Los Angeles – where the whiff of danger was as strong in the air as the pungent aroma of hairspray – but punk's DIY spirit wasn't lost on the young men of The Obelisk (or Malice, as they were soon to be known). In fact, at least to Lol Tolhurst, being based in Crawley had its advantages. "On reflection, I think it was a pretty good atmosphere for what we ended up doing," he said. "On one hand we were close enough to the capital to know what was going on, but we were far enough removed from it to not feel part of any scene. All those little towns, like Horley and Crawley, spawned a lot of unusual characters. That shaped our attitude to most things. We weren't city boys and savvy with all that, but we had our own quirky atmosphere that we grew up in."

And while punk would provide Smith, Tolhurst, Dempsey and the rest of their floating line-up with an attitude, if not a specific sound, the wave of post-punk bands soon to emerge would directly influence their music (once Malice had outgrown their limited repertoire of Hendrix, Alex Harvey and Thin Lizzy covers).

It didn't take a doctorate in logical thinking to figure that post-punk was the next evolutionary step from punk rock. Many of the basic beliefs stayed in place: the underground spirit ruled, the notion of "stardom" was anathema, long-winded solos were a no-go zone punishable by public humiliation, while the more austere the countenance, the better. Malice weren't exactly the most skilled band on the planet, so these essential, self-imposed limitations suited them perfectly.

Such acts as The Gang Of Four, Talking Heads and Wire, who all took an art-school approach to punk, led the charge of post-punk acts. In Manchester, a writhing, twitching vocalist by the name of Ian Curtis was fronting Warsaw, who would soon become Joy Division. The group's beginning was flawless: they'd formed immediately after members Peter Hook and Bernard Sumner had witnessed a crash-and-burn

Sex Pistols gig in Manchester on June 4, 1976. Curtis then responded to a "seeking singer" ad in the local Virgin record store. All of these bands would have a direct impact on the early music and outlook of Robert Smith and co, especially Joy Division – or more specifically, their second coming as New Order – who'd go as far as to accuse The Cure of plagiarism. Their claim wasn't without some basis in fact, either, but that was some way off in the future.

It wasn't just Sumner and Hook who would respond so powerfully to The Sex Pistols in that northern summer of 1976. Robert Smith was at a party during his last year at school when he first heard 'Anarchy In The UK'. "I remember thinking – 'This is it!' You either loved it or hated it; it polarised an entire nation for that summer. You had to make a choice: you were either going to be left behind or you were going to embrace the new movement."

A northern act that would have an equally tangible impact on the early songs and sounds of Robert Smith were Mancunians The Buzzcocks, who formed in 1975. The four-piece, who in their original formation comprised Howard Devoto (the former Howard Trafford), Pete Shelley (aka Peter McNeish), John Maher and Steve Diggle, aligned themselves more with the burgeoning New Wave scene at the time, although their buzzsaw guitar arsenal was the envy of most punk and post-punk hopefuls. But The Buzzcocks were fully aware of the past: such early, nervy outpourings as 'Orgasm Addict' and 'What Do I Get?' (and further down the line, 'Have You Ever Fallen In Love') managed to combine the restless urgency and futility of punk with the bittersweet melodicism of The Beatles and The Kinks. That was no small achievement – and it wasn't lost on Crawley dreamers Robert Smith and Lol Tolhurst.

In a 1999 discussion of The Cure's roots, Smith would namecheck various punk and post-punk outfits, including The Buzzcocks. "In the very early days, when we were just a three-piece, I wanted to be like Wire or [Siouxsie &] The Banshees," said Smith. "These were the people I emulated on a very immediate level. They were the generation immediately preceding me, literally by a year. They had a certain kind of power to them that transcended punk. I wanted The Cure to be that, but we never were. We actually sounded like The Buzzcocks in the early days, but I think that's because my songwriting was still in its very early stages. I think it was influenced by early Beatles [as

31

brought into Smith's world by his sister Margaret] – the sense of a three-minute guitar-pop song."

The almost-anything-goes aspect of punk and post-punk wasn't wasted on Smith, who'd quickly tired of his formal guitar lessons with "the gayest bloke I ever met". Learning by experience seemed much more natural to the free-thinking teenager. "What inspired me [about punk]," Smith said, echoing his bandmate Tolhurst, "was the notion that you could do it yourself. It was loud and fast and noisy and I was at the right age for that." Even in his early teens, Smith was smart enough to use and abuse the aspects of punk that suited him – and it had nothing to do with fashion accessories. "Because of not living in London or other big punk centres, it wasn't a stylistic thing for me. If you walked around Crawley with safety pins [or a black velvet dress, as Smith had already learned] you'd get beaten up. The risk involved didn't seem to make sense," he continued, "so luckily there aren't any photos of me in bondage trousers. I thought punk was more a mental state."

Embracing a punk state of mind, however, was not at the forefront of Robert Smith's world in the early months of 1976. He had more immediate concerns to deal with, such as his contempt for the regime at St Wilfrid's. The teacher/pupil relationship had deteriorated to the point where Smith was briefly suspended from school, although his father's active role on the school board ensured that it was a very short suspension. "They said I was disruptive, but it was a personal thing – I hated the headmaster," Smith said.

By this time, Smith had already developed the type of lively ego that would come in handy when he became an accidental pop star. "When I was in school," Smith said simply, "I thought I was better than the teachers." The truth, however, was that Smith's time at St Wilfrid's wasn't as tough as he would go on to tell the world. According to at least one of his St Wilfrid's teachers, Smith was popular, even with the teachers. ("Especially with the younger ones," I was told. "[He] was creatively anti–authoritarian, without being insolent – he was too well brought up.") According to Michael Georgeson, Smith and Tolhurst's Drama teacher from St Wilfrid's – he was also their Form Tutor and remains a close friend of Alex and Rita Smith – Smith's solid upbringing ensured that he never stepped too far out of line. "Robert was brought up in a caring and supportive family," Georgeson said, "and never displayed any undue unease in or out of the classroom at St

Wilfrid's. He was cheerfully co-operative, but very much his own man." Tolhurst, however, didn't leave quite the same impression on Georgeson. "Laurence Tolhurst was a pleasant enough boy," he said, "but lazy and with minimal talent. But he was a very good friend of Robert, who showed long-standing, patient loyalty towards Laurence." Georgeson knew little of Dempsey, apart from the fact that, like Smith, he was also popular.

None of this support did anything to diminish their enthusiasm towards the musical possibilities of Malice, the band formerly known as The Obelisk. Who knew what was in the future: maybe music presented the perfect opportunity for Smith and Tolhurst to steer clear of the workaday grind that they could see was a hell best avoided. "When it [The Cure] first started," Smith said, "I didn't have any objectives or ulterior motives other than not to have to work."

If middle-class, suburban Crawley was the unlikeliest spot for the birth of an influential and hugely successful band such as The Cure, they chose an even less likely venue to master the art of rock'n'roll. On January 23, 1976, Malice − whose floating line-up now included Smith, Tolhurst, Marc Ceccagno, Dempsey and another school friend called Graham − got together at St Edward's Church, Crawley, for their first "real" band rehearsal. Smith recalled the jam session in *Ten Imaginary Years*.

"I think it all came about because Marc Ceccagno wanted to be a guitar hero. Michael had a bass, I had got hold of a guitar and our first drummer, Graham, had a drum kit. His brother had an amp and a mic so he sang." The band then rehearsed every Thursday night, but soon began to experience a recurring problem that would plague their early progress: no one could actually sing. Smith, again: "One night we decided [the vocalist] couldn't stay, he just couldn't sing − and the same night, around the end of April [1977], Lol arrived and convinced us he could be the drummer. The problem was, he didn't have a drum kit, but we took him on anyway."

Dempsey, speaking in *Ten Imaginary Years*, remembers having "to teach Lol the drums. We had no aims. It was just something to do, something to talk about." Tolhurst repeated this when we spoke in 2005. "One of the main reasons we started the band was because we wanted something to do."

By October, Malice had not only fleshed out their repertoire with covers of Bowie, Hendrix and Alex Harvey songs – Smith clearly exercising his influence over the rest of the group – but had now begun practising three nights a week. Ceccagno, who was more taken by jazz, had dropped out, which meant that Malice were on the lookout for another guitarist. Enter Paul (Porl) Stephen Thompson, a man who would drift in and out of Cureworld for the next 30 years.

Thompson, the eldest of four children, was born in Wimbledon, in south-west London, on November 8, 1957. In 1962, the Thompsons briefly shifted base to Melbourne, Australia, before relocating to Crawley in 1964. Along with his sister Carol and brothers Andrew and Robert, Paul attended Southgate Crawley Infants and Junior Schools and then finished his education at Thomas Bennett Crawley Comprehensive School, leaving in 1974. When he met up with Malice, he was working as a waiter at nearby Gatwick Airport. He would usually turn up for rehearsals in his waiter's uniform, which was in sharp contrast to his free-flowing, almost Marc Bolan-like mane of wild curly hair. If every sleepy suburb was permitted only one rock star look-alike, Crawley's was definitely Porl Thompson.

The connection had come via Tolhurst, who was dating Thompson's sister Carol. (One for keeping it in the band, Thompson would much later marry Smith's younger sister Janet.) Thompson – who already had a certain notoriety around Crawley as a guitarslinger of note – had also previously met Smith when he was working at the counter of a local record store. The pair bonded over esoteric music. "He came in to buy *Songs Of The Humpback Whale*," said Thompson, "and we found we liked the same stuff."

Tolhurst was soon spending more time with Porl than his sister Carol. "Eventually I got more interested in talking with Porl about music, much to the chagrin of his sister who dumped me because of that. Then I said to Porl, 'Well, we've got a band going, why don't you come along?' Because he was the local guitar hero, we scored a coup with that."

"He had a real reputation when we were back in Crawley growing up," Smith confirmed. "He was *the* guitarist in Crawley." According to Tolhurst, "Porl was very artistic but he was in with a group of thugs [at Thomas Bennett school]."

When Thompson first became involved with the band that would become The Cure, Smith was savvy enough to realise that Thompson's status as a home-town legend might actually entice a few punters to see the band. "He was in the first incarnation of The Cure," Smith said in 1989, "because he was the attraction. We used to go play in pubs when we were 16; people would come see us purely because Porl was playing the guitar. They didn't even know the name of the group, it was just Porl playing guitar. So it was quite funny." Not laugh out loud funny, mind you, for someone with songwriting ambitions such as Robert Smith.

Again, given that Crawley was not exactly rock'n'roll ground zero, the band had to search for a venue to unleash the rock beast within. By this point, Smith was bored of their endless rehearsals. "We would jam," he said, "but I hated it. Why play another blues? Why change chords? Why not just stay on E?" Smith, at least, was definitely ready for their first public appearance. This time they chose Worth Abbey on Turner's Hill in Crawley, an institution that promoted itself as "an English Benedictine monastery in a changing world", with "a community of Roman Catholic Benedictine monks seeking to follow the Gospel of Jesus Christ within a framework provided by their rule of life and their Abbot". In hindsight, it seemed the perfect starting place for a band whose later albums would feature such titles as *Pornography*, *Faith* and *Disintegration* and who were often accused of inspiring an entire generation of God-less Goths.

So Malice unleashed their musical assault on the world on December 18, 1976, at the Christmas party for Upjohns, the company now managed by Smith's father Alex, who helped them secure the gig. But instead of plugging in and roaring their way through Hendrix's 'Foxy Lady' and Alex Harvey's 'Faith Healer' – or possibly something by blue-jean rockers Status Quo, whom Smith had checked out in 1971 and found "fantastic" – the band was forced to play unplugged and to operate under an assumed name. The tag Malice was considered not quite right for the hallowed grounds of Worth Abbey (where Smith and Mary would marry some 12 years later). So they turned up with acoustic guitars, and a bongo, no less, and sat on the floor and played. "That was the firm's dinner and dance," Tolhurst recalled. "We sat in the sort of minstrel's gallery in Worth Abbey with bongos and acoustic guitars and just played nonsense. Everybody politely clapped; it was the boss's son, so they had to be pleasant." The world of rock'n'roll remained unchanged, at least for the time being.

Two days later, Smith, Tolhurst, Dempsey and Thompson would reunite, briefly, with guitar man Mark Ceccagno. Amulet, Ceccagno's new, post-Malice combo, were booked to play a show at St Wilfrid's, and Malice managed to talk their way onto the bill. Smith, of course, also had to talk his way around his nemesis, the St Wilfrid's headmaster. Smith told him that Malice was a band that peddled jazz-fusion, which was perfectly acceptable, so they were given the green light to play. He did, however, neglect to mention that he was a member of the band.

Porl Thompson designed the stoner-ish looking poster for the show, which announced the gig as "A Special Christmas Bumper Bundle Party". "Jazz rock combo" Amulet were billed as "speshul gest [sic] stars". Nothing is known of the mystery band Bootleg, who were also mentioned on the poster as part of the evening's entertainment, although Michael Dempsey, for one, suspects that it may have been a ruse to inflate the entrance fee to 30p.

Smith, a reluctant vocalist at best, was yet to step up to the mic, so the band coerced Martin, a journalist from the local *Crawley Observer*, to take care of frontman duties. Completely unrehearsed, he rocked up in a three-piece suit, Manchester United scarf and motorcycle helmet, which he clung to throughout the show in fear of it being nicked. According to Tolhurst, the scribe-cum-vocalist's best feature was that he "did a good impersonation of David Cassidy". "We had about 100 rehearsals and knew six songs, so we thought we'd do it in public," said Smith. "The curtain opened and we were there, snarling. It was a disaster. I started with a different song and was one ahead all the way through without noticing until they started the last song and I'd already played it."

Their set, for what it was worth, included 'Foxy Lady' – later to be massacred by The Cure on their debut album, *Three Imaginary Boys* – 'Wild Thing', which Tolhurst attempted to sing, Bowie's 'Suffragette City', Thin Lizzy's 'Jailbreak' and a Smith original, 'A Night Like This', which would eventually turn up on The Cure's 1985 long-player, *The Head On The Door*.

Having bluffed their way in using the "jazz-rock fusion" ruse, Smith and co then started playing what he would describe as "loud, fast music". The racket was overwhelming – "a screaming wall of feed-back," according to Smith – and of the 300 people in the hall at the start of their set, most of them headed for the door. "There was another band on who were much more proficient than us," recalled Lol Tolhurst, "but it set the stage for what we were to become. It was a trial by fire. The response was fairly muted; everybody was sitting around the side of the hall."

Smith's take on the show was more extreme. As he saw it, because the band was playing so aggressively they qualified as a punk band, which didn't sit so well with the youth of Crawley. "Everyone hated us and walked out, but we didn't care because we were doing what we wanted."

In the type of scene that would be played out again and again at various times and in various locations during The Cure's early years, Malice's brief set ended in chaos. When Tolhurst stepped up to sing 'Wild Thing', a humiliated Thompson punched him, gobsmacked that he dared to desecrate a Hendrix number. It wasn't the last time a fist was raised in anger at a Cure show, although Tolhurst had some trouble recalling the ruckus when we spoke. "I don't actually recall any fights with Porl – at least not then," he said.

As for the band's first-time vocalist, he stormed off the stage with the farewell words, "This is shit", returning to his post at the *Crawley Observer* without so much as a glance back over his shoulder. As 1976 drew to a close, and Queen's 'Somebody To Love' and Abba's 'Money Money Money' slugged it out at the top of the pop charts alongside Showaddywaddy and Johnny Mathis, the dream was over for Malice. So Robert Smith, not for the last time, reacted accordingly: he split up the band.

Malice's temporary hiatus, of course, didn't quite rank with the subsequent splits in Camp Cure. There would be times when Smith – his judgement altered by drugs, paranoia, ennui, anger, Steve Severin (or a combination of each) – would swear on a stack of *Melody Makers* that it was all over for the band, usually to return to the grind within months. This time around, however, the rift lasted just beyond the Christmas holiday; by January 1977, the musical firm of Smith, Thompson, Tolhurst and Dempsey was back. While they continued the increasingly frustrating search for a vocalist, the Crawley four also had to consider their post-high school future.

What the band needed, more immediately, was a new and improved name. Not only was Malice now forever linked to the St Wilfrid's debacle of the previous December, but Smith felt that their moniker made them sound as if they were clones of camp rockers Queen, a band he truly despised. As far as Smith was concerned, the mincing Freddie Mercury had nothing on everyday hero Alex Harvey, so the name Malice had never been a comfortable fit for him. The idea for the tag Easy Cure came to them in the Smith family kitchen, during a January 1977 band meeting. And it wasn't an inspired choice.

"We decided we needed another name if we were going to start playing again," Smith figured. "One of our songs was called 'Easy Cure', a song written by Lol, and eventually, in desperation, we settled on that."

Smith, in fact, hated the name. "I thought it was terrible. I sort of remember sitting around arguing about what we were going to be called and in the end I think we just got bored of it."*

After his run-in with authority at St Wilfrid's which led to him being tagged "an undesirable influence", Smith still managed to pass nine O-levels. Even though Smith had vague plans of enrolling at university, his brief expulsion proved to him that academia or any kind of further education clearly wasn't for him. Smith knew where his immediate future lay: on the dole. Michael Georgeson told me that Smith's parents were very concerned about their boy's lack of interest in academia. "He was a great worry to his parents," said Georgeson. "The school, I seem to remember, took most of the blame for that."

Smith registered for Social Security forthwith, financing his musical addiction with money raised by flogging his father's home brew on the side. ("We'd steal five to six a week and sell them to old blokes of the area, and with the money we'd buy records.") According to Smith, his instructions to Social Security staff were very clear – not to put themselves out trying to find a job for this musician-in-the-making.

"It came to the point where I'd rather kill myself than get a job," said Smith. "I told Social Security to give the jobs to those who want them; I'd rather stay at home listening to music. But they'd tell me I had to work and I'd just ask, 'Why?' "

Smith had taken – and passed – the Oxford-Cambridge entrance exam, but more as a personal challenge than some gateway to the future. "I just wanted to see if I'd be able to get in," he said. Typically, he rolled up for his entrance interview in a woman's fur coat, and

---

* The name Easy Cure would later be adopted by an Italian Cure cover act.

wasn't accepted. He was, however, offered a place at Sussex University. "It was supposed to be the best university for drugs in the country."

Smith made a compromise with his father – he told him that he'd go to university if he was granted a year off to see where music led him. "But once I started the group and they realised I was serious about it, I wasn't just using it as an excuse to go around and get drunk all the time and pull women, they dropped all sort of ideas of me furthering my education."

As Lol Tolhurst saw it, this was a turning point in their lives. "We'd reached a point where we had to do one thing or another: take the safe path, go to university and so on. But we got to the doors of it and decided to do otherwise."

Smith, in fact, was convinced that the period that he spent on the dole, post-education, were possibly the best eight months of his life. It didn't hurt that Mary Poole, who actually had a job, would buy Smith's drinks at the many Crawley watering holes that they'd frequent in the mid-to-late Seventies. Robert Smith was in an enviable position: he had a band in waiting, a loyal girlfriend, home brew on tap, and a burning desire to do as little as possible. Lol Tolhurst was also enjoying this golden age. "We'd listen to his brother's really groovy records and drink home brew."

"I can't understand people wanting to work," Smith would declare in an early interview with *Shake* magazine. "I think the 'dignity of labour' is another myth propagated by employers. It's all just money. I mean, if you've got enough money to do what you want, then that's it really. I can't understand people needing to work to prove that they're worthwhile."

Interestingly, Smith would consider his lack of true faith one of the reasons for his raging apathy. Smith would talk about laying "myself open to visions of God, but I never had any. I come from a religious family and there have been moments when I've felt the oneness of things, but they never last. And I never think that I'm ever going to wake up and know that I was wrong. If God didn't exist and the search for meaning was futile, what was the point of having a job?

"When you have no belief in anything but yourself," he continued, "you tend towards apathy; you see no reason for doing anything and nobody can find a reason for you. I used to value nobody else's opinions."

While Smith's slack attitude to employment and God might sound like the usual mix of youthful arrogance and standard teenage rebellion, it wasn't as though he had that much to rebel against. The Sex Pistols might have sneered at the monarchy – John Lydon's tough London-Irish upbringing provided plenty of source material for his venom – while The Clash railed against racism and apathy, an outlook formed as much by education as angst. But The Cure came from comfortable, middle-class Crawley. If the band failed, there were jobs to be found in local firms, possibly with a little encouragement from supportive parents. Alex and Rita Smith may not have been overwhelmed by their son's (non) career choice, but they didn't throw their offspring into the street. Smith had the type of freedom of choice that many of his post-punk peers were denied, which goes a long way to explaining The Cure's decidedly apolitical outlook. Although they would go on to play many benefits and fund-raisers, the only thing they had to rebel against was the mundane, comfortable existence of the English middle class. 'Anarchy In The UK' it was not.

Yet when he was asked if he considered himself middle class, Smith bridled at the thought. "I hate the idea of classes," he said in 1984. "I think that's a stupid concept. I've never come across the concept of middle class. Middle class is a thing that the media likes to propagate – class divisions. I really hate it, it's stupid. I'm not working class, because I don't work, but then a lot of other people don't [work] either."

Lol Tolhurst, meanwhile, had undergone the obligatory careers vocation interrogation prior to leaving St Wilfrid's. "He said to me, 'OK, you're pretty good at chemistry and science, maybe you should be a chemist – and there's an opening at this firm.' They got cheap labour, really." When not working for Hellerman Deutsch, he attended Crawley Technical College. (Smith also enrolled there, principally to hang out with his bandmate.)

Dempsey had a similarly enervating chat with his careers advisor. "I had no idea," he told me. "I alighted on the word 'journalist' and he replied, 'Journalism – very competitive.'" Dempsey also left St Wilfrid's and decided against further education: Tolhurst had landed him a job at Hellerman Deutsch, testing cables and relays for Exocet missiles procured by the French military. ("I had no science knowledge at all," he laughs, looking back.) He then attended business school in Crawley, but had no real plans for a career in that world. "It was convenient, really," he replied when I asked him about this. He also found a job as a porter at Netherne Hospital, the local asylum, which he recalled as being "built on the Edwardian model – it was an extraordinary place, almost like a country house". A country house, that is, populated by mentally unstable inmates drugged to their eyeballs.

Undaunted by this, The Easy Cure, with Dempsey's help, would attend many of the parties held by the staff on the hospital's grounds. As for Porl Thompson, he continued with his fledgling design career – which would continue in tandem with his musical life – by enrolling at the West Sussex College of Design, although this wouldn't take place until 1979.

By early 1977, The Easy Cure had settled into a new rehearsal routine, this time in an annexe attached to the Smith household. Smith's parents had added a room to their Crawley home, and the group had virtually moved in, commandeering the space for rehearsals. "Our regular routine was three nights a week at the Smiths'," Tolhurst told me. "They remodelled their home for a family room but the band moved in for three years."

Gradually, more original songs came to life. Porl Thompson's tenure with The Easy Cure, inadvertently, also led to Smith developing his creative skills: as the band's rhythm guitarist, Smith was the first to master the basics of songwriting. As Smith saw it, songwriting was born out of necessity, not some insatiable creative desire that was eating him up inside. "The group was a way of doing something," he said, "but I found a lot of our songs better than those I was listening to."

Lol Tolhurst agreed with this. "I was talking with Michael Dempsey about this – a lot of people start bands thinking of people they liked and admired, but we started from the other direction. We decided what we didn't like and who we didn't want to sound like and what was left was what we played."

Smith was, however, drawing his nascent songwriting influences from a variety of reliable sources. One of those was veteran BBC Radio One disc-jockey John Peel. Smith tuned in to his nightly programme with all the intensity of an acolyte. But even a cocky kid like Smith had no inkling that his favourite DJ, the much-lauded Peel – a lone voice of credibility and taste in a sea of commerciality and musical fluff – would soon be championing the Crawley combo.

From the age of about 15, Smith had been a Peel convert, tuning in to his show every night. "That was the best part of the day. I heard [The Clash's] 'White Riot' and cut off all my hair [which was years away from growing into his trademark bird's-nest, admittedly]. The Buzzcocks, The Stranglers – I used to dream of making a record that John Peel would play."

What the newly named Easy Cure still needed, however, was a vocalist. Their *Crawley Observer* ring-in from the December show hadn't been seen since storming off the stage screaming, "This is shit", so the Crawley four knew they had to start looking elsewhere. The enigmatically named Gary X came and went during March 1977, followed by a man with an equally arresting name, Peter O'Toole (no relation to the blue-eyed boozer of the big screen), who made his public debut at a show to mark (belatedly) Robert Smith's 18th birthday, on April 22, at the local St Edward's Hall.

O'Toole's debut left absolutely no impact on Smith, who attempted to recall the gig in 1988. "I remember nothing at all so it must have been good."

But Robert Smith was coming to the realisation that no one else seemed to share the same musical mindset as the established members of The Easy Cure, even though Smith didn't fancy himself as a potential vocalist. "When we started, I wasn't the singer, I was the drunk rhythm guitarist who wrote all these weird songs."

Peter O'Toole, however, was still part of The Easy Cure when they spent another night around the Smith kitchen table, flicking through the pages of the music press, "trying to glean what was going on", according to Tolhurst. They spotted an ad in *Melody Maker*, searching for new talent. It was hard to miss, given that the ad's artwork was a very classy piece of prime Seventies sexploitation. To wit, two women were draped over a motorcycle in a particularly come-hither sort of way. The darker woman of the pair pointed her hard-to-miss hotpants-clad booty in the direction of the camera. "Wanna be a recording star?" the ad screamed in blazing red type. "Get your ass up," continued the text, which was strategically positioned next to the hotpants-wearing beauty. "Take your chance." It was followed by a phone number for German label Ariola/Hansa, along with the following details:

Hansa, Germany's leading pop label that brought you Boney M, Donna Summer, is auditioning in Britain. Top recording studios with video equipment. Only experienced groups, singer songwriters, age approx 15–30 should apply. For further details, phone numbers above and send tape, photo to Hansa Records PO Box 1 DT London W1A 1DT.

Even if The Easy Cure had any music-business savvy – and who has at this apprenticeship stage of their career? – they would have been hard pressed to find a less compatible label than the German-based Ariola/Hansa. Founded in 1964 by brothers Peter and Thomas Meisel, who also ran a publishing company called Meiselverlage, the Hansa label's first signings were European "schlager" artists (popular/folk musicians); these releases were distributed through Ariola, which signed such artists as David Hasselhof, Roger Whittaker, Snap and Eros Ramazotti. By the time they placed their "search for a star" ad in *Melody Maker*, Hansa had grown into a seriously successful label. Their roster featured such acts as Boney M and Donna Summer (and later Milli Vanilli, No Mercy and Lou Bega). If The Easy Cure had read the ad's not-so-fine print closely and considered the contents, they would have figured that Boney M and Donna Summer came from a different galaxy altogether to the Crawley hopefuls. Unlike Fiction, the label that would eventually be formed to provide a recording home for The Cure, creative development wasn't exactly high on the list of Ariola/Hansa priorities. They wanted to shift some units – their roster proved that.

But the real warning sign for The Easy Cure should have come in 1976, when Ariola/Hansa attempted to turn four blow-waved Brits, going by the name of Child, into the type of pre-fab pop outfit that would relegate The Bay City Rollers to pop's second division. It didn't work. The airbrushed quartet didn't score until September 1978, when their 'It's Only Make Believe' reached the UK Top 20 – but by then The Cure had learned all they needed to know about Ariola/Hansa.* Regardless, the business aspects of making music were a long way from

* Slick, sleek pop moodists Japan also signed with Ariola/Hansa on the strength of the 1977 "talent wanted" ad, recording three albums for the label. Not surprisingly, frontman David Sylvian denied that their method of recruitment was simply part of some tacky "talent contest". "No, it wasn't like that," he told an interviewer. "They saw pictures of us and became interested. We had nothing to do with the talent contest." OK, if you say so.

the minds of Smith, Thompson, Tolhurst, Dempsey and O'Toole when they joined forces around a tape recorder in the front room of the Smith household in April. This first recording of The Easy Cure was sent to the London address of Hansa, preceded by a band photo. The Easy Cure prayed to the rock'n'roll gods and then got back to rehearsing. It was the only time they would enter a talent comp – and for good reason, as it transpired.

While their application – or, more accurately, their photo – was doing the rounds of the Hansa office, another performance opportunity arose on May 6, this time at The Rocket, a Crawley local (now known as The Railway). The gig only came about through a choice piece of opportunism by Tolhurst. It was Sunday lunchtime and Tolhurst discovered that Marc Ceccagno's band, Amulet, who'd been witnesses to the Worth Abbey debacle, wouldn't be able to make their scheduled set at The Rocket that night. So The Easy Cure drummer made the call and offered their services. The publican shrugged and figured, "Why not?"

"We realised we needed to play in front of a real audience at some point," Smith figured, reasonably enough, "so we rehearsed all afternoon and went down and played. We went down quite well."

Well, not quite, according to Lol Tolhurst. "The first show there was absolutely abysmal. There were about 15 people there looking in their beer, trying to ignore what was going on on stage."

Although the band's songs-in-development were unlike anything else being heard in Crawley at the time – hardly an Olympian achievement, given the limited competition – any attention The Easy Cure received was based on the flashy axework of Porl Thompson. Yet by this time, the band was experimenting with such minimalist mood-pieces as '10.15 Saturday Night' and 'Killing An Arab' – songs that balanced both silence and sound in their arrangements. Thompson's chops seemed to be a tad superfluous.

While fledgling songwriter Smith clearly saw Thompson's tricky playing as excessive to The Easy Cure's needs, he also insisted that Thompson wasn't overly excited by the band's direction. "He didn't actually like what we were doing," Smith commented in 1989. "We didn't really like what he was doing either."

Michael Dempsey, however, could spot Smith's future intentions for the band's sound, even at this nascent stage. "We didn't have to be virtuosos. He stripped away everything that we didn't like – in fact, we never said we liked anything, really."

While both The Easy Cure and Thompson returned to neutral corners to consider the future, a telegram arrived from one Kathy Pritchard, addressed to a Robert J. Smith of Crawley, Sussex. Its message was simple. It read: "Please call Hansa Records urgently." Easy Cure's rough-and-ready demo tape (and, crucially, their cheap mug shot) had done the trick. Smith called the number and an audition was arranged at Morgan Studios in London on May 13, 1977.* Justifiably excited, the band caught the train to London, set up in the studio and ran through a couple of songs while the Hansa staff videoed the band. With the benefit of hindsight, Tolhurst admitted that the presence of a video camera should have tipped them off to Hansa's intentions: they were searching for the next Child, not some post-punk upstarts.

"They videotaped us, which should have been the first clue, but we failed to get the significance of it all. We realised after: they'd had a hit with Child, all pretty boys, and that's why they videotaped us. We were all young boys so they'd do the same with us."

Of all the members of The Easy Cure, only Smith seemed unsure about Hansa's intentions. Dempsey recalled that after the first try-out, "Robert was very circumspect – the others not so. But we were just so green."

Hansa had seen enough. By May 18, only five days after the band's Morgan Studios audition, they sent a contract to The Easy Cure, offering them a five-year deal. The band convened for an emergency meeting at the Smith household. If nothing else, they were realists – given that they hadn't been besieged by A&R sharks waving lucrative contracts, the band decided to sign up. "Well, it wasn't like we could choose who we were going to sign to," Smith explained much later. "There wasn't a queue down the road."

Tolhurst, for one, was shocked. "We were amazed. How did that happen out of all those people that applied?"

The band's following did build with further gigs at The Rocket – as many as 300 locals turned out for these shows. But again, it seemed to be Thompson's playing that was drawing the crowds, not Smith's

---

* The studio, later known as Battery, has since closed down.

swiftly developing and oddly curious takes on punk rock. It also helped that Tolhurst and Smith's older brothers encouraged all their mates to attend these shows. Such rough-and-ready cuts from the time as 'Heroin Face', recorded at The Rocket in 1977, would end up on the 2005 reissue of *Three Imaginary Boys*.

"Whenever we played," Smith said, "we thought it was awful – there was loads of feedback and you could never hear anything except Porl's guitar." Smith had set up a bare-bones sound-mixing unit, which he operated while the band played, but it didn't seem to help. Smith was convinced that their regular gigs at The Rocket came about purely because of Thompson's "guitar hero" status. "That's the only reason we kept getting re-booked."

The increasingly sceptical Smith also suspected that The Easy Cure was merely providing a background soundtrack for Crawley locals on a big night out. After all, The Rocket was hardly The Marquee. "We had a really drunken following," he said, "and we were really just a focal point, an excuse for people to go out, get drunk and smash the place up."

While the bar staff at The Rocket swept up the broken glass and fag butts from another Easy Cure show, the band had to deal with a more immediate challenge – and it had nothing to do with Porl Thompson's axegrinding or the choice of songs for their upcoming Hansa demo. Their vocalist with the movie-star moniker, Peter O'Toole, returned from a kibbutz in Israel and informed his bandmates that rock'n'roll was not the life for him. He quit the band on September 12. Smith made a key decision: he figured that he might as well become their singer, if for no other reason than there was no one else he knew who could do the job. It was a decision he'd been edging towards for some time.

"We went through about five different singers," Smith said. "They were fucking useless, basically. I always ended up thinking, 'I could do better than this.' So gradually I started singing a song, and then it was two songs. I thought I couldn't be any worse [than his predecessors] so I decided to be the singer."

It was no smooth or immediate transition from "drunk rhythm guitarist" to accidental frontman for Robert Smith. The band subsequently went through a brief "instrumentals only" phase, while he slowly developed the nerve to open his mouth and sing. And Smith's public debut as vocalist and rhythm guitarist of the now four-piece Easy Cure wasn't the highest point of the band's early career. "I was paralysed with fear before we went out," Smith said. "I drank about six pints of beer, which . . . was enough to knock me over." While the lager helped lubricate Smith's vocal cords and ease his stage fright, it didn't do a lot for his memory.

"I was singing the wrong song," he remembered. "Of the first three songs, I started on the second song. They carried on playing. No one even noticed. So I thought, 'If I can get away with that, I can be the singer.'"

While it may not have arisen out of any grand design, what Smith the vocalist wisely chose to do was to stay true to his speaking voice: just like his guitar playing, his singing stuck safely within his limitations. "I think the weirdest thing about the way I sing," he would comment, "is that most of the time it's how I talk." It provided the band with one of their more distinctive early musical traits: it wasn't as if Smith was singing a tune, it was more like he was talking directly to you, which increased the all-round creepiness of a song such as 'Killing An Arab'. So what if his pitch was flatter than Loftus Road, the home ground of his beloved football team, QPR?

The Easy Cure appeared at a free show on October 9 in Queen's Square, Crawley. The positively named Peace Jam — with poster art, once again, from the pen of Porl Thompson — was arranged by James and Consuelo Duggan, who'd organised approximately 100 similar shows in Ireland. Three hundred punters turned up for the event, which was talked up by the Duggans as a chance for people "to listen to the music and think about peace, not just for Northern Ireland but everywhere". Smith's father Alex, meanwhile, stood stage front with his trusty Super 8 camera, documenting the largest show of The Easy Cure's career to date. (This footage would turn up on the video companion to their first best-of collection, entitled *Staring At The Sea – The Images*.)

The local rag, the *Crawley Observer*, was sufficiently impressed to provide the band with their first press coverage. The paper was especially excited when they learned that the local lads had signed with Hansa for the lofty figure of £1,000.

Beneath a headline that read: 'Rockin' To The Top', the article documented The Easy Cure's seemingly rapid rise. "The band, all aged between 18 and 19, was one of 1,400 bands to answer an advertisement in the *Melody Maker*," they reported. "Only 60 bands were selected for an audition in London from which eight groups [Japan being one of the other winners] were offered a contract by Hansa, a leading German recording firm. The group's first single will come out on the Antlantic [sic] record label." In his first documented public comment, Robert Smith – who was soon to develop a notoriously hot and cold relationship with the media – was still in shock. "It all happened so fast," Smith said of the Hansa deal, "but now we are really looking forward to making our first record."

The Easy Cure had no trouble spending Hansa's £1,000 advance on new equipment. They would, however, have problems appeasing Hansa's commercial expectations when they got comfortable in London's SAV Studios for the first of two recording sessions for the label (the second was at Chestnut Studios). They laid down five originals during that first session. The song list featured 'Meathook', which would reappear on their debut album in 1979, and 'See The Children', whose questionable lyrics painted Smith as a dirty old man in teenager's clothing. There was certainly an uneasy air of queasiness about lyrics which talked of passing sweets through a fence and wanting to join in the children's games. Other tracks recorded were 'I Just Need Myself', 'I Want To Be Old' and 'Pillbox Tales', which would resurface as the B-side of 1978's 'Boys Don't Cry' and then, again, some 27 years later on *Join The Dots: B-Sides And Rarities*.

But Hansa wasn't interested in Cure originals. They'd sent the band tapes of songs they deemed suitable for their new signing, including 'I Fought The Law' – later brilliantly covered by The Clash – and 'The Great Airplane Disaster'. At Hansa's request, they also covered The Beatles' shouter, 'I Saw Her Standing There', Bowie's 'Rebel Rebel', along with originals 'Little Girl', 'I'm Cold' (another track to resurface on 2004's *Join The Dots*) and, most crucially, 'Killing An Arab', but in a much slower version than the track which would become their official debut single in 1978. The band managed to cut their own tunes only via an impressive act of stealth, as Tolhurst would recall. "When somebody had gone out for a cup of tea we'd persuade the engineer to record some of our songs."

If any indicator was needed of the wilfully non-Hansa direction that Robert Smith's slowly developing songwriting talent was taking, it was evident in 'Killing An Arab', a sparse, skeletal meditation on murder and nothingness. The track – which over its life would stir up plenty of attention from such groups as the National Front and America's Anti-Arab League – was directly inspired by an incident in the book *étranger (The Stranger)*, written by renowned French existentialist Albert Camus, which had been part of Smith and Dempsey's St Wilfrid's reading list. As heroes go, Camus was as peculiar a choice for Smith as everyman hero, Alex Harvey. (An early Cure press release would zero in on the Camus connection, declaring that the band was inspired by "punk and the Penguin Modern Classics".)

Albert Camus was born in Mondovi, Algeria on November 7, 1913, to a French Algerian (*pied noir*) settler family. His mother was of Spanish extraction. His father, Lucien, died during World War I's Battle of Marne in 1914. Camus endured a tough, poor childhood in the Belcourt section of Algiers. He eventually became an author and philosopher, one of the principal luminaries of existentialism, along with Jean-Paul Sartre, another hero of the young Robert Smith. Camus – who died in a car crash in 1960 – was best known for *The Outsider*, which was based on his theory of the absurd. In the first half of the novel the protagonist Meursault is a cold fish, virtually a walking corpse. It is Meursault's inability to reflect on the nature of his existence that leads him to murder. Only by being tried and sentenced to death is Meursault forced to acknowledge his own mortality and the responsibility he has for his own life.

If there was one passage in Robert Smith's dog-eared copy of *The Stranger* that left the deepest impression, it was the following, which occurred immediately after the murder by shooting that formed the narrative and moral heart of the book:

> I took a few steps towards the spring. The Arab didn't move. Even now he was some distance away. Perhaps because of the shadows on his face, he seemed to be laughing.

While its roots lay in a deeply profound, if worryingly emotionless study of alienation, Smith would regularly play down the song's intentions. "'Arab' was a great rabble rouser when we played it live," Smith would say, "but it was almost a novelty song." Smith would defend the song with a touch more levity in a 1978 interview with *NME*. "The song's dedicated to all the rich Arabs who go to Crawley college discos to pick up the girls," he joked, before adding that 'Arab' was "not really racist, if you know what the song is about. It's not a call to kill Arabs. It just happened that the main character in the book had actually killed an Arab, but it could have been a Scandinavian or an English bloke. The fact that he killed an Arab had nothing to do with it really."

Hansa, however, had trouble identifying with (or even locating) the "novelty" aspects of a track going by the name of 'Killing An Arab'. In fact, they had trouble identifying with any of the songs recorded by The Easy Cure during the two 1977 sessions. Hansa countered by offering The Easy Cure tunes that they had earmarked for teen-sceners Child. The band politely demurred.

"They wanted us to be another Child," Smith said with some disdain in 1978. "We were even offered a song that Child would eventually put out as a single. [And] they were giving us these really old songs to cover. We couldn't believe it," Smith said. "This was summer 1977 and we thought we'd be able to do all these outrageous songs we'd written and all they wanted from us were versions of really banal old rock'n'roll songs." Smith also slagged off the label's choice of "unsympathetic" producers whom Hansa had attempted to team with The Easy Cure.

Almost 30 years later, Lol Tolhurst still laughs at some of the meetings held between band and label. "We'd go and see them and they'd say, 'We don't like your songs. Not even people in prison would like this.' I have no idea why they said this. [But] we thought that was the way the music business worked." On one occasion, the band met with Steve Rowland, Hansa's A&R rep, in a London office that the label had hired by the hour. "All the time we were talking to him, we felt that he didn't hear a thing we said. He just had this plan about how he was going to make us big stars."

While The Easy Cure reconsidered the merits of signing with Germany's biggest independent label, they were headed towards another clash. But this time their adversaries were the law – and the National Front. On October 16, in between the two Hansa studio sessions, they were booked to play Felbridge Village Hall. The show's poster, with type by Smith and design by Thompson, featured a drawing of a gormless looking character (many believe it is the band's first public piss-take of Tolhurst). The Easy Cure were to be supported by the not-so-legendary Mr Wrongs rock disco, which turned out to be a Crawley school friend who came equipped with a turntable and his private stash of Led Zeppelin and Lynyrd Skynyrd vinyl albums. Admission was 30p, but, as the band would soon regret, the crowd was encouraged to bring their own booze.

The beneficiaries included the Arthritis & Rheumatism Council but the evening attracted the interest of both the local police and the National Front – obviously interested in any act with a provocative song called 'Killing An Arab' – neither of whom helped make the night any calmer. The police eventually brought the show to an abrupt and early end, while Smith and Tolhurst's brothers and their crew introduced various National Front members to the car park's asphalt.

The year 1977 had been a strange one for The Easy Cure. They'd found it relatively easy to secure shows in and around Crawley, having become semi-regulars at venues The Rocket and Laker's at Redhill, and they'd also snagged a record deal. But Hansa's intentions had left them feeling queasy, while Smith wasn't so sure that the band's small but devoted following were as keen on the nuances of 'Killing An Arab' or 'Heroin Face' (another early Easy Cure number, which would surface years later on the cassette-only add-on to their 1984 *Concert* album) as they were on Porl Thompson's string work.

They agreed to end the year with a New Year's Eve show at Orpington General Hospital, which had been arranged by Dempsey's brother-in-law. He actually had plans to become The Easy Cure's first manager, going so far as to print up 500 business cards emblazoned with the message: "Easy Cure For All Occasions". Better still, the Orpington Hospital gig guaranteed the band £20. It wasn't quite the £1,000 that Hansa had thrown their way, but given that almost 12 months ago to the day they'd been rocking the St Wilfrid's School under the name Malice, £20 was hard to resist.

Smith was definitely up for it: the show was a chance to kick out the jams and forget about their ongoing hassles with Hansa. "Well, we thought, 'We'll play anywhere for £20,'" Smith recalled, "but when we arrived, we realised it was full of 40- and 50-year-olds and trainee managers." As the night wore on, Smith learned that it wasn't just Hansa executives who were distressed by 'Killing An Arab'; the crowd was in the mood for favourites, not sparse, austere deliberations of French existentialism.

Speaking in *Ten Imaginary Years*, Dempsey also realised quite early on that the Orpington General Hospital may not have been the perfect venue for a strong-willed band with a limited repertoire of golden oldies. "They wanted a dance band and we really had no grasp on anyone's tunes but our own. We were also expected to play two sets but we knew right from the outset it was dangerous because we played our first set to a lot of booing and hissing. Luckily they weren't sufficiently drunk at that stage to be anything more than vocal."

Although Porl Thompson's Fender-bending antics may have still seemed superfluous to The Easy Cure's needs, he did come in handy at this year-ending show. In between sets, Thompson, who'd once been a guitarist-for-hire with local cabaret acts, mentioned that he knew his way around the 10-tissue weepy 'Tie A Yellow Ribbon'. So the band decided to use it to open their next set.

As Smith would relate, "We went back and started playing it and this roar of approval went up, but after bashing away at the chorus for six or seven minutes, this bloke threw a bottle and we ended up in the car park getting beaten up by several punters who wanted their money back."

It's hard to imagine that too many of the fans at the Orpington General Hospital could really summon up the strength to thump a group of hearty 18-year-olds. But the show was enough for Dempsey's brother-in-law, who trashed his Easy Cure calling cards and terminated his services as the band's manager-in-waiting, forthwith. In some ways, the gig was as much a turning point for the band as their battle with Hansa: they knew that they simply weren't cut out to play the favourites. As Smith stated in 1988, "We didn't want to learn loads of other people's songs just so we could, because that way we would have become yet another pub band."

During January, the band and Hansa agreed to undertake one more recording session, this time at London's PSL Studio with producer Trevor Vallis at the desk, a man who would go on to work with such acts as Marillion, Bucks Fizz and Peter Cetera. (Hansa had previously tried to link the band with producer Gary Taylor, former bassist for GTO Records' signing Fox.) The deal was very clear – Hansa had provided a relatively well-known producer, so the band should adhere to their label's plan and cut some no-brainer hits. At least, that was the plan.

At the third and what proved to be final recording session for Hansa, The Easy Cure obliged their master and cut one cover, their second take on 'Rebel Rebel', along with originals 'Plastic Passion' (another track destined for *Three Imaginary Boys*), 'I Just Need Myself' and 'Smashed Up', a song which Robert Smith would state was "the worst thing we ever recorded". By now, the band knew that the situation with Hansa was untenable: the label wanted safe versions of established hits, The Easy Cure wanted to find the middle ground between punk rock, Beatles songcraft and Albert Camus. And Hansa had no plans to get the band on the road, which was essential if they were to earn some kind of living. To make matters just that little bit worse, Lol Tolhurst was hit by a bus. As Robert Smith recalled, the band propped Tolhurst up in the pub, easing his pain with brandy. "He spent the rest of the day playing drums and bleeding. It was cack."

Smith and the band realised that the Hansa deal was a dead end. There was no way either party was going to compromise. "On top of all this," Smith added, "I had suddenly realised that I actually hated the songs we were doing and that even if Hansa liked them, we wouldn't follow through." (Of course this didn't stop the band re-recording three of the songs from the Hansa sessions – 'Meathook', 'Plastic Passion' and 'Killing An Arab' – for their subsequent debut long-player.)

By February 19, a dejected Easy Cure was back at their regular Crawley haunt, The Rocket. This time around they were supported by a punk band called Lockjaw, whose numbers included bassist Simon Gallup. Born in Duxhurst, Surrey, on June 1, 1960, before moving to Horley as an infant, Gallup was the youngest of five children (he was one of four boys). Again, like both Tolhurst and Smith, there was a sizeable age gap between Gallup and his nearest sibling, Ric, who was almost seven years his senior. Gallup had attended Horley Infants and Junior schools, then Horley Balcombe Road Comprehensive School. By the time his path crossed with The Easy Cure, he was holding down a job at a local plastics factory. It was hardly the rock'n'roll dream that dedicated Kiss fan Gallup had been hoping to live out. However, his brother Ric worked in a Horley record store, situated at the rear of an electronics shop, so Simon had been exposed to the punk singles that were pouring out of London, which would have an immediate and very tangible impact on Lockjaw.

Gallup was aware of Lol Tolhurst, mainly through reputation. Tolhurst was dating a girl that Gallup knew from school; she would often boast how Tolhurst was a "hard man". Tolhurst confirmed this. "Simon, when he saw me in the street, used to cross the road. As he got to know me he realised that was far from the truth."

Lockjaw had also endured a tough introduction to the music industry. They'd sent a very rough demo tape to a label called Raw Records, who, in Gallup's words, "thought we were this really good suburban band – but in fact we were shit." On being signed, Raw Records introduced Lockjaw to the world with the single 'Radio Call Sign', backed with 'The Young Ones' on the B-side. It sank without trace.

"They were a raw punk band," Tolhurst said of Lockjaw. "Their shows were very much the same: lots of stage invasions, people pogoing, stuff like that."

Lockjaw had snared the support slot at The Rocket on the strength of their Raw Records single, but it turned out to be their only appearance at the venue, mainly because, as Smith recalled, "The place was torn apart." Robert Smith took note of Gallup and his band; he, Tolhurst and Dempsey even started hanging out with Gallup at his brother's record store.

During March, The Easy Cure – and Hansa – realised that they needed to come to some kind of conclusion about their unsteady alliance. The band was insistent that the stark 'Killing An Arab' should be their debut single, while Hansa were just as insistent that it was a career-killer. By March 29, when Hansa officially rejected the song as a single, band and label parted. And the split was permanent.

The Easy Cure, understandably, were devastated by their first not-so-successful foray into the music business. From then on they would display a certain wariness towards the fiscal side of the world in which they moved – eventually reaching the point where Smith turned down all offers for use of the band's music in ads (at least until the early 21st century), thereby turning down millions of pounds in potential earnings. What he took away from the terminated Hansa deal was a sense of caution, plus the rights to all the originals they'd recorded during the three sessions.

According to Tolhurst, that was one of the smartest moves Smith ever made. "It all came to a sticky end but luckily Robert remembered to ask them to let us keep our advance and asked for the rights for our songs back. Robert's always been like that; he's always been aware it's our stuff. [Otherwise] Hansa would still own the rights to some of our stuff."

Subsequently, two Cure songs would emerge from the Hansa debacle. The first, a straight-up dismissal of the label entitled 'Do The Hansa', would emerge as an extra B-side on the 1986 re-release of 'Boys Don't Cry'; it also appeared on the *Join The Dots* collection. The other Cure song influenced by their tug-of-art with Hansa was, intriguingly, the 1987 single 'Catch'. At the time of its release, Smith revealed that the Hansa's execs would listen to their material and then advise them: "You write good songs, but there's never a catch."

During April, the now label-less Easy Cure once again hooked up with Simon Gallup and Lockjaw, this time at a show at Laker's. A bond was starting to develop between Gallup and Smith, despite the former's love of Kiss, the hideously successful cartoon rock outfit that The Cure considered "horrendous" (Lol Tolhurst's words). Post gig, they spent the rest of the evening drinking together, not stopping until two in the morning. "We became good friends," said Smith. Smith and Gallup would also learn that they shared a gently twisted sense of humour: their idea of fun was to ask the DJ at their shared gigs to play such funky pop cheese as The Bee Gees' 'Night Fever', "so we could disco dance while all the punks pogoed about", according to Smith. While he may have quickly warmed to the attitude of punk, Smith found it hard to fully conform: he'd only just dropped his flares in favour of straight-leg jeans, while he definitely wore his hair on the wrong side of his shoulders.

The Smith/Gallup alliance would ultimately have a major effect on the band's future. They would hang out at the Red Deer club in Croydon, where they'd check out such seminal punk acts as The Vibrators, The Buzzcocks and The Clash. Throughout much of The Cure's life, Smith had a tendency towards forming alliances – with Lol Tolhurst, Simon Gallup, Fiction label head Chris Parry and with video director Tim Pope – that would have a very tangible impact on the success (or otherwise) of the band.

But in early 1978 the shifts starting to take place in The Easy Cure camp were slight, as the Gallup/Smith bond started to form and the band's sound slowly expanded. During April, Smith bought a Bon Tempi organ and a WEM amp, to go along with his much-loved Woolworth's Top 20 guitar. Smith had heard Elvis Costello's benchmark record, *My Aim Is True*, and made a sonic discovery. "They were the sounds I wanted," he decided.

One sound the band didn't desire, however, was the wail of Porl Thompson's guitar. By May, the situation had become quite complicated: not only did Thompson refuse to play the guitar chords Smith suggested, but he'd also started dating Smith's sister Janet. "We'd be rehearsing in the house when my mum and dad were out," Smith said, "and he'd be somewhere else with my sister." Rather than confront the problem head-on, Smith, Tolhurst and Dempsey decided to abandon rehearsals for a couple of weeks and then simply fail to tell Thompson when they resumed.

"We were becoming more and more stripped down," Smith would relate afterwards, "and leaving him just short gaps [to play]. Eventually it became absurd – we'd be playing something like '10.15' and there'd be like a 16-bar section where he could play lead guitar. So we came to an agreement and he left."

Thompson formally left the band on May 3. Given their reluctance to deal with the Thompson problem directly, it seemed that their Easy Cure tag was becoming worryingly apt. The band staged a mock wake for their dear departed guitarist, at a Rocket show entitled 'Mourning The Departed'. To the backing of some solemn organ music recorded by Smith, they conducted an on-stage séance and Smith, resplendent in priest's robes, played the entire set with a crucifix-shaped piece of wood nailed across his guitar.

Thompson was relatively at ease with the decision, accepting that punk was rendering his "fast" playing anachronistic. He was even in the crowd at his own musical wake, as Robert Smith would attest. "Porl arrived in a hat and an old mac, and we didn't know he was in the audience until – just as we finished playing – he walked up and poured a pint of beer over Lol's head. Suddenly we were friends again."

Soon after his rock'n'roll wake, Thompson signed on at art college, while also playing with a couple of bands more suited to his flashy stringwork, A Lifetime Of Trials and The Exotic Pandas. But as with most people and players who would become Cure insiders, it wasn't as though Thompson was cast adrift forever. He would eventually return to the band, as well as becoming heavily involved with their record artwork via his company Parched Art.

The Easy Cure now had to make a few big decisions about their immediate future. For the first time in their short lives they were playing as a trio, which suited Smith's plans to strip back their sound. Smith had also decided to strip back their name: he figured that the tag Easy Cure sounded too American, "too hippyish", and opted to shorten it to a very simple The Cure. Not for the first time did Smith piss off bandmate Tolhurst, who'd inadvertently created the band's name with his 'Easy Cure' song. Smith, however, was adamant. "I hated it," he said, "which put Lol's back up. The Easy Cure sounded stupid so we just changed it. I thought The Cure sounded much more it." The Cure was almost starting to look more and more like a serious rock'n'roll band. While Dempsey may have possessed the more traditional good looks (he actually resembled a Seventies version of Lemonhead Evan Dando), both the curly-haired Tolhurst and Smith, with his floppy fringe and predilection for leather jackets, brooded in a way all serious young things should.

The rechristened trio also decided to have one last shot at recording some of their own songs. If this failed, Tolhurst, Dempsey and Smith knew that a life of drudgery in Crawley was probably all they had to look forward to. And that was more like a sentence. "We see so many of the people we went to school with doing absolutely nothing," Smith said at the time. This simply wasn't part of their master plan.

Chapter Three

"I hope this reply isn't too much of a bring-down: when you sell your first million albums, you will know we were wrong."

— BBC rejection letter, 1978

CRAWLEY, Sussex, might have felt like the suburb that time forgot, but it was a bustling metropolis in comparison to Lower Hutt, New Zealand. Located just north of the capital Wellington, the area had been colonised by Colonel William Wakefield in 1839, who acquired 110,000 acres of flat and fertile land from the local Maori. Not much has changed over the subsequent 170 or so years – like much of New Zealand, Lower Hutt is a green and pleasant land, possibly even sleepier than Crawley.*

Lower Hutt was the birthplace of John Christopher Parry, who would come to play a key role in transforming Crawley hopefuls The Cure into budding stars (and beyond). Parry's background had more than a few similarities to the men of The Cure: he came from a place that didn't rank too highly on the barometer of cool, and he was raised in a very large family. But whereas Robert Smith was one of four children, and Lol Tolhurst and Simon Gallup were both one of six, Parry topped them all – he had no less than 10 brothers and sisters.

Parry's musical life began in 1964 when he was recruited to drum – playing without a drummer's stool, as it turns out – for a New Zealand outfit calling themselves Sine Waves. By 1966, the band, now renamed The Insect, had developed a reputation playing at high school dances, youth clubs, socials and – to prove that no gig was too weird – Bible classes. The New Zealand music industry was hardly a world-beater in the Sixties, but it was competitive. The Insect, now called Fourmyula, entered and won a National Battle of the Sounds

---

* Lower Hutt did eventually acquire some kind of legend, when several scenes for the *Lord Of The Rings* trilogy were shot there.

competition in January 1968. Their prize was a journey to the UK aboard the *Sitmar*.

For any antipodean band of The Beatles' generation, the UK was the rock'n'roll mecca. Not only were the Empire ties still relatively strong, but it also seemed as though all the great sounds of the time – the Merseyside acts, The Rolling Stones, The Animals – emerged from the Old Dart. Such Australian stars as The Easybeats and The Master's Apprentices had done hard time in the UK, trying to replicate their domestic glory; Fourmyula were set to do likewise.* But before Fourmyula set sail, in February 1969, the band lived through a record company spat that would strangely echo that of The Easy Cure and Hansa.

Their label, HMV, were adamant that a cover of Martha & The Vandellas' 'Honey Chile' would be a sure-fire hit. The band wanted to go with an original, 'Come With Me'. Eventually they backed down, put their tune on the B-side of the single, and looked on with a knowing, satisfied grin as DJs opted for the original over the safe-as-houses cover. 'Come With Me' became a major domestic hit. No wonder Chris Parry experienced a strange sense of déjà vu when he eventually met up with The Cure: he'd endured exactly the same kind of muddle-headed record company logic as them.

The UK, however, didn't exactly embrace Fourmyula. The band watched more shows than they played, while they managed to secure only one session at Abbey Road, where they covered a track called 'Lady Scorpio' which became another hit at home but was met with a deafening silence in the UK. After a four-month stay they returned for a homecoming gig with the intention of showing the locals exactly what was happening overseas. They launched into Led Zep's 'Good Times, Bad Times' and then powered their way through a set of covers that they'd experienced first-hand in the UK. Their fans stared in slack-jawed, gobsmacked disbelief. Fourmyula, reluctantly, went back to the winning formula.

Fourmyula made one more assault on Europe, in 1970, establishing a reasonable fanbase in Scandinavia (they even changed their name to

---

* The migration continued for years after, with such acts as AC/DC, The Saints, The Go Betweens, The Triffids and the Nick Cave-led Birthday Party all relocating to the UK, along with Kiwi acts The Clean and The Chills, amongst others.

Pipp, a Danish word meaning "mad"). But like so many antipodean hopefuls before them, it all fell apart and they disbanded later in the same year.

Chris Parry had seen enough of the UK to realise that there were a hell of a lot more music biz opportunities there than in the Land of the Long White Cloud. While his fellow Pipp-sters hightailed it home, he stayed in London, marrying in 1971. He then spent two years studying marketing before securing a job in the International department at Phonogram Records. Then in 1974, via a connection who happened to be friends with Wayne Bickerton, Polydor's head of A&R, Parry was offered an A&R role. (In the same year, he became a parent for the first time.) His first signing, the Chanter Sisters, had a modest hit in 1975. Parry had come a long way in a short time from thumping the tubs for Fourmyula. He'd also learned some handy lessons about the machinations of the music industry, which he was about to put to practical use.

By 1976, Parry could sense the cultural change occurring in rock. He made a point of checking out all the key punk bands that were making a serious noise: the Pistols, Siouxsie & The Banshees, The Clash. Bearded and draped in a heavy coat, Parry was hard to miss at these shows – he looked more like a lumberjack than a talent-spotter. Parry was moving in the same circles as Caroline Coon, a high-profile stringer for *Melody Maker* who'd also helped found Release, an organisation dedicated to offering legal advice to under-agers facing drug charges. Release had the help of such A-listers as The Rolling Stones and The Beatles, which had helped to up the profile of both Coon and her organisation.

Her memories of this flashpoint in punk history are as strong and evocative now as they were when she was a star reporter for *Melody Maker*. "I loved what was going on," she told me. "I wanted to break this story [of punk]. I thought I could tell it better than anyone else on Earth." Coon, naturally, had some fairly sizeable obstructions to overcome: at the time, *Melody Maker* was manned, as she sneered, by "hippies and pub-rock fanatics – neither paper [*Sounds* or *Melody Maker*] took this breaking story seriously. *Melody Maker* refused to take my advice that this was one of the most significant events in rock'n'roll – partly because I was a girl." Finally Coon had a win: her seminal report on punk in the July 28, 1976 issue of the mag was arguably the first article to document the new movement, hitting the streets just ahead of her rival-cum-fellow-true-believer, *Sounds*' reporter John Ingham.*

Today, Coon has no strong memory of Parry, but does recall that "some record company execs were vile, some were lovely. We might have gone to the same gigs."

Chris Parry, meanwhile, was dealing with the same kind of trouble as Caroline Coon: he simply couldn't convince his senior colleagues at Polydor that punk was more than just a blip on the rock'n'roll radar. Most of his signing suggestions were rejected by the label.

In fact, despite Parry's rapid climb up the corporate ladder, by the time he first heard The Cure he was in fear of being known as much for the bands he missed out on as those he signed. Parry had witnessed a typically anarchic Sex Pistols show at Barbarella's in Birmingham in 1976 and raced back to London, imploring his Polydor bosses to sign the punk rock banner-wavers. Likewise The Clash. He'd later tell Lol Tolhurst about the experience. "He told me about seeing The Clash with people from Polydor and there was some kind of mini riot. This bottle exploded behind their heads and his colleague said, 'That's it, we're not signing them.' That was the attitude. I think he was the only guy among all the A&R people in London who could see what was going on."

Parry was annoyed by Polydor's wariness, admitting he was "pretty pissed off" by their refusal. Despite his keen antennae for punk, Parry lived in fear of being tagged a three-time loser – the kiss of death for any A&R man worth their damaged liver. Then he was given a tip from future Pogue, Shane McGowan, to check out Woking-class zeroes The Jam, who were playing The Marquee on January 22, 1977. Playing oddly angular takes on classic Britpop, and led by the fierce Paul Weller, The Jam were convincingly real. Parry walked away convinced that this was the band that could not get away. "I was determined I wasn't going to miss out again," he said.

Though they didn't necessarily fit in with the punk acts that were

---

* Coon eventually scored the prized job of Singles Reviewer for *Melody Maker* and was immortalised in song by The Stranglers in their 'London Lady'. Her punk encounters were documented in *1988: The New Wave Punk Rock Explosion*, which was actually published in 1977.

cheerfully blowing major label budgets all over London at the time – the Jam's heroes were Modfathers The Who and the Noël Cowards of pop, The Kinks – Parry spotted The Jam's star potential. He signed them on February 15, barely three weeks after the Marquee gig, and went on to score co-production credits for their first two albums, *In The City* and *This Is The Modern World*, both of which emerged in 1977.

By May 1978, at the same time that The Cure headed into the tiny Chestnut Studios in Sussex to cut their first demos as a trio, Parry had added Siouxsie & The Banshees, Sham 69 and sister act Doreen & Irene Chanter to his impressive roster of signings. He'd also signed Otway and Barrett, a punk-era duo, whose singer, John Otway, had tracks produced by The Who's Pete Townshend. While with Polydor, they produced an unlikely one-off hit, 1977's 'Cor Baby That's Really Free'. Parry's star – unlike that of The Cure – was clearly in the ascendancy. He even turned up in Julien Temple's iconic feature film *The Great Rock And Roll Swindle*, which charted The Sex Pistols' rapid rise and deadly freefall. It was pure method acting: Parry played one of a team of pissed-off A&R men in the film.

The Cure, meanwhile, had recorded a new batch of demos on May 27, with cash borrowed from Ric Gallup. The band had started to spend more and more time at Gallup's Horley record store, where he turned them on to singles from such mysterious labels (at least to the Crawley three) as London's Rough Trade. They'd also moan to him about their disastrous Hansa deal. After several months of this, as Tolhurst told me, Gallup was fed up. "He'd commiserate with us but then he said, 'OK, I'm tired of seeing you sitting round feeling sorry for yourselves; why don't you make another demo and send it around to the other labels?' He ended up paying for the recording sessions."

This collection of songs (three of which would make the cut for their debut album) proved just how lean and skeletal their sound had become since shedding Porl Thompson. '10.15 Saturday Night' opened with the sparest of all possible interplay between Tolhurst's drums, Dempsey's bass and Smith's guitar, before the band locked into a mean garage groove. Smith, meanwhile, pulled off a fair impersonation of a leaking tap as he documented the despair of the loneliest time of the loneliest night of the week. Sad, lonely and blue, Smith variously waits for the phone to ring, sobs, and finds himself spellbound by the damned relentless dripping of his tap. Smith then unleashes a sparse guitar solo which helps sustain the overwhelming sense of gloom, if only from a teenage miserablist's point of view. The song was an early favourite of Smith's, who'd planned to team '10.15' with 'Killing An Arab' as the band's debut release (a double A-side), because '10.15' was "more representative of what we were trying to do [at the time]." Smith had written both '10.15 Saturday Night' and 'Killing An Arab' in 1975, when he was 16.

"'10.15 Saturday Night' was written at the table in our kitchen," Smith revealed in the liner notes for the 2005 reissue of *Three Imaginary Boys*, "watching the tap dripping, feeling utterly morose, drinking my dad's home-made beer. My evening had fallen apart and I was back at home feeling very sorry for myself."

Elsewhere, 'Fire In Cairo' was another spare, tense strum, propelled by a chorus that, while understated, had all the singalong potential of any Buzzcock punk-pop anthem. It's a mouthful – "F I R E I N C A I R O" – but Smith's mantra-like chant (reinforced by some savvy multi-tracking in its finished version) gave the song exactly the kind of impetus he was seeking.

But of the four demos recorded at Chestnut Studios, 'Boys Don't Cry' was the most immediate and accessible. If there was one song from the band's early songwriting efforts that precisely captured the minimalist, post-punk, post-Porl Thompson direction in which Smith was steering the band, it was 'Boys'. Again, Smith's aching heart drove the song's central lyric: despite his protestations to the contrary – boys don't cry, apparently – you got the distinct impression that he'd shed a few tears during its writing.

When asked about what would become a signature tune for the band, Smith said that it was his attempt to write a classic pop song, with a definite Sixties influence. "In a perfect world," he announced in 1985, "that would have been number one."*

Despite Smith's dreams of chart glory, at the time, Dempsey was still holding down his porter's job in the psychiatric hospital, while Tolhurst continued working at Hellerman Deutsch. Because he was still officially unemployed, Smith took on the role of correspondent, as

---

* Smith, typically, would have mixed feelings when asked about 'Boys' at various times during the life of The Cure, even describing it as "naïve to the point of insanity".

he mailed out their new demos to virtually anyone who might be willing to listen. With the exception of Hansa, of course.

The letter that accompanied their demo tape couldn't have been any more precise. Along with some basic information (Lol 19 Drums / Mick 19 Bass / Robert 19 Gtr/Vocals), it spelled out their mission statement:

> "Hello," it read, "we are The Cure. We have no commitments. We would like a recording contract. Listen to the tape. If you are interested please contact us at the above. Please return the tape in the enclosed S.A.E." The letter was signed, "Thankyou, Robert THE CURE."

While this introduction to The Cure was doing the rounds of London's record labels, the band played their 'Mourning The Departed' show for Thompson at The Rocket on July 9, then five days later drove down to Brighton for another double-header with Gallup's band Lockjaw.

Gradually the replies trickled in – and none were positive. In late June 1978, Phonogram and then Island said thanks but no thanks. The trio had also sent an entry to the BBC's 'Band of Hope and Glory' competition, which was part of the *David "Kid" Jensen Show*. The BBC's response, dated June 29, was typical of the feedback they were receiving. "Unfortunately, we cannot use your group," wrote Tony Hale, Radio One Producer, "but that isn't to say that your tape is without interest or that the group is not good enough. It's just that the particular combination of qualities we are looking for isn't quite there." In a final note, which would prove to be deeply ironic given the success of The Cure over the next few decades, Hale signed off with the following: "I hope this reply isn't too much of a bring-down: always remember that music is a subjective area, so that when you sell your first million albums, you will know we were wrong."

While the BBC's response would provide some smug satisfaction for the band further down the road, it didn't help solve their immediate predicament, which only worsened when Virgin and then EMI also gave them the knock-back. The band did, however, receive expressions of interest from United Artists and Stiff. Of the two, the second was definitely the label of choice for The Cure, mainly because it was the home of Elvis Costello. But the label execs failed to show at an early Cure gig, as planned, and the proposed deal fell apart. "We were so upset when Mr Stiff didn't turn up," Smith said. "We thought he was going to be different, but he was just like all the others."

Over at Polydor, Chris Parry settled down to his usual weekend ritual of test-driving the seemingly endless supply of demo tapes that poured into their offices each week. He'd grab a pile every Friday night, just as he was heading home for the weekend. Parry was flicking through the Sunday sports pages when he dropped The Cure's cassette into his tape player. '10.15 Saturday Night' was the track that grabbed him – on hearing Smith's "drip, drip, drip" refrain, he found himself playing the tape again. 'Boys Don't Cry' also caught his ear.

Having had such stellar success with suburban three-piece The Jam, Parry's A&R radar started twitching like mad when he checked the return address and the line-up of The Cure. Maybe chart lightning did strike twice in the same (suburban) place. Tolhurst was, and still is, convinced that Parry imagined The Cure to be another Jam in the making. "He thought, 'They're kind of young, they're sharp with some stuff and they're outside of London – and nobody knows about them except for me.'" Michael Dempsey agreed. "Yes, I see the logic in that."

Parry was no fool. He did admit to the appeal of signing another pop/rock trio when he was interviewed for *Ten Imaginary Years*. "The idea of a three-piece excited me and that this little cassette had come from the backwoods and no one else had touched it. My reaction was it had mood, it was atmospheric and I liked it." So much so that he wrote to the band on July 21. His missive cut to the chase, reading: "Dear Robert, I would like to meet the Group [sic] and suggest that you telephone my secretary, Alison Korsner, who will arrange a meeting." Smith did exactly that and a get-together was arranged for August 10.

While speaking on the phone, Parry had asked if the band would play in London, but Smith refused: the trio wasn't so sure that playing before an away crowd (if anyone showed) would inspire a record company's support. And the band had already been burned in a similar manner by Stiff. Instead they agreed on a sit-down meeting at Polydor's office in Stratford Place.

Although the trio arrived on time, they were made to wait for Parry, who, as Dempsey would recall, turned up looking slightly sheepish, "as though he'd committed some criminal act". With his airbrushed hair and what Dempsey would describe as "craggy jowls", the band decided that Parry was a dead ringer for Libya's Colonel Gaddafi. As first impressions go, it was hardly a winner. (Smith would confess to being a "bit disappointed at first".) After an introductory chat in his office, Parry decided that a midday tipple was in order, so he took the trio to a nearby pub. Smith remembered it as being "a pleasant afternoon, really", as did Dempsey when we spoke. The close link between The Cure, music and alcohol was forged over several jars of Directors bitter with their manager/label boss/publisher/booking agent-in-waiting. "I liked him," Dempsey said. "He was quite direct – he wasn't a bullshitter."

To Smith, Parry seemed unlike anyone he'd previously met in the music industry – he was certainly nothing like the suits at Hansa. And unlike the Stiff staff, he'd actually turned up, albeit late. For starters, Parry had bird shit on his shoulder, which he didn't seem to notice, while he kept spilling beer on his shoes as he spoke with the band and boldly mapped out their future. "[He was] the first person we'd met involved in the business who didn't take himself seriously," Smith said. "He seemed to be doing it because he liked it."

As for Parry, he quickly discerned the three very different characters of The Cure. "I liked Dempsey's understated sense of humour," he said. "Lol was flapping around here and there, but it was obvious that Robert was the leader and had views on things. [He was] checking me out more than the others." Parry was also aware that the band had the intelligence to cut through the usual music biz hype. "They [had] a certain type of fatalism and sharp humour attached with all this nonsense. No one takes things too seriously."

With neither party too scarred by their first meeting, Smith suggested that Parry check out the band playing on home soil. For Smith, it was partly a challenge to see if Parry would turn up at the show, which was held at Redhill Laker's Hotel, Redhill, on August 27. That would be a real test of his commitment to the band.

The Cure was booked to support The Hotpoints, who – being a jazz/funk fusion outfit – were hardly a band in sync with these post-punkers. But not only did Parry go to see The Cure, he also arrived with a friend, Dave Alcock, whom an excited Tolhurst mistook for Bee Gees' manager and all-round entertainment Svengali, Robert Stigwood.

While their set still included such Smith faves as Hendrix's 'Foxy Lady', it was gradually loading up with Cure originals, including such cuts as '10.15 Saturday Night' and 'Killing An Arab'. Parry, standing on the floor where the band was playing (only the headliner actually got to use the stage), was suitably impressed. He turned to his friend Alcock and shouted: "This band are gonna make me an awful lot of money."

"It's not that I'm very money orientated," Parry would correct later on, "it just came out that way." What Parry saw in the band was a certain "universal appeal", which he couldn't help but translate into monetary terms. Truth be told, Parry was hungry for success. As Lol Tolhurst would tell me, Parry was irritated by the human interaction side of the music biz. "I can always remember him saying that he wished he could invent a machine that could write hit songs for him and that way he wouldn't have to deal with us monkeys."

After their set, Parry invited the trio for a post-gig drink at a nearby pub, the Home Cottage. As far as Tolhurst was concerned, it was over those few drinks that their future with Parry was sealed. "We liked him immediately for lots of reasons. Although he was sharp and business-like, after the show at Laker's, we went to this pub that sold this really strong bitter. He drank loads of it and made quite a fool of himself. We immediately liked him for that reason; he wasn't afraid to be an idiot."

Over those few jars of rotgut, Parry spelled out his grand plan for The Cure – but it wasn't quite what the three had expected to hear. While they had anticipated a fairly rudimentary offer from Polydor – "we figured Polydor, great, big label, lots of money," Tolhurst said – Parry admitted that he was becoming increasingly frustrated with the slow-motion grind of the corporate machinery. He knew how important it was to get a new band such as The Cure into the studio quickly and capture their freshness and raw energy on tape, before they either broke up or broke down.

Parry wanted to form his own label, and he wanted The Cure to be his first signing. Polydor would still be involved in the deal, however, because Parry realised two things: their distribution and marketing muscle couldn't be denied, and there was no point in burning any bridges. Polydor could definitely help Parry, and The Cure, make that "awful lot of money" he'd roared about on the dance floor at Laker's.

Smith, Tolhurst and Dempsey were, in Smith's words, "obviously a bit disappointed" that he wasn't asking them to sign directly to

Polydor. "But as he explained his ideas for the label, we started to like what we were hearing and decided to give it a go." Tolhurst agreed, if somewhat reluctantly. "We thought, 'Hmmmm, OK.'"

They agreed to sign with Parry, but only when he settled on a halfway decent name for his new label. Smith couldn't stomach Parry's original idea, Night Nurse, so Parry countered with 18 Age, which Smith found equally useless. A bemused singer asked his new boss a key question: "What happens when we get to 20?" Eventually, all parties agreed on 18 Age/Fiction (the "18 Age" part of the title was eventually discarded in 1982). On September 13, 1978, they signed a six-month deal.

Parry had other acts in mind for Fiction, namely Billy MacKenzie, later of The Associates, who was signed within days of The Cure. With his new signings and a grand plan for his label, Parry now had enough confidence to chuck in his A&R Manager position at Polydor. Fiction was his future.

By September 17, he also had enough confidence in his new charges to try to stir up some media excitement. After all, what was a new band without a buzz? ("He made things happen quickly," said Dempsey.) The Cure had another gig booked at Redhill, so Parry – now christened "Bill" by the band, a tag that would stick – brought along Adrian Thrills, of the *NME*, to check out their show. Never a man to miss an opportunity, Parry force-fed Thrills Billy MacKenzie's album *Mental Torture* during the drive. While Thrills held off in his judgement of The Cure, he felt that Mackenzie's album had lived up to its name. As Parry recalled, "He said it *was* mental torture." Thrills would become the first music scribe to write a Cure feature, but that was still a few months in the future.

Now that Parry had a new band and a new label, he needed some music. He booked the trio into Morgan Studios on September 20 – the same studio where The Cure had endured some of their futile sessions with Hansa, which had generated little more than tension. But plenty had changed in the six months since The Cure had parted ways with the Germans: they'd shed a guitarist, gained a new boss and label, and developed something that resembled a future plan. Even the rejection letters from EMI, Island, Virgin and all the other labels didn't seem to hurt the trio as much as they once did, now that Fiction Records was handling them. Parry might have seemed just a little odd, but he was ambitious. And the Fiction office – the empire currently comprised Parry and another ex-Polydor staffer, Ita Martin – was also located in the Morgan complex, which was convenient, especially if they needed some beer money.

With Parry working the desk, The Cure recorded some familiar tunes ('10.15 Saturday Night', 'Killing An Arab', 'Fire In Cairo') along with 'Plastic Passion' and 'Three Imaginary Boys' during the September 20 session at Morgan. In order to keep costs down, the recording was conducted during the graveyard shift. The band finished at 5.30 on the morning of the 21st, forcing Tolhurst to call in sick to his employer, claiming he had boils on his backside.

While Parry was happy enough with the results, he knew that The Cure also needed to be road-hardened. All their gigs at this stage had been in the safe surrounds of their home turf, at either The Rocket or Laker's. It was unlikely that *NME* would make them cover stars if they hadn't played anywhere apart from a few gigs in Crawley's High Street. Parry booked them a pair of shows with Wire, at the University of Kent, Canterbury on October 5 and the following night at the London Polytechnic.

It was a bold, probably foolish move on Parry's part to partner his Crawley neophytes with critics' favourites Wire. Though they may have emerged from the heart of the punk and post-punk movement, which had also inspired Smith and Tolhurst, Wire was rapidly outgrowing the stylistic limitations of the form. They would prove this at these shows.

Wire had joined forces at Watford Art College in 1976, when guitarists Colin Newman and George Gill formed Overload with AV technician (and third guitarist) Bruce Gilbert. With the recruitment of bassist Graham Lewis and drummer Robert Gotobed (aka Robert Grey), the first Wire line-up was established.

After some fumbling early dates in London, Gill was ousted and the reborn Wire opted for a pared down, experimental sound. A chance meeting with EMI's Mike Thorne, who was recording groups for a live punk album, resulted in two Wire tracks appearing on his compilation *The Roxy, London WC2*. By the time they'd signed to EMI in September 1977, they were itching to record, quickly, before they lost interest in the material, abandoned it and moved on. If there was one constant in a career based on action and reaction, it was their creative restlessness.

By October 1978, when The Cure opened for them at the University of Kent, Wire had just returned from their first US dates, on the strength of their previous two well-received albums. Produced by Thorne, 1977's furiously paced *Pink Flag* comprised 21 highly original tracks (each clocking in at barely 90 seconds). "On a formal level," wrote *Rolling Stone*, "it's an astonishing achievement, pulling punk away from the rock revivalism of The Sex Pistols and Clash without sacrificing its energy or gut-level impact." But within a year they'd delivered the remarkable about-turn that was *Chairs Missing*, which, with the introduction of keyboards, was even tagged "early Pink Floyd" by some tough critics. The near-perfect tune 'Outdoor Miner' might have become a hit, if it wasn't for some disruption at EMI. Robert Smith was no fool – he could see that Wire were streets ahead of The Cure in terms of music, ideas, appearance, the works.

After their first support slot, the gulf between The Cure and Wire was obvious. Smith admitted that he was "horrified". Tolhurst, however, reacted differently. "Wire were the first band we played with that definitely had 'it'," he says. "I think we realised after playing with them that we were going to be able to do our music and be able to find an audience for it, too."

Smith, Tolhurst and Dempsey were so startled by the Wire experience, in fact, that they almost crashed their van on the way home from the show – money being so short at this stage, they were required to drive home after most shows, a risky endeavour that would shorten Dempsey's term in The Cure. The next night they went one worse – they didn't even show up for the gig. But the cause of their no-show was out of their hands. They were relying on a Horley local, a man with a van named Phil, to get them to the show at the London Polytechnic. But his motor broke down on the trip north and by the time they reached the venue, Wire was already on stage. The Cure's offer to play after the headliner was firmly, politely refused.

Backstage, Chris Parry was fuming at the trio's amateurish approach. If the band was that casual in the future, he shouted, "You'll never get another booking again." Having vented his anger, Parry and the band adjourned to a pub, where Smith, Tolhurst and Dempsey – showing more than a little spunk, given the night's calamity and their label head's mood – floated the idea of "turning professional". Despite Tolhurst's vague plans of becoming a research chemist, it wasn't as if the trio was beholden to potentially rewarding positions outside of the band. But Parry, who was drunk by this stage, acquiesced, agreeing to a minimum wage of "£25 a week or something". The money offered may have been barely enough on which to survive, but Parry's decision gave the band a true sense of purpose.

For Lol Tolhurst, turning pro was a revelation. "That was a strange feeling for me because I remember walking around town and feeling like I was on vacation. 'OK, this is all going to stop in a few weeks.' After a few years it dawned on me that this is my real job."

Within the week, on October 12, Parry had the band back in their second home, Morgan Studios. Their plan was to record enough songs for a debut album.

A glance at the charts in late 1978 would suggest that punk's planned global takeover had never happened: maybe it was still a dream lodged somewhere in the mind of Malcolm McLaren. *Grease* was very much the word in the UK, as the rubbery-hipped John Travolta and squeaky-clean Olivia Newton-John let the world know how hopelessly devoted they were to each other; the Fifties retro musical also spawned the hits 'Summer Nights' and 'Sandy', which were lodged in the business end of the UK Top 10. Only Irish vagabonds The Boomtown Rats, with 'Rat Trap', reminded listeners that there was supposed to be some kind of revolution happening in the world of music. But they were a lone voice in the wilderness, surrounded by such pop fluff as Leo Sayer's 'I Can't Stop Lovin' You', The Jacksons' 'Blame It On The Boogie' and The Commodores' 'Three Times A Lady'. And – maybe just to remind The Cure of their Hansa nightmare – Boney M's 'Rasputin' was also in the Top 10.

The charts weren't that much healthier on the other side of the Atlantic – the US Top 10 was dominated by either the cast of *Grease*, remakes of creaky old standards (Donna Summer's 'MacArthur Park'), blue-collar rockers such as Bob Seger ('Hollywood Nights') and Australians impersonating West Coast soft rockers (Little River Band's 'Reminiscing').

Those who weren't helping *Grease* to the top of the pop charts and the box office were coughing up the cash to help The Rolling Stones become the US summer's top-grossing act. They netted a handy $6 million. Elsewhere, the four members of Gallup faves Kiss unleashed their own solo albums, piano man Billy Joel scooped the pool at the Grammys, and CBS Records hiked up album prices to a hefty $8.98. It was as though punk rock had never happened.

Back in Morgan Studios, Chris Parry was starting to wield his influence over The Cure, steering their songs in a direction he felt was right for his new signing. They were still studio novices, so they had no way of articulating what they felt these songs needed. All Smith knew was that he was hoping to find some kind of unholy alliance between the two "Bs": The Banshees and The Buzzcocks. "I really liked The Buzzcocks' melodies," he said, "while the great thing about the Banshees was that they had this great wall of noise which I'd never heard before. My ambition was to try to marry the two." He'd fail, at least with these early sessions.

Of all the bands that moved in and out of The Cure radar during their career, there was none – certainly in their formative years – that played a bigger role than Siouxsie & The Banshees. They formed a kinship, of sorts, with The Cure: not only would Smith become a Banshee for an extended period of time, playing guitar with them both in the studio and on stage (at a time when he was uncertain about the future of The Cure), he and Banshee bassist Steve Severin would form a bond based on chemical over-indulgence. Smith would also take some fashion leads from Siouxsie – in fact, he was convinced that The Cure's sizeable Goth following was a direct consequence of his time as a Banshee.

Just like Peter Hook and Bernard Sumner of Joy Division, Chris Parry and numerous other music industry players from the Seventies, the Banshees began as a direct result of a close encounter with The Sex Pistols. Both Siouxsie Sioux (the former Susan Dallion) and future Banshees bassist Steve Severin were part of a notorious group of Sex Pistols hangers-on called the Bromley Contingent. The Banshees formed in September 1976, with original drummer John Simon Ritchie soon to reinvent himself as the doomed Sid Vicious of The Sex Pistols. They played their debut at the legendary Punk Festival at London's 100 Club – their setlist comprised exactly one song: a near-Satanic desecration of 'The Lord's Prayer'. Vicious soon departed for life as a Sex Pistol and was replaced by Kenny Morris, while original guitarist Marco Perroni moved on to Adam & The Ants. His spot was taken by John McKay.

Siouxsie was not the most articulate or eloquent of vocalists, but there was a raw power behind her delivery that made her an irresistible force. "A vital connection between punk and psychedelia," in the words of *Rolling Stone*, the Banshees' 1978 debut LP *The Scream* was a key album in post-Sex Pistols Britain. The Banshees weren't just drawing on such revered UK acts as Roxy Music and David Bowie, they were also pointing the way forward for everyone from The Cure to The Mission, Sisters Of Mercy, All About Eve and numerous other bands who would form, either directly or otherwise, because of the Banshees. They even scored an unlikely hit with the very atypical, richly melodic 'Hong Kong Garden', which raced into the UK Top 10 in September 1978, not long before The Cure had returned to Morgan with Parry.

As for The Cure, their hassles continued in the studio. Because Parry was funding the sessions, Smith felt that their label boss and producer "had us over a barrel". Band and producer's method of dealing with their frustration manifested itself in very different forms – Smith would sink into a sulky funk, slumping in a corner of the studio, Parry would unleash his temper with extreme prejudice.

But Parry also truly believed that he had a "production concept" for the band. Rather than flesh out the trio's sound, as he did to some success with The Jam, he wanted to strip it "right down to the bones". He was enamoured of Smith's voice and words, but felt that after the amped-up onslaught of punk, listeners would be searching for something more elusive, more "mysterious".

Parry felt that he had a clear idea of what was good for The Cure, whereas Smith only knew what he didn't want for the band. "We had many arguments," Parry would report. "I'd think, 'Fucking hell, I've got enough problems trying to sort out the label without this.' Why can't they see I've got their best interests at heart?"

Lol Tolhurst's memories of those first sessions for Fiction are much less complicated than Smith's. "We went in and recorded our songs. Chris and Mike [Hedges] were at the desk, we sat at the back and when we got bored we went home." Dempsey agreed. "We went in and simply recorded our entire live set."

But in engineer Hedges, the band found an unexpected ally, who would come to play a key role in both the sound and success of The

Cure Mk I. When Hedges was hired by Parry and first encountered The Cure, during October 1978, his CV was underwhelming. He was a tape operator and engineer, who'd assisted on such recordings as Central Heating's 1977 album, *Heatwave*, the 1978 London cast recording of *Evita*, and *Paraphernalia*, an album by jazz saxophonist Barbara Thompson. So far, it was hardly a career of note. However, within a year of recording with The Cure, Hedges would work with Robert Smith's teenage hero, Alex Harvey, engineering 'The Mafia Stole My Guitar', the title track of Harvey's only solo album. He would also engineer *Candidate*, the album from Cockney Rebel Steve Harley. Much later he would work with Dido, U2 and Travis.

Lol Tolhurst was a big admirer of Hedges; he was convinced that he was the right man at the right time. "He was still fairly young and he'd grown up in that studio system where he had a lot of good recording knowledge. You had to go through a whole apprenticeship to become a recording engineer and he'd done that. What he didn't have necessarily in terms of a creative vision he could make up technically. He was very good for us.

"He was, and is, a great person, very intelligent, a truly great Englishman in the best sense."

The Cure's situation was hardly unique: a trio of novices walks into the studio with vague plans and have trouble adapting to this strange new environment (relatively new in the case of The Cure). It's a common occurrence throughout the history of rock'n'roll. When American punk/funk upstarts The Red Hot Chili Peppers were making their long-playing debut, the tension in the studio was so bad that their producer, Andy Gill, developed cancer, their engineer left the studio screaming, never to return, and Gill eventually took the master-tapes hostage until he was paid. The situation in Morgan Studios wasn't quite that extreme.

"The band didn't really know what was going on," according to Mike Hedges. "Everything was new for everyone except Chris. Robert knew what he wanted but he didn't know how to express it. We used very little technology. He [Smith] just wanted to use his old [Woolworth's] Top 20 guitar and a cheap HH amp, which was the worst in the world for distortion."

Smith's insistence on using the HH amp led to another late-night argument with Parry. Although their producer felt the amp was suitable for some songs, it literally fell apart after the recording of their debut album's title track 'Three Imaginary Boys'. Smith was clinging to this cheap amp and his bargain-priced guitar like some kind of security blanket. Parry was livid.

"I thought, 'Jesus, here I am investing money in an album for some git who refuses to listen to reason.' So I said, 'Fine, if you wanna be a punk band, all dirgey and stupid, which you will be if you continue to use the equipment you've got, you can. But you'll be thrown off the label.'"

If there was one positive aspect of the sessions that would spawn *Three Imaginary Boys*, it was the presence of The Cure's neighbours, The Jam. The Woking three-piece, whom Parry had signed the year before, were cutting their second LP, *This Is The Modern World*, in the studio next door. Parry was juggling production of both records. Because The Cure were working on the cheap, at night, they would sneak into the studio when Paul Weller, Bruce Foxton and Rick Buckler had finished for the day, and "borrow" their gear. Tolhurst recalls using Buckler's drums for almost all of the *Three Imaginary Boys* sessions, mainly because he "had a pretty ropey old drum kit". Smith obviously wasn't such a punk purist that he couldn't resist the temptation to use The Jam's more cutting-edge, Polydor-financed equipment. Maybe some of their melodicism (and good fortune) might rub off.

Over the course of three graveyard sessions, The Cure had cut a total of 26 songs. Their final night of recording was on October 25, after returning from an uninspiring show supporting the long-gone Young Bucks at the Windsor Castle in London's Harrow Road. According to Tolhurst, "For all intents and purposes we could have been playing our first show at The Rocket in Crawley. It was 10 people looking in their beer." But that show was another key moment in the Chris Parry/Cure relationship, because Parry pulled them aside before going on stage and suggested, strongly, that they needed to develop some kind of image. Smith, in particular, was now very uncertain as to whether his new label boss and surrogate manager shared the same mindset as The Cure. "That sowed some seeds of doubt," said Smith. "I mean, Bill [Parry] could have waited until after the show to have his say." Smith would eventually explain the band's non-existent image this way: "As a group, we weren't particularly affiliated with anything. There was no left wing, no right wing, no nothing." Dempsey agreed, telling me that "we never said we liked anything, really." The band that had been formed out of resistance to the 9-to-5 grind was still keeping their distance.

At this point in their musical lives, The Cure didn't so much have an image as an anti-image – they were still a long way removed from their wild-haired, lipstick-smeared, black clad, sexually indeterminate signature look of the Eighties and Nineties. Michael Dempsey favoured corduroys and Hush Puppies – Parry thought he "looked a dork" – Smith was fond of a shapeless, nondescript coat and Tolhurst, according to Parry, "used to turn up wearing any sort of trousers and shoes, a white shirt and a bit of a beard. I thought, 'These guys are the dog's breakfast – the music is great but they look like shit.' " The band's concerns, however, were alleviated somewhat by the cash that Parry forked out to help them spruce up their wardrobe. Smith and Tolhurst would soon be seen sharing a leather jacket, which turned up in many of their early live and promo shots.

Parry's road-hardening plan for The Cure continued through October and November 1978, as the band supported The UK Subs and then Generation X. While it's unlikely that he had the luxury of picking and choosing support slots, Chris Parry was demonstrating a knack for connecting them with acts of wildly different backgrounds, profiles and mindsets.

The UK Subs, when The Cure opened for them at the Moonlight Club in West Hampstead, were in the strange position of being known as punk-rock survivors. Helmed by singer Charlie Harper, The UK Subs had been in action since November 1976, when Harper had heard The Damned and experienced a musical rebirth, quickly killing off his existing band, an R&B flavoured combo called The Marauders. The UK Subs (a shortened form of their original tag, The Subversives) outlined their plan of world domination from Harper's place of business, a hairdressing salon in south London. Not surprisingly, Harper sported a flawless perm. They'd cut several John Peel Sessions on BBC Radio One in 1977 and 1978, eventually scoring a record deal with the GEM label. In 1979, they were even the subject of a Julien Temple directed film documentary, entitled *Punk Can Take It*.

Lol Tolhurst had previously met Harper at the Croydon Greyhound when Harper actually asked him to join the Subs. He politely declined the offer. Robert Smith's take on their shared bill at the Moonlight

Club was that it was "a fucking glorious night", even though The UK Subs were members of one of punk's most loathed clubs – ageing rockers. "I remember they said, 'Hey, we gotta use your gear, man,'" said Smith, "and I said, 'You can't call me *man*. This is 1978.'" To Smith's recollection, The Cure's set that night was one of their most aggressive and best. The trio would be photographed outside Harper's house in Clapham Common for a *Melody Maker* feature which ran on March 24, 1979, Smith and Tolhurst stunning in their Miss Selfridge's jackets.

As for the brilliantly (and presciently) named Generation X, they were led by William Broad, one of the many punk scenesters who set up camp in Sex, the boutique operated by Malcolm McLaren and Vivienne Westwood. He may have been a Beatles-fancying child of the Sixties, born in Middlesex and raised, briefly, in Long Island, New York, but Broad embraced the punk life as though he was born to it. He dyed his hair blond, renamed himself Billy Idol and joined proto-type punk act Chelsea. Two months later he'd joined forces with bassist-cum-punk provocateur Tony James and formed Generation X. They may have worn the gear and sneer of street punks, but Generation X knew their way around a catchy pop song, reeling off a string of UK hits in 1977, which included 'Wild Youth', 'Ready Steady Go' and the cleverly titled 'Your Generation'. They even covered John Lennon's 'Gimme Some Truth' on their self-titled 1978 long-player, giving away their classicist's roots. Generation X were also the first punk act to star on *Top Of The Pops*, a moment that had almost the same gravitas as Bowie's star turn in 1972.

The Cure, however, probably weren't that familiar with Generation X's pedigree when they arrived at High Wycombe on November 24 for the first of a string of support dates. They were preoccupied with negotiating with Gen X's sound and lighting man, who insisted that The Cure pay £25 for use of the house gear. The band responded by lugging in their own gear: the two Yamaha A40 bins they'd been using as a PA, an HH mixing console, set up on stage, which Smith operated on cues from fans in the audience, and a pair of lamps, which the band parked on either side of the stage. By the time of their next show, at Northampton Cricket Club, their display of moxie so impressed the headliner's crew that they offered The Cure free use of Generation X's equipment.

Parry may have put The Cure on a token wage, but money was still tight: after each show with Generation X, they'd drive back to Parry's house at Watford and crash on the floor. It was only on November 30, when they played at Tiffany's in Halesowen – and were attacked by skinheads afterwards – that The Cure were actually granted the luxury of a hotel room. And even then it was mainly for show, because Parry knew some Polydor brass were coming to the gig.

Robert Smith has always been a man fond of a tipple and he very graciously accepted the offer of free Southern Comfort from the Polydor staffers. So graciously, in fact, that he spent a good part of the night with his head down the toilet, throwing up his freebies. Tolhurst was imbibing with as much gusto as Smith, but restrained from vomiting until they reached their shared hotel room. Then he let loose in the room's sink and all over the carpet. They checked out quickly the next day.

Even in this early, relatively freewheeling chapter of The Cure's career, Michael Dempsey was quickly learning that he wasn't built for life on the road. Sure, he agreed that this new world was "fun", but he had trouble adapting to his seemingly endless hangover and the indifferent reaction of most crowds. "He's a funny character," Tolhurst said in 2005. "As friends we still get on pretty well; we might even record some things in the future. But being on the road, especially at that lowly level, demanded a certain constitution. It's like being in the army – you don't get much sleep, you get up, go full pelt for a few hours and then head off somewhere else. He used to bring a lot of multi-vitamins and pills and remedies with him; he was always slightly under the weather. Whereas Robert and I had fairly robust constitutions; we could do it for month after month without suffering too much."

Dempsey was also troubled by the band's many risky, late-night road trips. "Because of Parry's 'economy'," he said in 2005, "we didn't stay in hotels, so we'd be driving huge distances, almost falling asleep at the wheel. And we not only drove ourselves, but we lugged our own equipment. I did it reluctantly; I don't think I particularly enjoyed it."

An innocent enough incident occurred after their October 3 gig at the Bristol Locarno which the band believe led to them being ejected from the Generation X tour. It began when Tolhurst wandered through the backstage area, in dire need of a toilet. Although warned not to enter, he pushed past a security guard and strolled into the gents, to discover that Billy Idol was "introducing himself" to a female fan. Undeterred, Tolhurst went about his business, calmly spraying Idol's foot with pee as a farewell gesture.

"I found Billy in, shall I say, a rather compromising position with a young lady in the bathroom," Tolhurst said. "I was desperate to relieve myself, he wouldn't budge, so I did the best job I could. Unfortunately some of Billy was in my trajectory." (Years later, Tolhurst met Idol again in New York. "He gave me the strangest look as he was trying to piece together where he remembered me from. I didn't remind him.")

The Cure and Generation X would share one more bill, on December 5 at the California Ballroom in Dunstable, but even then, according to Smith, it was only because The Cure were the only act available at short notice. "The toilet incident obviously didn't go down too well," Smith explained, "but, as well as that, we were beginning to get too good a reaction and that made them nervous."

Tolhurst confirmed this when I spoke with him. "As I recall, it [the bathroom encounter] was the excuse they needed to eject us from the tour. We had been going down too well, I think."

The day before their Dunstable finale, The Cure recorded their first of many sessions with the hugely influential BBC Radio One DJ John Peel. Peel was a veteran of pirate radio station 'Wonderful' Radio London (the "Big L") who had joined the BBC in 1967. Alongside everyone from Captain Beefheart to T. Rex, The Undertones to The Sex Pistols, Joy Division and The Buzzcocks, The Cure was one of the many independently minded acts that Peel would not only champion at the apprenticeship stage of their careers, but throughout their musical lives. Their debut Peel session featured four band originals: '10.15 Saturday Night', 'Fire In Cairo', 'Boys Don't Cry' and 'Killing An Arab'. It was just the seal of credibility that the band needed.*

The Cure endured another indifferent gathering on December 8, at The Corn Dolly in Oxford, when drunken yobs repeatedly yelled for "that drip drip drip one". The band responded by playing '10.15 Saturday Night' over and over again. Yet in spite of narrow-minded

---

* When Peel died on October 25, 2004, Smith posted this eulogy on the band's web site: "Passionate, honest, generous, intelligent, funny, a truly great man – we will miss him terribly."

yobbos, Tolhurst's piss-stained encounter with Billy Idol, and Dempsey's wariness about life in the back of a van, The Cure's luck and their profile were slowly improving. On December 16 they received their first national coverage from the British music press, courtesy of Adrian Thrills, the scribe hand-picked by Parry three months earlier to check out the band at Redhill.

Under the headline, 'Ain't No Blues For The Summertime Cure', Thrills documented the band's brief history. He noted Smith's fondness for his Woolworth's Top 20 guitar and laid out the evolution of the band, analysed their head-butting with Hansa and their eventual signing by Parry and Fiction. It may have been Smith's first formal sit-down with the music press, but he was already developing the type of spiky one liners and catty put-downs that would become his trademark. When asked about Hansa's plans, Smith delivered his witty kiss-off about how "it got to the stage where we would have become the Barron Knights of punk", while dismissing the tunes offered to them by the German indie as "really banal old rock'n'roll songs". Smith also defended 'Killing An Arab' for the first but by no means the final time. Thrills described the song as appearing "at first glance, irresponsibly racist", before detailing its erudite roots. Smith handled this potentially prickly subject with the steady hand of a press veteran. After making his jibe about the song being dedicated to all the wealthy Arabs seen hanging about Crawley discos, Smith tried to downplay the song's meaning, once and for all. "It's not really racist," he said, "it's not a call to kill Arabs."

Even though Thrills' depiction of The Cure as "an abrasive light-metal trio" was way off the money, the writer was clearly impressed by the brooding young men from Crawley. "The Cure are like a breath of fresh air on the capital's smog-ridden pub and club circuit," he wrote. "I suggest you catch The Cure immediately."

Thrills' favourable feature had a very immediate and tangible effect – not surprising, given the follow-my-leader nature of the UK press (and the punters who devoured the music weeklies). When The Cure walked on stage at the Hope & Anchor in Islington, a week later, the place was packed. Even though Smith was running a temperature of 102 and was self-medicating with Night Nurse and Disprins, the band was a hit. Rick Joseph of *Melody Maker* was in the crowd and fancied what he saw, despite Smith's physical shortcomings.

"This was a cruel date on The Cure's calendar," he began, worryingly, going on to outline Smith's illness, Tolhurst's unstable drum kit and the low-rent venue, which, he wrote, "displayed the charm of a cross-Channel lorry deck". But just like Thrills before him, Joseph could spot the band's rising star. He praised their "crisp set", stating that in spite of their setbacks, "The Cure . . . salvaged this unluxurious event from oblivion through their own embryonic music talent and their ability to inject a dose of enjoy-serum into the Mivvied corpuscles of punters present." In short, The Cure rocked, returning for a pair of encores.

To Michael Dempsey, London shows such as this were the highlight of his tenure with The Cure. "They were landmark moments," said Dempsey. "But there were diminishing returns from then on. It was like drinking – the first one was great, but it's downhill from there."

As for Chris Parry, his decision to jump the good ship Polydor appeared to be justified. His new signing had the songs, the leather jacket, the support of the famously fickle music press – now all The Cure needed was some music in the marketplace. In December, the band's debut single, 'Killing An Arab', backed by '10.15 Saturday Night', was released. In an effort to capitalise on the good press and get something in the stores before Christmas, Parry was forced to release their single on Small Wonder Records, at least for the initial pressing of 15,000 copies. Small Wonder was a grass-roots indie label operating out of a record store in Walthamstow, east London, which had scored some small-scale success with the bands Punishment Of Luxury and The Leyton Buzzards. The deal was this – by effectively sub-letting The Cure for these 15,000 singles, Fiction could undertake some free market research, gauging the public's response to the band's improving profile. And if the first pressing sold out, Fiction would be sufficiently cashed-up to press another 15,000.

But despite Parry's best efforts, the band's debut didn't reach the stores in time for Christmas, so The Cure missed out on the chance to go head-to-head with The Bee Gees, whose 'Too Much Heaven' was the single of the season (alongside the desperate plea that was Rod Stewart's 'Do Ya Think I'm Sexy'). Even Robert Smith might have noted the irony that The Barron Knights' 'A Taste Of Aggro' was also riding high in the Yuletide charts.

What Parry did manage to do, however, was place 'Killing An Arab' on the Polydor punk compilation, *20 Of Another Kind*, which emerged in March 1979. The Cure found themselves back in the company of shaghound Billy Idol and Generation X, along with Parry signings The Jam and Sham 69 (who both contributed two songs, not surprisingly, given that the Fiction label boss compiled the album).

Although Robert Smith disliked the sleeve design for 'Killing An Arab', it was certainly striking. A stark, piercing pair of eyes – the reversed-out image of an old man's face – glared from the cover, while the flipside, in an almost laughably literal interpretation of the song, featured the image of a small dripping tap (you know, as in "drip drip drip"). It was the first of several disagreements between Parry and Smith on the look of the band and their music, even though Parry admitted he "wasn't terribly concerned" when Smith screwed up his nose at the cover art. Parry didn't want his rising star to get involved in such subjective discussions – he just wanted him to keep writing quality songs. Which was something Parry was sure The Cure had produced with 'Killing An Arab'.

"I knew the punters would like it," Parry declared. "It was something you could pogo to, so it was a winner for punks and . . . those were the people I really wanted to get at – the people who read music papers, the active ones."

Despite its delayed release, the music weeklies' response to 'Killing An Arab' was favourable and immediate. And before the end of the year, Small Wonder had 2,000 orders for the single. The upswing in the band's fortunes came as a shock. "One minute we were nothing," Smith said, "and the next we were the New Existentialists."

Music writers were engaged in some healthy one-upmanship in an effort to claim first reviewing bragging rights for The Cure's debut single. *Sounds*' Dave McCullough edged out his rivals, reviewing 'Arab' on January 13. Amidst the usual overly clever waffle, McCullough did manage to cut to the chase: "The A-side is . . . nice and fresh and crisp and funny. Quaint. You immediately love it." He did the band a sizeable favour by also reviewing the flipside, '10.15', noting that "it hits upon the sparseness in rock'n'roll like no other record has in, oh, as far back as I can think. There's scarcely any playing in the song at all. Everything is left to your imagination." McCullough had justified Robert Smith's decision to move away from Porl Thompson's guitar heroics in just a couple of sentences.

Melody Maker, who'd covered the band's January 8 show at the Moonlight Club in West Hampstead, were next in line to talk up 'Arab'. Ian Birch likened the song to Siouxsie & The Banshees' recent excellent single. "As 'Hong Kong Garden' used a simple oriental-styled riff to striking effect," Birch figured, justifiably, "so 'Arab' conjures up edginess through a Moorish-flavoured guitar pattern."

NME's Tony Parsons was another convert. Writing in the January 27 issue, he praised Smith's vocals, a surprising move given that his voice was hardly the key weapon in The Cure's limited arsenal: "Those vocals – taut, terse, tense intonation, very much wired and emotional, the scream that a nervous system might make on the verge of metabolic breakdown." Then, in an observation that echoed Smith's self-imposed separation from the working stiffs of Crawley, the writer compared Smith's forlorn vocals with "that feeling you get watching the faces on the workaday tube ride after stepping out at dawn for the third time without sleep". It was a little confused, sure, but the message was clear enough: The Cure was officially credible.

Even legendary *NME* scribe Nick Kent signed up, turning his attention to '10.15', calling it "something of an isolated vignette, hopefully portraying a whole mood of rejection".

Sounds could sense sufficient momentum in The Cure bandwagon to make the band cover stars of their January 27 issue. Again, Dave McCullough wrote the piece, entitled 'Kill Or Cure', taken from an interview conducted – at the band's request – in the Natural History Museum. If the choice of venue was designed to prove how far removed they were from the London cool school, it was lost on McCullough. He seemed preoccupied with the baby-faced looks of the band, especially Robert Smith. "They look so young it's not true," he wrote. "Robert resplendent in baggy, singularly silly and unhip pants. They look younger in the way that most grammar-school kids from fairly safe family backgrounds look younger. Unexposed and clean."

Of course McCullough wasn't a crystal-ball gazer: there was no way that he could know that within five years Robert Smith would become a walking cadaver, as he did his damnedest to try to destroy himself during his prolonged "chemical vacation". But that was way off in the future – right now The Cure had to finish their debut album.

Chapter Four

"I'm the Hoover, Robert's the lamp stand and Michael's the fridge."

– Lol Tolhurst

BY early 1979, Morgan Studios had begun to feel like The Cure's second home. They'd returned there on January 8 to continue work on the set of songs that would eventually become *Three Imaginary Boys*, breaking only briefly for a show at the Nashville in west Kensington on February 9. It was there that they had their second close encounter with the National Front. This motley crew of hairless bovver boys were convinced that 'Arab' – which had sold well enough to warrant a second pressing by Fiction – was a call to arms for Arab-haters everywhere. They stood outside the gig, handing out propaganda that referred to the song, as if it was some kind of new National Front anthem. Robert Smith shook his head, dismayed by their naïve take on his Camus-inspired tune, and continued playing as fights broke out in the crowd. The sparring matches inside Morgan seemed timid by comparison.

With the benefit of both hindsight and the privilege of being a pampered (and much loved) rock star, Robert Smith would continually write off *Three Imaginary Boys*, insisting that if he'd had more control, the record would have been a much more satisfying, rounded debut. But at the time of its making, the 19-year-old didn't speak the language of the studio, and had no way of translating the sounds he was hearing onto tape. And neither he, Tolhurst nor Dempsey were confident enough to question the work of Hedges and Parry. So, understandably, the more seasoned pair took control of the production.

Michael Dempsey wasn't the only member of The Cure to question Parry's studio expertise, but he was the only one to say so on the record. When I asked him whether Parry deserved the production credit he received for their debut LP, he replied enigmatically: "The producer sat in the seat with producer written on it." Being an ex-drummer, Parry devoted much of the band's limited studio time at Morgan to nailing the perfect drum sound, while Tolhurst spent hours tapping away at a snare. "His focus in the studio would be on the drums, getting a good drum sound, which was natural enough," Tolhurst told me. The rest of the sessions raced by, with a minimum of overdubs and some additional lead guitar from Smith. "Everything was done in one or two takes," Tolhurst said. "Maybe there was a couple of overdubs on the whole album. We played it as we would play our set."

Despite the quick-fire nature of the sessions, The Cure actually emerged with more songs than were required for *Three Imaginary Boys*. These cast-offs included 'Pillbox Tales', which would appear as the B-side of the 'Boys Don't Cry' single; the little-heard 'World War', which would end up on the 2005 reissue of *Three Imaginary Boys* and – in a snappy retort to their former German bosses – a faux-disco romp entitled 'Do The Hansa'. This wouldn't be heard until the 1986 re-release of 'Boys Don't Cry' – and even then only as a bonus B-side.

Of these rejects, 'Pillbox Tales' was noteworthy because its lyrics were mainly written by Tolhurst. As Tolhurst told me, "The strange thing about 'Pillbox Tales' is that it started off as an ode to a girlfriend of mine who I would meet at an old World War II gun emplacement in the woods in Horley." To Smith, the song was essentially written for boozy punters, "so we could bang out a couple of minutes of thumping 150bpm emergency drunk music".

'Do The Hansa' was equally transparent (and throwaway), a kiss-off to their first label, Smith muttering unintelligible comments in mock German. To Smith, 'Hansa' was a "nonsense song. The faux German is quite funny, as is some of the playing." To Tolhurst, "I think we just enjoyed our chance to have a little revenge and poke fun at their lack of vision." The track also proved that the band didn't know how to handle much outside their limited post-punk repertoire. This might explain why it was buried in The Cure archives for seven years.

While Parry, Hedges and assistant Mike Dutton finalised *Three Imaginary Boys* in studio 4 at Morgan, The Cure began a four-week-long residency at London's Marquee. By this point, The Cure's set was virtually all originals, bar their crash-and-burn take on Hendrix's 'Foxy Lady'. They opened their Marquee debut with '10.15', then moved through 'Accuracy', 'Grinding Halt', 'Another Day', 'Object', 'Subway

Song', 'Foxy Lady', 'Meathook', 'Three Imaginary Boys', 'Boys Don't Cry', 'Plastic Passion', 'Fire In Cairo', 'It's Not You', 'Do The Hansa' and the obligatory set-closer, 'Killing An Arab'. Their set the following Sunday night was identical, apart from a reprise of '10.15'.

Their 40-minute bracket, in the words of *Melody Maker*'s James Truman, was "compact, perfectly conceived and performed with control and vigour". The astute Truman would compare The Cure to such post-punkers as Wire, Pere Ubu and The Buzzcocks. He even likened Smith to Television's legendary Tom Verlaine, only "younger, fresh-faced, spitting out lyrics and rolling off lightning guitar phrases in a jumble of sustained discord and harmonics". Truman also praised the timekeeping of Lol Tolhurst.

In his final analysis, Truman heaped some serious praise on a band that was still floundering around for a sound to call their own. "The Cure are doing what few other of the new bands have done, writing traditional melodic songs, embracing experiment to a point short of self-indulgence and at the same time being intelligent about it. They are very young. They will also be very successful."

By the time Truman's review hit the streets, the word had spread on The Cure – The Marquee was full for each of their Sunday night residencies, which almost made the crowd's constant gobbing tolerable. One of their support acts was Joy Division, already developing a legend of their own, although Smith was too nervous to pay much attention to the doomed Ian Curtis and his fellow Mancunian gloomsters.

Lol Tolhurst still has fond memories of their Marquee residency. He felt that it was during this month of Sundays that The Cure proved they were more than some trio of suburban hopefuls with a Camus fixation. "My favourite memory," he said in 2005, "is standing outside The Marquee before we played, watching the people coming in and listening to them talking. I recall a couple walking by, and on seeing the 'House Full' sign outside, exclaim: 'House full? For The Cure?' I think that's the point we realised we were onto something."

While Smith and the band were clearly chuffed by all this high praise, they were in for a shock. A few nights after their final Marquee slot, as the band got ready for a set at The Pavilion in West Runton, Chris Parry gave them a sneak preview of the album cover artwork, which was designed by Bill Smith (who'd also worked on the 'Killing An Arab' cover). Smith was mortified. Though he was hardly expecting a glorious, full-colour portrait of the trio, he wasn't anticipating this drab, ambiguous cover shot of a lamp, a refrigerator and a Hoover. The rear image was just as enigmatic – rather than spelling out song titles, Parry had used symbols to designate each track. ('Accuracy' was represented by a target, and so on.) It was a radio programmer's nightmare and an aesthetic bummer.

So what was Parry thinking? Just this: "I thought, 'Let's make it completely dispassionate, let's pick the three most mundane things we can possibly find.' My problem with The Cure was: here was a band without an image but with strong music so I thought, 'Let's make it completely without an image.'"

Smith knew he couldn't win the argument – when he complained, Parry simply told him that it was too late to change anything. But Smith's dislike of the artwork lingered for years. As late as 2000 he would dismiss it as "a bag of shite".

"It was all Parry's idea. He had this idea of the group that I reluctantly went along with. He even chose which songs should go on the LP."

Dempsey's reaction was the flipside of Smith's, which says something about their markedly different personalities. "I didn't particularly hate it – I still don't," he said when we spoke. "None of us were particularly against it, although Robert later said he was." Dempsey felt that Smith's concerns weren't so much about the image itself, but more because he didn't have any control over the decision. And Lol Tolhurst? He simply decided who was who. "I'm the Hoover, Robert's the lamp stand and Michael's the fridge."

In fact, when I asked him in 2005, Tolhurst felt that too much had been made of Smith's reaction to the artwork: he certainly didn't express his concern at the time. "We were presented with this cover by Bill Smith – the same thing with 'Killing An Arab' – and we went, 'OK.' We didn't know any better so we went along with it."

"There was a mysticism to artwork that we didn't fully grasp," added Dempsey, "and we didn't want to rock the boat too much – we didn't have the confidence."

The band continued to tour in the lead-up to the album's late May release, playing in Cromer, Chippenham, Chesterton (where the band's roadies were busted) and Westford. They also played a hometown Crawley show at Northgate Community Centre, this time with

Amulet as support, on April 29. It was another benefit for Dr Tony Weaver and once again the local league of the National Front gatecrashed the gig. According to Smith, "They ringed the community centre and tried to burn it down while we were playing."

This would draw some undesirable press, as did an incident at a show at Bournemouth Town Hall, where a woman attacked her boyfriend, resulting in a headline that read: "Man Loses Ear At Pop Concert". But more upbeat press started to roll in, too. On March 24, *Melody Maker* ran an Ian Birch interview with the band, in which Smith outlined his "less is more" approach. He also explained his stay-at-home nature. "I don't really socialise with Mick or Lol. I never socialise with anyone, really." But all this attention was a prelude to *Three Imaginary Boys*, which was finally released on May 5.

Robert Smith would become one of *Three Imaginary Boys'* harshest critics, slamming the album at regular intervals pretty much from its release onwards. He would even go so far as to declare that if it turned out to be the band's first and last long-player, "I would have been disgusted if it had been my only testimony to music." Smith wrote the songs that were recorded for *Three Imaginary Boys* with no real idea of The Cure's audience or the type of musical direction in which he was hoping to steer the band, hardly a new situation for a band still serving its apprenticeship. And it showed.

"We were playing about 50 songs at the time," he would state, "mostly in pubs and to people who didn't care if we fell over and died. I wrote most of them by myself [despite the shared songwriting credits with Dempsey and Tolhurst] without thinking they'd ever be heard by more than 30 people at a time. Chris Parry picked what he thought were the best of the 30 we recorded."

Tolhurst's take on *Three Imaginary Boys* wasn't so extreme. "The truth is, up until the first record we had no idea," he said to me. "When we made the first record we thought, 'Well, maybe that's it, we might never make another one.' We didn't have a master plan; we didn't really have one until the mid-Eighties. We were pretty young; we didn't have any idea of what was going to happen. That naivety comes across when I hear the records now. In some ways that was our saving grace."

Smith's criticisms were the typical responses of an ambitious musician with a sound in his head but no real understanding of how to capture it on tape – and who wasn't in the position to flex any muscle when it came to final song selection. And Smith didn't hold back – he'd slam the album's rapid-fire turnaround, its wayward song selection, its artwork, its lack of musical focus, Lol Tolhurst's limitations as a drummer – and he had a handy fall guy in Chris Parry. Smith, more often than not, would blame virtually all of *Three Imaginary Boys'* shortcomings on his producer-cum-manager-cum-label-boss. But, of course, it took some time before Smith uttered many of these criticisms.

"The first one is my *least* favourite Cure album," Smith would tell *Rolling Stone* in 2004. "Obviously, they are my songs, and I was singing, but I had no control over any other aspect of it: the production, the choices of the songs, the running order, the artwork. It was all kind of done by Parry without my blessing. And even at that young age I was very pissed off.

"I had dreamed of making an album," he continued, "and suddenly we were making it and my input was being disregarded. I decided from that day on we would always pay for ourselves and therefore retain total control."

Smith would admit that he felt the album was heading in the wrong direction almost from the first recorded note. "I distinctly remember thinking, 'This isn't sounding the way I want it to.'" What he was aiming for was a bare-bones sound, stripped down and unembellished, something the band would achieve on a few tracks but not the entire album. "When we came to record," he said, "I didn't really have the time to do what I wanted to do and I didn't have enough clout to do it, either." Smith felt that Parry "tricked" him into recording songs that Smith wasn't mad about, just so the band would have plenty of choice when it came to determining the final track listing. (Neither of his bandmates can recall Smith saying this at the time of its release, however.)

"Chris Parry told us to record every song we had and we'd work out what went on the album afterwards. I trusted him, but in the end he just chose what went on there." Smith would nominate such tracks as 'Object' and their cover of 'Foxy Lady' as throwaways that should have been kept for B-sides, at best. "They were diabolical and I hated them – they were the dregs of what we were doing." By the time the sessions had ended in February 1979, Smith was already sketching the songs that would appear on the far more accomplished (if wrist-slashingly bleak) *Seventeen Seconds*. If Smith had learned one thing from their *Three Imaginary Boys* experience it was this: he vowed to be involved with the production of every future Cure album. Unlike many of Robert Smith's proclamations, he has stayed true to his word – he's co-produced each of their subsequent 11 studio albums.

Of course, *Three Imaginary Boys* wasn't quite as poorly conceived as Smith wanted the world to believe, either in 1979 or 2004. If it were, it seems likely The Cure would have been laughed off the pages of the music press, never to return. (And there were other distractions in May 1979, such as adapting to the reality that arch Conservative Margaret Thatcher had just become the UK's first female PM.) The band and Parry were savvy enough to open the album with their ace, the tense '10.15 Saturday Night', as taut a track as you were likely to hear in 1979, Joy Division's 'Transmission' included. '10.15' rolled into 'Accuracy', another Sahara-dry moment of post-punk despair, a song so stripped back it's almost naked. It's a classic case study of Smith's half-spoken vocal style, which he'd just about mastered, even at this early stage. 'Grinding Halt' – which would become a feature of the band's upcoming Peel session, for reasons other than the song itself – had all the herky-jerky rhythms of New Wave, Smith's staccato rhythm guitar and Tolhurst's minimalist drum fills echoing the sounds of XTC's recent, excellent *Drums And Wires* album. Tolhurst wrote the original song, but Smith took a knife to the lyrics, paring them back to their absolute minimum.

'Another Day' slowed down the pace of *Three Imaginary Boys* significantly – the song's murky sound was a precursor to the type of narcotic haze that hung over subsequent Cure albums *Faith* and *Pornography*. Rather than rhyming couplets, Smith spat out fragments of lyrics – "shades of grey", "I stare at the window", "the eastern sky grows cold" – which wielded the same kind of gloomy melancholy that would lead to his peer Morrissey, of The Smiths, being crowned Britain's bedsit guru, the most miserable man in Manchester.* A muddled middle-

---

* Smith's verbal assaults on Morrissey would make for some of the most quotable quotes of his inconsistent relationship with the press. "I loathe the Morrissey kind of wallowing in despair," he'd announce in 1989. "I don't find it very entertaining to be around someone who's morose all the time."

eight, where the song effectively comes to a halt, didn't do 'Another Day' any favours, but the song is a handy sonic signpost for the future sound of The Cure. (As was 'Winter', an out-take from the *Three Imaginary Boys* sessions.) To Smith, 'Another Day' was purely about boredom and repetition. It showed.

'Object' returns to the more urgent pace of 'Grinding Halt', Smith's vocals drenched in so much reverb that it seemed as though he was trying to out-Orbison The Big O himself. (What Smith would have done for just an ounce of the majesty of Roy Orbison's voice.) Like much of his lyric-writing on the album, Smith's message is ambivalent, as he plays off the disparate meanings of the words 'object' and 'objection' in a clever and faintly erotic fashion. It's not clear if Smith was enjoying his time as an object of desire, or whether he was holding up a sign reading "hands off". It's unlikely that Smith knew himself, although he would admit that the song was written as a joke, a "pastiche of a sexist song". It was a theme Smith would later master with the pure cheese of 'Let's Go To Bed'.

'Subway Song' is the band's indifferent attempt at rock'n'roll noir; the song comprising little more than Dempsey's rumbling bassline, Smith's finger clicks and some very rudimentary harmonica. It stumbles along haphazardly until a piercing scream breaks the silence, making for a truly jarring ending. But it wasn't a patch on The Jam's 'Down In The Tube Station At Midnight', that was for sure. At the time, Smith had been telling people he'd known of someone who'd been murdered in the subway, so the song obviously grew out of Smith's twisted sense of mischief.

From there, *Three Imaginary Boys* headed further downhill with the band's diabolical take on Hendrix's 'Foxy Lady', which included Michael Dempsey's one and only Cure lead vocal. A cursory listen to their desecration of the Hendrix masterpiece proves why: Dempsey half-raps, half-whines his way through Hendrix's tale of seduction like the bastard offspring of Ian Dury and John Lydon. ("It's not one of our better songs," Dempsey admitted, when I asked him about it.) How a Hendrix lover such as Robert Smith allowed 'Foxy' to make the album's final cut remains a mystery to this day. As the band insisted, the song selection was based on what worked live – and 'Foxy Lady' had been a standard in their live set since the time of Easy Cure. Adam Sweeting of *Melody Maker* was being generous when he said: "Imagine

Hendrix without the guitar flash, phasing and stereo trickery and you're left with a sparse, twitching skeleton."

By the time of 'Meathook', The Cure was rapidly running out of musical and lyrical ideas. Smith rambles on about a trip to the butcher, as if these mundane observations contained some of life's great mysteries, while behind him the band scratches around for something resembling a tune. Fortunately, it's all over in a bit over two minutes. If 'Meathook' was the song of a band short of ideas, 'So What' headed even further into the land of filler-dom, as Smith – now well and truly out of lyrics and drunk to boot – read out loud the details of a cake icing and food decorating set off the back of a sugar packet.

Made all the more droll by Smith's inclusion of the usual promo-speak designed to entice housewives who bake – Give your cakes that professional look! – he slurs a list of the packet's contents: turntable, nine-inch icing bag with high definition nozzles, adaptor and 15-inch food decorating bag with piping nozzles. It was clear that Smith had fallen a long way from the deconstruction of Albert Camus and existentialism of 'Killing An Arab'. The sound of the sugar packet being scrunched into a ball at the song's close might as well have been Smith casting his verdict on the direction of not just the song, but the entire *Three Imaginary Boys* record. "Funny," Smith would say of 'So What', "it seemed like a good idea at the time."

However, the album wasn't a complete train wreck. A slightly more polished version of 'Fire In Cairo', one of the first songs recorded during the September/October 1978 sessions with Parry, provided a few moments of quiet despair, while Smith's catchy, singalong chorus displayed some early signs of his million-dollar melodicism. 'It's Not You' was more filler, most likely included because its propulsive energy had been generating some lively pogoing (and gobbing) at Cure shows.

But if a track such as 'Another Day', with its dimly lit, overcast mood, was some kind of pointer for the band's musical future, then the album's title track (based on a Robert Smith dream) may well have been the blueprint for what was to follow. As a vocalist, Smith had found a melancholic mood rarely heard this side of one of his teen favourites, Nick Drake, even if the band's electric backing was much spikier than anything that could be found on *Five Leaves Left*. And such snatches of lyrics that include a plea for help, concern about the future and a deep feeling of emptiness would establish Smith's reputation as the guru of gloom, the only man who could out-Morrissey Morrissey. Smith's voice, which trailed off as the song drew to its close, sounded like a man lost in the wilderness. It was hardly the soundtrack to an afternoon of hedonistic bliss, but 'Three Imaginary Boys' was a brooding, evocative end to a muddled, misdirected album.

"The atmospherics of a song like 'Three Imaginary Boys'," Smith concurred, "was an example of where I wanted us to head."

Despite Smith's concerns about virtually every factor of their debut – most of them uttered well and truly after its release, of course – the album was generally well received. *Sounds'* Dave McCullough, giving Parry high praise as the "essential fourth Cure", which must have pained Robert Smith greatly, was all over the album like a cheap suit. The successful recipe, according to McCullough was this: "Take three intelligent, sheepishly good-looking, nice middle-class boys who have a flair for original, stylish music and who don't mind leaving their souls in the hands of a fourth streamlined, highly successful party." He even praised their massacre of 'Foxy Lady' – hell, McCullough even thought that the lifeless artwork was "a witty metaphor".

Critic Adam Sweeting also heaped on the praise, suggesting The Cure was looking backwards in order to move punk forwards. "I can't remember a band which has displayed such a basic format so richly since The Who . . . it's like an introspective reverie on a wet afternoon." Despite a miscue with the album's title – he called it *The Cure*, which was some 25 years too early – *Melody Maker's* Ian Birch was another true believer, declaring that "the Eighties start here". Labelling their debut "masterful", Birch – just like *Sounds'* McCullough – doles out equal amounts of praise for band and producer, admiring Parry's "intuitive understanding of The Cure psyche" which allowed each member "an equally dynamic share of the action". Taken by the "distinctive material" and the band's ability to move through many moods ("anger, disillusion, scorn, wistfulness and humour"), Birch signed off with this major rap. "This is great pop that you should waste no time discovering. The missing link between The Kinks 1966-style and the Banshees 1978-style? The lean and friskily alert music of the Eighties? Find out for yourself."

Trouser Press also signed on as Cure converts, comparing the band with Talking Heads and Wire. "Like both those groups," they announced, "The Cure concern themselves with creating sound patterns using the barest palette available – one guitar, bass, drums and voice." In other words – well, XTC's, actually: *Drums And Wires*.

Unexpectedly, the album spent three weeks in the album charts, peaking at number 44, holding its own in a UK chart dominated by a reasonably healthy mix of quality pop/rock (Blondie, The Police, Bowie and Squeeze all had charting records at the time) and the usual fluff, including pop castrato Art Garfunkel and such disco leftovers as Boney M, Eruption and Amii Stewart.

But neither the band nor Chris Parry was ready for the *NME* backlash, heaped out by Paul Morley. He may have found 'Killing An Arab' "pleasurable", but Morley wasn't quite so charmed by *Three Imaginary Boys*. In a review that's admirable for its relentlessness, Morley took issue with virtually every aspect of the band's debut long-player. For starters, Morley felt – not inaccurately – that the band had no true idea what, if any, message they had to share with the world. "The lads go rampant on insignificant symbolism and compound this with rude, soulless obliqueness. They are trying to tell us something. They are trying to tell us they do not exist. They are trying to say that everything is empty. They are making fools of themselves."

But Morley was only just warming up. Quite justifiably, he slagged the album's "mysterious" artwork (even if he misread Dempsey as the Hoover and Tolhurst as the fridge), figuring that Parry's "no image" concept had backfired. "All this . . . fiddling about," he wrote, "aims for the anti-image but naturally creates the perfectly malleable image: the tantalising enigma of The Cure. They try to take everything away from the purpose and idea of the rock performer but try so hard they put more in than they take out. They just add to the falseness."

Eventually Morley got beyond the band's image and set to work on *Three Imaginary Boys*' tunes. They didn't do much for him, either. He described them as "willowy songs [that] wallow in the murk and marsh of tawdry images, inane realisations, dull epigrams". His lengthy and at times quite justified hatchet job ended with this one final kiss-off to The Cure. "In 1979 people shouldn't be able to get away with things like this. There are too many who do. Fatigue music. So transparent. So light and – oh, how it nags."

The Cure, up until this point, had been blessed with the perfect media relationship. Through their earliest days, when they played covers for drunks in Crawley and then throughout their Hansa tribulations, they'd been ignored. This worked to their advantage when *Melody Maker*'s Rick Joseph reviewed their Hope & Anchor show and the jury returned with a positive verdict for 'Killing An Arab': at the time they were still a fresh, new band, the kind of act that most writers would like to claim they'd discovered. Hell, they'd even been nominated as ground zero for the Eighties, according to Ian Birch. Now the relationship was starting to sour.

"I think a lot of people in the music press thought we were manufacturing our image in some way," Lol Tolhurst figured, "and it was as though they were trying to find the 'truth' behind our 'mysterious façade'. In truth, we were probably quite naïve, so what they really saw was that naivety mixed with our genuine desire to communicate our emotions. I think the music press was no different from the mass populace – we tended to polarise people."

Parry had also led a relatively charmed life up until the publication of Morley's review. He'd signed and produced critics' darlings The Jam and the Banshees. *Rolling Stone* had gone into raptures about the former's debut, *In The City*, blessing the album with four stars and stating that it "stood out from the class of '77 . . . [it] barrels along at a pogo pace." They'd been just as effusive when it came to Siouxsie & The Banshees' 1978 debut, *The Scream*. Not only did they also receive the four-star treatment, but *Rolling Stone* believed that "their debut draws a vital connection between punk and psychedelia", going on to namecheck The Cure and The Psychedelic Furs as bands directly influenced by the Banshees.

So Smith and Parry – much to their credit – responded as any self-respecting music fan would to Morley's damning review. They wrote a letter to Morley at *NME*. Admittedly, Smith did actually concur with some – but not all – of the writer's barbs. "[But] what irritated me," Smith said, "was that I agreed with some of what he said but the bit about the packaging making claims for social validity was nonsense. He was saying that we were trying to do something and then not achieving it, which was obviously not true."

In a 2000 interview, Smith conceded that there was some merit to *Three Imaginary Boys*, but that was more a result of the band's musical shortcomings – especially Lol Tolhurst's bare-basics drumming skills. "People picked up on it, because it sounded very different from anything else at the time," he said. "Because Lol couldn't drum very well, we had to keep everything very, very simple. Our sound was forced on us to a certain extent."

The band didn't connect that well with another journalist who wielded some influence. Nick Kent, one of the most widely read (and quoted) music writers of the time whose best work was compiled in *The Dark Stuff*, simply found them hard to like. In a May 19 *NME* piece called 'A Demonstration Of Household Appliances', he sensed that the band just didn't feel that comfortable discussing their music. Kent was right on the money, given that Smith would admit that he didn't think *Three Imaginary Boys* "sounded like The Cure at all". They were very much a band-under-development, who hadn't quite decided which direction their music should take.

Although Kent admitted that The Cure was neither "rude nor cliquish", he got the sense that "the ongoing interview situation is not one that they feel particularly at home with, that they find the process bemusing, almost quaint in its ridiculousness". Running through the individual band members, Kent found Tolhurst "the most democratic and business-like" and felt that Smith was "the creative, shoulder-shrugging one". Dempsey left no impression on him at all. "Between this pair," Kent wrote, "Dempsey blends in without adding any partic-ular dimension." However, Kent's criticisms seemed more personal than professional, advising that The Cure should be watched closely. "What will follow may well be some of the finest pop of the Eighties."

The band's response to this new-found criticism was simple and direct. At their next Peel show appearance − Peel had championed 'Killing An Arab', spinning it most nights on his show − they altered the lyrics of 'Grinding Halt', inserting grabs of Morley's panning of their album, tearing strips off his lofty prose stylings and laughing away his claims about "the tantalising enigma of The Cure".

Still, The Cure and Parry were uncertain about their next move. Smith, whose songwriting confidence was growing in sync with his hair, was tuning into Captain Beefheart and German minimalists Can, as was Tolhurst. They realised that there could be a lot more to The Cure than lyrics read verbatim from food decorating sets or the stripped-back garage rock of 'Grinding Halt'. Yet that was exactly the track that was chosen as the next single from *Three Imaginary Boys*, although the decision was a half-hearted one, at best. Only 1,500 promo copies of the single (backed with 'Meathook') were pressed and dispatched to UK clubs and radio stations. It was more a teaser for the album than a genuine second seven-inch.

Again, the *NME* spewed venom. This time the writer was Ian Penman who, when he was in the mood, could be even more verbose – and incomprehensible – than Morley. "The Cure's particular hypothesis," he wrote in mid-May, "concerns a situation of non-forward moving national community activity. Got that? This is the sort of thing we in the Brill Building call a 'hype'." End of review. It was also the end of Fiction's plan to go forward with 'Grinding Halt' as a second single from *Three Imaginary Boys*. They dropped the idea as swiftly as Penman dropped his arch barbs. (The Tolhurst-penned track eventually found a life on the soundtrack to the 1980 punk flick *Times Square*, alongside tracks from David Johansen, The Patti Smith Group and Roxy Music.)

What The Cure could do was tour, which is how they spent the rest of May (and much of 1979, in fact: they played over 100 shows that year). There was no venue too small, or suburb too obscure, for The Cure, as they rolled through Northwich, Newport (twice), Halifax, Stafford, Birmingham, Sheffield, Yeovil, Portsmouth and Norwich, during the month of their album's release, with all the relentless forward motion of one of Rommel's tanks. Yet *NME* remained unconvinced, despite the band's improving profile. They unleashed another spray when reviewing their May 29 show at the Limit Club in Sheffield, going so far as to label them "mutton dressed as lamb". Robert Smith's lack of trust towards the music media was developing, along with the trio's growing skills as a live outfit.

On June 1, The Cure van docked at Carshalton Park for yet another show. While they were hopelessly mismatched with Mod revivalists Secret Affair and The Merton Parkas, the *Quadrophenia* vibe of the night – the film based on The Who's album had just been released – would help inspire a future Cure single, 'Jumping Someone Else's Train', a bitter put-down of bandwagon jumpers and assorted wannabes. The *Record Mirror*'s Philip Hall was at the show, but walked away under-whelmed. "Lots of ideas but little identity," he declared. As Smith scowled and continued scribbling new lyrics in his notebook, The Cure kept on touring, swinging through Liverpool, Cheltenham, Milton Keynes, Swansea – basically anywhere that would have them.

By June 17, they returned to London for their first headliner since March's month-long Marquee residency. But again, the band drew the wrong kind of press notices, this time from Mike Nicholls at *Record Mirror*. It seemed as though *NME*'s thumbs-down had marked the band as targets for every other music paper.

"Did you know they were the Pink Floyd of the new wave?" Nicholls asked with more than a little snippiness. "Well, Robert Smith carries off an admirably Syd Barrett drone and their general art school and smoke bombs approach has definite hippy appeal. The Cure can consider themselves prime contenders for the Most Frustrating Band of the Year award."

In the Fiction bunker, Chris Parry shrugged and released 'Boys Don't Cry', backed with 'Plastic Passion', as the next Cure single, on June 26. While *Melody Maker*'s Ian Birch acknowledged that 'Boys' was a live highlight, he found the single version "ordinary". *NME*'s Paul Morley, however, had changed his tune, embracing The Cure like a long-lost sibling. "'Boys Don't Cry' is a light trippy riff, with an eloquent one-string motif, chatty, ambiguous, yearning vocals and a series of understated, unexpected twists," he declared. "It is classic new pop. I still find the *Three Imaginary Boys* LP as empty as a yawn . . . [but] this is magnificent."

Clearly there was some back-pedalling at work in Morley's gushing review, but the song was far and away the finest three minutes of The Cure's life to date. Even Smith knew that, admitting that, in a righteous world, the track should have reached the top of the charts. As a prime example of old-before-its-time pop classicism, the song still rates highly several decades after its release. It proved that The Cure could be a much more adroit, tuneful outfit than *Three Imaginary Boys* suggested.

Later in the year, Parry would add 'Boys Don't Cry' to his second *20 Of A Kind Compilation*, but only as something of a consolation prize for his band. Every bit as sure as Smith as to the commercial potential of 'Boys', Parry felt that his former label Polydor had stitched up the band, failing to give the single the push it deserved. "'Boys Don't Cry' was my pick for the Top 10," insisted Parry. Of course it didn't get anywhere near the money end of the charts.

In between July shows, including another London gig at the Lyceum, alongside The Ruts, a clearly disappointed Robert Smith undertook the first of many non-Cure projects. Simon Gallup's brother

Ric had graduated from working in Crawley's one reasonable record store to setting up his own label, christened Dance Fools Dance. Smith was the label's other co-founder. A Smith "discovery", 11-year-old drummer/guitarist Robin Banks and 12-year-old shouter Nick Loot (aka The Obtainers), were the label's first release, albeit in a massive pressing of 100 copies, which were flogged to friends and family for 50p apiece. They'd dropped a cassette in the letter box of Smith's parents' house and he was smitten. "The songs were brilliant," he said. With Smith producing, The Obtainers cut 'Yeh Yeh Yeh' and 'Pussy Wussy' at Morgan. The pair of songs made the single's A-side.

"They were two strange kids from our town . . . they probably hung around the record store that Ric Gallup worked in," Tolhurst told me. "One was fairly 'normal', in a strange way. The other was quite a character, like a teenage John Lydon, complete with sneer. Basically one banged pots and pans and the other sang in a voice not dissimilar to Mark E. Smith of The Fall. I think their main objectives were to live up to their name and obtain as much as they could all the time, which they did pretty well!"

But more significantly, Smith's pal Simon Gallup was now in a band called The Magazine Spies. With their name shortened to Magspies, their track 'Lifeblood And Bombs' was used as the single's B-side. Gallup's future wife Carol Thompson – no relation to Porl – sang backing vocals on the track. Just like The Obtainers, Gallup had slipped Smith some music via the family letter box, leaving him a copy of Shane Fenton & The Fentones' 'I'm A Moody Guy'. The message wasn't lost on Smith. "He thought I was a moody bastard."

It may have been a throwaway track, cut simply for laughs (and for the king's ransom of £50), but the Gallup/Smith alliance was clearly growing stronger. Smith's relationship with Lol Tolhurst had deep roots, despite his cutting remarks about Tolhurst's limited musical repertoire. But that wasn't the case with Cure bassist Michael Dempsey. He and Smith had never really connected and that was only heightened by their endless hours squeezed into the back of the Cure Maxi van (which was actually a retired Upjohns' vehicle – prior to that, the band got about in a van that Dempsey bought from a pig farmer). With The Cure, as with so many bands, the need to relate to each other was just as strong off stage as it was on. And this just wasn't happening with Dempsey and Smith. "I never really knew Michael," Smith admitted.

"We never had that much in common. If it weren't for the group, I wouldn't have socialised with him at all because I don't think we particularly enjoyed each other's company." Lol Tolhurst was now drummer and go-between. "It was always that I was Robert's friend and he knew Michael and Michael was my friend and he knew Robert. I was always in the middle."

Dempsey wasn't coping especially well with the touring life, either, regularly falling ill, despite guzzling vitamins by the handful.

Smith and Gallup, meanwhile, were getting tighter with each beer. Every Saturday, Smith met up with Gallup and his mates at their local in Horley. "I thought it would be great if Simon was in the group," said Smith. "It would be much more fun." Both Smith and Gallup were diligent curry eaters, too, which made their connection even stronger.

Heartened by The Magspies' experience and their boozy Saturdays, Smith was now very serious about finding a place in The Cure for Gallup. But there was still the matter of Michael Dempsey to deal with. For the time being, however, Smith and Gallup decided to collaborate on another project. If The Obtainers seemed like the dodgiest case of child exploitation this side of the Industrial Revolution, what became known as the Cult Hero was weirder still. The idea came out of another beery night at Gallup's local in Horley.

Full-figured postman Frank Bell was one of Horley's stranger legends: when not stuffing letter boxes he was often spotted hanging out with the local wrecking crew, decked out in a T-shirt that proclaimed: "I'm a Cult Hero." Robert Smith had met him and was taken by his bold personality. Smith was convinced that the mailman had all the makings of stardom. When Bell's name was mentioned in the pub one night, Smith had a brainwave: "I thought, 'Get him in the studio and write a disco song.'" And that's exactly what Smith did. He invited Gallup, Tolhurst, Porl Thompson and his teenage contenders The Obtainers to help out, along with a gaggle of Horley locals. Smith also invited his two sisters not only to attend, but play at the sessions: Janet plucked a bass and Margaret sang backing vocals. The song was cut at Morgan with Mike Hedges, although Chris Parry was given the producer's credit.

When it was eventually released in December 1979, the single 'I'm A Cult Hero' (backed with 'I Dig You') was hardly the type of pop cheese to stop a nation in their tracks or change the course of popular music. Only 2,000 copies were pressed. As *NME* would report, 'Cult Hero' was "a bit of discofied nonsense concocted by the group and a drinking buddy that should never have seen the light of day". But it achieved several things – firstly, Frank Bell's dream of stardom was realised (especially when the song became a novelty hit in Canada the next year, selling upwards of 35,000 copies). And Robert Smith, still smarting from the *Three Imaginary Boys* cover fiasco, grabbed the chance to design the artwork, which was based on a Howlin' Wolf LP. And, most crucially, it strengthened the bond between Gallup and Smith.

Michael Dempsey was on holiday when the session was planned. By the time he returned, Gallup had already mastered the bassline. Dempsey was relegated to adding some synth lines. As good-natured as the Cult Hero indulgence obviously was, Dempsey knew that his time as Cure bassist was as good as over. "Robert was tiring of me," Dempsey said. "He'd clearly mapped out in his mind what was happening next. Simon was very easy-going, as was Lol, who would always find a way to make things work, but that was less a characteristic of mine." Dempsey could also see that Gallup's pared-back style of playing was much more suitable to the future Cure sound. "Robert stripped away a lot; he took out an awful lot [from the band's sound]. He wanted to go down a very dark and uncompromising road and Simon was perfect for that."

But Dempsey's time wasn't quite over yet. By July, there was sufficient interest in the band for them to make their first overseas trip, albeit a simple hop across the Channel to Holland. They played at an open-air festival on July 29 at Sterrebos. It was hardly a keynote gig in the early life of The Cure – Tolhurst recalled that "it was pissing with rain" and the band played in constant fear of electrocution – but it did show that Parry's goals for The Cure stretched beyond the borders of Old Blighty. He had the band earmarked for world domination, which wasn't surprising, given that it was his money being thrown in their direction.

Back in London in early August, Parry made an introduction that would have a radical, almost terminal impact on The Cure. Smith was at a Throbbing Gristle show on August 3 at the YMCA off Tottenham

Court Road. He was standing at the front when the stench from what he thought could have been car fumes forced him to retire to the bar. There he bumped into Parry, who then introduced Smith to Banshee bassist Steve Severin. It seemed an innocent enough incident: label boss introduces one rising star, Smith, to another, Severin. But if Parry had any idea of how dangerous this liaison would become for The Cure, he would have grabbed Smith and braved the car fumes. Within a few months, Smith would be suffering an advanced case of divided loyalties.

Smith was quite a sight – he was decked out in sunglasses and a green Charlie Cairoli suit. Severin laughed when he laid eyes on him. "I was there in a bright-green check suit," Smith recalled, "and Severin came over to me and said, 'What the fuck do you think you're wearing?' I loved that." A bond, of sorts, was immediately formed. Although Severin had been a fan of 'Killing An Arab' (Parry had slipped him a copy), he seemed more bemused than impressed by Smith. His first move – once he got past Smith's suit – was to ask him how on earth he could be in a band and still live in Crawley. He just couldn't comprehend how anyone could live somewhere other than London, the centre of Severin's universe. Smith shrugged and replied that Crawley was more peaceful. "We just chatted over a few drinks," Smith said, "which set the scene for the next five or six years, really."*

At this point, Smith had yet to witness a live Banshees performance; he'd only heard 'Hong Kong Garden' when it was spun by indie guru John Peel. But during his early trips to London, in late 1978 and early 1979, Smith couldn't help but notice graffiti splattered about the capital that screamed: 'Sign the Banshees'. "It seemed to be everywhere," said Smith, "and it gave them a mythic quality in my mind before they'd even released a record."

Smith and Severin seemed more an odd couple than like-minded reactionaries – Severin, alongside Siouxsie, had been part of the infamous punk crew the Bromley Contingent, while Smith had watched punk from the sidelines in Crawley. Severin was also four years older than Smith. But the pair shared a freethinking musical spirit, while Smith – although he wouldn't admit it – must have envied the credibility that

---

* When asked to give an interview for this book, Severin requested an "appearance fee" of £200, which was declined.

Severin and the Banshees had established with both press and punters.

Even before they signed to Polydor, the Banshees were receiving all the right kinds of notices. Their now legendary desecration of 'The Lord's Prayer', at their debut show on October 2, 1976, was described with the kind of gushing prose reserved nowadays for royal nuptials or Tinseltown premieres: "The prayer begins. It's a wild improvisation, a bizarre stage fantasy acted out for real." Paul Morley, the *NME* scribe who would carve up *Three Imaginary Boys* like some crazed wood-chopper, delivered this typically ambiguous Banshees bulletin in January 1978: "They could be the last 'rock' group. The only 'rock' group. They are not a 'rock' group. They are 20th century per-formers." Even in the midst of Julie Burchill's brazen pillorying of their debut long-player, *The Scream*, she did list those things she loved about Siouxsie: " 'Hong Kong Garden', the way she treats her audience like muck . . . I even kind of liked the way she danced on *Top Of The Pops*." Surely Robert Smith would have jumped if he'd been offered this kind of press in exchange for Morley's windy assault on The Cure's debut LP.

A few weeks after Smith and Severin's first exchange, on August 29, Severin helped The Cure score the support slot for the Banshees. An unholy alliance was under way.

In early September, the band was briefly back in Morgan Studios to cut their third single, 'Jumping Someone Else's Train', the tune inspired by the Mod revival Smith had witnessed several months earlier. Smith would characterise the opening guitar chord as "sub Pete Townshend", another nod in a Mod direction. Although it hardly made an impres-sion on the charts when it appeared in November, 'Jumping' was an impressive kiss-off from Smith, proof positive of the improvement in his songwriting and the growing sense of assuredness in his lyrics, which were actually penned in the bar at Morgan. But the session was just as significant for the single's B-side, 'I'm Cold', which turned out to be Dempsey's final recording with The Cure. Smith had been writing a lot of the material that would make their next album, *Seventeen Seconds*, and Dempsey's dislike of the material showed. "We'd had a couple of rehearsals," Smith said, "and he didn't like the new stuff." At the same time, Fiction labelmates The Associates had been trying to poach Dempsey from The Cure and this wasn't something that Dempsey was totally averse to. He said as much to Smith. "I said, 'I think they're great – I think they're better than us.' "

Just to demonstrate how strong the ties now were between the Banshees and The Cure, Siouxsie added a backing wail to 'I'm Cold'. Smith had encouraged her to sing on the track, as he spelled out in the liner notes to *Join The Dots*, where 'I'm Cold' was given a second life, some 25 years after its recording. "I wanted Siouxsie to sing on a Cure song because I admired what the Banshees were doing and I wanted them to be part of The Cure story," Smith said. The track was a regular from the band's early gigs at The Rocket in Crawley, but was slowed down to a neo-psychedelic drone for the single. Smith was impressed by the playback of the song, at full volume, late at night at Morgan, but wasn't totally convinced he'd achieved his aim of displaying the "darker, heavier side of the band". But that would come, and soon.

The Cure/Banshees double-header continued on September 5 at the Ulster Hall in Belfast. As a precursor to the drama that was about to go down, The Cure arrived on time, but their gear didn't; eventually they played after the Banshees, using borrowed equipment. But that was a minor glitch compared to what happened the next day in Aberdeen.

Maybe the Banshees should have seen the signs: British PM Thatcher was in town and the city was crawling with security.* While Maggie spoke, the Banshees had an in-store signing of their album *Join Hands*. The store had ordered 200 copies, but Polydor had only delivered 50, which virtually walked out the door. The Banshees' manager, Nils Stevenson, sold his stash of albums to the store's owner to cover the demand, but Banshee drummer Kenny Morris and guitarist John McKay chose to start handing out the albums for free. When the store-owner advised them of their poor grasp of economics, the pair retaliated by refusing to sign any more autographs. A band huddle ensued and McKay and Morris stormed out of the store and the band. By the time the other Banshees returned to their digs, the vexed duo were on a train back to London, their tour passes safety-pinned to their hotel room pillows, which had been shaped to resemble human bodies.

Smith had sensed some inner-Banshee tension during their opening

---

* Such was the tension surrounding the grocer's daughter from Grantham at this time that it was deemed necessary to install fortress-like iron gates at the entrance to Downing Street, a legacy of her confrontational political style that remains to this day.

show in Bournemouth. After The Cure's set, Severin and Siouxsie had been extremely sociable backstage, while McKay and Morris maintained a stony silence. As Smith recalled, "If we bumped into them and said hello, they'd just turn their heads away like superstars."

When The Cure finished their set at the Aberdeen show, they found that there were two Banshees missing and an advanced state of pandemonium breaking out backstage. "Get back on stage!" Stevenson shouted at them, so The Cure continued playing, debuting a still lyric-less version of 'Seventeen Seconds'. Severin and Siouxsie then joined them for a crash-and-burn take on 'The Lord's Prayer'. The show was over – and so, it seemed, was the Banshees.

Back at their hotel, Siouxsie, Severin and The Cure addressed the problem in a logical fashion: they got smashed. During the course of the night, Smith offered his services as stand-in guitarist, an act of generosity that was also tinged with desperation: it was important for The Cure's profile that the show go on, too. Severin smiled and said that they'd prefer to go ahead with their plan to audition some new guitarists. While the Banshees tried out the usual hopefuls, The Cure returned to Holland for the New Pop Festival, where they played before 10,000 Rotterdam fans. The Banshees may have been on the skids, but the cult of The Cure was growing.

The Banshees' auditions for a guitarist proved futile, despite the support of the BBC's John Peel, who sent out an appeal during his show. So they relented and decided to ask Smith to join the band as fill-in stringman. Smith's only proviso to becoming an occasional Banshee was that The Cure retain the support slot. Severin and Siouxsie agreed. Although Lol Tolhurst, now nicknamed "The Fatman", had offered his drumming services, the Banshees hired tub-thumper Budgie, formerly of punk outfit The Slits (and later to become Mr Siouxsie). So, with some kind of order restored, the double-header returned to the road at Leicester on September 18.

Smith boasted that he wasn't fazed by his dual role of opener and headliner. "I don't remember it being difficult," he said. "After what we'd been doing for the past two or three years, it was a piece of piss, really." When asked his opinion by the *Crawley Observer*, Dempsey's only concern was for Smith's staying power. "I only hope Rob has enough energy," he replied. *NME*'s Deanne Pearson, who'd joined the roadshow at the Leicester pit stop, suspected otherwise when she reported on the tour's progress. "[Smith] looks ill," she wrote, "thin and pale. [He] isn't eating properly, isn't sleeping properly, his mind a constant whir of activity."

Not the kind of guy to walk away from either a piss-up or an alliance, Smith began spending the bulk of tour downtime with Severin; Tolhurst also became part of what Smith described as a "group within the groups". But Smith would travel separately from Tolhurst and Dempsey; he would ride in the Banshees' cosy bus, at their insistence, while his two Cure bandmates tagged behind in The Cure's famously unreliable green Maxi van.

By tour's end, the relationship between Smith and Dempsey had soured. He was out of the band immediately after the final Banshees' show; *NME* announced the split on November 10. Dempsey insisted that he was "booted out" of the band – but he was also ready to sign on as bassist in The Associates. This opened the door for Simon Gallup to join the band.

Asked about the split, Smith stated that life in The Cure had become "like a job". "The differences were between him [Dempsey] and me. The more it went on, the more unbearable it became," said Smith. "The Cure part of the show was always uncommunicative and teeth gritted. As soon as I got in the Banshees' van, it was all over [with Dempsey]. I think the final straw came when I played Michael the demos for the next album and he hated them. He wanted us to be XTC part two and – if anything – I wanted us to be the Banshees part two. So he left."

Dempsey's departure actually played out this way: after the tour, Smith began recording home demos of songs that would make up the bulk of *Seventeen Seconds*, using his sister's Hammond organ, a drum machine and his prized Top 20 guitar. Armed with new lyrics, written mostly during one night in Newcastle where he'd come out second-best in a punch-up, Smith was ready to give Tolhurst and Dempsey a preview of the album-under-development. As Smith would report in *Ten Imaginary Years*, "Lol was really excited but Michael was . . . well . . . cool."

"We were around Robert's house a lot playing early versions of 'A Forest' and things like that," Tolhurst remembered. "That was the point Michael wasn't quite into it. I've always liked Michael; he's a good friend. I've come to the conclusion that while we really like each other, he's hard to work with. He has very fixed ideas about where he wants things to go."

Annoyed by Dempsey's cool take on these new songs, Smith jumped to his feet and sprinted to Gallup's house, asking him on the spot if he wanted to join The Cure. When Gallup reminded him that The Cure actually had a bassist, Smith replied, "If you come and play bass, he won't be able to, will he?" Gallup didn't have to think too hard about his next move, because he'd just about resigned himself to his factory job and evenings at the pub with Carol Thompson. Tolhurst drew the short straw and was told that he had to phone Dempsey and break the news.

"I called Michael up and said, 'I don't really think we want to play with you any more,' it was very uncomfortable. I still liked him as a person but it was difficult to see how we could continue playing as a band. It was strange.

"We were English and we really didn't know how to talk to each other that much," Tolhurst added. "We were good friends, but things close to the heart, well, we didn't know how to say it to each other."

"When it was actually put to me," said Dempsey, "it was unexpected. He [Smith] was single-minded and strong-willed enough to know what he wanted to do next. It must have been a huge relief when I wasn't part of the band." Dempsey told me that Smith was even thinking about dispensing with The Cure moniker. "He put it that he didn't want to have The Cure name any more. I could have it if I wanted."

Dempsey felt that he and Smith were actually quite alike in some ways – and he couldn't recall a single argument from his time with the band. "Smith and I are similar in that taciturn English manner, or at least [we were] at that time."

But there were key differences between Dempsey and the world of The Cure: for one, he wasn't much of a drinker. And, as he readily confessed, he had troubles with the often sedentary life of a rock band. "You need the capacity to do nothing for a long time, which is not so much in my temperament."

Parry kept his distance – he figured that if he tried to prevent the inevitable, it might be the end of The Cure. "I thought they were the perfect pop trio, better than The Police, better than The Jam. But Robert wasn't interested and he closed the doors."

'Jumping Someone Else's Train' was released just prior to Dempsey's farewell, on November 2. The reviews were mixed. "There are hints that the formula is wearing a little thin," commented *NME*, "but it's the best of their new songs." Writer Chris Bohn figured that, "The Cure's biggest problem is trying to replace the innocent charm which helped flesh out the bare bones of their early singles." More positively, reviewer Alan Lewis was seduced by the "harsh but detached tone of the song". "Someone should get a medal for the sound quality," he announced.

But 'Jumping' wasn't an important song for The Cure; it was more of a holding pattern as the new trio got ready for their public debut, in Liverpool on November 16. Though the songs he was writing were as black as night, things were going Robert Smith's way: he wanted to strip back The Cure's sound even more, and Gallup's super-minimalist basslines would provide the perfect backbone. And he was now surrounded by two drinking buddies. Life was good.

Chapter Five

"If we'd become furniture movers, then we'd have got in all the people we liked: it was really a question of attitude and outlook. Simon had that; that's always been what got people into The Cure."

– Lol Tolhurst

AS Robert Smith and Lol Tolhurst readied the new Cure in November 1979, they decided to hire keyboardist Matthieu Hartley as well as Gallup. It was a curious decision, given that Gallup's lugubrious, single-note signature was designed to pare The Cure's sound back to the absolute minimum. But the decision to hire Hartley was based on reasons not entirely musical, even though he'd been a bandmate of Gallup's in Magspies. Not only was he a hairdresser by trade, which the band might find useful as they headed into their big-haired era – Tolhurst, though, insists he never cut the band's hair during his brief tenure – he was also another Horley buddy of Gallup's. The reasoning ran along these lines: how could Gallup's drinking buddies resent them when The Cure had demonstrated that they were an equal opportunity employer?

As Tolhurst told me, "We asked Simon's friend Matthieu along as well because we figured he'd feel more comfortable about joining the band." (Smith would be even pithier: "They've added a new dimension to the group – pissheads.") Tolhurst admitted that Gallup's playing was not the most important reason for his joining the band. "I'd see over the whole life of The Cure that an attitude was more important than anything else," he said. "If you had the right attitude and can play a little bit, that was more important than anything else. If we'd become furniture movers, then we'd have got in all the people we liked: it was really a question of attitude and outlook. Simon had that; that's always been what got people into The Cure."

As for Hartley, Smith had no idea whether his synth lines would be useful, or even necessary, for The Cure's sound, but his somewhat accidental decision proved crucial: towering walls of synths (though not necessarily played by Hartley) would have a monumental impact on The Cure's future sonic direction.

Born on February 4, 1960, in Smallfield in Surrey, Hartley, like so many of those in The Cure, was the youngest of three; exposure to their older siblings' record collections would shape the career direction of many Cure members, Hartley included. He'd lived in Smallfield until 1968, then the family shifted to Horley, where he attended Balcome Road Comprehensive between 1972 and 1976, alongside Simon Gallup. When Robert Smith decided Hartley was right for the band, he'd spent the previous four years as an apprentice hairdresser.

Hartley had no hesitation in signing on for The Cure. But he was also under no illusions about his role in the band. "I said yes immediately because the prospect was so exciting. My role was reasonably detached, though. I just did what Robert told me to."

Lugging his Korg Duophonic synthesizer – the perfect machine for the sound Smith was after, as it turns out, because it was virtually impossible to play more than a couple of notes at once – Hartley, along with Gallup, was broken in during a fairly heavy end-of-year touring schedule. Their first gig – the opening night of the Future Pastimes Tour – was on November 16 at Eric's in Liverpool. Not the kind of man to miss an opportunity, Parry loaded the bill with his other protégés, The Associates, whose line-up now included Michael Dempsey, which must have made for some uncomfortable silences backstage. "There was a certain awkwardness to it," Dempsey agreed. "But it was OK." The Passions were also on the bill.

It was hardly a dazzling debut for the new Cure: they arrived late and discovered there were only about 100 punters left at the gig. Undeterred, the quartet bellied up to the bar, ordered more drinks – they'd enjoyed a sociable few on the drive to Liverpool – and played on, regardless of the meagre attendance. Even though a slurring Smith had some trouble associating certain lyrics with their rightful songs, he declared that the band's debut wasn't just successful, it was "a new start". As for fresh recruit Gallup, he was impressed by the free beer, which was a whole new experience for him.

Smith talked up the new Cure in a discussion with *Record Mirror*, a conversation that also contained a few not-that-subtle digs at the distance between himself and Dempsey. "If you're in a band," Smith said, "and you're playing together for a concentrated period of time, you have to get on with each other – unless you're only in it for the money, which we're not. It's not so much the unity of thinking, because everybody thinks differently, but the unity of ideas. And despite what the press think there's no hierarchy in The Cure. If there's one drink on the table we all fight for it."

Smith may have played up The Cure as a hierarchy-free zone, but the reality was that he was gradually moving further towards his role as band leader. It was a tough ask for a 20-year-old, but it was a role that Smith would grow into over the next few years, to the point where he virtually became The Cure. Parry, for one, would have liked Smith to step forward much sooner, as Tolhurst explained to me. "I can remember meetings with Chris – I don't think he enjoyed having meetings with me and Robert. I think it was divide and conquer. The two of us could gang up on him, more than anything else, and he would have to acquiesce to whatever it was we wanted. Robert resisted [becoming band leader] until the middle of the Eighties."

The Future Pastimes Tour rolled on, filling the London School of Economics, then, in back-to-back shows from November 20 to 24, they played Preston, Manchester, Bradford, Newport and Coventry. After winding through venues in Birmingham, Portsmouth, Norwich, Durham and Wolverhampton, the tour came to a close at Crawley College on December 7, a homecoming of sorts for the band. But it wasn't all gravy – some local skinheads started smashing the place up while The Cure played. As for Gallup, earlier in the day he'd been given a taste of small-town jealousy when he'd wandered into a record store and was informed that "my mate's much fucking better than you are [as a bassist]. I don't know why you got the job." The band wouldn't play another home-town show for four months.

In a post-tour post-mortem, Smith admitted that life on the bus – the three bands shared a ride – had been "good fun", which was hardly surprising now that he was surrounded by not just his old playground sidekick, Tolhurst, but Gallup as well. The soundtrack to Walt Disney's *The Jungle Book* had been on repeat in the van, so all the bands could now belt out 'The Bear Necessities' without a lyric sheet. Although Fiction-mates The Cure and The Associates got along swimmingly, Smith learned that The Passions had "peculiar ideologies" that didn't sit well with him and the rest of The Cure.

But that was a minor concern. The now four-piece Cure weren't just sounding like a "proper" band, but on stage they were beginning to resemble a group of serious young post-punkers, rather than a gang of barely legal suburbanites who weren't quite sure whether – or where – they belonged. Smith was growing more assured as a frontman, while Gallup's not-quite-so-wasted Sid Vicious looks gave the band sizeable cred with the polytechnic crowds. While their set still included such tunes from their *Three Imaginary Boys* period as 'Boys Don't Cry', 'Fire In Cairo', 'Accuracy' and '10.15 Saturday Night', they were also breaking in such newer, moodier pieces as 'M' (Smith's pet name for his girl-friend Mary Poole), 'Play For Today', 'Seventeen Seconds' and, crucially, 'A Forest'.

The band was now sufficiently confident (and in demand) to head to Europe again, playing 11 shows that included stops in Paris, Amsterdam and Eindhoven. By mid-January of the new year, they returned to the now familiar Morgan Studios with Mike Hedges to begin work on what would become their second long-player, *Seventeen Seconds*.

During the making of the album, Smith would play a cassette over and over again: it was virtually all he was listening to at the time. The tape contained four totally disparate and seemingly unrelated songs, which Smith later confessed all contained elements of what he was trying to recreate with The Cure's second coming. One song was Van Morrison's sprawling, mesmerising 'Madame George', from his landmark 1968 album *Astral Weeks*. This much praised work was a sustained study of introspection, a journey deep into the mystic from the bellicose bard of Belfast. The next track was 'Fruit Tree', a sadly beautiful cut from Nick Drake's 1970 album *Five Leaves Left*. The sparse, dimly lit beauty of the song gelled perfectly with the heavy atmospherics Smith was trying to bring to life on *Seventeen Seconds*. "It's a morbid romanticism," Smith confessed when asked about his Nick Drake obsession, "but there is something attractive about that."

The third track on Smith's perfect mix tape was the Aram Khachaturian ballet piece, 'Gayaneh Ballet Suite No. 1. Adagio', that appeared on the soundtrack to Stanley Kubrick's *2001: A Space Odyssey*. The film was another bleak, minimalist masterpiece, much fancied by Smith. As with Nick Drake, it was Smith's brother Richard ('The Guru') who'd turned him on to the seminal Kubrick odyssey.

And the final track on the tape must have conjured up some mixed memories for Robert Smith – it was Jimi Hendrix's live take on Dylan's rock'n'roll Armageddon, 'All Along The Watchtower'. The cut was taken from Hendrix's UK swansong, his festival-closing set at the Isle of Wight Festival. That was also Smith's first true rock'n'roll experience, an event he recalled as "two days of orange tent and dope smoke". When not wearing out this four-track cassette, Smith also had Bowie's *Low* on repeat. The high point of the Thin White Duke's "Berlin phase", whence he retreated to escape the coke-induced ennui of a prolonged spell in LA, the Brian Eno-produced *Low* fluctuated between such glorious high IQed pop as 'Sound And Vision' and introverted, experimental instrumentals. It was very clearly a key album for Smith and *Seventeen Seconds*, an epic downer that somehow still managed to sound startlingly original and icy cool.

"[With *Seventeen Seconds*] I was trying to get a combination of all the things I liked about those four things," Smith explained when the subject of his "master tape" was raised, "even though they were so disparate."

Seventeen Seconds was not exactly laboured over in the studio. The new four-piece Cure cut the album with Hedges in 13 days, after rehearsing the shortlisted songs at Smith's parents' house during the first week of January. All 11 tracks were recorded at Morgan between January 13 and 20; the album was mixed from February 4 to 10. The swiftness of the recording was as dictated by economics as it was the band's sharp studio focus – although more than one producer who worked with the band would tell me that The Cure rarely entered a session unprepared. "We mostly had it all before we got to the studio," Tolhurst explained. "That's why it was pretty quick." But *Three Imaginary Boys* hadn't been a hit, so there simply wasn't a lot of money in the recording kitty. The brevity of the sessions was possibly also dictated by the fact that the band's drug consumption, although active, hadn't reached the Bolivian-fuelled highs (and lows) of their next album, *Faith*. And again, as I was told by Phil Thornalley, who produced their fourth album, *Pornography*, the mood in the studio didn't necessarily equate to the grim tunes the band was recording. For Gallup, having endured the slog of a factory job, the recording was like one sustained party. "Staying up until three in the morning, drinking . . .," he rhapsodised. Producer Hedges had equally positive memories of the making of *Seventeen Seconds*. "When I try to remember it, all I can see is a party." Smith related how the band slept on the floor of Morgan's studio one, "to get that us-against-the-world feeling".

Smith, as he promised (threatened, actually) after *Three Imaginary Boys'* unsatisfying studio experience, co-produced the album. The band's one non-studio activity during the recording of the album was another Holland jaunt on January 15.*

Chris Parry would relate how Smith was a very different man this time around. During the making of *Three Imaginary Boys* Smith seemed unsure about how much creative control he could exercise – and then complained about it forever after. But during the *Seventeen Seconds* sessions he took over. When Smith caught Parry tinkering with a snare drum on the first day of recording, he issued his manager-cum-label-boss a simple directive: "Don't bother, Bill, it's not what we want." Equal parts impressed and vexed, Parry backed off – his creative involvement with the band was being reduced with each new session.

"I had to ask Bill not to come into the studio," said Smith, "because he was trying to produce the record and I wanted to do it with Hedges. I knew exactly what sound I needed for *Seventeen Seconds* – I wanted it to be inspired by Nick Drake with the clear, finished sound of Bowie's *Low*." Smith was justifiably proud of his co-production efforts, to the extent that he sometimes forgot that Mike Hedges was seated alongside him. "We did it on our own," he said in 1996, "and everything about it was exactly what I wanted. I produced it, although they [presumably Parry] said I wasn't capable. *Seventeen Seconds* is a very personal record, and it's also when I felt The Cure really started."

"After the first album, Parry wasn't privy to the workings of the band that much," Tolhurst added. "He'd turn up to the studio but we didn't let him in on much; we kept things pretty close. He might say that he knew how to remix something so we'd give him the fader and get Hedges to re-route it so he was adjusting the high-hat or something."

If The Cure was hoping to maintain one sustained melancholic mood with *Seventeen Seconds*, they couldn't have done it better. The album locks into a sombre groove from the opening track and doesn't

---

* A live take of 'In Your House', recorded at this show, made its way to 1984's odds-and-sods collection, *Curiosity*.

Easy Cure's Robert
Smith, Michael Dempsey
and Porl Thompson in
1977, before their
fateful meeting with
Hansa Records.

BELOW: Original Cure bassist and co-founder Michael Dempsey: "None of us had a really strong vision of being superstars."

TOP RIGHT: Phil Thornalley, Cure bassist and record producer, 1984-1985. "Those early Cure records had a sound, but not one I would try to get," he said.

MIDDLE: Lol Tolhurst, one of Crawley's Three Imaginary Boys: "We went to school on the same coach," Robert Smith said. "But he made no impression on me whatsoever."

ABOVE: Simon Gallup, who joined The Cure in 1982, lived in fear of Lol Tolhurst. "Simon, when he saw me in the street, used to cross the road."

St Wilfrid's Comprehensive School, where the battlelines were drawn on David Bowie, "between those who thought he was a queer and those who thought he was a genius." (Nick Crocker)

ABOVE LEFT: Porl Thompson with Michael Dempsey at an early gig on Crawley Bandstand, 1976.

Hello ,

We are THE CURE .

Lol 19 Drums
Mick 19 Bass
Robert 19 Gtr/Vocals

We have no commitments . We would like a recording contract
Listen to the tape . If you are interested please contact
us at the above.
Please return the tape in the enclosed S.A.E .

Thankyou ,

Robert.

Robert   THE CURE .

Tolhurst, Dempsey and Smith (from left), circa 1978. "He was a postman one Christmas," Tolhurst said of Smith. "That lasted about a week. I don't remember him having any other full-time job."

SUPPORT ANTHONY WEAVER CAMPAIGN

BENEFIT   GIG

The CURE

AND

AMULET

SUNDAY APRIL 29   7:30
NORTHGATE COMMUNITY CENTRE

The poster for a benefit gig for their former teacher, Dr Anthony Weaver. The National Front, thrilled by 'Killing An Arab', crashed the gig.

Robert Smith, self-medicated
with Night Nurse and Disprins,
plays London's Hope & Anchor,
January 1979. (Justin Thomas)

ABOVE: Lol Tolhurst,
Hope and Anchor gig, 1979.
"All the punk stuff started
happening and we realised,
'hey, we can do this'."
(Justin Thomas)

LEFT: Michael Dempsey at
the same Hope & Anchor gig.
"They were landmark
moments," said Dempsey.
"But there were diminishing
returns from then on."
(Justin Thomas)

Three Imaginary Boys in the Natural History Museum, January 1979. Lol Tolhurst, Robert Smith and Michael Dempsey (from left). (Paul Slattery)

Dempsey, Smith and Tolhurst (from left), a band without a clue. To Smith, The Cure was "just the best way to avoid getting up in the morning". (Richard Mann/Retna UK)

Lol Tolhurst, Matthieu Hartley, Simon Gallup and Robert Smith,
circa 1979 (from left). "They've added a new dimension to the group,"
said Smith, " they're pissheads." (LFI)

Seventeen Seconds line-up, 1980. Keyboard player Hartley
fully understood his (brief) role in the band. "I just
did what Robert told me to." (Paul Slattery)

In the midst of 'A Forest', *Top Of The Pops*,
April 1980. "Our records always go down after we do *Top Of The
Pops*," said Smith. "We actually do the show as a career move
to stop ourselves from becoming too famous."

BELOW: One of Simon Gallup's first Cure gigs was sharing a bill with Michael Dempsey, whom he'd replaced. "There was a certain awkwardness to it," Dempsey confessed.
(Philippe Carly - www.newwavephotos.com)

TOP RIGHT: Hartley, prior to his departure in 1980. "Fans used to ask me if I liked Joy Division and, I mean, they were exactly the kind of group I can't stand."
(Philippe Carly -www.newwavephotos.com)

MIDDLE: Lol Tolhurst, fast becoming the band's target. "We beat him up, wind him up, frame him up, but he understands," according to Hartley.
(Philippe Carly - www.newwavephotos.com)

ABOVE: Robert Smith during The Cure's Seventeen Seconds period. "When I try to remember it," he admitted, "all I can see is a party." (Philippe Carly - www.newwavephotos.com)

let go until the final strains of the closing title track have drifted off into the sonic horizon. It's virtually impossible to accept that this is the same band that made the patchy, unsteady *Three Imaginary Boys*.

It opens with the stately instrumental 'A Reflection', a conversation between strummed guitar and solitary piano; a sound that Smith had purposefully designed to set a contemplative mood for the entire record. The sombre, sober track brings to mind such dimly lit meditations as those on Brian Eno's 1977 long-player, *Before And After Science*. It's followed by 'Play For Today', another song that was in development not long after the *Three Imaginary Boys* sessions. Although it shuffles along at a fair clip, unlike much of the album, 'Play' still maintains an appropriately solemn, downbeat mood. Smith would relate that the song dealt with "the fraudulent aspects of an insincere relationship", but his lyrics were secondary to the downcast mood of the song, and the album.

Smith's vocals are barely audible on 'Secrets', although if you tune in closely you can make out his lyrical design, which was to craft a song about missed opportunities, and the dream he held of "hopelessly wishing to have the courage" to seize the day. (Smith stated that this muffling was intentional: "The voice was supposed to be so you could almost barely hear it.") The very hollow-sounding Eighties production style that dates a song such as 'Play For Today' isn't so evident with 'Secrets'; it's yet another twilight mood piece, where Smith and band were in a mood so blue that it made their Mancunian peers Joy Division seem like a fun-loving dance band by comparison. The pensive, slow-burning 'In Your House' follows, Smith's snake-like guitar line wrapping itself around a lyric that dealt with "feeling uncomfortable in someone else's presence, but always returning". The song was a perfect example of Smith's desire not to deviate from the one mood during the entire album; it's an unwavering, unapologetic study in sorrow and bleakness. Though not quite as grim as such future long-playing downers as *Pornography* or *Disintegration*, *Seventeen Seconds* isn't a record for the young at heart. That was especially true when you consider the fact that it emerged in the spring of 1980, at a time when the charts and airwaves were ruled by such irrepressibly upbeat pop fluff as Lipps Inc's 'Funkytown', Paul McCartney's 'Coming Up' and Jermaine Jackson's 'Let's Get Serious'.

The following track, 'Three', was somewhat sinister, dominated by a creaking keyboard and Tolhurst's rock-steady, one-step-at-a-time drumbeat which pushed it along at a virtual crawl. Smith described how 'Three' dealt with what he called "the eternal triangle" but that's virtually impossible to determine, given that his vocal was buried so deeply in the mix. 'The Final Sound' goes one step further into the abyss; the soundscape was so positively Gothic in tone you could almost be fooled into believing that it was lifted straight from the soundtrack of some Hammer Horror gorefest.

'A Forest', the next track, is the definitive early Cure mood piece, a strikingly original and authentic slice of Smith songcraft that would feature on most Cure setlists for the following quarter of a century. Just like his 'Three Imaginary Boys', 'A Forest' was, allegedly, based on one of Smith's childhood dreams, where he was trapped in the woods, unable to find any way to escape. (Typically, Smith would then do a backflip and deny it all. "It's just about a forest," he said.) As Smith's guitar – which sounds as though it was recorded from somewhere deep inside a wind tunnel – entwines itself with another of Tolhurst's no-nonsense rhythm patterns and Gallup's plodding bassline, the track slowly yet relentlessly builds to a genuinely eerie crescendo. 'Boys Don't Cry' may have been the band's first three minutes of timeless pop, but 'A Forest' was deeper, more profound, a genuinely stirring, unsettling six minutes of sound. It was *Seventeen Seconds'* centrepiece and, as it transpired, the band's first legitimate hit. Chris Parry thought the song was "wonderful – a most pleasant surprise".

Simon Gallup would recall that 'A Forest' was a song with an indefinable running time. In fact, sometimes the people playing it didn't actually know when it would end. "[It] was one that just used to go on and on. The drums would stop, Robert would carry on playing guitar and I was never sure when he was gonna stop so I'd just carry on after him. Then I got some effects pedals and I found I could experiment and make all sorts of bizarre noises."

Smith also knew the song was crucial for the band; it definitely pointed the way forward. "[It was] the archetypal Cure sound," he said in 1992. "It was probably the turning point when people started listening to the group and thinking we could achieve something, including me."

"With 'A Forest' I wanted to do something that was really atmospheric, and it has a fantastic sound," Smith continued. "Chris Parry said, 'If you make this sound radio friendly, you've got a big hit on your hands.' I said, 'But this is how it sounds. It's the sound I've got in my head. It doesn't matter about whether it's radio friendly.'"

'M', a crisply strummed valentine to the love of Smith's life, Mary Poole, followed 'A Forest'. Though it would be a stretch to call it a love song, this mid-tempo ballad came as a relief in the midst of the album's almost terminally heavy emotions and all-round broodiness. All Robert Smith would say, when asked about the song's meaning, was to state that it was "about a girl" – although he would later admit that another Albert Camus story, *A Happy Death*, had a major influence on the lyric. But anyone close to the band knew the truth about 'M'.

Seventeen Seconds' closing pair of numbers, 'At Night' and the title track, maintain the deep, dark mood with a steely-eyed intensity. The former, a slow-grinding plod that was once again held in place by the metronomic thud of Tolhurst's drums, contained a lyric inspired by another literary purveyor of the paranoid, Franz Kafka, whose story gave the song its title. The song seemed so insistent on maintaining an overwhelming sense of despair that the band would have gladly kept playing its slow-motion groove for another hour. As for the title track, the album's closer, Smith's lyrical inspiration was more oblique; he stated that it was derived from "an arbitrary measure of time – one that seemed to be suddenly everywhere once the song was written". While that was hardly the most concise and easy-to-follow explanation, few of these studies in solemnity were dictated by lyrics or anything resembling a message; Smith would readily leave that to the Bonos of the world. He was more intent on pursuing a single mindset in the manner of Nick Drake's *Five Leaves Left* or Bowie's *Low*, albums that played such crucial roles in dictating the tone and style of *Seventeen Seconds*.

"I knew exactly what I wanted to do with *Seventeen Seconds*," Robert Smith declared years later. "I knew exactly how I wanted it to sound and I didn't want anyone to interfere with that. Anyone who wanted to play more than one piano note could go and do it somewhere else." Producer Hedges was impressed by the band's sharp focus: they were barely recognisable from the novices who made *Three Imaginary Boys*. "I really appreciated the musical direction – morose, atmospheric, very different to *Three Imaginary Boys*," he said. "I followed Robert's instructions – he wanted a certain sound." (Not only would *Seventeen Seconds* become a career-saver for The Cure, it proved that Hedges was much more than some in-house studio journeyman. His career was also set in motion.)

The Cure didn't realise just how influential an album they'd created with *Seventeen Seconds*. As late as 2004, Red Hot Chili Peppers' guitarist/songwriter John Frusciante would swear allegiance to *Seventeen Seconds* and its sequel, *Faith*, revealing that both albums were major influences on his band's mega-platinum 1999 comeback *Californication*. There can be no question that the band's gloomscapes achieved far more than simply becoming a sonic touchstone for the Goth movement.

Smith felt much closer to *Seventeen Seconds* than *Three Imaginary Boys*. "During *Seventeen Seconds*, we honestly felt that we were creating something no one else had done," he would tell *Rolling Stone*. "From this point on, I thought that every album was going to be the last Cure album, so I always tried to make it something that would be kind of a milestone. I feel *Seventeen Seconds* is one of few albums that genuinely achieved that."

With the album now wrapped, The Cure returned to the Lakeside at Crawley on March 18 for their first home-town show since the pre-Christmas debacle at Crawley College. Their last Crawley concert had been marred by surly skinheads and local jealousies; this time around it was a much better-natured gig. Porl Thompson even jammed with the band for their encore of 'Cult Hero'. Clearly inspired, Smith subsequently pieced together The Cult Heroes for their one and only gig, opening for The Passions at The Marquee in London five days later. (Smith had obviously forgiven his Fiction labelmates for the "very peculiar ideologies" which he felt had marred their late 1979 tour.)

For the Marquee gig, Smith roped in the true cult hero, Horley postman Frank Bell, plus two local schoolgirls and his Cure buddies. Fuelled by enough booze to stop a football team, and cheered on by around 400 Horley and Crawley locals, The Cult Heroes flashed back to 1973, rocking their way through a Top 10 set that Smith had taped from one of Jimmy Savile's Sunday radio programmes. It was unlikely that any post-punk outfit had even contemplated covering Thin Lizzy's 'Whiskey In The Jar', Sweet's 'Blockbuster' and Gary Glitter's 'Do You Wanna Touch Me (Oh Yeah)', but it said something about the brotherhood being shown on stage. Those who could stand up fell about laughing.

With time to kill before the release of *Seventeen Seconds'* first single, this was the first of several Smith cameos. He also added backing vocals to The Associates' upcoming long-player and then became a temporary Strangler, playing guitar for the pop-punk pioneers at the Rainbow Theatre in Finsbury Park, as part of a fund-raiser for their recently busted bassist Hugh Cornwell. As well-intentioned as all this was, it was really only a lead-up to the main event, the release of the first single from The Cure's second coming.

'A Forest' appeared on April 5. It was backed by the live staple, 'Another Journey By Train', an instrumental remake of 'Jumping Someone Else's Train', which had carried the prosaic working title 'Horse Racing'. "The name [change] came about because the demo rhythm went from sounding a bit like galloping horses to sounding kind of like a runaway train," the ever-logical Simon Gallup explained. But 'Another Journey' wasn't the cut that most critics were interested in: with 'A Forest' they were witnessing a new Cure, a band who'd undergone both physical and spiritual changes since their not-so-successful *Three Imaginary Boys*. The reviews were mixed, even if the commercial response to 'A Forest' was outstanding by Cure standards.

NME's Julie Burchill, later to become a million-selling writer of bodice-ripping fiction, was no Cure fan, as proved by her earlier hatchet job on the band. She found 'A Forest' equally unsatisfying. In her review of the single, she accused the band of "trying to stretch a sketchy living out of moaning more meaningfully than man has ever moaned before . . . without a tune, too." Inadvertently, she had given Smith credit for not doing things in small steps, but it was hardly the type of upbeat press coverage for which the band was hoping. However, there were other reviewers who spotted how far the band had advanced from their scratchy, indifferent debut LP. "This isn't what you'd call an immediate song," wrote another critic, "but there's something very attractive about it." Co-producer Smith was also given kudos in the same review, which declared that 'A Forest' "has the [band's] best production to date."

The year 1980 also marked the point when The Cure's reach extended beyond Europe and the UK. 'Boys Don't Cry', backed with '10.15 Saturday Night', was given a release in Australia and New Zealand through Stunn Records, a New Zealand-based indie label run by Terry Condon, a school pal of Chris Parry's. A second version of the seven-inch, specifically for the Kiwi market, added 'Killing An Arab', making for a very rare (and collectible) three-track single. Accordingly, the band's reputation started to build south of the equator, with such alternative-before-their-time radio stations as Sydney's 2JJ jumping all over 'Boys Don't Cry'.

As rewarding as it was to build a fanbase in Parry's part of the world, he also had larger plans for The Cure. In February 1980 a repackaged version of *Three Imaginary Boys*, re-titled *Boys Don't Cry*, became the band's first North American release. Featuring a cover image as un-informative as the parent album – three palm trees of varying sizes in an Egyptian setting that just reeked of 'Killing An Arab' – *Boys Don't Cry* compiled eight tracks from *Three Imaginary Boys* plus the A-sides of their first three UK singles and 'Plastic Passion' and 'World War', a hitherto unreleased cut from the band's early Morgan sessions for Fiction. This rejigged Cure debut album was also released through Stunn in Australia and New Zealand.

Parry was sufficiently buoyed to book the band's first US tour, which commenced on April 10. Rather than launch a full-bore assault on the US of A, which could consume months and eat up many thousands of pounds, Parry focused on eastern US cities with the type of college radio (and new music fans) that would embrace this strangely angular, moody UK quartet. The band opened their rapid-fire tour at Emerald City in Cherry Hill, New Jersey, then played three nights (April 15 to 17) at Hurrah's in New York, with a Boston show at the Allston Underground on the 20th.

At their first New York gig, The Cure opened their show with 'A Forest', a sure-fire mood-setter. The rest of their set balanced such standards as '10.15', 'Boys Don't Cry', 'Arab' and 'Plastic Passion', with roughly half of *Seventeen Seconds*. The band and Parry knew there was no great logic in playing too many songs that weren't available in US record stores, especially in those pre-download days. Jon Young, a writer for US mag *Trouser Press*, was in the thick of a crowd that he would describe as "restive". Smith struggled to deal with a loudmouth who was "shouting incoherently as if he'd expected Bruce Springsteen". Eventually he stopped the band and simply asked the punter what he wanted, which Smith would interpret as "piss over Portobello Road – or something". But Smith had the last laugh when the heckler came backstage afterwards and sucked up to the band.

While Smith might have displayed enviable levels of confidence both in the studio and when it came to dealing with the great unwashed, he wasn't so sure that they'd be offered another US junket in any great hurry. So while Stateside, the band played tourist, staying up all night and then kicking on at first light to soak up the sights. Simon Gallup, meanwhile, remained impressed by the relatively new sensation (for him) of backstage riders – while in North America, his tipple of choice was Southern Comfort. Smith's 21st birthday fell while they were in Boston; the band and Parry partied with prejudice at what Smith recalls as "some art media event". Smith toasted the day by turning up for their final US show 90 minutes late, then taking a very stoned ride on the bonnet of a car driven by an equally wasted Parry. When Smith tried to change a flat tyre, he broke his thumb, although it took some time for the signal to travel from Smith's digit to his brain. "I'd just reduced it to pulp," he later said.

Back in the UK immediately after their Boston show (via an unplanned detour to Cape Cod), Smith was already showing signs of wariness when it came to dealing with the press. (This would reach chronic proportions as the band went larger and larger Stateside.) Speaking with *Record Mirror*, Smith exhibited mixed feelings about their first US tour. "[We were] being bombarded by people who all ask the same questions and all want to shake your hand," Smith reported. "You just find yourself getting sucked into the whole rock'n'roll trip which we're trying so hard to get away from."

Smith's comments were a touch disingenuous, because on April 24 The Cure were lined up for their debut *Top Of The Pops* appearance. Starring on this weekly pop institution was hardly the kind of move that would guarantee a band street cred but it did expose The Cure to several million viewers, which couldn't hurt their gradually improving career, even if the sight of Smith's Elephant Man-sized thumb was enough to scare off impressionable teens.

Smith had conflicting emotions about appearing on *Top Of The Pops*. His conscience was pricked by what he described as the "anti-everything" side of his nature, telling him that the show represented all that was wrong with music: it peddled cookie-cutter pop as lip-synced by airbrushed stars. (It should be made clear, however, that The Cure kept good company on their *Pops* debut: Blondie, The Undertones, Dexy's Midnight Runners and Bad Manners also appeared.) But there was also a more pragmatic side to Smith's nature. "I was convinced we should do *Top Of The Pops* because I realised, even then, that if we didn't do it, someone else would – and it made no difference to the majority of people watching whether we played or not." What Smith didn't know was that future *NME* writer Andrew Collins became one of many new Cure converts via their debut *Top Of The Pops* spot, in almost the same way that Smith fell for Bowie eight years earlier. "I first fell in love with The Cure, aged 15, on April 24, 1980," Collins wrote. "They were . . . a trio [sic] all disconsolate and shy and looking at their feet, and yet producing this strangely beautiful pop song which I must have first heard on John Peel, as that's where I heard everything first." So the band's time wasn't completely wasted.

(Robert Smith would maintain many unsteady relationships during The Cure's long life, none more so than that between him, his band and this not-so-venerable UK pop institution. Smith always felt uncomfortable appearing there. In 1985, he stated that his discomfort was "mainly because I can see the audience and they always look so fed up. I always feel sorry for them. They go expecting a big party – and it's the most awful experience; you can see it on their faces. Besides, I'm not much good at pretending I'm having fun." Almost all Cure cameos on the show would be swiftly followed by the single they were trying to flog taking a chart nosedive. "Our records always go down after we do *Top Of The Pops*. We actually do the show as a career move to stop ourselves from becoming too famous," Smith figured.)

Gallup and Hartley, meanwhile, were much more enthused than Smith about appearing. The laconic Tolhurst laughed it off. "All you could see on the telly," Tolhurst said afterwards, "was Robert's huge bandage moving up and down the neck of his guitar. It was hysterical."

The footage from their *Top Of The Pops* cameo was intertwined with images of a forest, for the Dave Hillier-directed video for 'A Forest'. Smith's thumb was by far the star of the clip, the band's first. "We came across looking very morose and disinterested," said Smith, "which we were."

Despite the throbbing in Smith's thumb, The Cure returned to the road, starting yet another British tour at the West Runton Pavilion in Cromer on the night following their TV debut. Ending at the Rainbow Theatre in London on May 11, the band played 16 dates in as many days. 'A Forest', meanwhile, surreptitiously made its way to number 31 on the UK single chart, their highest position by far. As The

Cure bandwagon rolled on, reviews began to trickle in for *Seventeen Seconds*.

The response from *Record Mirror*'s Chris Westwood typified the uncertainty that critics felt towards the album: no one was really quite sure what to make of this brand new Cure. "Why don't The Cure come out of their shell?" Westwood asked. "This is a reclusive, disturbed Cure, sitting in cold, dark, empty rooms, watching clocks." In a typically arch Nick Kent review for *NME* entitled 'Why science can't find Cure for vagueness', the critic wasn't totally convinced by the band's impenetrably dark side, even if he did open with the valid point that The Cure were a band in a hurry. "Few have covered so much territory in such a brief space of time," he observed. Kent was right: in roughly the same time that many bands take to master 'Louie Louie', The Cure had delivered a handful of singles of increasing quality, played upwards of 100 shows and cut two long-players. Kent, however, felt that the album failed to deliver fully the type of pent-up tension at which most of the songs hinted. Referring specifically to 'A Forest', Kent wrote that "the scenario, once created, soon sounds limp, devoid of any tension or mystery. It's a symptom throughout *Seventeen Seconds*."

"To many," Kent concluded, "*Seventeen Seconds* may seem a valid progression. I, however, find it depressingly regressive. Even so, I await their next move with great interest."

On May 18, 1980, Ian Curtis, the Joy Division frontman crowned "one of the most talented performers and writers in contemporary rock music" by *NME*, committed suicide. Curtis' final video, the haunting, darkly beautiful 'Love Will Tear Us Apart', had been shot only a couple of days after the release of *Seventeen Seconds*. *Closer*, an album that was equal parts farewell to Joy Division and eulogy for Curtis, appeared in July. Robert Smith was, frankly, stunned.

"I remember hearing *Closer* for the first time and thinking, 'I can't ever imagine making something as powerful as this.' I thought I'd have to kill myself to make a convincing record."

But Robert Smith wasn't quite ready to top himself just yet. After their final UK show at The Rainbow in London's Finsbury Park, The Cure crossed the Channel for their first full European tour, playing a festival in France alongside The Clash and UFO that fell apart in a volley of riots and tear gas, and then being arrested (but not charged) for indecent exposure during a late-night romp in Rotterdam. While still in Holland for a series of outdoor dates, *NME* ran a piece called 'Days Of Wine And Poses', written by Paul Morley, the same stringer who'd written off *Three Imaginary Boys* as "fatigue music". Writer and star-in-the-making were far more polite this time around: as it turned out, Morley was a fan of *Seventeen Seconds*.

The article provides some insight into Smith's hot-and-cold affair with the press. When Morley effectively pissed all over *Three Imaginary Boys*, Smith and band responded by writing the critic a vitriolic reply and then, during a Peel session, turning 'Grinding Halt' into a poison-pen letter directed at the black heart of the *NME* scribe. But when they met, Smith had a confession to make: he wasn't that big a fan of their debut LP either; he'd listened to the album maybe "three times" before moving on to *Seventeen Seconds*. As Smith and Morley loosened up over a bottle of vino, the real Robert Smith began to appear. "Smith is soft where I imagined he would be hard," Morley wrote. "He's not a big softie. He's always on a fine line between agitation and boredom and such a balance turns out faintly, deviously charming." When Morley asked Smith if he took himself seriously, Smith replied: "I do take myself seriously but there's a point beyond which you become a comic figure."

Smith was also uncertain about the live incarnation of the band: were they on stage to entertain or enlighten? Or was their job purely self-satisfaction – the audience be damned? "It's very selfish when we go on stage," Smith said. "It matters what the audience thinks, but I write songs for myself. I'd prefer it if we really impressed a lot of people who'll like us for a long time rather than give someone a good night out who'll forgot it next week."

In the same interview, Smith would own up to a dangerous temper, but he wasn't the physical type. As Tolhurst had already mentioned, there was a certain Englishness at work here – emotions were best kept to oneself. "I don't throw tantrums or anything like that," he said, "so rather than smash the room up I write things down. It's a release."

As their seemingly endless 1980 tour continued, Smith and Gallup, especially, found new outlets for their bad vibrations. The pair was in the process of developing a more than lively interest in Bolivian marching powder, and had virtually given up on sleeping. They spent much of their downtime in a near catatonic state, Walkmans glued to their ears. Smith was still dealing with his mixed feelings regarding Ian

Curtis' suicide: did it really mean that in order to have his band taken seriously, he had to follow suit? It was not exactly the ideal environment for new recruit, Matthieu Hartley. Tolhurst, as always, remained the band's target: without him as class clown it was likely they would have ended up killing each other. Even Hartley got in on the action, as he revealed in *Ten Imaginary Years*.

"Dear old Lol, he's the master," the keyboardist said. "We beat him up, wind him up, frame him up, but he understands. He knows we have to release our tensions in some way and he's the target." (Snapshots from the time usually show Tolhurst buried up to his neck in sand on a beach somewhere.) What Tolhurst didn't know – couldn't have known, really – was that he was setting himself up for the biggest of all possible falls a few years further down the road.

The band's relentless touring schedule – they played over 80 shows between March and November 1980 – also meant that their entourage was increasing. The Cure crew now included a roadie named Elvis, a former Teddy Boy who, according to Smith, dismissed the band as "a right scruffy bunch of cunts". Their tour manager was Welshman Lawrie Mazzeo, a bloke with a passion for fine dining and a habit of short-changing hotels. Then there was Mac, their lighting man, who was with the band during the 6.30am romp in Rotterdam that ended with a public indecency incident.

By the time The Cure reached New Zealand on July 24 for their first antipodean tour, the roadlag was starting to set in. Posters promised Kiwi fans the chance to 'Get a Dose of the Cure' – the recently released *Seventeen Seconds* had charted well there, as it did in Holland and France – but as the band shuffled between Auckland, Wellington, Christchurch and Dunedin, playing nine shows in all, the heaviness of the songs they were playing was starting to wear them down. "We'd played too much and were becoming very jaded," Smith recalled. It was also during this tour that Smith dropped his first tab of acid; he spent most of the mind-stretching experience taking photos of his reflected image in a hotel room mirror. (In one picture "there are about 2,000 cocktail toothpicks stuck on me," Smith revealed in 2003. "In that skin, in those things – I looked like a porcupine.") And while in Auckland, the band let off steam with some hotel room redecorating, smashing a door and several fittings and fixtures. This time around Mazzeo settled the bill before they checked into another hotel.

Smith downplayed the incident the next day. "We're not the type of band to smash furniture," he said. "We're not The Who. It was just part of our working day. It was obvious they preferred us to leave so we went to another hotel." As much as Smith tried to dismiss it as another day in the life of The Cure, it was hardly the type of publicity they needed on the eve of their first Australian tour. These boys mightn't cry, but they sure knew how to drink (and drop LSD).

Although their Oz tour was a success – Australia would embrace the band with the same fervour as North America in a few years' time – it was a tough time in camp Cure. It didn't help that the planned Australian itinerary had mushroomed to 24 shows. And like Michael Dempsey before him, Hartley had developed a serious case of road fever: the Auckland incident had escalated out of a minor run-in with Smith that went completely off the rails. "It just started to go all wrong with Matty," Smith said. "He was getting very grumpy, very tired and moaning that he couldn't get any vegetarian food – lots of things upset him." To Smith's recollection, Hartley used to take out his anger on Tolhurst, the band's in-house punching bag. Nonetheless, the band managed to set a new house record at Sydney's Bondi Lifesaver, packing 2,200 fans into a venue that was built for maybe half that many at a very tight squeeze.

When the band stopped in Perth, on the west coast of Australia, en route to Europe, they knew that Hartley needed to face up to the fact that he just wasn't built for the road, or the band. His snoring did nothing to help his relationship with his bandmates, either. And again just like Dempsey before him, Hartley wasn't too enthused about the increasingly grim direction in which Smith planned to take The Cure. "[It was] not my style of music at all," Hartley would state. "Also I was treated strangely, childishly. Robert stopped talking to me. So did Lol. I'd had enough. [Fans] used to ask me if I liked Joy Division and, I mean, they were exactly the kind of group I can't stand. I realised that the group was heading towards suicidal, sombre music – the sort of thing that didn't interest me at all."

The band played one final show, in Stockholm on August 30, before finally making it home to the UK. They'd been away for a particularly tough six weeks and hadn't had a genuine break since March. When Parry collected his charges at Heathrow, the cracks showed in a very obvious way: while Smith, Gallup and Tolhurst squeezed into the front of the pick-up, Hartley was left in the back, sardined with the band's gear. Once Hartley arrived home, he decided to save Smith a call: he rang the bandleader and told him he was quitting The Cure, having lasted only nine months.* Smith didn't hold any grudges. "Matty was really good about it," he revealed. "He phoned me up and that was it."

---

* Interestingly, he now lives near Smith in Bognor Regis, working in a photographic store and still playing music.

Chapter Six

"I was 21, but I felt really old. I felt life was pointless. I had no faith in anything. I just didn't see there was much point continuing with life."

— Robert Smith

NICK Kent had been understating the band's case when he noted that they had covered so much territory in such a brief space of time. Most bands would have pleaded temporary insanity after such a ruthless slog of a tour, and gone underground until at least the new year. Not so The Cure. Almost immediately Smith, Gallup and Tolhurst chose to head back to Morgan Studios, at the end of September, to start work on their third album, once again with Mike Hedges producing.

It turned out to be a major miscalculation, not least because they were all very jaded when they drifted into Morgan on September 27, barely a month having passed since Hartley's last stand in Stockholm. Among the new tunes they attempted to capture on tape over the next three days were 'All Cats Are Grey' and 'Primary'. While both would eventually make the cut for the album that became *Faith*, neither was recorded satisfactorily during this first session at Morgan. Smith had been hoping for something "funereal", instead "they just sounded dull". Unfortunately for the band, this aborted session would set the tone for *Faith*. Whereas both *Seventeen Seconds* and *Three Imaginary Boys* had been turned around in record time, the recording of their third album became an odyssey that saw the band bounce between almost as many studios as they would record songs.

Tolhurst, for one, knew that the band wasn't ready for another LP. "The Cure existence on the road wasn't the kind where you could write songs," he said to me. "We had to write so much of *Faith* in the studio." But, as he explained, it simply didn't enter their minds to withdraw from the musical front line. "We never thought about going home and not doing anything for six months," he said. "Our contract said to make an album a year and we did that."

The Cure was always striving for financial self-sufficiency; by the time of *Faith* they'd pretty much achieved that. Their records were relatively cheap to produce and constant touring helped to pay the bills. Regardless, it was a true low point in Robert Smith's life. "I was 21," he said in 1985, "but I felt really old. I had absolutely no hope for the future. I felt life was pointless. I had no faith in anything. I just didn't see there was much point continuing with life."

But before Smith could get too involved with thoughts on the value of his existence, The Cure figured that if the studio wasn't working for them, they'd best get back out among the faithful. They returned to the road on October 3, revisiting the Stockholm venue, The Rockpalais, which had been the site of their last show with Hartley five weeks earlier. Over the next three weeks the new three-piece Cure bounced between Bremen, Munich, Amsterdam, Brussels, Bordeaux and Hamburg, working hard on consolidating their burgeoning European fanbase. This 27-date tour of Scandinavia, France, Germany and the Low Countries ended on October 31 at Rodange, where they played at The Blue Note. The band may have been fast running out of steam, but the tour achieved its purpose: almost every show was a full house, while *Seventeen Seconds* climbed into the Top 10 in Belgium and the Netherlands, where The Cure, a band still without anything resembling a definable look, found themselves in the company of such very image-savvy acts as Abba, Queen, The Stray Cats and Spandau Ballet. It was almost enough to distract them from the tricky task of making their third album.

Back in the UK, The Cure decided to round off their most active year yet with a series of campus shows (and then only universities that were open to the public). It was smart positioning on the part of Parry: if the music press critics were having trouble with The Cure, then best focus on their Penguin Classics-reading fanbase. After all, who needs good press when people are buying your records? (As proved by 'A Forest', which had become an unlikely Top 40 hit in April.) And rather than hire the usual hopefuls as support acts, the band asked for demo tapes to be sent to them, in order to give a new band a shot in each town they visited. It all made perfect sense. To celebrate, The Cure planned an end-of-year party by hosting a Christmas show (the first of many), to be held at the Notre Dame Hall, just off London's Leicester Square, on December 18. Also on the bill for this invitation-only affair were Cure peers the Banshees and The Associates, as well as The Scars and Tarzan 5.

Although the night was soured by the death, 10 days earlier, of John Lennon, the only Beatle to survive punk with his legend intact, Smith and the band celebrated in typical Cure fashion: they got stupendously pissed. Freed up after a six-month stretch during which the band had played in 13 different countries, they had the perfect excuse to have a seriously big one. All Smith could recall of the night was that "we were all really loud on stage and there was a lot of screaming and a lot of drinking". Echoing their one-off Cult Heroes set earlier in the year at The Marquee, The Cure saw out 1980 with a sloppy cover of a rock'n' roll chestnut, Gary Glitter's 'Do Ya Wanna Touch Me (Oh Yeah)'.

It had been a strange year for The Cure. They'd moved on from the mistakes of *Three Imaginary Boys* and released an album that was much truer to the sound that Robert Smith could hear playing inside his head. (Image, though, was still an issue – the Andrew Douglas photo on the cover of *Seventeen Seconds* was just as enigmatic as the household appliances shot of their debut.) They'd toured relentlessly and dabbled with life as a four-piece before settling once again as a trio. The band had also attempted the seemingly unthinkable by trying to cut two albums in a year, an attitude that would soon be absurd in a music world about to be overrun by marketing departments intent on squeezing every last breath of life out of each album they release. The memory of the aborted sessions at Morgan might have soured a remarkably lively year for The Cure, but Smith and the band knew that they couldn't waste too much energy contemplating what they couldn't change.

As another year under Thatcher's repressive regime dawned, Smith began to spend more and more time in the many churches of Crawley, and the theme of the band's next album started to emerge. Previously Smith had vague plans for a record "of ideas", but he now wanted to concentrate on faith – or the lack of it, in his case. Smith would take a notebook with him, scribbling away while the services continued in their solemn, austere fashion. Such sombre, hymn-like songs as the album's title track and 'The Funeral Party' would be bold attempts on Smith's part to capture the idea of religion and devotion on tape. While taking it all in, Smith was about to make a discovery that would put the fear of God in him – if he could only believe in the existence of a higher being, of course.

"I'd think about death and I'd look at the people in the church and I knew that they were all there above all because they wanted 'eternity'. I realised I had no faith at all and I was scared."

At the same time, Tolhurst's mother Daphne, possibly his biggest supporter, had become gravely ill. Smith and his long-time musical and personal ally would spend hours locked in earnest conversation about the subject of death. The eventual passing of Tolhurst's mother (on June 21, two months after *Faith*'s release) and the subsequent death of Smith's grandmother would weigh very heavily on The Cure's third album. "I think that marked a point for us starting an adult life," Tolhurst said.

As January rolled into February 1981, the plan for *Faith* was relatively straightforward: time had been booked at Morgan's studio one, which had proved a touchstone for their sophomore album, between the 2nd and the 11th. While *Seventeen Seconds* might have been a surprisingly efficient recording process, done and dusted within a few weeks, *Faith* was a case of trial by studio. The sessions continued throughout February, as the band bounced between a variety of studios: Red Bus, Trident, the Roundhouse and the legendary Abbey Road. The problems that Smith was encountering with his lack of faith extended into the music-making process: recorded tracks were repeatedly scrapped and both the inner-band relationship, and the understanding between Smith and producer Mike Hedges, reached boiling point.

Smith would unleash his anger on his bandmates and ever-present roadie Gary Biddles, especially when they were off getting wasted while Smith was trying to record his hushed, pensive vocals. As Smith would recall, the band had laid down the basic beds for the tracks in a "completely disinterested way, as if someone else was doing it and not us. [And] whenever I started to sing, the whole atmosphere went black."

The band's recently discovered thing for cocaine wasn't helping the album's unproductive sessions, either. "I was taking a lot of coke during the making of that album," Smith would confess in 2000, "and it was a very difficult and cranky atmosphere. Everything we did was wrong. I was permanently red-eyed and bitter and *Faith* didn't turn out how I wanted it to at all. I remember finishing the vocals off at Abbey Road and just feeling incredibly empty." The two impending deaths in the Tolhurst and Smith family, plus the gloomy legacy of Ian Curtis, which Smith just couldn't seem to shake, only made the *Faith* sessions tougher. Lol Tolhurst cut to the chase when he explained to me that "I listen to *Faith* now and don't think it's as realised as *Seventeen Seconds*."

Chris Parry, meanwhile, had been allowed to attend these sessions, but didn't enjoy what he was hearing. And, of course, the extra sessions, in increasingly slicker and higher-priced studios, were hitting the Fiction head where it really hurt: his bottom line. Parry would never disclose a figure, but did say that *Faith* "cost a lot more than it needed to".

While Parry worried about the mounting recording costs, the band was trying to prepare themselves for another reality – they were soon to start touring the same songs that had been so difficult to record. No wonder they were burying themselves under a pile of Colombia's finest. Finally, by the end of February, their third LP was completed. It had tested a lot more than The Cure's faith: it had been a bloody ordeal.

If *Seventeen Seconds* had been one long, sustained downer, a 10-track meditation on misery, then *Faith* sank even further into Smith's spiritual abyss. During the album's slow-burning opener, 'The Holy Hour', Smith's voice is again buried in the mix, a spectral presence in a turgid sludge of effects-heavy guitar and plodding bass and drums. And this was the same band that delivered such a melodic, immediate, Sixties-flavoured strum as 'Boys Don't Cry'! 'The Holy Hour' had started to take shape in Smith's imagination as he sat through Catholic Mass at Crawley's Friary Church one Sunday night; much of the album was written from Smith's attempts to unravel the enigma that was the Catholic faith, an ongoing presence during his upbringing. Smith was spellbound by the faithful (although he didn't count himself among their number), as they responded to the catechism. 'The Holy Hour' was one of several *Faith* tracks road-tested before it was committed to disc by the three moodists of Sussex. By the time of its recording, it had been fine-tuned to such a degree that there was absolutely no flab on the track. Nor was there the slightest suggestion of joy. The tone of *Faith* had been well and truly established.

'The Holy Hour' was followed by 'Primary', a natural successor to 'A Forest'. Powered by the dual basses of Smith and Gallup, another of

Tolhurst's steady-handed, bare-boned drum patterns and Smith's lost-in-a-wind-tunnel rhythm guitar, 'Primary' was an urgent, precisely crafted mood piece, every bit as evocative as 'A Forest'. Smith spits out the elliptical lyrics – which he would admit were inspired by the notion of dying very young, "innocent and dreaming" – as though they've left a poisonous taste in his mouth. The next track, 'Other Voices', was dominated by Gallup's thudding, insistent bassline before Smith unleashed a war cry that wouldn't have been rejected by Hiawatha himself. There's much talk of "empty rooms" and "distant noises/ other voices" during 'Other Voices', a track whose key inspiration had been drawn from one of Truman Capote's precise studies of Southern Gothic, *Other Voices, Other Rooms*. While it wasn't essential that Smith's wordplay made any kind of literal sense – the guy was no Truman Capote, after all – his lyrics seemed perfectly matched to the epic sense of doom and gloom that hung over *Faith* like a dark cloud. Just like 'A Forest' on *Seventeen Seconds*, 'Other Voices' had the feel of a mantra: it seemed as though the track could continue forever, snaking its way into the deep-black night.

The following track, 'All Cats Are Grey', did nothing to alleviate the all-consuming sense of despair – in fact, if anything, the five-and-a-half-minute Goth rock hymn tightened the noose just that little bit more. As with 'Other Voices' (and 'Killing An Arab', 'M' and 'At Night' previously), the track drew from a literary source: this time around it was Mervyn Peake's *Gormenghast* trilogy, Gothic novels published between 1946 and 1959 that could be read as an allegorical study of post-war Britain. These novels are so revered that they've been compared with the prose of Charles Dickens and J.R.R. Tolkien. Interestingly, the three books, *Gormenghast*, *Titus Alone* and *Titus Groan*, don't go anywhere in a hurry, not unlike The Cure's *Seventeen Seconds* and *Faith*. As one literary critic noted, "Peake's command of language and unique style set the tone and shape of an intricate, slow-moving world of ritual and stasis." Sound familiar?*

'All Cats Are Grey' unwound slowly, Smith's graveyard vocal held back until the track was almost at its midway point; by that time, the band had hooked remorselessly into one seriously bitter groove. More

---

* Smith also referred to Peake's trilogy of novels in the song 'The Drowning Man', referring specifically to the third book in the series, *Titus Groan*.

than anywhere else on *Faith*, or *Seventeen Seconds* before it, Smith sang with the solemn conviction of someone who'd caught a glimpse of humanity's true heart of darkness and didn't fancy what he'd seen. Just like 'A Forest' before it, the track was Smith's attempt to capture a recurring nightmare he'd been suffering, in which he repeatedly found himself lost in a series of caves, unable to find any way to escape. Scary stuff.

Joy Division's *Still*, reviewed by *NME* six months after *Faith*, may have been celebrated as a record that "confronted . . . and discovered the causes of the current depression [and found it] to be rooted in spiritual rather than material impoverishment", but Smith seemed even deeper in the bottomless pit of despair than the doomed Curtis. (Although The Cure lacked a eulogy with quite the same grace of Joy Division's 'Love Will Tear Us Apart'.) 'The Funeral Party' took Smith's obsession to its naturally bleak conclusion, a monumental wall of keyboards draped over the track like a black shroud, as Smith wailed and moaned and thrashed about like some poor unfortunate struggling to find a way to deal with his demons. The song was lifeless, tuneless, a good old-fashioned plod, yet strangely seductive and listenable at the same time. (Smith would state, later on, that he'd stretched the song's theme of death to include a consideration of his parents' eventual death and, naturally enough, his own demise.) At this mid-point of the album the question lingered: how much lower could The Cure go?

'Doubt' answered that question with a crisp, relatively clean strum of Smith's guitar and a tempo that suggested there was some life left in The Cure just yet. It's no less a bitter, angry rant than what preceded it, as Smith spilled what he would describe as "the anger and frustration at the pointlessness of everything"; it's just that the band had virtually ground to a halt with 'The Funeral Party' and obviously decided to pick up the pace a beat or two with 'Doubt'. But the overwhelming sense of bleakness returns with 'The Drowning Man', another slowly uncoiling, downbeat mantra of misery, a song that also mourned the death of innocence and what Smith referred to as "blind love". If cocaine was the drug that launched a million all-nighters, it clearly had the reverse effect on The Cure – it seemed as though the Bolivian marching powder that he'd been hoovering throughout the sessions only helped Smith tap into the pessimistic side of his nature. 'The Drowning Man' typified that.

The Cure's third album closed with the title cut, 'Faith', a track that stretched Smith's morbid mood by an epic seven minutes. Any listener who, by this time, hadn't totally succumbed to the album's overbearing feeling of despair, now had no choice but to capitulate (if they hadn't run screaming from the room already). Smith's voice was reduced to an agonised whisper, the backing of Tolhurst and Gallup was a heavy-legged crawl. If *Faith* were a soundtrack, it was the score to the most wrist-slashingly turgid film ever made. But Smith would defend the closing track in subsequent post-mortems on *Faith*. He firmly believed that, just like the grim last track of their next long-player, *Pornography*, the song offered a faint flicker of hope, the briefest ray of sunshine in a record that promised very little in the way of good vibrations. It was all relative, of course. According to Smith, 'Faith' was "as optimistic as I could get".

Throughout *Faith*, Robert Smith was ruthless with his use of sound and texture to reinforce a mood; he spared the suffering listener absolutely nothing as he unleashed all his pain and suffering and woe while drenching the band's sound with Gallup's rumbling bass, Tolhurst's spare, sparse drumbeats and the occasional wall of synths. Joy Division's similarly shroud-like wall of pain just didn't seem so bleak when played back-to-back with *Faith*. Smith may have cried "there's nothing left but faith", as the title track slowly, sadly crept off to its eventual death, but you were left asking how much faith the guy had after such a merciless exercise in bleakness.

Robert Smith would wear his "Guru of Goth" mantle like some crown of thorns, but he did nothing to dissuade Goth's true believers with *Faith* – by directly referring to Peake's *Gormenghast* novels, Gothic benchmarks, he was clearly staking out his spot as top Goth on the block. Smith mightn't have been quite ready to join Ian Curtis in taking that final leap into the unknown, so instead he opted to craft an album so low, so heavy-hearted, that it should have come with a warning about being played to those of a nervous and/or fragile persuasion.

With the Picture Tour (as the *Faith* album tour would be known) looming, the band took another unusual tangent regarding their support act. The idea of having local bands submit tapes, and then using a different act in each city they visited, worked reasonably well with their late 1980 tour, but Smith could see its limitations. While he believed that some of the bands hired passed the quality control test, there were other factors that could get in the way of a big night out. "The trouble is," Smith said, "if we arrive late for a soundcheck or if something goes wrong we've got to make a choice – either the support band gets a soundcheck and you get half as long as you need, so your sound's awful and the audience is disappointed, or the support group doesn't get a soundcheck and you get a good one and the audience is pissed off all the way through the support act because they can't hear anything." The solution was simple: dispense with the support act altogether.

Smith had a totally new plan. He approached various film schools, pitching the idea for some kind of short film to take the place of an opening act. He also offered to cough up the cash. But the response was collectively cool, so Gallup's brother Ric was hired. He produced a stark animated piece called *Carnage Visors*, the title being a dark twist on the term rose-coloured glasses. But the film, which was shot in Gallup's garage, almost fell apart before its first screening – when he got the film back from the processors, he realised that the light exposures had been incorrectly set and the on-screen result was even darker than the music that The Cure would be playing. Gallup was forced to start from scratch, re-shooting several months of work in a few days.

The *NME*'s response to the film, when it eventually debuted on the Picture Tour, was muffled. "It's not very good," they reported, "just a series of evolving shapes for people to look at while Smith's austere soundtrack further imposes the correct conditions of The Cure's entrance." (A Google search will reveal, however, that something of a *Carnage Visors* cult has developed amongst serious Cure-aholics. Several websites are dedicated to Gallup's unsettling animated short.) The Cure must have learned something from the drawn-out experience of recording *Faith*, because they cut the accompanying music in record time. On March 16, after a few days of rehearsals, the trio, fuelled by numerous bottles of wine, and ably assisted by a Dr Rhythm drum machine, recorded the 27-minute instrumental soundtrack in a few hours at Point Studios. This recorded version of *Carnage Visors* would find a home on the flipside of the cassette release of *Faith*.

But before *Carnage Visor*'s public debut, the first single from *Faith* was released. 'Primary' was backed with 'Descent', a *Faith* out-take that, just like its A-side, featured a trade-off between the duelling basses of Smith and Gallup. 'Descent' remained an instrumental because, as

Smith admitted, "I didn't want to write any more words. I'd written all I needed for the *Faith* album and really had nothing more to say." The single appeared in late March, sitting very comfortably amidst the chart fodder of the day, which included such lightweight fluff as Shakin' Stevens' 'This Ole House', Kim Wilde's 'Kids In America' (more of her later) and the watered-down Joy Division of Ultravox, whose 'Vienna' had been embraced as the soundtrack for the puffy-sleeve-loving New Romantic generation. The rumbling, discontented Gothic groove of 'Primary' was a hard sell. However, it was a significant achievement on the band's part – and tangible proof of their improving profile – that the single charted as high as number 43.

A second *Top Of The Pops* appearance on April 16, however, didn't contribute much to the single's chart value. It began badly when the presenter, Radio One jock Peter Powell, couldn't remember The Cure's name or whether they were making their *Top Of The Pops* debut (they weren't). Things then went downhill real fast, as the band obscured their instruments with clothing, just to remind the few million looking on that "live TV" was an oxymoron. Backstage, the very serious young gloomsters of The Cure did their level best to steer clear of the other names on the bill, missing out on the chance to form lifelong bonds with such like-minded peers as Bucks Fizz, the Nolans and Girlschool. A bad time was had all round.

The reviews for 'Primary' were as ambivalent as The Cure's petulant approach towards the fame game. *Melody Maker*'s Adam Sweeting, every inch The Cure banner-waver, called it a "triumphant return" after the heavy going and "limpid wanderings" of *Seventeen Seconds*. He wrote that 'Primary' was "unbearably urgent, matching a new-found sense of space with a brilliantly focused precision . . . [it] is a far better pretext for a national holiday than the forthcoming Royal Wedding." The review by *Sound*'s David Hepworth, however, typified the response to an even darker, even bleaker Cure than had been heard on 'A Forest'. "I do wonder," he wrote, "how long The Cure can continue to prop their songs against the same chord progression, with its clambering bass and deadpan drums. At the moment their fast song (this one) sounds just like their slow one speeded up."

NME, meanwhile, sat somewhere between the two. "Smith's dry, lost vocal," noted Chris Bohn, "tells of an unsettled individual listening out for a strange guiding voice, while the band play an attractively doomy tune." *Record Mirror*'s Simon Tebbutt neatly summed up the single's musical mood when he observed how the band "sounds incredibly bored". Back in Crawley, Robert Smith pondered this: if the critics noticed how bored the band was sounding on record, what chance did The Cure have when they would be forced to relive the album night after night for the next six months?

Faith finally made its miserable presence felt in stores on April 11, reaching a UK chart peak of number 14. Though as uninformative and enigmatic as previous sleeves, the cover image was the Parched Art (Porl Thompson and his colleague Undy Vella) take on Bolton Abbey, a small village near Skipton in what is now North Yorkshire. It was a site that Smith knew extremely well: when he was a nipper, during family holidays in the Yorkshire Dales, he'd play in the grounds of the ruined abbey beside the River Wharfe. It is here, at a local landmark known as the Strid, that the river narrows and the current surges. According to Dales folklore, you can jump the river at this point, but if you fall short the seething current will drag you under and you'll almost certainly drown. "It's one of my oldest memories," he'd admit.

This was Thompson's first Cure LP cover, although he had designed the sleeve for the 'Primary' single. It was yet another case of The Cure keeping things very close to home, Thompson, of course, being an ex (and future) member of the band, and husband-to-be of Smith's sister Janet.

Unimpressed by The Cure's two prior album sleeves, Thompson, who was studying design in West Sussex, approached Smith and told him that his Parched Art could do a far better job. In a textbook case of method designing, he threw himself into the gig, ditching college and hanging out with the band in the various studios where the album was recorded. Despite all that, and his insistence that Parched Art were the right men for the job, the *Faith* cover image is no great progression from what came before. Smith, however, didn't seem to mind, because Thompson and Vella would also design the covers for *The Head On The Door* and *The Top*. Thompson would also help out with the sleeve for *Pornography*.

The year in rock 1981 would be a banner time for all things Goth, with the release of such albums as Joy Division's swansong *Still*; Siouxsie & The Banshees' *Juju* and Bauhaus' *Mask*. Though every bit as grim, *Faith* wasn't destined to be so highly regarded. It was 'Primary' all over again; critics were uncertain exactly what to make of all this useless misery – was the Thatcher regime to blame or was it simply the weather that made Robert Smith so bloody grim?

Adam Sweeting was among the few champions of the album, noting that it should definitely be filed in the "uneasy listening" corner of the record store. He felt that there was something about *Faith* that could get under your skin. "Mostly," he commented, "*Faith* is a sophisticated exercise in atmosphere and production, gloomy but frequently majestic. You may not love it, but you'll become addicted to it." *NME* grumbled that The Cure were now leaders of "the new songwriting category known to experts as Grammar School Angst", although they did admit that there was an upside to the new album. "It's very well played, beautifully recorded – and says absolutely nothing meaningful in a fairly depressing way."

Mike Nicholls, from *Record Mirror*, was a tad less generous with his praise, comparing the band unfavourably with PiL, John Lydon's post-Sex Pistols experiment in noise. "The Cure remain stuck in the hackneyed doom mongering that should have died with Joy Division," he figured, not unreasonably. "[They] are lost in the maze of their spineless meanderings . . . hollow, shallow, pretentious, meaningless, self-important and bereft of any real heart and soul." In short, Nicholls figured, *Faith* stank.

When he revisited the album and the ensuing Picture Tour more than 20 years later, Robert Smith wasn't that thrilled by *Faith*, either. He was convinced that the death of his grandmother and Tolhurst's mother's illness (there had also been a death in the Gallup family) had cast a dark pall over the record, a murky, morbid gloom that was almost tangible in its songs. "The initial demos that we did in my mum and dad's dining room are really quite upbeat," Smith said. "Then, within about two weeks, the whole mood of the band had completely changed. I wrote 'The Funeral Party' and 'All Cats Are Grey' in one night, and that really set the tone for the album.

"A lot of people around the band began reacting badly to the fact that we were becoming successful, on a very limited scale. There was a lot of jealousy and sour grapes and people saying, 'You've changed!' We *had* changed because we weren't going to the same pubs all the time, because we were touring Europe. So we lost a lot of friends, and we became much more insular. We would just drink ourselves into oblivion, and play these songs."

Accordingly, the Picture Tour was a grim affair, tinged with more than a little sadness, although the band's use of Pink Floyd's PA gave their live set an earthquaking sonic boom. (Smith had namechecked the Floyd's *Ummagumma* in early discussions of *Faith*, when he owned up to admiring records that were "built around repetition". He also included Benedictine chants and Indian mantras on his list.) Smith was suitably impressed by the Floyd PA after the band gave it a test run at Shepperton prior to the opening date at Friars in Aylesbury. It was roughly 10 times the size of their previous PA and was hardly likely to break down with the frequency of their old gear. "At the moment," Smith said with some insistence, "it's reliability we want."

Within a few dates of the Picture Tour – so named because of the screening of Ric Gallup's *Carnage Visors* – The Cure had settled on a setlist to which they'd remain faithful for their next eight months. The opening trio of songs would typically combine *Faith*'s 'The Holy Hour' and 'Other Voices' with *Seventeen Seconds*' 'In Your House', setting a resolutely bleak mood for the night. Their sets were now running to around 20 songs, but with the exception of a smattering of pre-*Seventeen Seconds* tracks ('Killing An Arab', '10.15 Saturday Night'), Tolhurst, Smith and Gallup stuck very rigidly to the downbeat, downcast mood that permeated their two most recent LPs. The Cure's legend as the ultimate overcoat band, Gothic gloomsters obsessed with death, was firmly established during 1981.

The morbidity of the music they were playing also started to seep into the band's psyches off-stage. In the past they'd managed to balance onstage austerity with off-stage boozing and high jinks, but the unrelenting bleakness of these shows was like some social experiment gone horribly wrong. "I didn't realise what effect it would have on the group," said Smith. "I thought we could just merge the [new] songs in live, and the other [older] songs would balance, but it affected everyone. Those songs had a downward spiral effect on us – the more we played them, the more despondent and desolate we became."

The Cure's ever-increasing fanbase wasn't quite prepared for these funereal dirges and the trio's increasingly long faces. Even during the first week of the tour, at an Oxford show covered by *Melody Maker*, the rock'n'roll natives were becoming increasingly restless. While an

140

agitated audience yelled out unrequested requests – 'Forest', '10.15 Saturday Night', 'Killing An Arab' – the band ploughed through their recent material with a cold, steely-eyed intent. As *Melody Maker* noted, there wasn't a lot of love felt between band and punters. "The Cure were about four numbers into their set. As they paused for breath between songs, yells [for older songs] went up around the hall. We've paid our money and we want hits, dammit. Singer and guitarist Robert Smith stepped to the microphone and said, 'This one's called "The Funeral Party".' I thought I saw the hint of a smile."

Rival rag *NME* witnessed a similar uneasy atmosphere at their Reading show three nights later, April 26, at the Hexagon, but they did admit that the show displayed a reverence and solemnity that bordered on the "religious". "They allow a sense of doom and fatalism to hang over them with a sense of personal election," they reported. "At times they seem more impressed by their own exclusive use of a doomy vocabulary than convinced of it, white ghouls taking glamour from their pallor."

It was an astute take on The Cure circa 1981. In much the same way that they'd one day be pigeonholed as cute, huggable, big-haired pop freaks, as captured in their string of hit singles and made-for-MTV Tim Pope videos, they were now stuck in a ghoulish rut, playing the part of the voice of doom. Smith would become so wrapped up in the role he was playing that he'd sometimes leave the stage in tears.

There were, however, occasional flashes of good humour: a show at Dublin College on May 22 would be remembered mostly by the band because they barricaded themselves inside a beer tent. (The show itself was a half-baked set played to uninterested locals.) Two weeks later, at Freiburg in Germany, there were almost as many people on stage as there was in the crowd – The Cure clearly didn't have quite the pull in Deutschland as they did in neighbouring France. Smith spent most of the night seated at the front of the stage singing, pretty much to himself, and then got pleasantly smashed with the few punters who'd braved the stifling 90-degree heat.

But these were rare moments of drunken joy. The Picture Tour bottomed out, hitting a low point on June 24, when the band played at the Terrein Serviem at Sittard in Holland. Having just completed their set, and with the crowd expecting an encore, Tolhurst was given an urgent message to call England immediately. When he did so, the voice at the other end had a simple, shocking message: "Your mother's dead." The band went back on stage and started playing 'Faith', but after what was possibly the most unbearable minute of his life, Tolhurst stopped, his shoulders drooped. The show was over.

The next day the band returned to England for Daphne Tolhurst's funeral, playing the tape of the previous night's show during the service, as well as a handful of Daphne's favourite Cure songs on acoustic guitars. A few hours later, over many drinks, Tolhurst insisted that the show must go on. If it didn't, he might just lose his mind.

"When we were in Germany," he told me, "I came back to see her; she was staying with my sister who was a registered nurse. I knew she had about a month. I told everyone on the crew that if I got a call about her before a show, tell me afterwards because there's not much I can do.

"We were in Holland when my brother called. I drove down to Amsterdam that night, flew back, saw everyone, made the funeral arrangements and then kept touring because I figured that's what my mother would want. Those few following nights after were the weirdest shows I'd ever played.

"There's a little causeway at the top of Holland and I remember driving along that a day or two after she died, and I saw these swans on one side in the freshwater and also in the sea, which always struck me as very weird," Tolhurst continued. "I think that was a pivotal time for me about the way I would then think about things and write about things. Up until then a lot of what we wrote about came out of books and not out of real life. But we were now able to talk about what was happening to us and how they happened; that came to a pinnacle in *Pornography*."

For the immediate future, however, Tolhurst was on the verge of unravelling: his downward slide into chronic alcoholism had begun. "Since my mother died, for at least six months, every single restraint I had went straight out the window. I was sad, really, a lot of that was grief."

The Picture Tour took another bleak turn two weeks later, during a festival show on July 5 at Werchter in Belgium which featured the unlikely pairing of The Cure on stage before blue-eyed soul mannequin Robert Palmer. Palmer's road crew had threatened to pull the plug if The Cure didn't stop playing, but their tour manager shouted to them that they could play only one more song. As they lurched into 'A Forest', Smith had an announcement for the crowd: "This is the final song because we're not allowed to carry on any more," he stated. "Everybody wants to see Robert Palmer, I think." Smith, Tolhurst and Gallup transformed the song into a nine-minute-long plod. When they finally neared the song's end, with Palmer's seething road crew looking on, Simon Gallup started up a chant of "fuck Robert Palmer, fuck rock'n'roll". Minutes later, Palmer's crew took their revenge, tossing The Cure's equipment off the back of the stage, and trading blows with the band. The Cure wore their "us against the world" attitude like a badge of honour, and the tour dragged on.

In between these European festival dates and the band's next North American tour, The Cure paused to record a new single, again with Mike Hedges producing. The band had finally outgrown Morgan studios; this time they recorded at Hedges' Playground Studio (which had been named by Smith, as it turned out). The track 'Charlotte Sometimes' was recorded over two days, July 16 and 17. Not only inspired by, but also named after the Penelope Farmer book – subtlety not being one of Smith's strongest points – 'Charlotte Sometimes' wasn't a major Cure single, but it marked a subtle transition from their grim past to their poppier future.

Cut during the same recording pit-stop, 'Splintered In Her Head', the B-side of 'Charlotte Sometimes', was equally noteworthy because it was a very clear sonic signpost to their next album, *Pornography*. (The title was also taken from a line in the Penelope Farmer book.) The song emerged from a random drumbeat with which Smith had been tinkering. "The intention was that the song should complement 'Charlotte'," Smith admitted in the liner notes to *Join The Dots*, "that it should have the same kind of vibe. And despite my slightly deranged harmonica playing, I think it does. There are also definite signs of the *Pornography* stuff to come."

But the video for 'Charlotte Sometimes' was a major mistake, ranking among the worst of the band's small-screen career. On the advice of Chris Parry, it was directed by Mike Mansfield, who'd made numerous videos for current band du jour Adam & The Ants. The clip was shot in the grounds of Netherne Hospital, where erstwhile Cure bassist Michael Dempsey had worked. Smith had hoped for something "really mysterious", but the video's cold, sterile mood didn't do anyone any favours. When 'Charlotte Sometimes' was released in October, the album art featured a typically oblique, cryptic cover image, which was actually a shot of Mary Poole, which had been snapped by Smith at a Scottish castle in 1980. The song crawled to number 44 in the UK singles chart.

Within a week of the single's recording, The Cure was in New York for a double-header at The Ritz. But the band barely made it through the first night intact. Smith and Gallup had cheerfully gulped down two Quaaludes apiece, which had been offered to them backstage. They must have been super strength, because Tolhurst, in the uncommon role of straight man – he'd been to the dentist that afternoon and was advised against drinking for the day – genuinely feared for the barely conscious pair's lives, as he escorted them to various New York clubs.

"I had to carry both of them into the clubs, which I'm sure they don't remember as they spent the rest of the night sitting on some couches pretty much unconscious," Tolhurst said. "I attempted to get Simon to the bathroom at one point to splash some water in his face as he looked like he could depart at any time. Unfortunately I couldn't hold him up over the sink so he nosedived straight into the porcelain, which must have hurt later.

"Then a club patron came over to me, as it was obvious that I was having some difficulty holding Simon up, and offered to help. But before I could say or do anything he started blowing some unspecified powder up Simon's nose. Simon regained consciousness just long enough to think the man was attacking him so he started stamping on the poor guy's feet. Then he fell back into his stupor once more.

"Eventually I thought I'd better get them back to the hotel to sleep it off," Tolhurst continued. "The only way I could persuade them to come with me was by starting a fight with Simon so he would get up and run after me straight into the back seat of a taxi to take us to the hotel. Once there it took me about an hour to persuade Simon that he didn't need to brush his teeth first, he should just go to bed.

"We didn't have a lot of money back then so we were all sharing a suite of rooms. I finally pushed them both in the direction of the bedroom. Then I heard Simon back up again trying to brush his teeth. At this point I abandoned the effort and went to bed myself. The next day was funny."

The tone was set for the rest of their North American tour and the upcoming August shows in Australia and New Zealand: Smith was so freaked out by the usual well-wishers after their Hollywood show at the Whisky A Go Go on July 27 that he took refuge in his hotel room, in tears. A few nights later, while in Auckland, New Zealand, Smith tracked down Severin, who was in Scotland with his fellow Banshees. The Cure frontman felt that he needed to give his new pal a sneak preview of 'Charlotte Sometimes', which he promptly played down the phone to Severin before falling asleep. However, a dangerously drowsy Smith hadn't hung up the phone. The next morning, The Cure was down $480.

A review of The Cure's 15-song set at Christchurch, on August 6, aptly showed the uncertain response the band was copping from both press and fans throughout the Picture Tour. "The Cure concert was tiring, sometimes difficult, an accessible barrier, no fun, but deserved respect," David Swift wrote in local newspaper *The Press*. "The band was not close to the audience, but earned accolades all the way." Bizarrely, Swift likened bassman Simon Gallup to Thin Lizzy's rock'n' roll gypsy, Phil Lynott, a comparison that would have provided one-time Lizzy lover Robert Smith with a rare chuckle. Swift's response to the night's opener, *Carnage Visors*, was to shrug and wait for the main attraction. "I do not think anyone will remember the film," he surmised. As for the band's dour frontman, Swift felt that the only hint of personality that Smith demonstrated all night was his T-shirt, which was emblazoned with the image of tragic Hollywood bomb-shell, Marilyn Monroe. Death was all around.

The band then crossed the Tasman to Australia, where they found a way to deal with the seemingly non-stop requests for their more access-ible, pre-*Seventeen Seconds* tunes: physical confrontation. "They were expecting a lighter, poppier show," Smith figured, reasonably enough, "and . . . we started with 'The Holy Hour' and 'All Cats Are Grey', seven minutes of atmosphere."

The mood darkened when the band returned to Canada for a series of shows, followed by a month-long tour of France, which ended with a rough night at Toulon's Theatre D'Hiver on October 23. By this stage of their increasingly violent and seemingly never-ending tour, Smith and Gallup had developed an unspoken understanding: when Smith started to unstrap his guitar, Gallup knew that it was time to leap into the crowd "to settle accounts".

Smith would recall in *Ten Imaginary Years* that much of the tour was, to him, a blur of angry crowds and his own fragile state of mind. (He and Gallup were obviously still recovering from their Quaaludes encounter in New York.) "I don't really remember many of those shows," Smith said. "I was getting to the manic stage that was going to lead to *Pornography*. I was due for a break – too much of everything, no respite."

If only it could have been that easy. The band had a final lap of the UK scheduled before they could take the time to check their heads and determine if this pain (both physical and existential) was really worthwhile. The support act for the last British leg of the Picture tour was punk poetess Lydia Lunch, who had teamed up with the Banshees' Steve Severin, the man who had been appalled by Smith's green check suit when they first met a couple of years earlier. This new collaboration called itself 13.13. Not only would the bond between Severin and Smith tighten during these dates, but Lunch and Robert Smith would also form their own unholy alliance.

Born only five weeks after Smith, on June 2, 1959 in Rochester, New York, Lunch was already a veteran at 22 when she first met Smith during the tour. Lunch was seemingly born to punk. At the age of 16 she was a key player in New York's 'No Wave' scene, shrieking and chanting at the front of Teenage Jesus & The Jerks, who contributed four cuts to Brian Eno's highly regarded *No New York* compilation, a snapshot of the short-lived scene that also spawned such acts as James White & The Blacks, and Defunkt. Lunch had also starred in three 8mm movies by filmmaker Vivienne Dick, before recording the pivotal *Queen Of Siam* album with a band that included ex-Voidoid (and future Lou Reed) guitarist Robert Quine and a bassist calling himself Jack Ruby (real name George Scott), who'd played alongside John Cale. By the time Lunch was heading the very fluid line-up of 13.13, she'd shifted base to California. Steve Severin was at her side by the time Lunch arrived for their first show at the Lyceum in Sheffield on November 25. She'd been personally invited by Smith to join the tour. And Also The Trees, who would soon be working in the studio with Lol Tolhurst, were also on the bill.

When I spoke with Lunch in late 2004, she retained strong, very deeply felt memories of the tour, which she expressed in her typically potent mix of prose and poetry. "At the time," she said, "I was experimenting with the spontaneous explosion of *The Agony Is The Ecstasy* [a

Smith, Gallup and Tolhurst (from left), early 1982. "I'm not much good at pretending I'm having fun," Smith would later reveal. (LFI)

Video maker Tim Pope. During the legendary clip for 'Lullaby', Pope had Smith lowered repeatedly into a furry black hole "full of some sticky gunk that looks and smells like Airfix glue". (LFI)

Robert Smith on the set of the Pope-directed clip for 'The Walk'. According to Pope, "I don't think either of us had a fucking clue." (LFI)

In 1983, The Cure become 'The Lovecats', a ditty inspired by Smith's love of Walt Disney's *The Aristocats*. "An amateurish pop song," said it's author. (LFI)

On the set of 'The Lovecats'. Pope had to convince the owner of the derelict terrace in Primrose Hill that he was a potential buyer. That's Lol Tolhurst in the cat suit. (LFI)

Siouxsie & The Banshees, featuring Robert Smith
(far right), on the set of the 'Dear Prudence' video in
September 1983. "My involvement was based mainly on my
friendship with Steve Severin." (LFI)

Team Cure, circa 1983: Andy Anderson, Phil Thornalley,
Tolhurst and Smith (from left). Anderson's lethal magic
mushroom tea spiced up many long nights on the road. (LFI)

Porl Thompson, Boris Williams, Smith, Gallup and Tolhurst
(from left), *Kiss Me* era. Smith almost killed most of the
band one night during sessions for the 1987 album. (LFI)

Smith on stage at Wembley, 1985.
By then The Cure was an unstoppable
force, with a hit album and two
high-rotation MTV videos.
(George Chin/WireImage)

Smith with his teenage sweetheart and
now wife, Mary Poole, the inspiration
for 'Lovesong'. "She would have
preferred diamonds, I think," Smith
figured. (Richard Young/Rex Features)

Smith, with Lol Tolhurst (in sunglasses) rides the Orient Express,
1986. The band ran up a record bar tab while on board, somewhere
between £1,500 and £2,000, a figure which emerged during the Lol
Tolhurst court case. (Richard Young/Rex Features)

A close-cropped Robert Smith, 1986. Without his daily writing regime, "I'd have just got up in mid-afternoon and watched TV until the pubs opened, then gone out drinking." (Lynn Goldsmith/Corbis)

The Cure, 1987, about to become the oddest pop stars on the planet. "That was the accomplished version of The Cure," said Tolhurst. "Put us all together and it was the best gang in town." (George Chin/WireImage)

The diminishing role of Lol Tolhurst (second from right) becomes clear. Smith said that if Tolhurst had stayed in the band, "Simon would have thrown him off a balcony". (Mauro Carraro/Rex Features)

Gallup, Williams, Thompson, Smith, Roger O'Donnell and Tolhurst (from left). "I couldn't see why he was in the band," O'Donnell said of Tolhurst. (Neal Preston/Corbis)

Smith and Poole's wedding day, August 13, 1988.
"We just got married to have a nice day," Smith said soon after.
"It's really dumb but I was sort of overcome." (LFI)

The Cure founder and its one permanent fixture, Robert Smith,
the face that launched a million Goths. (Adrian Boot)

work which would eventually be released in 1982 as an EP cut with The Birthday Party]. Never has there been a more appropriate title."

Clearly the shows were as tumultuous for Lunch as they were for The Cure, as she would go on to explain. "Take musicians who have never played together before, throw them on stage with the vague theme of 'follow the lyrics' – [playing] sad songs about death, decay and murder – and encourage them to illustrate. Pray for the best, expect the worst."

Whereas The Cure's method for dealing with audience apathy and agitation during this tour was to resort to physical violence, Lunch and 13.13 just powered on, while the crowds stared, unsure what to make of the wild scene they were witnessing. If there was one thing that both 13.13 and The Cure took away from the Picture Tour, it was this: they'd been through a heavy learning experience. "The tour taught me," Lunch said, "especially in front of thousands of black-clad sad romantics, that my instinct has always been to improv wildly, madly, with force of insight, even if said experiment creates an atrocious, hideous din to which no one – sometimes even the self – is not in tune with. This is far better than repeating, night after night, a set song list whose tedium is far more aggravating than the frightening sounds, like that of a naked wound, seething in agony, amplified to an unbearable fevered pitch of near hysteria."

As for the tour itself, Lunch doesn't remember it as being an overly sociable time – it was hardly a laugh riot backstage. Instead she remembered it being "one of the darkest periods for everyone I know". Lunch told me there were three common denominators on the Picture Tour: "drug abuse, depression, alcohol". In fact, Lunch's own set was so physically and mentally draining – screaming blue murder at the top of your lungs to a stony-faced crowd can do that – that most nights she didn't have the energy to hang around until the show was over. Instead she'd simply collapse in a heap.

As arduous and draining as those dates turned out to be, Lunch and Smith maintained what she described as a "long-distance relationship" well after the tour ended on December 3. Smith must have felt strongly about their time together: he even had a "mystery" inscription dedicated to Lunch carved into the run-out groove of the vinyl of one of their early albums (most likely *Pornography*).

"I always found him terribly sweet, sensitive and shy," Lunch told me, offering quite a different take on a man who was sometimes known to jump into his audiences and physically sort out all non-believers. In an effort to continue their relationship/friendship, Smith and Lunch created a small montaged book of poetry and photographs which would bounce between them over the ensuing years. "I still have it," she told me. "[It contains] pieces of hair, photos of ghost-white dolls with no eyes, criminal tales of love gone sour. A beautiful little funeral book."

It would be a serious challenge to find a symbol more apt for the Picture Tour than Smith and Lunch's "beautiful little funeral book". The Cure – and Smith in particular – had pushed themselves danger-ously close to the edge over the past eight months. They'd alienated audiences, tested their own toxic capacities and found themselves con-tinually questioning the very reason they were making music in the first place. When asked about the *Faith* period in 2004, Smith could see it was clearly a Cure low point.

"When we toured on the back of this album, the mood was so sombre," he recalled. "It wasn't a particularly healthy thing to do because we were reliving a really bad time, night after night, and it got incredibly depressing. And so I kind of have mixed feelings about *Faith*."

When the tour finally ground to a halt at the Hammersmith Palais on December 3, rather than retire to their respective Crawley recovery centres – Smith was still bunking with his parents; it wasn't until 1985 that he bought a London flat, in Maida Vale, which he shared with long-time, long-suffering partner Mary Poole – The Cure jumped straight into their next project, their fourth album, *Pornography*. It would turn out to be the longest, darkest night of a career that, to this stage, could have desperately used an injection of something just a little upbeat and life-affirming. Robert Smith simply couldn't resist the temptation to dissect his own black soul and then put it on public display.

Chapter Seven

"We wanted to make the ultimate, intense album. I can't remember exactly why, but we did."

– Lol Tolhurst

THE Picture Tour had almost been a career-ending slog, a maze of dispirited crowds, wasted nights and non-stop travel. But rather than pause and regroup, the trio of Smith, Tolhurst and Gallup barely took the time out to reintroduce themselves to friends and family before they began sessions for their fourth album. This time around, Smith in particular felt that he wanted to work with someone other than producer Mike Hedges – ideally someone younger and a little more flexible in their working methods. Parry and Smith, jokingly, had made a wager with Hedges that if the single 'Charlotte Sometimes' flopped, then they'd look elsewhere for a new producer. Maybe they weren't kidding after all. Hedges' contribution to The Cure had been vital, especially in the making of *Seventeen Seconds* and *Faith*, albums that helped to define the darker side of Robert Smith's muse. But the band and Parry knew it was time to experiment. Hedges made their decision easier when he opted to produce Siouxsie & The Banshees' *A Kiss In The Dreamhouse* album instead of making another Cure LP.

Producer-in-the-making Phil Thornalley had been recommended to the band by studio veteran Steve Lillywhite. Thornalley had been Lillywhite's studio engineer and general sidekick during the making of The Psychedelic Furs' 1981 breakthrough long-player, *Talk Talk Talk*. (A rough and tumble studio encounter, as it turned out, with frequent punch-ups interrupted by the occasional recording of songs.) Thornalley had worked with virtual hit machine Lillywhite during various other RAK studio sessions. Thornalley was no Cure insider, but he wasn't a complete stranger to Parry. Their paths had crossed when Thornalley was the tape operator on the *All Mod Cons* album in 1978, a hit for Chris Parry's other suburban three-piece, The Jam. Thornalley, however, played down any strong connection to The Cure when we spoke in late 2004. He insists he was simply "a name on a list" when he was eventually hired by the band over the Christmas/New Year break.*

If Robert Smith was serious about being on the lookout for someone with a different approach, background and age to Mike Hedges, he couldn't have made a more astute choice than Thornalley, who was Smith's junior by about eight months. Born in Warlington, Suffolk, on January 5, 1960, Thornalley was one of two boys, his brother Jonathan being a couple of years older. Thornalley didn't come from an especially musical family, although, as he told me, his childhood neighbours were musically inclined, which is where he first developed a taste for rock'n'roll. By the time he left Culford School at Bury St Edmunds, in 1978, Phil Thornalley had already played in several fledgling outfits. "But that didn't look like the route for me. I was interested in being a producer and songwriter and the studio seemed the right place for me."

Very much the right teenager in the right place, Thornalley scored a plum job: a sound engineer apprenticeship at London's legendary RAK Studios where he started work in 1978. There were few better places to learn studiocraft, especially for someone like Thornalley, who had a real flair for thinking-person's pop. Established in 1976, RAK Studios (and the RAK record label) was the baby of Mickie Most, who'd produced The Animals' seminal 'House Of The Rising Sun' (in 15 minutes!), amongst other benchmark hits from the Sixties. Most was very much a man with an ear for the charts, subsequently signing such multi-million-sellers as Suzi Quatro, Smokie, Kim Wilde and Hot Chocolate to the RAK label. Pop-lover Thornalley couldn't have hoped for a better boss or mentor. (Later, as part of pop outfit Johnny Hates Jazz, Thornalley would record with Most's son Calvin Hayes, who was the band's keyboardist, and Mike Nocito, the co-engineer of *Pornography*.)

"He was fantastic; no other producer has come along like him," Thornalley said of Most. "His instincts were totally commercial but refreshingly so, because his sessions were over very quickly. He knew if

---

* That list also included Kraftwerk producer Conny Plank, who met with Smith and Tolhurst at this time, but, tragically, died shortly afterwards.

something was a hit or not." By the time Chris Parry and Smith chose to work with Thornalley, initially for one day in what Thornalley would describe to me as a "probationary trial", he was the house engineer at RAK.

The Cure's approach to recording the album was hardly typical. As Nocito told me, a first day of recording is usually spent "just getting the drum sound right". Yet The Cure came in and played their entire album, from bleak start to grim finish, in one hit. Both Thornalley and engineer Nocito were stunned. Then Smith, Tolhurst, Gallup and Parry retired to consider their verdict: was Thornalley the producer they needed? ("I think they were deciding if they liked my attitude," said Thornalley.)

As his bandmates and manager chewed it over, Smith spent a weekend in a windmill in Guildford (I kid you not) where he fine-tuned most of the album's lyrics in a stream-of-consciousness out-pouring. Still dazed and confused by the band's ruthless Picture Tour, Smith had decided that his new lyrics should head into even heavier territory than *Faith* or *Seventeen Seconds*, if that was humanly possible. "I really thought that was it for the group," he said in 2003, looking back at another of his darkest hours. "I had every intention of signing off. I wanted to make the ultimate fuck-off record, then The Cure would stop. Whatever I did next, I would have achieved one lasting thing with the band. So *Pornography*, from the moment we started it, we knew that was it."

"I had two choices at the time," Smith said in another discussion of *Pornography*, "which were either completely giving in [thereby emulating Joy Division's Ian Curtis] or making a record of it and getting it out of me. I'm glad I chose to make the record. It would have been very easy just to curl up and disappear."

His poison-pen lyrics now prepared, Smith and the band re-convened. Obviously they approved of Thornalley, because by Christmas 1981 they'd agreed to make the album with him. Yet in spite of the band's slowly rising star, Thornalley was, if anything, under-whelmed by the moody trio. To him, they were just the next act on the RAK schedule, slotted in between sessions with such hit machines as Hot Chocolate, Racey and popstress Kim Wilde, who worked in the next studio at RAK while The Cure unleashed their fourth album. The Cure sometimes passed Wilde in the corridor, having just finished another all-nighter – most sessions for *Pornography* running from around 8pm to breakfast time. By this time of the morning, The Cure would be "looking fairly deranged," as Smith would relate. Ms Wilde was not amused. "I think I scared the hell out of Kim Wilde," Tolhurst told me. "I cornered her once and had a big long conversation about nothing. She was ready to go to work and I was ready to go to the pub. But she was game."

Thornalley would defend RAK's musical egalitarianism. "[Everything else was] full-on pop," Thornalley told me, "not particularly dark and meaningful 'art', although legitimate in their own right." In fact, the only song of The Cure's that Thornalley had heard was 'Killing An Arab', and even then it was via a random spotting on the radio. "Those early records had a sound, but not one I would try to get. I worked at the studio and The Cure was just the next group that came in," Thornalley explained to me. "That was my job. There was no pontificating on my part; it was very unpretentious. One day it could be a middle-of-the-road singer, the next day an orchestra, then The Cure for three weeks. You just get on with it, you know.

"I had no real knowledge of the history of the band. Perhaps that was positive, because I had my own feelings on good sounds. I'd learned a lot from Mickie Most and Steve Lillywhite, who tended to be more aggressive in their approach. They tried to get some excitement on the tape as opposed to coldness."

Thornalley quickly came to understand the hierarchy within The Cure: Smith was an interested and willing student in the craft of recording, while the less technically inclined Tolhurst and Gallup left Smith alone in the control room and concentrated on getting their parts right. "Simon and Lol weren't as interested, but from a recording point of view, they were experienced; they were well-rehearsed," Thornalley figured, reasonably enough. "They'd obviously done it many times before. That was very refreshing. They knew where things belonged; they knew what was going on."

As Thornalley recalled, Smith spent a lot of time trying to be as actively and creatively involved in the production of the album as possible. As harmless as that sounds, the studio system was then very much stuck in the old school, BBC mindset: the talent's rightful place was on the other side of the glass, while the producer and engineer ruled the control room. Smith's studio attitude bordered on heresy.

"Robert was very interested in the studio and I think, in some respects, he thought it was cool that someone who was a bit younger than him had learned how to use the studio," said Thornalley. "He was always looking over my shoulder; in fact, on that album, he had his hands on the desk. In those days the engineer or the producer would growl at the artist if they got too close. They tried to make it as mystical as possible."

More than most bands, The Cure has a fantastic legacy of myth making. Of all The Cure long-players, *Pornography* remains the one album frequently singled out by converts and critics to be the most tortured and arduous for them to capture on tape. Smith himself added to the aura surrounding *Pornography* by insisting that he spent most of its three weeks' recording completely wasted. "We slept very little during the recording," he said in 2003. "There was a lot of drugs involved." In another interview, Smith insisted that he couldn't even remember making much of the album. "We probably drank and took more drugs than we should have – an interesting process, but one that would kill me now."

If the band's documented history is to be read as the Gospel according to Saint Bob, Lovecat Robert Smith used up several of his nine lives just trying to get the record made. But this theory is based on selective memory and the incredibly bleak and pessimistic gloomscapes captured by Thornalley and the band. A healthy dose of spin, at least on Smith's part, also comes into play. Yet to their first-time producer, making *Pornography* was almost the perfect studio experience: Thornalley spent three weeks (from their one day of demos to the final mix) working with a band who came into the studio fully rehearsed and prepared to make a seriously heavy album. There were no overdoses, no hissy fits, no breakdowns. There was, however, a hefty £1,600 in the recording budget to cover the band's cocaine intake, according to at least one studio staffer whom I spoke to. With Thornally and Nocito un-involved, most nights would begin with several heart-starting lines of blow; sometimes four or five hours would pass before any work was attempted. And Smith wouldn't even consider attempting vocals – which were usually recorded in the very early hours of the morning – unless he was "pretty hammered", as co-engineer (and teetotaller) Nocito would tell me. Yet this was hardly uncharacteristic behaviour for a young rock band in the studio.

"I don't remember [the sessions as] being dark and doomy," Thornalley said. "The music was obviously dark, but as for the process, I don't recall there not being any laughter. I think there was. Maybe Robert was the tortured artist and the others maybe weren't so emotionally involved." Engineer Nocito agreed that it wasn't all gloom and doom during the making of the album, although he did admit that the weather (it was a cruel English winter) and the late hours didn't make for the most ideal working environment. "It's hard to be lively at four in the morning," he told me.

Smith, typically, offered up a much darker version of the album's recording – he likened it to the creepy comic film *Groundhog Day*, where Bill Murray's tortured newsman character is forced to relive the same day time and time again. "You knew what you were going to be doing, what drugs you were going to take," Smith insisted. "You knew how you were going to feel the following morning. It just became a sort of bizarre routine.

"At the time," Smith added, "I lost every friend I had, everyone, without exception, because I was incredibly obnoxious, appalling, self-centred. The tension in the studio was palpable, really. In a strange way it was sort of fun to do because it was so bad." Maybe Smith and Thornalley were recalling different albums: who can really tell?

From my research, the only time Smith and Thornalley truly clashed was very early in the recording. When a session wound down at 9am, the very nocturnal Smith told RAK studio staff to expect him back at 3pm, which gave Thornalley and Nocito the chance to catch only five or six hours of much-needed sleep, at best. Smith did this for several sessions, but rarely rolled into the studio before 8pm. Thornalley, understandably, was fed up and questioned Smith's professionalism. A brief flare-up ensued but, from then on in, Smith was a little more realistic when it came to nominating a starting time. The mood swiftly improved, to the stage where band and RAK staff were allocated nicknames: Thornalley was from then onwards known as "Da Vinci", engineer Nocito was "Mitch" and Smith was "Sandy", named after a *Crossroads* character. (Nocito's nickname has stuck to this day.)

Phil Thornalley believes that Lol Tolhurst has been harshly treated in the documented history of both *Pornography* and the band itself. According to Robert Smith, Tolhurst the drummer was about as useful as trying to clap with one hand tied behind your back. Smith insisted that Tolhurst needed the help of his bandmates just to get through the *Pornography* sessions.

"I don't want to be slanderous," Smith said at a 2003 press conference, before doing just that, "but Lol had, at times, a very limited range."

Smith has also stated that during the *Pornography* sessions he and Gallup chose to stand on either side of Tolhurst, sticks in their hands, drumming with him "because he was physically too weak to do it – and we wanted a big, booming sound". And Smith has repeatedly said that Tolhurst's key role in The Cure was that of band mascot-cum-whipping boy, the willing and frequent target of his and Gallup's scorn. It would seem that his musical role was minimal, almost non-existent. (Smith's views of his fellow Cure founder, admittedly, have been clouded by the court case Tolhurst would later bring against him and the band. It's hard to give a balanced opinion of an obviously pissed-off former confidant when he's dragged you through the courts.)

Thornalley disagrees with Smith's low estimation of Tolhurst's creative worth. Thornalley felt that Tolhurst was a rock-steady drummer, whose solid time-keeping formed the core of *Pornography*'s grim wall of sound (what *NME*'s David Quantick would refer to as "Phil Spector in hell"). "I think Lol was a good drummer; he wasn't a great drummer but he was really, really steady," Thornalley said. And the producer was a reliable witness; he'd been amazed by the sheer number of diabolical drummers in punk and post-punk bands with major record deals who'd recorded at RAK. Most of these so-called time-keepers had trouble staying awake, let alone staying in time. "It was so hard getting good drum sounds because they couldn't play. But Lol could play; he could stay in time and that's the basis of that record, the mantra of the drums. They start off on one pattern and stay there. He was solid; he kept up that two-bar riff."

"Lol was limited but that doesn't mean someone's not good," continued Thornalley. "It's a shame. His work on those earlier albums is unique and that's kind of what you want to be when you're a musician."

Engineer Nocito agreed with this take on Tolhurst. "Everybody knew Lol wasn't a great drummer, but he was great for The Cure. If Boris [Williams, future Cure drummer] had played on *Pornography*, the record wouldn't have been anything." (Post *Pornography*, when Nocito saw the band on tour – he even recorded a Glasgow show on the RAK mobile recording unit – he would continue to be in awe of Tolhurst's fists-of-iron. "I remember being so impressed by Lol, because you kept wondering if the thing was going to fall apart, yet somehow he kept it all together.")

Tolhurst told me that his so-called "mantra of the drums" was, in part, the result of buying new gear. He'd bought a huge snare drum, somewhere between 10 and 12 inches deep, from The Specials' drummer John Bradbury. He also acknowledged that the room they used in RAK was perfect for the cavernous rumble of the drums that can be heard all over the album. "We just wanted something that was very powerful," he said. "This room we used in RAK had this huge ceiling; it made them much louder and reverberant. It fitted the tone of the material.

"The songs were pretty sharp and angst-filled; the big booming sound seemed right. It was one of my favourite memories playing drums. It was angry but restrained as well; we wanted to make the ultimate, intense album. I can't remember exactly why, but we did."

During their several weeks of recording *Pornography*, The Cure adopted a siege mentality. They decided to bunker down in the Fiction offices, which weren't too far from the RAK Studios. Smith made himself a tent-like construction in one room of the Fiction camp, situated on the floor behind a settee. He'd fastened a blanket to the wall with a drawing pin, which created a sort of rough and ready lean-to. And he was very much the master of his domain.

"We took over Fiction and wouldn't let anyone in the door," Smith recalled in *Ten Imaginary Years*. "I had all these little bits, things I'd found in the street and taken back to my nest. It really got out of hand."

When Tolhurst, Gallup and roadie Gary Biddles weren't holed up in their own room at Fiction HQ, or hoovering their way through their £1,600 of coke (the budget was topped up after a week, apparently), they were building a mountain of beer cans in the corner of RAK Studios, or distracting Smith with their sloshed off-mic capers. At the time, the rest of the band was thrown by Smith's seriousness, although Gallup would eventually understand his attitude. "He had to concentrate 20 hours of the day and we only had to do it for 12." (Thornalley: "Robert resented that because he was trying to make a statement.")

156

At the end of each night's recording, Thornalley was under strict directions to stop the cleaners from touching the sky-high pile of beer cans. He was, however, allowed to usher into the studio some Cure fans who worked at a nearby off-licence; they had the plum job of delivering the band's nightly supply of beer. To The Cure, this aluminium edifice marked the progress of the album just as vividly as the tapes of each song. "It was very difficult to explain to the cleaner every day – 'don't touch the cans'," Thornalley said. "The stench must have been appalling." Engineer Nocito learned a tough lesson when he attempted to clean up this rapidly expanding mess: Parry gave him a serious dressing-down. "I think he might have let me empty them, though," Nocito laughed.

"We built this mountain of empties in the corner," Smith said, "a gigantic pile of debris. It just grew and grew." Smith still has a photo of their beer can Himalaya, as does Tolhurst.

Despite Smith's assertions that his fragile state of mind had reached breaking point during the making of *Pornography*, Thornalley recalled that there was only one break during the three weeks. And that was because Smith underestimated the potency of some industrial-strength acid that he'd swallowed when the coke ran out – it wasn't due to any type of mental collapse or tortured artist syndrome. "Yes, some very strong acid was dropped," Thornalley confirmed with a laugh. "There was a complete lack of focus [for one day] but then everything came back to normal." As normal as life could be in the midst of all-night binges and a five-foot-high pile of beer cans, of course.

"I remember getting to the studio," Tolhurst said, "and I'm sitting in a chair. Robert's at my feet and he suddenly started laughing uncontrollably. I turned to Phil and said, 'Oh dear, I don't think we'll be recording today.' Robert spent the next two days hidden behind the couch under a pile of sheets."

In spite of The Cure's football-team-worthy consumption of ale and Colombia's finest both during and after each recording session, Thornalley only witnessed one night of genuine Caligula-like behaviour. And even then it was when the sessions were over and The Cure hooked up with the Banshees and fellow Fiction labelmates The Associates for a monumental post-sessions piss-up. Producer Mike Hedges also joined the party, as did Ric Gallup, who organised a special screening of *Carnage Visors* for the night (he'd just done likewise during the album's mixing, screening the film on the RAK studio wall). "That was pretty debauched," Thornalley said quietly.

As for inner-band politics, if there was any serious tension within The Cure it completely bypassed Thornalley. The Cure didn't seem to bear any grudges, either, because former members Matthieu Hartley and Michael Dempsey visited the band during the making of the record. However, Thornalley did have a pretty thick skin, which rendered him immune to any in-fighting, if it did exist. "I'd been in situations with The Psychedelic Furs where there were fist-fights in the studio," he told me. "I was kind of numb to the band politics that were going on." As for engineer Nocito, he was impressed by Smith's quick wit and stunned by his deeply sarcastic nature. Tolhurst, in particular, would be the frequent victim of Smith's vocal sparring. Interestingly though, Nocito felt that the bond between Tolhurst and Smith was tighter than that between Smith and Gallup. "Lol and Robert were very close," Nocito told me. "Simon, if anything, was the easiest to talk to of the band."

In fact, Lol Tolhurst could sense that the sheer intensity of the music they were making, and the band's strong focus on making the album, had started to drive a wedge between Smith and Gallup. By the end of the subsequent tour, they'd resort to speaking with their fists. "By *Pornography* it was still very much democratic but the very nature of what we were doing made it difficult, especially between Robert and Simon," said Tolhurst. "Simon liked to come to the studio, play whatever he had to play and then relax, but the very nature of *Pornography* meant we had to be on all the time. That was the seed right there of Simon's departure. It was a very intense time."

Chris Parry, meanwhile, once more kept his distance during the making of the album. Maybe being the number two target of Smith's sarcasm – " 'Bill' would get it almost more than anybody," Nocito said – made him wary. He only intervened when it dawned on him that there obviously wasn't another 'Boys Don't Cry' or 'A Forest' amongst the album's nine dense tracks. The chance of extracting a single from *Pornography* was about as likely as clearing away The Cure's beer-can mountain. Parry admitted that he was bored by the album, with the possible exception of the track 'A Strange Day'. He'd wander into the sessions at 10 o'clock most nights, but could only endure a few hours before heading for the door. At the same time Parry understood the simple necessity of a song for radio, and thought he could salvage something from 'The Hanging Garden'. He instructed both his star and Thornalley to polish the song. Thornalley and Smith tried, but the producer feels that it was time (and money) wasted.

"Under pressure from Chris Parry we [worked on] 'Hanging Garden'" – which was finally released as a single in July 1982, clawing its way to number 32 on the UK chart – "to add something more catchy. I think we spent more time on that [than any other track on the album] trying to make it more palatable to radio programmers." These were the same radio programmers, of course, who were currently spinning such hits as Bananarama's 'Shy Boy' and Hot Chocolate's 'It Started With A Kiss'. A ditty about the "purity of animals fucking", set to some primal jungle drums, was always going to be a tough sell.

But Smith was on a different wavelength to Parry. Although he wasn't averse to a hit record, he simply wasn't as obsessed by the charts. His dream was to create an album that would be seen as a statement of serious artistic intent from a songwriter hoping to say something more profound than "boys don't cry". And if it didn't work, then fuck it, The Cure was over and he'd move on.

Though Thornalley admits that he didn't really connect with Smith's message – "I didn't know what he was on about, frankly; I was 21 and wasn't on the same emotional level with him in any sense, emotionally or artistically" – they did bond when it came to sonic exploration. He and Smith would experiment with what were then known as "found sounds", a concept that was introduced to the mainstream by the recent release *My Life In The Bush Of Ghosts*. This landmark album was a collaboration between a pair of like-minded rock'n'roll eggheads, Talking Heads' David Byrne and studio pioneer (and erstwhile Roxy Music keyboardist) Brian Eno.

Inspired by this ground-breaking LP, Smith and Thornalley would flick between TV stations, searching for random grabs of noise to record and incorporate into *Pornography*'s murky soundscape. During one night of exploring, they not only found the perfect sound bite, but also chanced upon the album's title, when they discovered a televised debate between two unlikely opponents: feminist Germaine Greer and *Monty Python* comic Graham Chapman. Their discussion topic was, of course, pornography. A few seconds of their "deconstructed" version of the debate can be heard at the opening of *Pornography*'s title track.

"It was one of those very weird coincidences," said Thornalley. "Around that time it was considered quite cool to put a microphone next to the television and record whatever as a kind of effects track. It just so happened that the discussion we recorded was a debate about pornography. A very strange coincidence."

Polydor, who were responsible for distributing and marketing the band's releases through Parry's Fiction label, weren't that impressed by the title *Pornography*. When *NME* revealed the album's proposed name in early March, a humourless Polydor spokesman made this comment: "Whether or not it actually goes out under that title remains to be seen."

The title of the new Cure album, however, was a minor concern for both Polydor and Parry when they were given a preview of the album at Mike Hedges' new Camden studio, The Playground. If *Seventeen Seconds* and *Faith* had suggested that you were listening to a band dealing with some genuine pain, *Pornography* was the sound of death, pure and simple. Parry summed it up when he stated: "The first album was done in naivety, the second with clear cut-vision, the third under difficulty and *Pornography* was all those three rolled into one. It was a mess." (Parry may have taken some consolation from the fact that *Pornography*, unlike *Faith*, came in on budget, even if there was plenty of red ink in the column marked "cocaine".)

Smith, as he had with 'Charlotte Sometimes' and 'Killing An Arab' and 'At Night' before that, drew some of his lyrical ideas from the literature he was consuming at the time (when he wasn't frying his brain, of course). During a break on the Picture Tour, Smith had become obsessed with books on psychiatry, clinical insanity and what he categorised as "mental health in general". The line "a charcoal face bites my hand", which emerges from the sonic murk of the track 'A Short Term Effect', was lifted directly from his most recent reading.

But as Tolhurst explained earlier, the ideas behind other *Pornography* tracks came from actual life experiences: 'The Hanging Garden' documented yet another wild night for Robert Smith, when he wandered around his family's garden, stark naked, after hearing what he thought was the noise of cats outside. Smith would later note that 'The Hanging Garden' also dealt with "the purity and hate of animals fucking . . . seeing someone fucking a monkey doesn't particularly shock me". The track 'Siamese Twins' – Smith cut the vocal with Mary Poole looking on – was inspired by something similar. As for 'A Strange Day', it was, in Smith's words, "how I would feel if it would only be the end of the world". 'Cold' was directly influenced by Smith's hefty drug consumption of the past two years, as were parts of 'A Short Term Effect'. And the lyric for 'The Figurehead' came to Smith after a Hamlet-like experience during the making of the woeful 'Charlotte Sometimes' video, when he unearthed a skull in the disused asylum that was the shoot's location. Alas poor Yorick, indeed.

As uplifting as all this sounds, Smith's po-faced lyrics were nothing compared to the barely alive dirges contained within *Pornography*. The album opened with 'One Hundred Years', a song that Smith characterised as a soundtrack to "pure self-loathing and worthlessness". And few albums began with an opening line as overbearingly nihilistic as "it doesn't matter if we all die". It was a mission statement that The Cure swore by. "Nihilism took over," Simon Gallup would state many years later, when asked about the *Pornography* period. "We sang 'it doesn't matter if we all die' and that is exactly what we thought at the time." Smith explained it this way: "If I hadn't written those songs, I would have become a fat, useless bastard. I went through a period of thinking everyone was fucked and then I started to write these songs. I channelled all the self-destructive elements of my personality into doing something."

If the robotic rhythms of Lol Tolhurst and Smith's mercilessly bleak opening line made 'One Hundred Years' a tough introduction to *Pornography*, the track went even further downhill from there. In an increasingly gloomy frame of mind, Smith wailed about the killing of patriots, unspecified pain and dread, and, curiously, morbid laughter while a small object tumbles from someone's mouth as the track built in intensity like the whirring of a dentist's drill. As miserable as 'One Hundred Years' was – many view both the track and its parent album *Pornography* as the sound that launched a million Goths – Smith does use the song to drive his point home: from here on in, even more so than *Faith* or *Seventeen Seconds*, this is uneasy listening. The ultimate "fuck off" album had begun.

Tolhurst's truly primal thumping of the tubs is dead centre of the mix during the following track, 'A Short Term Effect'. Teamed with the wooden-legged, almost atonal bass of Gallup and another of Smith's

161

howling-into-the-abyss vocals, the effect is incredibly claustrophobic. Again, Smith dealt in scattershot images rather than finely crafted rhyming couplets as he spat out lyrics that in their evocation of a covering of earth suggested nothing less than a funeral. This was intoned as readily as The Beatles once harmonised "won't you pleeeeeaaase help me", and it was genuinely creepy, the sound of a man slowly unravelling.

'The Hanging Garden', the track Parry had earmarked as the album's one commercial possibility, swiftly followed, but you'd hardly say it offered any respite from what came before. When Smith barked "fall fall fall fall into the walls" it's as if he's opened the door to one of his worst nightmares, which was really saying something. The pace of Tolhurst's jungle drums is upped just a notch here, but the overall sound is as overwhelming and unrelenting as anything else on the album – or anything else that would be heard during this year of the Goth, when not only The Cure, but expat Aussies The Birthday Party (*Junkyard*), Smith's strange pal Lydia Lunch (*The Agony Is The Ecstasy*), Siouxsie & The Banshees (*A Kiss In The Dreamhouse*) and the Pete Murphy-led Bauhaus (*The Sky's Gone Out*) all unleashed the dogs. There were others waiting in the wings, too: within a year, The Birthday Party barked out their *The Bad Seed* EP, while The Creatures – whom *NME* would tag "the Sonny and Cher of the psychiatric ward" – delivered *Feast* and the Southern Death Cult released their self-titled debut. It was the best of times, it was the most Goth of times.

'Siamese Twins' continued where 'The Hanging Garden' left off: it was not so much a song as a death march, the merciless plod of Tolhurst's toms teamed with a rare splash of keyboards (all three members played keys during the sessions). Even the act of lovemaking is reduced to something primal, brutal and ugly by Smith, as he coughs up lines about writhing beneath a red light and the Siamese twins of the title as if he were describing a sweaty wrestling match. Halfway through the song he effectively gave up, moaning how it would be best for him to be left to expire since he'll soon be forgotten. No wonder the black trenchcoat brigade took to *Pornography* like moggies to catnip: Smith had written the guidebook to eternal damnation. 'Siamese Twins' typified just how grim this album truly was.

A brief moment of respite followed, as Smith's squiggly guitar line brought a rare suggestion of melody to 'The Figurehead', but his vocal was still delivered from an emotionally cold and distant place. He twice repeated a line about meaning nothing as if they were the last half a dozen words he would have the chance to utter, while the song plodded ever onwards to the closing mantra about never being uncontaminated again. As hard a listen as *Pornography* was, full marks to The Cure for their dogged pursuit of a single sound: this psychodrama of an album rarely wavered in tone during its 35 grim minutes.

'A Strange Day', not surprisingly, is more of the unholy same, yet another soundtrack to the demons that were doing in the head of Robert Smith (so much so, as it turns out, that only a few notes in, Smith actually announces the fragmentation of his head). As with 'The Figurehead' before it, Smith makes a half concession to melody with another wiry, knotty guitar line – you'd hardly call it a riff – but it's half-submerged beneath another of his venomous lyrics. This time he depicts a day where he stumbles into deep waters. Smith believed there was no way out – although, admittedly, he wasn't ready to go the way of Ian Curtis.

'Cold', the next track, lived up to its name; it was a creaking, slowly creeping ode to nothingness, in which Smith howled into the void how he was in an embryonic state, dreaming of being interred and becoming a memorial to bygone days with all the walking-corpse-like blankness of The Sister Of Mercy's Andrew Eldritch. Yet unlike Eldritch – who was still a few years away from his own Goth rock masterwork, 1987's *Floodland* – it was hard to believe there was even the hint of a sense of humour, albeit morbid, at play here: if Smith really wanted to kill off The Cure, he'd just written their eulogy.

But wait, there's more: the title track then brought this epic downer to a thankless close. It opened with the muffled snatches of the Germaine Greer/Graham Chapman debate, as sampled by Smith and Thornalley, before it locked into yet another of the band's thudding, ill-tempered grooves. Should this continue, Smith warns, the outcome will be fatal. It was the perfect kiss-off from an album that had "band suicide" smeared over it in the blood of Tolhurst, Gallup and Smith. That much said, there was just the briefest ray of light in this closing track to the album that would effectively be the last rites of The Cure, Mk 1, as Smith vowed to fight his melancholic blues and, inevitably, find his cure. What Smith couldn't have known was that that cure would come in the shape of an eccentric English videomaker and a totally different musical outlook of his own. But that was some way off in the distance.

Pornography would prove to be enormously influential. Several decades later it would be namechecked as a career-starter by such nu-metal monsters as The Deftones and System Of A Down. And those who considered themselves true Cure lovers, not just blow-ins seduced by the pop songs and big hair, firmly believed that *Pornography* was the definitive Cure album.

Of course it was a tough sell on its release in May 1982, even though the album reached a chart high for the band, peaking at number nine. As *Rolling Stone*'s Mark Coleman would astutely point out in 1995, albeit with the benefit of hindsight: "Though *Pornography* is revered by Cureheads as a masterstroke, normal listeners will probably find it impenetrable." *Pornography* turned out to be the kind of album – just like Lou Reed's junkie soap opera, *Berlin*, or Bowie's coke-fuelled *Low* – that required some distance and a good few years of music history to be really appreciated.

Reviews filed some 20 years later typically found much more to like about the album than critics did in 1982. The following review typified that revisionist attitude: "With *Pornography*, [Smith] entered the downward spiral that prompted the greatest music of his career. The title track is sheer hell as Smith abandons music altogether. But the remaining tracks are among the finest the Eighties had to offer. 'One Hundred Years', with its grinding riff, 'Siamese Twins', with its stuttering beat, and 'The Figurehead' ("I laughed in the mirror for the first time in a year") are Gothic studies in terror par excellence. Nothing sounded like *Pornography*, not even other Cure records." *Uncut* followed suit in August 2004. "On its release," they noted in the midst of a Cure cover story, as the band entered a third wave of popularity, "*Pornography* was met with bafflement and disgust. It's actually a masterpiece of claustrophobic self-loathing."

But in the summer of 1982, *Pornography* was a hard album to love. In his *NME* review, which ran on May 8, Dave Hill opened with this warning: "It [*Pornography*] won't improve your social life or relieve you of your load, and this music proves an antidote to nothing much at all, though it may clear out your system . . . this record portrays and parades its currency of exposed futility and naked fear with so few distractions or adornments and so little sense of shame. It really piles it on." Though a great deal more reverential than Paul Morley's demolition job on *Three Imaginary Boys*, it was hardly a glowing recommendation from Hill, especially in light of the praise heaped on the Banshees' *A Kiss In The Dreamhouse* LP, which emerged a few months later. "Beyond all wildest hopes and dreams," *Melody Maker*'s Steve Sutherland noted when dissecting the Banshees' third and best-known album, "beyond all past suggestions and momentum, beyond all standards set this year, *Dreamhouse* is an intoxicating achievement." It was pretty clear who was top of the Goth rock hierarchy: and it wasn't Crawley's Three Imaginary Boys.

Yet, perversely, *Pornography* became a hit, of sorts, somehow finding its place in the UK Top 10 alongside such far more chart-friendly acts as ABC, Madness, Duran Duran and Malcolm McLaren's latest creation, Bow Wow Wow. The latter's oddly beguiling and wildly catchy 'I Want Candy' was fast becoming the summer anthem of 1982, along with such other hits as 'Happy Talk', a reworking of the Rodgers & Hammerstein song from *South Pacific* by Damned outcast Captain Sensible, and Yazoo's 'Don't Go'. Robert Smith might have felt decidedly uncomfortable in the pop spotlight, but producer Phil Thornalley, for one, was chuffed with *Pornography*'s small-scale success. "That was my first effort as producer – and my name was on the charts," he told me, just as thrilled 20 years later.

The Cure, meanwhile, had more pressing matters to deal with. They had yet another tour lined up, which would consume the trio for the best part of three months. The Fourteen Explicit Moments Tour began to cast its ghoulish spell with shows at the Printemps de Bourges on April 10 and at the Top Rank Skating Bowl in Plymouth on April 18, with Zerra 1 opening the night. Even at this early stage of the itinerary, Smith had some inner-band tension to deal with – Tolhurst may have been the usual recipient of Smith's razor-sharp sarcasm, but The Cure frontman had really started to fall out with Gallup.

"*Pornography* was an intense period of mindlessness," Smith would go on to admit. "I was just full of rage. I felt I hadn't achieved what I wanted to. I thought everything was coming to an end. I hated Simon – who was my lifelong friend – more than anyone else in the world. The whole thing was a complete mess." And Smith's growing camaraderie with Steve Severin wasn't doing The Cure any favours, either.

Severin's idea of a good time was to hang around backstage at Cure shows and either hide Tolhurst's drinks or spike them with LSD. At the same time he'd be in Smith's ear, trying to entice him over to the Banshees' ranks as a full-time member. "I was always asking Robert to disband The Cure and join the Banshees," Severin admitted. "I was definitely sowing the seeds of discontent."

Tolhurst, interestingly, had no problems with Severin, despite his divisive role in the world of The Cure. "I love Steve," Tolhurst said as recently as 2005. "We had many a crazy night on tour or in clubland. [But] given the Banshees' history with guitarists, I'm sure he thought about luring Robert away."

Their setlist from that opening show in Plymouth exposed Smith and The Cure's miserable mindset at the time, as did Porl Thompson's grisly painting of animals falling from the sky, which fluttered behind the band. The plan had been to use Thompson's image – clearly influenced by the lyrics of 'The Hanging Garden' – as the album art, but he missed the deadline. So they enlarged the image which Thompson had painted, and used it as the stage backdrop instead. 'The Holy Hour', which opened most of the Picture Tour shows, had been ditched as the set opener, replaced by the equally morbid 'The Figurehead'. 'M', 'Cold' and 'The Drowning Man' followed in rapid, relentless succession. Clearly intent on pleasing no one but themselves, The Cure then plunged even deeper into the murky existential waters of their recent albums, as they worked through 'A Short Term Effect' and 'The Hanging Garden'. In fact, they were a good eight songs deep into the set before they unleashed something resembling a hit, 1981's 'Primary', only to head deeper into the gloom with 'Siamese Twins', 'One Hundred Years', 'Play For Today', 'A Forest' and 'Pornography'. Reluctantly, they tacked on two older, more familiar tracks, '10.15 Saturday Night' and 'Killing An Arab', before signing off with 'Forever', a rarely heard (and unrecorded) track.

Both the running order and the setlist rarely changed as the band moved through Bristol, Brighton, Southampton, Sheffield and New-castle. When *Pornography* finally made the record stores, they were in London, playing a 20-song set at the Hammersmith Odeon. By this time the band had fully embraced their recently introduced onstage look, which would soon become a Cure signature: they smeared cherry-red lipstick around their eyes and mouths, which would smudge and run as soon as the stage lights kicked in, giving the impression that the trio were bleeding. "[It looked] like we'd been smacked in the face," said Smith. It seemed the perfect look to accompany the torrid, ugly music they were making.

Tolhurst, Gallup and Smith were also at the early stages of their big-haired period. Heavily inspired by the skyscraping flat-top that actor Jack Nance sported in *Eraserhead*, David Lynch's eccentric freak-out-cum-nightmare of a film, Smith and Gallup, especially, were starting to test the acceptable limits of just how high their hair could reach, while Tolhurst – whose locks were naturally curly – adopted a style that made him look like a drink-sodden Byron. (The puffy sleeves that the band would soon sport pushed that image to its logical fashion-victim conclusion.) But that was yet to come: at the time of *Fourteen Explicit Moments*, the trio's towering hair and bleeding-face make-up exacerbated the impact of the brutal music they were unleashing on the public. This was a freak show.

Melody Maker's Steve Sutherland, a music correspondent embedded deep inside Goth rock territory, unleashed a written assault on the band's latest tour that made Paul Morley's slagging seem little more than empty words. "Seldom have three young people in pursuit of a clutch of aimless atmospheres achieved so little with such panache," he wrote. "The Cure – that's a joke. More like a symptom." Reluctantly, Sutherland accepted that his word meant nothing to The Cure faithful, lost children who lapped up all this ghoulishness, but that didn't stop him describing Tolhurst, Smith and Gallup as "three updated Al Stewart bedsitter boy students [ouch] squeezing their pimples and translating Camus prose into Shelleyian stanzas." In short, he thought The Cure sucked.

NME were a little less brutal when they covered the band's show at The Dome in Brighton on the night of Smith's 22nd birthday. Smith had obviously liked his and Thornalley's experiment in "found sound", because the band recycled the strange, garbled gurgles at both the beginning and end of 'Pornography', which closed their set (they returned with a three song encore of '10.15', 'Killing An Arab' and 'Forever'). But critic Richard Cook could sense some dissent in the ranks of The Cure. "The Cure felt dissatisfied with this performance," he wrote. "Smith, on his birthday, looked dejected and tired. If this is second-string Cure then their best must be very close to the edge."

Oh how right Cook was: The Cure was so close to the edge that a hefty push and a few ill-chosen words would have destroyed them completely. As Fourteen Explicit Moments headed to the continent on May 5 – their Rotterdam show at De Doelen being their first since the Hammersmith Odeon – some major cracks were opening up. There were any number of contributing factors: Gallup blamed the European heat and the intensity of the music; Smith believed that Gallup had started to taunt Tolhurst because "he couldn't get to me", while faithful roadie Gary Biddles felt that part of the problem was Gallup's increasing popularity with audiences. Smith also felt that Gallup was jealous of the increased attention he was receiving as Cure frontman.

And Smith was still being eaten up by the realisation that, unlike Ian Curtis, he wasn't prepared to make the ultimate sacrifice for his music. He had what he would later describe as a "genuine passion for being alive. Life never got that painful for me," Smith said. "Even when the void opened up before me, I always thought, 'The sun will rise whether I'm here or not, so I may as well be here for as long as I can and try to find some enjoyment.'" But Smith did feel the heavy weight that came with The Cure not being regarded as "serious" as Joy Division because they chose life over death – as stupid and puerile as that seems. He was learning that rock'n'roll was a fickle business, even in matters as weighty as life and death.

Whatever the cause of their tension, this once-tight combo were now solitary men. After most shows, Gallup preferred to hitch a ride with The Cure crew rather than travel with his bandmates, while Smith was spending more and more time alone, holding up the bar in numerous hotels before retiring to drain his mini bar, occasionally sleeping it off in the bath.

During the Picture Tour they'd sometimes fought with audiences, but now The Cure was fighting with everyone – with each other, surly staff in European clubs, even the occasional biker gang. Smith, in particular, had crawled away from some of these clashes very much bruised and battered. Even members of their crew were throwing the odd punch at each other in anger. By the time the bloodied and disgruntled Cure bandwagon rolled into Strasbourg on May 27, for a show at Hall Tivoli, almost everyone involved was eagerly anticipating the end of the tour, which was just two weeks away in Brussels.

After yet another brutal show, played to a bewildered audience,

Gallup and Smith were drinking on separate floors of a Strasbourg club. Gallup, along with his new buddies in the road crew, was finishing up for the night when he was told by a member of the bar staff that he hadn't paid for his drinks. Gallup, apparently, had been mistaken for Smith – the usual conflicting evidence, however, doesn't clearly indicate exactly who was in the wrong. Whatever the case, Gallup decided he'd had enough of Smith, so he walked over to his Cure bandmate and thumped him.

As Gallup saw it, Smith had seemed oblivious to his dilemma. "I was knackered but the [barman] took me up to the bar and Robert appeared to see what was going on. I hit him, he responded and we had a fight."

"He didn't want to pay for his drinks because he thought I wasn't paying for mine," Smith explained. "I told him to shut up and he punched me. It was the first time he really laid into me; we had an enormous ruck."

Lol Tolhurst, meanwhile, was holding up the bar with members of Zerra 1. "I was talking with Paul and Grimmo of the opening band," Tolhurst said to me. "Someone came over and said, 'I think there's been a fight and Simon and Robert have left the club.' I thought I'd carry on because I was having a nice time. When I got up the next morning, the tour manager told me that they'd both gone; they'd got separate flights home.

"I thought about putting a wig on [Zerra 1's] Paul Bell, playing a tape of the previous night and keeping the lights low, [that way] we could keep going. I thought better of it and a couple of days later they came back and finished the tour. But the writing was on the wall for Simon."

Smith's father also had a hand in keeping the show on its rocky road. When Smith unexpectedly arrived on his doorstep, he lectured his son on his responsibilities as an entertainer. "People have bought tickets," Smith senior admonished his son. "Get right back out on tour."

But the damage was very clearly done. The Cure was headed for a serious fall and it was impossible for anyone to stop it from happening. The inevitable crash happened on June 11 at the Ancienne Belgique in Brussels at the last show of the Fourteen Explicit Moments Tour. Backstage, a clearly fed up Smith announced that he was going to be the drummer for the evening's show. Gallup figured that if Smith were going to be contrary, he'd do likewise: therefore he was going to play guitar. Tolhurst walked over and strapped on Gallup's bass. Though no one would say it out loud, there was an air of finality: the three could sense that this was the end of The Cure, possibly forever. So rather than go out with a whimper, they chose to say goodbye with a racket. "I thought, 'I'm not going through this pantomime,'" Smith revealed. "I knew it was the last chance we had to make this memorable in the worst possible way. I'd never played the drums in public; I don't think Lol knew which way a bass went."

Somehow the set proceeded, the newly configured band reeling off such 1982 standards as 'Siamese Twins', 'Primary' and 'One Hundred Years' in rapid succession. But by the time the quarrelsome Cure could begin their last song, 'Pornography', roadie Gary Biddles – who was very much from the Gallup camp – grabbed the mic. He had a simple message for the crowd: "Robert Smith is a cunt." (Smith insisted he also shouted: "Tolhurst's a wanker.") Smith, still in a violent frame of mind, threw his drumsticks at Biddles, striking him in the head; then Gallup jumped into the fray. Tolhurst, meanwhile, brushed his curls out of his eyes and continued grappling with his bass. "That was pretty morose that night," Tolhurst recalled. "I think Gary Biddles was jumping around the stage saying various things about Robert and I. He was part of the Gallup alliance." When the melee had finally been halted, the three knew that the dream was well and truly over. As far as Robert Smith was concerned, The Cure was dead.

"By the end of the tour, we weren't in the best of health mentally," Smith wildly understated when asked in 2003 about the brawl that ended the first stage of The Cure's career. "Night after night playing those songs – most nights after the shows were pretty demented as a response to what we were doing musically. I was in a really depressed frame of mind; I was taking an awful lot of drugs – anything and every-thing [bar heroin, Smith has stated more than once]. Inevitably, it sent your mental equilibrium awry."

Tolhurst admitted that their drug consumption wasn't helping the band's problems, but felt their troubles ran deeper than whatever they were putting up their noses. "I don't think it [coke] makes people reasonable; it exacerbates things. But I also think the problems were there and would have come out sooner or later." He also felt part of the band's problems related to the timing of the tour – *Pornography* hadn't been released in many of their ports of call, which meant they were playing unfamiliar songs to unprepared crowds.

"The main thing that's true is that it was the first tour we'd been on without releasing the album [to coincide]," Tolhurst said. "We were touring and playing the songs for an album that nobody had heard. They'd booked us into some huge halls in Europe and there we were playing songs that nobody knew in places that were half full. And we were perhaps not in the best frame of mind; maybe we should have taken a break before going out on tour."

As for Smith, he was dissatisfied with the music his band was playing – he felt they were seriously underachieving. "I was really disappointed with what we were doing," he said. "I thought we should be going somewhere else, not in success terms, but I thought we should be making music that was on a par with Mahler symphonies, not pop music. I just felt that I was not doing what I wanted to do. [It was] your classic early twenties crisis."

But the truth was this: Robert Smith had succeeded brilliantly. His master plan for *Pornography* was to cut the ultimate fuck-off album, a stark, raw, fearless farewell. Not only had he achieved that, thereby alienating many of The Cure faithful, but he'd also managed to drive a bloody stake right into the heart of The Cure themselves.

As soon as the crew had cleared away the debris from their final show of the tour, Tolhurst, Smith and Gallup were on a flight home, Smith sleeping all the way. When they landed at Heathrow, a grumpy Smith turned to Gallup and mumbled a cursory "bye" to his bandmate and close pal. The two Cure allies wouldn't exchange another word for 18 months.

Chapter Eight

"My reaction to all those people who thought that The Cure could only be pessimistic and predictable was to make a demented and calculated song like 'Let's Go To Bed'."

– Robert Smith

HIS band may have been falling apart around him, but in one crucial aspect, Robert Smith was a lucky man. Over the past three years and three Cure albums he'd suffered a very public meltdown and done his best to alienate his audience, his friends and his bandmates. But the one constant in his life was Mary Poole, his long-time girlfriend. Even when he'd sunk lower than he thought possible, with The Cure having crashed and burned at the end of a period Smith described as "more like a rugby tour than a Cure tour", Poole stood by her man. Smith was smart enough to recognise her remarkable, unswerving faith in him and acknowledge how much she helped him keep his head together.

"I was quite out of sync, a bit disturbed," Smith said of his hard times in the early Eighties. "I knew then that Mary was the girl for me, because she stuck by me. But everyone I know reaches a point where they throw out their arms and go berserk for a while – otherwise you never know what your limits are. I was just trying to find mine."*

By mid-1982, Smith truly believed that he couldn't sink any lower: he had some major healing to do. "I'd reached a spiritual low point around that time," he'd confess. "Inevitably there followed a physical decline. I couldn't be bothered any more. It took quite a few different things to bring me out again." Poole, of course, was the one person who could get through to Smith and help him recover. "Mary was the

---

* Smith would repay Poole's loyalty many times over as The Cure's commercial worth increased, sometimes in very material ways. Allegedly he once renegotiated the band's record label deal with a proviso: that a jet-black Porsche be delivered to Poole before he put pen to paper.

biggest motivating force," Smith agreed. "There's a great advantage in knowing someone for so long, being the same age and from the same background. You know what the other person means and what they're going through." But Smith was a pessimist at heart and realised that it would take more than physical comfort and soothing words to help him out of his existential funk. "They can't tell you that everything is going to be all right because you both know, deep down, that it probably won't be all right. At the same time, it was good having someone I didn't have to pretend to. I had no reason to be anything other than what I was."

Smith had returned from the Fourteen Explicit Moments Tour a physical wreck, a 23-year-old with worrying drug, booze and psychological problems. Unlike previous years, where he'd simply thrown himself back into the music, this time he paid attention to what his body and head were telling him: he needed a break, and badly. After briefly checking in with the Banshees – whose company Smith clearly preferred over his pissed-off Cure brothers – who were making their *Kiss In The Dreamhouse* album, he and Mary disappeared for a month's camping-cum-detox in Wales. (Smith's brother Richard had bought a farm there.) During this holiday, Smith abstained from all mind-alterers – although beer was permitted, of course. Tolhurst, meanwhile, drifted through Europe for several weeks, while a disgruntled Gallup returned to his Horley crew at the King's Head pub, uncertain about his musical future.

Chris Parry and Fiction had more immediate concerns: they needed their cash cow, The Cure, to keep generating product. Accordingly, 'The Hanging Garden' was finally released as a single in July, in a rich assortment of seven-inch (backed with a live take on 'Killing An Arab' from the Manchester Apollo gig on April 27) and bonus-track versions. It was even packaged as a four-song double pack, with a gatefold sleeve, which also included the live version of 'Arab' along with 'A Forest'. (During 1983, 'The Hanging Garden' would be The Cure's first Japanese release. In late 1982, as part of a four-track release called 'The Singles', it would be the band's final Australian release on Stunn Records, the label run by Parry's school pal Terry Condon.)

The single did reasonable business for a band that was as good as dead, reaching number 34 on the UK singles chart. It wasn't exactly causing nightmares for such chart-toppers as Irene Cara's 'Fame' and

Hot Chocolate's 'It Started With A Kiss', but its middling success demonstrated that despite Smith's best efforts, not all Cure fans were completely alienated by the band's self-destructive rampage. *NME* journalist Adrian Thrills, however, was not among the converts. "The Cure have drifted disappointingly and indulgently from the idyllic pop invention of their younger days," he wrote with some scorn, "a decline in standards reinforced by the inclusion of the original versions of 'Killing An Arab' and 'A Forest' on one portion of this double pack." Thrills may have been wrong on some minor points – the recordings of 'Arab' and 'A Forest' were live takes – but his point was well made. It seemed that even Chris Parry lacked the confidence in The Cure's new music; what other reason was there to include these old standards on the band's latest release?

Chris Parry was going through a marriage break-up during the second half of 1982, which may have been some motivation for him to try to keep The Cure together: what could be worse than losing both your wife and your flagship band? The cash would prove useful, too. So Parry made a key decision. If Smith wanted to kill off The Cure as their fans knew it, Parry reasoned, then why not try to reinvent the band? His master plan was for them to lighten up on the bleakness and delve deeper into the pure sense of melody that had carried such early tunes as 'Boys Don't Cry'. All Parry now had to do was get the band back together.

It wasn't hard for Parry to talk Tolhurst around: there was none of the tension in their relationship (at least at this stage) that existed between Smith and the Fiction head. Tolhurst would frequently visit the Fiction offices and Parry would take the time to inform him as to exactly where it all went wrong for The Cure. Surprisingly, it wasn't that much harder to convince Smith that reinventing The Cure as a pop band was a good idea. As Parry stated in *Ten Imaginary Years*, "It appealed to Robert because he wanted to destroy The Cure anyway; he was up for it."

But before The Cure could undergo their makeover, Smith had two more immediate tasks to undertake: one musical, one dictatorial. The magazine *Flexi-Pop* had approached Smith about recording a song for a promotional flexi-disc. Because The Cure didn't actually exist at the time, Smith asked Severin to help him record a mournful tune called 'Lament', which he'd written while in Wales with Mary. They pieced it together during a one-off session at London's Garden Studios; the flexi-disc was given away with *Flexi-Pop* issue 22, which featured ABC's Martin Fry in a studied, studly pose on the cover.*

Smith's next step, as he gradually re-immersed himself in a musical world that as recently as July he'd "despaired about", was to advise Tolhurst that his drumming days were over. His grand plan was to move Tolhurst to keyboards. Tolhurst began taking piano lessons, but his keyboard skills were, at best, limited: everyone that I asked about this would admit that his prowess didn't stretch much beyond two-fingered noodling, although he has moved way beyond that with his post-Cure bands Presence and Levinhurst.

Producer Phil Thornalley, soon to return briefly to the inner sanctum of The Cure, suspected that Tolhurst's new role was part of a Robert Smith scheme. "He wasn't a very good keyboard player. I don't know what went on there. I guess Robert wanted to expand the rhythm pattern of the band." *Pornography* co-engineer, Mike Nocito, also felt there was something slightly suspicious about Tolhurst's change of instrument. Both Thornalley and Nocito knew that Tolhurst's drumming was perfect for The Cure, so what other reason could there be behind Tolhurst's sideways move?

When I asked Tolhurst about his shift, he insisted that it was an effort on his part to embrace new technology and keep the band moving forward. "At that point it was just the two of us; The White Stripes hadn't been thought of yet, and we thought, 'How are we going to do this?' Even during *Seventeen Seconds* there was some kind of electronic element to the drums that I'd been fascinated by. It seemed a natural evolution from playing the drums to the keyboards, which are rhythmic as well. Going into the electronic era more than anything else, that's what we really wanted to do."

During September and October, Parry co-ordinated what would become known as the 'Art Under The Hammer' sessions, where the new two-man Cure demoed various ideas for their perfect throwaway pop song. At the same time, Simon Gallup had split with his wife Carol, with whom he had two children, Eden and Lily. This left Gallup

---

* Parry obviously had little involvement in the project because there was no editorial in the mag on The Cure. The typical trade-off for a free song is a free feature. As for 'Lament', a more polished take would appear on 1983's *Japanese Whispers* collection.

as the latest resident of the Fiction office, which is where he accidentally learned about the movements of his two estranged bandmates. One morning he fielded a phone call from a fan, who asked a simple question: "Where are The Cure recording?" This was news to Gallup – neither Smith nor Parry had got around to advising him officially that he was out of the band. "I wanted to talk it over [with Smith]," Gallup said, "but after the fan's call I knew it was too late. For the next six months I was bitter and sour and, even after that, when I saw them on *Top Of The Pops*, I kept thinking, 'That should be me.'"

Along with session man Steve Goulding, formerly Wreckless Eric's drummer, Tolhurst and Smith settled down in Island Record's in-house studio to record 'Let's Go To Bed', a co-write that, at least on the surface, was another of Smith's great "fuck-offs". The core of the song was also written during Smith's Welsh retreat with Mary. In its original, slowed-down form, the song could have fitted on *Pornography*. But Robert Smith wasn't a fool; in fact, he was one very smart operator. He knew that if The Cure's pop experiment sank like a lead balloon, he could defend himself by dismissing it as a lark. That way the band's credibility would remain intact. But if the song was a hit, well, maybe it was time to reconsider The Cure's future direction.

Smith had drawn lyrical ideas from some deadly serious sources – French existential literature, drug-fuelled dreams, ugly, sordid images – but he did a complete about-turn with 'Let's Go To Bed'. "When I wrote 'Let's Go To Bed'," he said, "I thought it was stupid. It's rubbish. It's a joke. All pop songs [of the time] are basically saying, 'Please go to bed with me.' So I'm going to make it as blatant as possible [and] set it to this cheesy synth riff – everything I hated about music at the time. It was junk. Lol and I recorded it, Fiction put it out and suddenly we're getting 15 plays a day on American radio. Sod's law, isn't it?"

"My reaction to all those people who thought that The Cure could only be pessimistic and negative and predictable was to make a demented and calculated song like 'Let's Go To Bed'," he said in another analysis of the track. "The purpose was to specifically destroy our image and then somehow start it all over again."

Smith, of course, was underplaying The Cure's case. 'Let's Go To Bed' might have been totally disposable – as late as 2001, Smith was still writing it off, declaring that the "bassline has been played wrong for almost 20 years" – but what great pop wasn't? Displaying considerable stealth, Smith was moving The Cure closer to the Madonnas and Duran Durans that were all over 1982's charts like a rash.

But The Cure also needed a different look to go with their updated sound. The big hair and bleeding eyes look that had been sprung on the public during their last tour was a great start: now that ghostly image needed some brightening up. They couldn't have found a better makeover man than director Tim Pope, whom Parry hired to film the clip for 'Let's Go To Bed', on the strength of a promo showreel that included his video for Soft Cell's 'Bedsitter'. The choice was perfect: Pope was still a relative newcomer, with all the edginess that that entails.

Like many video directors, Tim Pope was pretty much ready for any gig that he was offered before he signed up to direct 'Let's Go To Bed'. He'd directed videos for Altered Images' 'Happy Birthday' and 'I Could Be So Happy', The Psychedelic Furs' 'Love My Way', Wham's 'Young Guns (Go For It)' and Visage's 'Pleasure Boys'. He'd also directed a quartet of Soft Cell videos for the songs 'Sex Dwarf', 'Torch', 'What' and 'Bedsitter', the track that would catch the eye and ear of Chris Parry. While that proved his music video directing chops, he'd also worked on ads (his client list would include Energizer batteries, Kellogg's Rice Krispies and Pizza Hut) and had spent time working at the BBC. Curiously, Pope's first major project involved training politicians how to cope with TV appearances, so ego-stroking was something he understood deeply. But of all his projects, Pope's relationship with The Cure would become his best known, a career-maker that would lead to him directing high profile clips for such platinum-plus acts as The Pretenders, Fatboy Slim and Hall & Oates, as well as scoring Hollywood directing gigs for *The Crow* series of films.

Cure videos, up until the time that Pope was recruited, had been pretty dreadful affairs. Smith, as much as anyone, was aware of that – he described Mike Mansfield, who directed the 'Charlotte Sometimes' clip, as "really useless". He also dismissed the video for 'The Hanging Garden', which was directed by Chris Gabrin, who'd worked with Madness on their 'Grey Day' and 'Shut Up' clips, as "really awful". "They wanted to make us look serious and we wanted them to make us look like Madness." It failed on both counts.

Lol Tolhurst agreed. "Those videos were unmitigated disasters; we weren't actors and our personalities weren't coming across."

On the small screen The Cure came across every bit as po-faced and dour as the music they were making. But in Pope they'd found an empathetic soul. Crucially, Pope was willing to experiment with this relatively new form just as much as The Cure was willing to tinker with their public image as serious young things. It proved to be the perfect union.

"What you see in Tim Pope videos was the personality of the band," said Tolhurst. "I read something where he said we're either the most intelligent people in the world or the most stupid and he couldn't make up his mind which. That's what I liked about The Cure: we took what we did seriously but we didn't take ourselves seriously. We always had this sense of the absurd and he was the first person to illustrate that."

According to Phil Thornalley, who would be part of The Cure when Pope directed 'The Lovecats' video, the understanding between Smith and Pope was quite profound. "[Pope] and Robert seemed to be on the same wavelength. [He was] an English eccentric, but not in that slightly 'Ooh, I'm a bit mad' way. Very creative guy. You know that people are really good when they're not defensive. Anybody could offer any ideas and when he might have dismissed it, he would consider it. That's a good sign."

Tolhurst also admired the English eccentric in Pope. "That's really the reason we liked him. All the towns we grew up in had these eccentric characters. Tim Pope would have fitted in. He had these strange, abstract thoughts: that appealed to us much more than someone who was slick and smooth. We liked people who were deranged."

Parry had sat down with Tolhurst and Smith after 'Let's Go To Bed' was mixed, and threw around ideas for the accompanying video. That's when Parry recalled seeing Pope's promo showreel. "I investigated and found he was fairly new to the game and a bit freaky. It was worth the risk because for the first time ever, we'd choreographed it – we asked him what he thought and he said, 'Great.' Robert was after something quirky, something that took the piss out of the other pop songs that the song was supposed to be in competition with."

Pope (or "Pap" as he would be known in The Cure universe of nicknames) had some knowledge of The Cure's music, and – not unreasonably – figured they'd be gloomy bastards. But once he met

"I will most certainly not be wearing black and lipstick in 2011,"
insists Robert Smith. "That's a guarantee." (SIN/Corbis)

Gallup, Bamonte, Smith, Williams and Thompson (from left).
"I can even imagine doing this at 60; I don't care what
others think," Smith said recently. (Ebet Roberts/Redferns)

Band of the Year at the Brits: "It's a fucking travesty,"
Smith said, "because I thought we were the best band the
year before as well." (LFI)

Chris Parry, The Cure's long-term manager. "Robert told me in 2000 that he hadn't spoken to Chris in six months," Tolhurst revealed. "He said he'd gone crazy."

"He was such a funny little chappy with hair that all stood up." - Video director Tim Pope on Robert Smith. (Steve Double)

Another day, another few thousand miles. "If I work the next one or two years with The Cure thinking I'd rather be at home, then I wouldn't be honest with myself." (Paul Harris/Contributor/Getty)

Wish-list, April 1993: Gallup, Boris Williams, Smith and former guitar
roadie-cum-munitions expert, Perry Bamonte (from left), outside
Hook End Manor, where the band had recorded 1989's
Disintegration album. (Steve Double)

Smith leaves court during the case of Tolhurst vs
The Cure, February 1994. "It's really stupid," Smith said.
"It'll cost him more than he can hope to win." Tolhurst's
lawyers came away $1million wiser. (Chris Taylor)

Drummer Jason Cooper joins The Cure, 1995. "My favourite memories before joining are listening to *Faith* and drinking cider," he admitted. (Steve Double)

Smith preaching to the perverted at Glastonbury 1995. Former bassist Phil Thornalley would describe touring with The Cure as "not for the faint-hearted". (SIN/Corbis)

The Cure strike a pose with Depeche Mode's Martin Gore, 1996. Daryl Bamonte, the Mode's former roadie, would eventually take over as The Cure's manager. (LFI)

Robert Smith saves the world in *South Park*, February 18, 1998. "When my nephews saw that, they worshipped me, but kept asking, 'What is disintegration, Uncle Bob?'" (WENN)

Record producer, Ross Robinson. Smith dismissed nu-metal as "horribly cynical", yet the ageing star and the Limp Bizkit producer got it together for 2004's *The Cure*. (Mick Hutson/Redferns)

Smith at David Bowie's 50th birthday at Madison Square Garden. When Bowie first invited Smith, he thought it was a crank call. "We disagreed on almost every point," Smith would later say. (LFI)

According to The Cranes' Mark Francombe, "luckily there are
500 Goths in every town in the western world, so The Cure's
albums still get bought." Certainly more than 500 people
desperately tried to obtain tickets for The Cure's Barfly gig in
March 2004 – tickets on eBay reportedly nudged the £2,000 mark.
(Heike Schneider-Matzigkeit)

The hands of time: Jason Cooper, Simon Gallup, Robert Smith,
Roger O'Donnell and Perry Bamonte (from left) at the
Hollywood Rockwalk induction of The Cure, April 2004. (LFI)

Robert Smith has no plans of killing off The Cure just yet. "As long as I make music with people I like it's wonderful; it's something most people dream of. (Kevin Estrada/Retna UK)

Smith he felt a genuinely strong connection. "I thought, 'This can't be the geezer who makes all these doomed out records,' because he was such a funny little chappy with hair that all stood up." When Smith and Pope were introduced, Smith had the strange (yet comfortable) sensation that they'd already met. "We had the feeling that we'd known each other for a long time." Smith would describe Pope as a "very surreal bloke" who "succeeded in bringing out the human side we tended to hide. He did a great job for The Cure." And so a match made in pop heaven was forged.

The relationship between Robert Smith and Tim Pope couldn't have been better timed. Music Television (that's MTV to you) was launched on August 1, 1981 when it aired The Buggles' satirical 'Video Killed The Radio Star'. Too right, brother: thanks to the seductive power of the moving image, a "buzz" video now had just as much commercial impact as a high rotation song on the radio. The music industry would never be the same again. Prince, Madonna, Duran Duran and such hair-metal acts as Mötley Crüe and Twisted Sister were all early MTV stars who understood the power of the moving (sometimes gyrating) image. All these acts quickly realised that the new music wasn't just about the song: if you had a wild, vibrant (and ideally raunchy) clip to accompany your new song, you were well on the way to hitsville. Looking fabulous was every bit as crucial as sounding good, which effectively killed off the few remaining prog rock dinosaurs and sensitive singer/strummers, who had no chance of competing with Madonna's mock-orgasmic acrobatics or Prince's pert buttocks. OK, The Cure was never going to be an especially sexy band – their female fans would rather comb their hair than fuck them – but their weird new look was tailor-made for Generation MTV.

Pope chose a studio in St John's Wood for the 'Let's Go To Bed' clip, which was shot in 13 takes. Pope wasn't overly impressed by the band's script outline – his actual response was "fucking hell, this is incoherent" – so instead he persuaded Smith, for the first time in his career, to actually perform. As stunning as it seemed for a man whose dark side rivalled Sylvia Plath's, Smith did just that: and Pope's camera loved him. Smith was adamant that there was a lighter side to The Cure that hadn't been tapped and he understood that it required an absurdist such as Pope to fully comprehend (and exploit) it. "There are other sides to what we do that I think are completely absurd and making videos is part of that process. Tim does see a side of the group which is, in essence, foolish."

And Pope truly brought out that Cure character in the clip for the jaunty, likeably lightweight 'Let's Go To Bed'. It opened with an overalls-clad Tolhurst, who, with his ever-expanding hair and tragic dancing, looked like some Thompson Twins reject, performing what seemed like semaphores. Although Smith looked quite stiff in the rapid-fire early scenes – Pope said later that Smith had been "very, very shy" – he quickly warmed to his new role as performer, conducting an animated conversation with two painted hard-boiled eggs before slapping paint all over the hapless Tolhurst. (He also got the chance to acknowledge Mary, whose name was scrawled on a pull-down blind in the middle of tiny set.) Sure, the make-up would get messier and the hair would get much larger (as would their budgets), but the video marked the birth of the new Cure: bright, vibrant and refreshingly goofy.

Inevitably, on its release in November, 'Let's Go To Bed' became a hit, reaching number 44 in the charts, but not before Smith and Parry conducted another heated debate about the direction in which The Cure should be headed. Contrary as ever, Smith wasn't so sure that 'Let's Go To Bed' should appear under The Cure moniker. He wanted to rename the group Recur, at least for this single. It was another cautious, clever step on Smith's part: if it failed, he could laugh it off in the same way as the Cult Hero indulgence. And if it somehow connected with the masses, he could call it a fluke. But Parry insisted that it was a Cure song – why build an audience just to confuse them? – and Smith reluctantly backed down. There was, however, one proviso: if the single reached the Top 20, Parry would release Smith from his contract and allow him to record a solo album. (Ah, the solo project, one of Smith's favourite discussion points. Despite many, many assurances that it was ready to roll at various downturns during The Cure's career, it still hasn't emerged as of early 2005, although several Cure LPs could have passed for Smith solo albums.)

Having lost his latest sparring match with Parry, Smith then set about destroying 'Let's Go To Bed' in a series of interviews designed to talk it up. "I don't think it's a Cure song," he told the *Record Mirror*. "This single has been released to get daytime airplay and it's disappointing to me because it's the first time we've ever been seen to be involved in current trends or fashions. For us to be seen bothering in an area I don't respect upsets me." And then, when speaking with *Melody Maker*. "I realised when I did it that it wasn't horrible enough, it just wasn't quite dumb enough to be commercial."

" 'Let's Go To Bed' was like going to a party," he told *NME*. "We made a record instead of getting drunk." Petulant as ever, Smith threatened to split the group if they ever made it to the top of the charts. "I'd never let us be seen to be competing to be a number one group," he stated. "It's all such nonsense." Cure critics agreed. In one review of 'Let's Go To Bed', an unimpressed observer wrote: "Let's not. Let's drone over a sub-funk backing and talk about the implications of it, eh Rob?" Yet, reluctantly, the review did acknowledge the track's commercial possibilities. "The insidious timing and uncanny production could well stick this little stocking filler a fair way up the charts."

While 'Let's Go To Bed' was doing just that, Smith took yet another unexpected about-turn. Unlike Tolhurst, Smith had a ready-made escape plan from the pressures of The Cure, which he put into action when there was more disquiet in the Banshees' camp. Severin, who'd drifted in and out of the 'Let's Go To Bed' sessions, once again got into Smith's ear: surely he'd rather be a Banshee, a "serious musician", than a member of this accidental pop band. When guitarist John McGeogh left the Banshees in November, Smith snapped up Severin's offer to rejoin the band.

Smith's timing couldn't have been worse for Parry and Fiction. Suddenly the label boss had a pop band on his roster: a genuine earner. Now their creative heart – and face – was running off for a tour that would consume every ounce of his energy for at least the rest of the year. And Smith also seemed to be heading straight back into a lifestyle that had almost killed him earlier in the year. As Severin would recall, the Banshees became very protective of their new recruit.

"The pressure [on Smith] from the record label was immense. They were always waiting in the wings like vultures. It was like, 'If we don't give Robert something to do with the Banshees, he'll be off doing something with The Cure, so let's think of something: a rehearsal, a festival, a photo shoot, anything to keep him away from Fiction.' We weren't going to play second fiddle to The Cure."

Robert Smith had, seemingly, found the perfect balance between a creative (and commercial) outlet in The Cure and an escape from that pressure with the Banshees. "While with them [the Banshees] I was making dark and Gothic music; at the same time with The Cure we were doing all these demented songs and videos. It was like having two separated but somehow parallel lives." But by mid-December 1982, *Melody Maker* was asking the very reasonable question: "Have The Cure Split? Is Robert Smith Joining The Banshees?" Smith was in particularly sharp form as he deflected questions from prime agitator Steve Sutherland.

"Do The Cure really exist any more?" Smith asked rhetorically. "I've been pondering that question myself. See, as I wrote 90 per cent of the *Pornography* album, I couldn't really leave because it wouldn't have been The Cure without me." The only clue that Smith would leave to The Cure's future was this: "Whatever happens, it won't be me, Laurence and Simon together any more. I know that." As for his Banshees future, Smith was equally vague. "As far as I'm concerned, I'm just doing this tour. Never believe rumours."

Lol Tolhurst bided his time with his first production role, working the desk for the self-titled debut of And Also The Trees. They were a moody Worcestershire quartet who'd formed in 1979; they'd been one of the local bands who'd opened for The Cure a few years earlier when they put out the call for unknown support acts. "Being 15 years old, it was a little surreal," Justin Jones, frontman of And Also The Trees, told me. "A thousand skinheads turned up thinking that we were going to be a punk band, shouting, 'Play something faster, you Dracula bastards.'"

"We really hit it off with Lol in the studio," Jones continued. "He was great fun and very generous." During the sessions, Tolhurst even approached Jones about playing guitar on a planned solo album, to fill in the gap while Smith was busy being a Banshee. Tolhurst did actually record some (to this day unheard) solo tracks with Zerra 1's Paul Bell, as well as undertaking some production work in France.

Yet Tolhurst was convinced that the bond that had developed between him and Smith over the past five years of The Cure was too strong "to ever let it fade away". "I was always sure that Robert wanted to head up his own thing with The Cure," Tolhurst said to me, "so I never worried about him leaving for good. I always viewed what he did with the Banshees and Steve as a musical vacation. I knew he would be back." Many others, however, must have questioned The Cure's future, especially when Smith would make such public declarations as, "I don't despair about losing touch with The Cure. It's more despairing to realise I'll never reach the heights of a Bach or a Prokofiev." That was hardly the vote of confidence that Cure-aholics needed.

Tolhurst remains unsure – even as late as 2005 – why his own attempts to keep The Cure on the rails at that time have been constantly underplayed by Smith. "I know what I did, what I contributed to The Cure; I'm still aware of that," Tolhurst told me. "It still seems strange now; to give myself reasonable credit doesn't seem to want to take away from what The Cure did; it doesn't hurt it.

"I'm not sure what it is – maybe Robert is scared that it will seem more to do with me than just him. For my own sanity, I have to ignore most of that. I know the truth about most of those things. [But] I'm sure Robert has his own version as well."

The Banshees' demands on their newly recruited guitarist were as physically and mentally draining as any of The Cure's previous stints of globetrotting, but with one key difference: Smith wasn't required to make the key decisions. They toured the UK until the end of 1982, then spent January and February of 1983 pushing the product in Australia, New Zealand and Japan. Initially, Smith was well pleased with the life of a hired guitarist. There were no songwriting expectations, no videos or records to make – all he had to do was turn up each night and play. "I'm just there," he told one journalist, when he was asked to define his role in the Banshees. "I'm just the guitarist with the Banshees. There's nothing formal, which is probably why it's working." When stretched, Smith admitted that the Banshees got a "bit fed up with me doing other things", but in early 1983 Smith had little else to do but play guitar. He even admitted to getting along well with the notoriously prickly Siouxsie Sioux. "I think it's because I don't take her too seriously," Smith figured. "It's novel for her to have someone to tell her to shut up because most people are too scared."

But trouble was brewing: 'Let's Go To Bed' had become a small-scale radio hit in the USA, especially on the West Coast. The Cure's limited audience there was rapidly building, all on the strength of one sweetly twisted pop pastiche and a quirky Tim Pope video. The Cure needed to capitalise on this.

And it didn't take long for Smith to become irritated with his role as hired-gun for the Banshees: he wanted to return to songwriting. "Eventually," Smith said, "I became frustrated because I couldn't have the same control over what they were doing [as he did with The Cure]."

"Siouxsie [is] quite [a] strong character," Tolhurst added. "He was never going to be more than the hired hand in that band and he knew it." But Smith's bond with Severin was tighter than ever. In fact, as Smith once stated, that alliance was eventually the only thing that kept him in the Banshees. "I don't think I was the right guitarist for them. My involvement was based mainly on my friendship with Steve Severin."

Chris Parry was becoming increasingly frustrated. He was convinced that the Banshees were simply cashing in on Smith's name, while Smith remained with them purely because he had some peculiar dreams of being in a "supergroup". Parry was also convinced that Smith had only agreed to the English leg of the tour, which would have taken him through to the end of 1982 – suddenly he was on the other side of the planet, with no plans to return until February 1983. Parry's first response was a little extreme: he tried to sue his recalcitrant star if he didn't return to The Cure. Smith, allegedly, called back and threatened to break Parry's legs. Parry's next move was surprisingly humble, especially for a man described to me as "brash" and "very good at business". He approached Smith and apologised for his legal threat. Backing down was not one of Parry's fortes – he'd held fast on everything from the cover art of *Three Imaginary Boys* to releasing 'Let's Go To Bed' under the name of The Cure. It didn't seem that apologising came naturally to Parry, but he'd do pretty much whatever was required to lure his star back.

"He was worried that people would think that The Cure no longer existed," Smith snapped, "but I didn't give a fuck – we could always re-form. I hated being looked upon as a source of money; being with the Banshees was a reaction against that."

While still chewing over his future in March 1983, Smith, for the first time in a long time, was a man without a band. Finally off the road, Banshees Budgie and Siouxsie Sioux were moonlighting as The Creatures, while Tolhurst was still working with And Also The Trees, which left Smith free for any offer that came his way. And that offer came from the most unexpected place.

Nicholas Dixon had recently been appointed choreographer by the Royal Ballet. Young and hipper than most people associated with such a high-brow art form, he approached Smith with the idea of writing a musical score for a production of *Les Enfants terribles*, Jean Cocteau's twisted tribute to love, death and incest. Smith was flattered by the offer but he was also pragmatic enough to realise that he was a little out of his depth. As a test, he proposed the choreographing of a Cure track; 'Siamese Twins', from *Pornography*. With Tolhurst briefly back on drums, a hat-wearing Severin playing bass and Marc Almond's Venomettes providing strings, Smith strummed the song live while two dancers twirled around him. Smith and Dixon's experiment aired on BBC2's *Riverside* programme in February. Despite a favourable response, their planned adaptation was put on hold (and remains that way, 20-odd years later).

Smith's next non-Cure project was much closer to his comfort zone. He and Severin had long been promising to throw themselves into a serious collaboration, something much more fulfilling than cameos on the BBC or sharing a stage as part of the Banshees. Smith occasionally slept on the floor of Severin's London flat, wearing layers of coats to prevent the English chill from turning him into a block of lipstick-covered ice. Clearly their connection was very strong. During March, Smith and Severin shifted base to London's Britannia Row Studios, a site owned by Pink Floyd, ostensibly to record a collaboration they entitled The Glove. (Tolhurst also used Britannia to mix And Also The Trees' *Shantel* album.)

The name was a nod to Smith's youthful love of The Beatles – the Glove was a character in the Fab Four's trippy 1968 cartoon *Yellow Submarine*, a peculiar, deadpan slice of hippie-era psychedelia littered with in-jokes and Beatles references. In one standout scene, as 'All You Need Is Love' chimes in the background, John Lennon has it out with the so-called 'Flying Dreadful Glove', one of the Blue Meanies' evil crew, in the ultimate battle between good and evil. (The Glove, of course, morphed into "Love" when it fell under the spell of The Beatles' music.) The Smith/Severin alliance was now official; its name was the perfect mix of Smith's love for The Beatles and their collective thing for twisted, trashy movies. The fact that the Glove possessed good and bad sides couldn't have been lost on the pair, either.

It would be a stretch to call The Glove a true musical collaboration:

it was more like a non-stop party, fuelled by acid and video nasties, with the Banshees, The Associates and Marc Almond's band playing bit parts. Smith would depict The Glove as "an experiment in disorientation". During the making of their *Blue Sunshine* LP, he and Severin made a peculiar pact: "There was this unspoken idea that we should make the album with as many different drugs as we could get our hands on." Acid was their mind-alterer of choice and the pair would gobble them down like aspirin. (Severin couldn't actually recall dropping any tabs during the actual sessions, but LSD can have that effect on you.) The party-cum-album-recording would begin most nights at 6pm and then continue for the next 12 hours, when the pair would retire to Severin's flat, where they'd come down while watching such shockers as *Videodrome*, *The Brood*, *Evil Dead* and Nicholas Roeg's more upmarket *Bad Timing*, which they'd watch in slow motion.* When not taking in these B-grade shockers, they'd take a pair of scissors to dozens of magazines scattered about Severin's flat, to create bizarre murals. The sessions and the party moved between Britannia Row, Morgan, Trident and the Garden studios, as the pair juggled their chemical indulgences and music-making.

"Acid used to make me feel very connected to Severin," Smith said. "We used to walk around London, living in this *Yellow Submarine* cartoon world. It was really upbeat and fun, because I'd got rid of all the bad stuff with *Pornography*. When you're taking acid with someone you really like, then it's really, really funny. It was a fantastic time, that Glove album."

The third member of The Glove was Jeanette Landrey, a former dancer and choreographer, and then girlfriend of Banshee drummer Budgie, who provided vocals for much of the album.† Although she didn't realise it at the time, Landrey's role was little more than session singer – and silent witness to the increasingly weird relationship that was brewing between Smith and Severin. "I don't know what I

---

* The genuinely unnerving Roeg film had a direct influence on the *Blue Sunshine* track 'Sex Eye Make-Up', as did a letter Smith had that was written by a madman and addressed to the Queen.
† Chris Parry had advised Smith not to sing on the sessions because of a potential problem with royalties. So Smith and Severin used a *John Peel Show* appearance to announce that they were seeking vocalists. Smith, however, did end up singing on two tracks.

actually expected," she said when the album appeared in August 1983, "but if I was offered something similar again I'd have a much clearer idea of the problems involved. I still feel like a faceless voice to some extent. It's very much Steve's and Robert's baby – but that was always clear so I can't complain."

Blue Sunshine took its title from one of the Z-grade horror flicks that were on repeat play in Severin's flat – "blue sunshine" being the name of an especially potent strain of acid.* And while it may have been recorded during some particularly high times, *Blue Sunshine* was treated with much reverence on its release, which was more a nod to Severin's involvement than Smith's. 'Like An Animal' was the lead single; Allan Jones' review in the August 13 *Melody Maker* was heavy with praise, declaring that this exercise in psychedelia packed the same kind of "spacious rush as The Byrds' 'Eight Miles High' ". Big raps. "Are The Glove the new West Coast experimental art ensemble?" Jones asked. "Whatever: like all good pop records, 'Like An Animal' sounds like it's always been there. The Glove may yet prove to be a real handful."

When they hunkered down with Steve Sutherland in early September, both Smith and Severin were guarded, insisting that this was a one-off experiment and they weren't quite ready to kill off their day bands. Smith seemed more interested in spelling out the process of making the record, rather than dissecting such tracks as 'Mr Alphabet Says' and 'Blues In Drag'.

"It was a real attack on the senses when we were doing it," Smith boasted. "We were coming out of the studio at six in the morning, watching all these really mental films and then going to sleep and having really demented dreams. Then, as soon as we woke up, we'd go virtually straight back into the studio, so it was a bit like a mental assault course towards the end." In another post-mortem on The Glove, Smith confessed just how draining the indulgence had been. "After that period with Steve, I was physically incapable of cleaning my teeth. The whole thing was unreal – a dream – and not something I'm likely to repeat in a hurry."

Despite his dental health issues, Smith's next move was even bolder (or, in hindsight, possibly more stupid). While Simon Gallup went

---

* The director of this 1978 gem, Jeff Lieberman, went on to call the shots on such Oscar contenders as *Satan's Little Helper*.

back to work with Cry (quickly renamed Fools Dance), an outfit he formed with another member of the ex-Cure club, keyboardist Matthieu Hartley, Smith decided that he could juggle recording duties with both the Banshees and The Cure. This, more than anything he'd lived through before, was very nearly Robert Smith's undoing.

Chapter Nine

"We always used to pretend we understood what each other was saying, but I don't think either of us had a fucking clue."

– Tim Pope on Robert Smith

IN theory, Robert Smith's master plan for the rest of 1983 and early 1984 seemed like the perfect juggling act. By recording and touring with the Banshees he was cast as a respectable musician, playing with a highly regarded band. As frontman and tunesmith for The Cure he had a ready-made creative outlet. And when Siouxsie proved too much for him to bear, or Parry started to put the squeeze on The Cure, he had the perfect retreat. In the back of his mind, though, he knew that a break wouldn't be such a bad idea. He even said it out loud when talking with *Flexi-Pop* magazine about the *Blue Sunshine* album. "I need a holiday," Smith said. "I keep making plans to go every week but every week I'm in another group."

In April 1983, The Cure made another fleeting return, this time performing on BBC's *The Oxford Road Show*. Smith was asked to perform 'Let's Go To Bed' and 'Just One Kiss', the UK flipside of 'Bed'. The ever-contrary Smith thought not – instead he said he'd prefer to play a pair of gloomy *Pornography* tracks, 'One Hundred Years' and 'The Figurehead'. Of course, there was a slight hitch: The Cure didn't actually exist, apart from Smith and Tolhurst. Parry had no plans to miss out on this plum gig, so he recruited Andy Anderson, who'd drummed with space rockers Hawkwind and, more recently, the band Brilliant. Anderson knew Smith; he'd helped out during the non-stop party that produced the *Blue Sunshine* LP. Bassist Derek Thompson of SPK signed up as temporary bassist. Unlike Smith's dreaded *Top Of The Pops*, their performance was live, and it had the desired effect on Smith: he loved the experience. Within a few weeks of the *Road Show*'s screening, Smith wanted to record another Cure single.

This time around, it would be just Smith and Tolhurst together in the studio. For the five-day sessions that would generate the tracks 'The Upstairs Room', which was written while bunking on Severin's floor, 'The Dream', a re-recording of 'Lament' – Smith's favourite track of the four, which he felt showed off his "romantic side" – and their next single, 'The Walk', the duo chose to work with chain-smoking producer Steve Nye. Just like Thornalley, Nye had learned from the masters, having started out as an assistant engineer to Beatles producer George Martin, at AIR Studios in 1971. Amongst many subsequent productions, he had worked with XTC and Roxy Music and had co-produced Bryan Ferry's solo outing *In Your Mind*. But Nye was best known to Smith for his work on Japan's *Tin Drum* album from 1981, widely regarded as the finest hour of these dedicated followers of synth-pop fashion.*

While Smith was searching for something just as infectious as 'Let's Go To Bed', he was also ready for some direction in the studio. "I thought it would be good to do something structured," he said, "to go in and have someone say to me, 'That vocal isn't any good, you'll have to keep doing it.'" In short, he didn't want another *Blue Sunshine*. And Jam Studios, where they chose to record the four tracks, had all the Smith essentials – a good pool table, a full fridge and a space where he could write.

Both the single and Tim Pope-directed video of 'The Walk' seemed like a very natural progression from the band's new beginning of 'Let's Go To Bed'. Beneath the song's electro-pop surface there was just a hint of the new romanticism that The Cure had previously dabbled with, but there was an insistency and melodicism at work that made it an ideal pop song for anyone who'd outgrown Culture Club. And while the on-screen Smith hadn't quite perfected the Lovecat persona that would soon make him a star, he seemed more at home in Pope's second Cure clip.

Shot against a stark black background, Tolhurst once again plays the fool, performing a herky-jerky dance in a child's paddling pool while wearing a dress (on his insistence, as it turned out). Smith, meanwhile, eyes the camera with a growing sense of assurance – hell, he even danced with the baby doll that was thrown around during the clip like a

---

* *Tin Drum* was another Hansa release, incidentally: to Smith it must have felt like 1977 all over again.

football. It didn't make that much literal sense – and who was the mysterious old biddy "signing" and mouthing Smith's lyrics? – but that was hardly the point. Tim Pope wasn't so sure himself. He would eventually come clean on the mysterious "understanding" he and Smith shared. "We always used to pretend we understood what each other was saying, but I don't think either of us had a fucking clue."

'The Walk' clip was shot at a studio only 400 metres from RAK Studios, where The Cure had hoovered up their budget while making *Pornography*. Phil Thornalley, who'd produced the album, decided to check out the shoot and check in on Tolhurst and Smith. It turned out to be a fortuitous meeting for Thornalley, as he would tell me. While he was watching the cross-dressing Tolhurst and Smith splash about in the kiddies' paddling pool, he was indirectly made an offer that he couldn't refuse.

"I'd gone up there to hang out for an hour, whatever," he told me. "They said, 'Simon's gone, do you know any bass players?'" Thornalley certainly did: himself. Although best known as an engineer and producer (and later a songwriter), Thornalley had been playing the bass in bands since his teens. And since working with the band on *Pornography*, his stock had risen considerably: his subsequent production credits included XTC's *Mummer*, Duran Duran's *Seven And The Ragged Tiger* and Julian Cope's *Sunshine Playroom*. He was seduced by the possibility of joining a band that was starting to have its own chart success: he'd achieved plenty, but hadn't actually played in a successful outfit. Thornalley, of course, also had an escape plan – he realised that he was merely a fill-in and could jump ship and return to the studio if it all got too much.

"It had a temporary feel to it," Thornalley said. "There was a festival in summer, a few dates in America." Of course, there was also a certain amount of ego involved in his decision, as Thornalley freely admitted. "It was lust for glory; the thought of being given a chance to be in a band that was playing theatres as opposed to toilets. It was a chance to see the world and whatever."

While Thornalley briefly returned to RAK, 'The Walk' became a hit. Smith knew something was up when his mother Rita told him that she liked the track. "She normally hates any Cure stuff I play her," he chuckled, as the song climbed to number 12 in the charts. The single's reviews, typically, sniffed at this second step in the band's new pop direction. "Robert Smith actually sounds in a fairly good mood here," reported *NME*, "but I'm sure it's just a silly phase he's going through." And then, another far more damning take on 'The Walk'. "I'd feel pretty sick if I spent all my royalty cheque earnings in an expensive recording studio only to come out with a load of fly-blown rubbish such as this."

Robert Smith, typically, did his best to side with his critics and play down his latest pop confection, when he said: "It occurs to me that a lot of idiots must be buying 'The Walk'."

The BBC had been very hesitant to play the Pope-directed video for 'The Walk' because – shock, horror – Tolhurst and Smith were wearing make-up. The simple solution was to compile another make-shift Cure line-up and undergo the torture of *Top Of The Pops* not once, but twice. Their first appearance was on July 7, with Anderson drumming, Tolhurst on keys and a shades-wearing Porl Thompson miming the basslines. They returned soon after, this time with the newly recruited Thornalley on bass. Looking on, regular Cure critics *Melody Maker* reluctantly accepted that something was happening here. "The Cure on *TOTP* was an event almost as absurd as Jimmy Savile's inanity," they reported. "They looked and acted bored, but all across the nation Cure fans, Cure converts and folk who can't tell The Cure from Culture Club and couldn't care less interpreted Smith's stifled yawns as enigmatic arrogance. Such is the power of reputation, such is the impact of dressing in black."

Much of what they said was true, but it wasn't a case of the mainstream bending to accommodate The Cure – it was more a case of The Cure lightening up on the misery and exploring their own heart of popness. The charts certainly hadn't undergone any type of radical change; when 'The Walk' began its march towards the Top 10, The Cure's chartmates were Paul Young (dripping all over 'Wherever I Lay My Hat [That's My Home]'), Eurythmics, Shalamar and Nick Heyward. It became even clearer that The Cure was on the rise when New Order, who'd risen from the ashes of Joy Division, accused the band of plagiarism: the Mancunian's 'Blue Monday', which appeared around the same time, bore some striking similarities to 'The Walk' – or was it the other way around?

"Plenty of people have ripped us off," barked New Order's Peter Hook, "but The Cure really take the piss sometimes." Some years later

Smith would defend himself when he revealed that if 'The Walk' was stealing from anyone, it was Japan, not New Order. And if there was any similarity between 'The Walk' and 'Blue Monday', he accredited that to the fact that both bands fancied six-string basses.

Of course New Order would have the last laugh, because 'Blue Monday' became the highest-selling 12-inch single of all time, breaking the band in the States and finally helping to put the legacy of Ian Curtis to rest. But Hook's comment said something about The Cure – they'd become serious players in the pop world, a band that couldn't be ignored.

With two hit singles on the trot, The Cure was now ready for a return to "serious" live work, rather than the pantomime of *Top Of The Pops* or their *Riverside* one-off (a two-off, actually, because Smith had returned there in July, this time with Severin, performing The Glove's 'Punish Me With Kisses'). The Cure agreed to headline the event known as Elephant Fayre, which was held in St Germans in Cornwall on July 30. They warmed up with two club shows in Bournemouth and Bath.

Smith could have used Elephant Fayre as an opportunity to road-test the brighter, bolder, more outgoing Cure as captured on 'Let's Go To Bed' and 'The Walk'. Instead he decided to use the event as a eulogy for The Cure that came before, the band that dared not smile. Their 18-song set was littered with their pre-Pope moodscapes: opening with 'The Figurehead', they droned their way through 'The Drowning Man', 'Cold', 'Siamese Twins', 'Pornography' and more, not even bothering to include their two most recent singles. But Smith knew what he was doing. "It was something of an obligation to play all the old songs," he said afterwards, "but that was the whole reason for doing it. I just wanted to play those songs just once more. [It was] like the end of an era for us, I suppose."

Melody Maker's Steve Sutherland could see the value of the new Cure, even if they were wheeling out the grim old songs just one more time. In his review of the set, he noted that The Cure's resurrection was the most unlikely second coming of the summer of '83. "A few months back," he stated, "if anyone had been laying odds on a summer artistic renaissance, The Cure wouldn't have even figured in the reckoning. [They] were, to all intents and purposes, widely considered a lost cause. But from something old sprang something new . . . it was a show of strength with the power of trance . . . The Cure['s] future will be well worth the wait."

Elephant Fayre clearly had the right effect on Smith: within five days The Cure was in the middle of a two-night-stand at New York's The Ritz, followed by shows in Toronto and San Francisco. 'Let's Go To Bed' had done the trick Stateside: whereas their last round of shows drew the usual long-faced types in overcoats, there were now more than a few Smith clones in the crowds. It wasn't quite Curemania, but their star was very clearly rising. Tolhurst spotted the evolution, stating that the band's American fanbase now included its fair share of screaming 14-year-olds. "I remember doing some personal appearance in a club and I couldn't believe it: there were a thousand people there singing along to the song. It was something that happened outside of us playing a show, it was completely new to us. I thought, 'OK, this is the Eighties, this is how it's going to work, let's go along with it.'" When a bra came sailing onto the stage, The Cure realised that their entire world had changed.

On the way home, Smith, Tolhurst, Thornalley and Anderson stopped over in Paris, where they hired the Polydor-owned Studio Des Dames for five days to record three tracks: 'The Lovecats', 'Mr Pink Eyes' and 'Speak My Language'.

If 'Let's Go To Bed' and 'The Walk' were the work of a band in the midst of a transition, 'The Lovecats' was the sound of The Cure as a full-blown pop group. And an excellent one, at that. Smith wasn't digging too deep for meaning – the song was inspired by Walt Disney's *The Aristocats*. "I knew all the words [to the film] by heart," Smith admitted. "I was completely obsessed." But of pretty much any pop song Robert Smith would ever write and record, 'The Lovecats' was a perennial, a song that would forever be associated with the bird's-nest-haired, smudged lipstick era of The Cure. As late as 2005, the song was still being heard everywhere: it was even used as a programme ID for a drive-time radio show on Australia's ABC, in between political updates from Canberra and weather reports. Ubiquity, thy name was 'The Lovecats'. Even the polka-dot shirt that Smith wore in the clip briefly became a fashion item *de rigueur*.

For Cure fill-in Phil Thornalley, the French sessions that resulted in 'The Lovecats' was by far his most enjoyable time with the band. Along with Smith and Parry, Thornalley co-produced the three tracks, which were subsequently mixed at RAK. "That was the best time with The Cure," Thornalley told me. "I was doing what I did best: I was producing, I was playing the bass. It was a great session. The studio was crammed with all these orchestral instruments and we did three tracks in five days. In many respects, given my background as a pop person, 'Lovecats' was my moment when I felt that I really shone with The Cure; it was the best record I ever made with them, mainly because everybody enjoyed it." Thornalley could barely comprehend that this was the same band – minus Gallup, of course – who'd made the terminal comedown that was *Pornography*.

"It's a great pop song," he continued. "Everybody did a great job, particularly Robert. It was nice to be making a record with him where he was being more poppy. And he is – he's written all these great pop songs, 'Boys Don't Cry', 'Friday I'm In Love', 'Inbetween Days'. I'd never seen that side of him."

As for Smith, he was more comfortable talking up the non-single cuts than 'The Lovecats', which he laughed off as an "amateurish pop song". 'Speak My Language' pretty much came out of nothing – or at least a bassline that he sang in the studio to Thornalley and Anderson, who jammed with him. "I made up the piano parts and the words as we went along," Smith said in the liner notes for *Join The Dots*. "Very jazz." 'Mr Pink Eyes' was a minor-scale slice of autobiography, flavoured by some blasts on the harmonica by Smith, that was written after the Lovecat caught sight of himself in a bathroom mirror after another bender. "Mr Pink Eyes was me," he admitted.

A Tim Pope shoot was organised as soon as the band touched down in London – Parry knew that 'The Lovecats' had hit written all over it. It was shot in a derelict terrace in England's Lane in Primrose Hill, a house that Pope only managed to rent when he convinced the landlord that he had plans to buy the dump.

Robert Smith was very clearly adapting to his newer, cuddlier small-screen persona, because he hogged the camera like some Hollywood hopeful throughout the clip, while Anderson and Thornalley quite readily accept their bit parts in the part-performance, part-pantomime clip. Thornalley was as pleased with the video as he was with his work on the track. "God knows what the neighbours thought," he laughed. "We started shooting around seven in the evening. It was good fun." Tolhurst, as usual, played Cure clown – this time he was decked out in a cat suit, which he continued to wear once the clip was wrapped, scaring the crap out of an early-rising Rasta who was wandering the nearby streets.

With 'The Lovecats' on simmer – engineer David "Dirk" Allen had some final tinkering before it was ready – another single from The Glove's *Blue Sunshine* was released. As curious as the track 'Like An Animal' was, it was merely a stepping stone along the way to 'The Lovecats', which appeared on October 25, quickly becoming The Cure's finest pop moment, reaching number seven. Even Steve Sutherland heaped praise on the sure-fire hit, although it wasn't held in quite the same regard as two singles which had preceded it, The Glove's 'Like An Animal' and The Creatures' 'Right Now'. But once again, by this time Robert Smith had moved on – back to the Banshees. It was part of a musical tightrope that he tried his best to walk for the next six months.

Maybe Smith just wasn't sure if he was ready for pop stardom or maybe he just fancied the idea of spreading himself thinly. Whatever the reason, he rarely had a moment to stop and think from September 1983 onwards. First it was an Italian gig and video shoot with the Banshees for their less-than-awesome cover of The Beatles' 'Dear Prudence', released a month before 'The Lovecats' to a far less excitable response. ("Siouxsie's . . . group are getting fogged and indecisive," noted *NME*, who felt that 'Prudence' was an "under-fed treatment of a dried-out chestnut.") There was also a Banshees show in Israel, after which Smith wrecked the group's car, followed by a two-night stand at London's Royal Albert Hall on September 30 and October 1, shows which were documented on the Banshees' double LP *Nocturne*. At the same time, Smith was already showing signs of the big fall that was to come, admitting, "If I went on like this for a few more months I'd be the next one to have a breakdown." Hardly the words of a guy enjoying his dual musical life.

On October 27, The Cure returned to *Top Of The Pops* for another run through 'The Lovecats', which continued its climb up the charts. It didn't matter that Smith forgot the song's lyrics: by this stage he was lucky to remember which band he was in.

Japanese Whispers was released in December, a stop-gap eight-song collection of The Cure's trilogy of pop singles – 'Let's Go To Bed',

'The Walk' and 'The Lovecats' – plus five B-sides. The album came with a warning, as word started to leak that Smith was considering an about-face to murkier emotional waters for The Cure. "Beware!" advised *Sounds'* Bill Black. "All the signs are that Smith intends to return to the plodding ground of past work for the next album, so get happy while you can." The most schizophrenic phase of Smith's musical life was summed up precisely on December 25, when he starred with both the Banshees and The Cure on the Christmas Day episode of *Top Of The Pops*, performing 'Dear Prudence' and 'The Lovecats'.

It wasn't as though he had much time to sit back and take it all in, because Smith was now doing the two album shuffle, bouncing between sessions for The Cure's *The Top* at Genetic Studios in Reading and the Banshees' *Hyaena* at Pete Townshend's Eel Pie Studio in Twickenham. By this time, the Banshees' record had been a stop-start project taking up almost a year. A typical Smith day ran like this, as he documented 20 years later, still stunned that he managed to survive with body and psyche relatively intact.

"I used to do the Banshees album at Eel Pie . . . then travel out to Genetic . . . in a taxi. [The Cure] were all staying in a pub, so I'd meet up with the others, who were all a bit pissed by then. I'd have a few drinks then go into the studio. We'd start recording at 2am. Then I'd go back to Eel Pie. I used to sleep in the taxi." For these manic six weeks, Smith was sustained by an especially potent brew of magic mushroom tea, courtesy of drummer Andy Anderson who, along with Tolhurst and Smith, formed the musical core of *The Top*. (Thornalley was AWOL working on Duran Duran's latest opus.)

Smith wasn't the only one who started to unravel at this time. Lol Tolhurst's alcoholism was exacerbated by The Cure's decision to set up camp in a pub while making *The Top*. "That's the beginning of where I was going to get worse addiction-wise," he said. "[I was] stuck out in the middle of the English countryside in the winter at Martin Rushton's studio. It was a recipe for disaster – and this is key – that we stayed at the local pub, the John Barleycorn, and they gave us the key, so we could come back at five or six in the morning and carry on. The landlord would cook us breakfast so we'd be up at eight in the morning drinking pints with breakfast, having been up all night."

The upside of their stint at the John Barleycorn was that it gave

Tolhurst the chance to become closer to new Cure drummer, the black, one-eyed Andy Anderson. "He was still pretty sane at that time," said Tolhurst. Also in the studio, strangely enough, was Nigel Revlor, a friend of Parry's who managed Pete Shelley. He was going through a divorce at the time and was hiding out at the studio while *The Top* was being recorded. According to Tolhurst, "He would come to the studio every night to sleep and escape home. He was there for the whole album – he'd wake up about six in the morning, shower, and then go to work. He was there for the whole time but I don't think he heard a thing."

Somewhere in the midst of his mushroom-fuelled balancing act, Smith also helped Tim Pope with his own record, the twisted novelty song 'I Want To Be A Tree'. It was a sentiment that Smith could fully comprehend, especially when the tension started to grow at Eel Pie. Smith would turn up for the Banshees' sessions and learn that the others had clocked off for a curry, leaving him to work with producer Mike Hedges. It didn't help that Severin, Budgie and Siouxsie felt, justifiably enough, that Smith wasn't giving them 100 per cent. Inner-band relations were right on the edge – and someone with an ego as healthy as Siouxsie couldn't have been comfortable when, during their Italian stopover a few months earlier, the tour poster read "Siouxsie & The Banshees With Robert Smith". Whose band was this anyway? Again, it was only Smith's friendship with Severin that kept him focused on *Hyaena* – or as focused as he could be given his schedule and his lifestyle.

It was inevitable that Smith would come apart. It had happened before, on The Cure's Picture and Fourteen Explicit Moments tours and in his relationships with erstwhile bassists Michael Dempsey and Simon Gallup and Fiction head Chris Parry. This time it was Smith's health that packed it in. Blood poisoning was cited as the official cause for his collapse, but a complete physical meltdown was closer to the truth. "It was like the vengeance of God," said Smith. "My skin started ripping apart, falling off. It was almost as though my body was saying, 'Well, if you refuse to stop, I will stop you.' I had everything you could imagine going wrong with me. I didn't exactly have a breakdown but I was like a clockwork toy that ran down." Smith knew that something had to be done when his body started to shake uncontrollably – and it had nothing to do with pre-show nerves or a bad chemical reaction.

Smith's crash led to one of the more bizarre resignations in rock'n' roll history. Asked to tour America with the Banshees in May 1984, he cried off, offering Siouxsie a doctor's certificate from the Smith's family GP stating that he simply wasn't up to the grind.* It was an interesting twist on the old standard "musical differences" – it's not often that a band member has backed out of a tour after actually taking a doctor's advice. But before his relationship with the Banshees reached that strangely formal nadir, Smith had plenty of business on both sides of the musical fence. There had been a Banshees single, 'Swimming Horses', followed by a tour in March, then a Cure UK tour in April on the back of yet another winningly eccentric single, 'The Caterpillar'. The Cure's obligatory *Top Of The Pops* spot, aired on April 12, gave some idea of how Smith felt: he and the band (which had now solidified into Smith, Tolhurst, Anderson and Thornalley) played their new single sitting cross-legged on stage. "We were knackered," Smith insisted. It showed.

The Cure's fifth album, *The Top*, and, finally, the Banshees' *Hyaena*, dropped a month apart: the former in May 1984 and *Hyaena* in June. It was the final move in a spectacularly productive (yet turbulent) time in Smith's life. Over the previous 18 months, he had delivered four hit singles for The Cure ('Let's Go To Bed', 'The Walk', 'The Lovecats' and 'The Caterpillar', all with the requisite Tim Pope videos); he'd also finished three albums – *The Top*, *Hyaena* and *Blue Sunshine* – for three different outfits, toured with both The Cure and the Banshees, and taken enough acid and magic-mushroom tea to lose several of his nine lives. Somehow he'd also managed to maintain his relationship with Mary; they were soon to move to Maida Vale, where they would set up base for several years. But by June 1984, with both *The Top* and 'Caterpillar' charting highly, he finally handed Siouxsie his GP-approved resignation. Robert Smith was a Banshee no longer.

In an interview at the time, Smith figured he was going through a mid-life crisis at the ripe old age of 25, hinting that, "The point where I stop working in contemporary music, I think, becomes increasingly close." When asked about his life as a Banshee, Smith was frank. "The stuff we did live was absolutely brilliant," he said, "but the recorded

---

* Smith would recall entering his surgery and seeing his doctor's face drop. "He said, 'Whatever it is you're doing, you have to stop.'"

stuff didn't really have the same definition and maybe it was a mistake to make that record [*Hyaena*]. A lot of it is good, but it's not cohesive enough to be great." And his current mindset? "Happy but very muddled," Smith replied.

Steve Severin, Smith's accomplice in The Glove and prime reason for his lengthy stay in the Banshees, wasn't so enthused, especially given that Smith had just served his notice to the band. Their seemingly unbreachable alliance was over. Many years later, when asked whether he'd maintained any kind of relationship with Smith after the split, Severin virtually wrote him off. "Robert has a tendency to edit people out of his life when he has tired of draining them," Severin snapped. "I have the impression that he lives in a rock star hermetic cocoon surrounded by sycophants. If so, he's welcome to it. I doubt we would have much in common any more."

Robert Smith wasn't a quick learner. He may have had a full physical collapse, his head and his body screaming for a rest, but he continued to tour with The Cure. After a trio of shows at London's Hammersmith Odeon, Cure 1984 (Smith, Tolhurst, Thornalley and Anderson) did the obligatory European run, concentrating on France, Holland and Germany, countries that didn't take great exception to their recent pop makeover. After a final date on May 31 at Utrecht, Smith turned his attention to talking up *The Top*, an album that sounded remarkably coherent, given its bizarre, fractured creation. Smith, however, wasn't so sure, damning it as "a really self-indulgent album – a reaction against 'The Lovecats' in a way. I had to get it out of my system, but there are songs on there that were really pointing the way to what I wanted to do."

Smith may have given credits to Anderson, Thompson and Tolhurst in *The Top*'s liner notes, but The Cure's latest was effectively as close as Smith would ever come to his much talked about solo album. Those credits give away some obvious clues as to Tolhurst's diminished role within The Cure, too: he was listed as simply playing "other instruments". Tolhurst was purely a physical presence in the studio, weighed down by Smith's obsessiveness and his own toxic problems.

"To be honest," Tolhurst admitted in 2005, "I played few keyboard parts on that album. The songwriting credits I have on *The Top* are for lyrics, really. I think this was the beginning of the downward spiral for me. The vision of The Cure was starting to evaporate for me; although

I was physically in the studio every day pretty much for the whole album, my soul was elsewhere, looking down into that horrible dark abyss which nowadays I am thankfully free of."

Tolhurst wasn't the only one on a downward spiral. Tim Pope would let it slip that Dave Allen, *The Top*'s co-producer, told him that Smith's manic self-obsession had made for some "terrifying" sessions. When *Melody Maker* likened Smith to Pink Floyd's doomed Syd Barrett in their uncharacteristically positive review of *The Top*, they were closer to the truth than they might have imagined.

"Trying to get to the bottom of *The Top*," the ubiquitous Steve Sutherland observed, "is a bit like trying to decide whether a happy lunatic would be better off sane. It's silly and sinister, perfectly amoral and completely incompatible with anything else happening now."

Hindsight being the great leveller it is, it's now much easier to unravel *The Top*. Along with its even more successful follow-up, *The Head On The Door*, which was released in August 1985, *The Top* was both an experiment and an each-way bet from Smith. He was trying to find a way to keep both sets of Cure lovers happy, providing enough upbeat pop tunes to satisfy those seduced by 'The Lovecats', without denying the overcoat and mascara brigade who'd understood *Pornography* to be the word according to Goth. This duality was reflected in Cure setlists from the time, too, where they attempted to present both sides of the band, including the epic downers ('Play For Today', 'One Hundred Years', 'The Wailing Wall') and the hits ('Primary', 'The Lovecats', 'The Caterpillar'). It was a fine balance that Smith would eventually perfect, much to his commercial, if not his critical, benefit.

The Top opened with 'Shake Dog Shake', where Smith unleashes possibly the creepiest shriek he would ever commit to tape – and that's saying something, because it's not as if his recorded history has been short of unsettling cries and feline-like screeches. But here he sounds truly possessed. Sonically, it does hark back to the swirling, claustrophobic soundscapes of *Pornography*, but 'Shake Dog Shake' isn't necessarily a warning of things to come. It was just a reminder that The Cure hadn't completely lost touch with their petulant past. The more restrained 'Birdmad Girl' follows, an early example of Smith's efforts with vocal experimentation. The song may be a morbid study of what Smith described as "insensible savagery", but there was a noticeable playfulness to Smith's voice, as he wrapped himself around a slithery guitar riff and a stark piano. ('Birdmad Girl' is one of only two Tolhurst co-writes on the album; *The Top* truly was Smith's album.)

The musical mood of the album, though not necessarily its lyrical tone, is pretty well established at this early stage, two tracks in – each bleak soundscape would be countered with something lighter and breezier. It was as if the juggling act he was trying to maintain with the Banshees and The Cure was also captured in his songwriting. For every 'Wailing Wall' – a Middle East-flavoured dirge that came to Smith when he was touring Israel with the Banshees – there's a baroque pop ditty such as 'The Caterpillar', with its rusty violin scratchings and toy piano interlude. Then there was the strangely seductive 'Dressing Up', a particular favourite of Smith's, a track that opened with what sounded for all the world like pan flutes, as if Smith had sampled wild sounds from some esoteric South American soundtrack. And 'The Empty World' featured a scaled-down military band, tin whistles and all. Added to that was the gently twisted title track, where Smith and co-producer Allen were so intent on capturing the sound of a spinning top that they devoted the bulk of one night's recording to doing just that. He'd come a long way from the three-nights-and-you're-outta-here rush that was the recording of *Three Imaginary Boys*.

Smith may have inched closer to the perfect musical balance on *The Top*, but his lyrical mindset was still set to pitch black. The screeching, insistent 'Give Me It' comes on like a warning, as Smith implores his protagonist to leave him alone so that he might be free to find affection as if he was documenting the last agonised cries of a dying man. Then there's 'Piggy In The Mirror', another song touched by the Nicholas Roeg film *Bad Timing*, a song that Smith described as "me hating myself again". When Smith invites us to follow him in his search for where the real pleasure might lie during 'Shake Dog Shake', it's not quite an invitation; it felt more like a dare. Clearly, it proved that Smith was feeling the strain of simply taking on too much, as he bounced between bands and schedules like some human basketball. And no Cure album would be complete without a literary loan: for *The Top* it was J.D. Salinger's turn. His short story, 'A Perfect Day For Bananafish' provided the title, if not the message, of 'Bananafishbones'. When asked about the song's meaning, however, Smith admitted that it was far more personal and much more in tune with the rest of *The Top*. "Again, me hating myself," he replied.

But if there was one song from *The Top* that summed up Smith's jumbled emotions (and senses), as he struggled to understand whether he was fronting a pop band-in-the-making or something far darker and heavier, it was the title track. While it was clear that Smith didn't have any immediate answers for his dilemma, at least he had finally worked up the courage to ask the question out loud, as he sang of being unable to care yet being equally unable to admit it without feeling an apprehensive sense of remorse. Smith knew that this was an important song for him, as simple as it seems when deconstructed. He referred to it as a classic case of "finally coming to my senses; [it's] something of a milestone lyric." Robert Smith wasn't totally free of his band's bleak past, but he was finding the courage to consider their poptastic future. *The Top* was proof of that.

Lol Tolhurst's role on the album (and in The Cure) might have been reduced to a couple of co-writes and "other instruments", but he seemed fully aware that The Cure was a band in transition. "With *The Top*, it was like 50-50, you know," Tolhurst said. "There were some days when we did things that felt sad and sort of claustrophobic and then some days it was like happy and up. So that accounts for the variation. [It was done] purely for that reason, just to sort of experiment and try and see if people would believe it was us. I suppose we like to confuse people, really. We're a bit mischievous." As for Smith, he revealed that he'd gone back to his old method of compiling a master tape of favourite songs while making the album, and playing it over and over for inspiration. The tape's contents – Billie Holiday's 'Getting Some Fun Out Of Life' and Pink Floyd's 'Interstellar Overdrive' – seemed to explain *The Top*'s sonic schizophrenia, or possibly the reason why, five years later, Smith would come clean and admit that the entire album was recorded in the wrong tempo. Wrong tempo or not, *The Top* spun its way into the UK Top 10.

August 1984 was the rarest of months for Robert Smith: he had no commitments other than to return to Wales with Mary, with the album still climbing the charts, and sift through hour after hour of Cure tapes – about 160 in all – for their live set, *Concert*. On its release in October, it appeared that Smith had the balance just about right, aligning the stark, bleak roar of 'One Hundred Years' and 'The Hanging Garden' with their almost-hits 'Primary' and 'A Forest'. Smith dug even deeper into the back catalogue for '10.15 Saturday Night' and 'Killing An Arab'. Of course Smith wasn't satisfied, but you'd hardly expect anything less. "Half of it is really good," he said, "and half of it is . . . interesting if you like The Cure, but if you don't you'll be bored by it. Very bored."

By the time *Concert* did appear, The Cure was back performing some concerts of their own. The next leg of their world tour kicked off in Wellington, New Zealand, on September 30. They wouldn't return home until the end of November.

It wouldn't have been a Cure tour without at least one meltdown and a departure: this time it was the turn of drummer Andy Anderson. But unlike most Cure road trips, where the unease takes some time to bubble to the surface, there was tension pretty much from the get-go. Temporary Cure-ist Phil Thornalley told me that when they reached Australia, there was clearly more brewing with Anderson than magic-mushroom tea. "The tension on that tour was rife," Thornalley said. "By the time we got to Australia there was already tension with Andy. It was strange and very sad."

The cracks had actually started to appear back in May, when Anderson flipped out in Nice when he was sprayed with mace after having been mistaken for an intruder. (Dressing Rambo-style, in combat fatigues, while marching down the corridor of a five-star hotel, blaring boombox on your shoulder, can cause that kind of confusion.)

"The first time in Nice was kind of interesting because I had to go with Parry to get him out of jail," Tolhurst said. "He came back in the morning in combat gear, boombox on his shoulder, shaved head, walking through the foyer of this fancy hotel. The security guy grabbed him and maced him, which wasn't the right thing to do, because he went into this fury. He chased the guy and started banging on a door of the room into which he thought he'd disappeared, but in fact it was the room of the daughter of the mayor of Nice. So he got carted off to jail.

"When Chris and I got him out, I spent three hours on the beach at Nice with him talking him out of going back to the hotel and finding the guy. Then the mayor said very kindly, 'If Mr Anderson leaves town today, there'll be no charges.'"

As Lol Tolhurst added, "We said to him, 'OK, you get another chance.'" The next time around, though, Anderson truly bottomed out. He and Smith had argued after a show in Sydney on October 12;

by the time they made it to Tokyo five days later, Anderson exploded.

Earlier in the night they'd played the second of two shows at the Nakano Sun Plaza Hall, and the band had ended up in a club until somewhere around four in the morning. Smith, who admitted to being "a bit sake-ed up", staggered off to bed. When he awoke, he found that Anderson had left a wave of destruction behind him, systematically attacking band and crew members and anyone else who approached him. Maybe the mixture of his magic-mushroom tea and the physically and mentally taxing life on the road sent him over the edge. There were even suggestions that Anderson had lost it after one too many jibes about his skin colour. "There was definitely some issues with racism," said Smith. "When we went to places like Japan, you'd notice things, people's attitudes, how difficult it was for him to get served in clubs. I think it really got to him."

Phil Thornalley was very reluctant to go into the specifics of Anderson's Tokyo rampage. He would say, however, that by the time The Cure reached Japan the Anderson situation was way out of control. "He wasn't a happy camper. As ever, touring with The Cure there was lots of drinking, drugs – it had just taken its toll."

"We had a German tour manager, Jade Kniep," Lol Tolhurst said to me, "who had spent some time in the military, which was fortunate as he was able to restrain Andy so he couldn't hurt himself or others. We had a meeting the next day and said to Andy, 'OK, we'll send you home to London and see what happens on our return.'"

As Tolhurst was to learn, Anderson had a history of erratic behaviour. "People said to us, 'Oh, you should get Andy, he's a really good drummer.' But no one told us that if you went on the road with him for too long, he went crazy."[*]

It was a classic Cure scenario: they were five days away from their first show of a US tour, at the Paramount in Seattle, and they were now one member short. Even though his own time with The Cure was fast running out, Thornalley proved to be the band's saviour, as he searched for a drummer who could fill in at a phone call's notice. His first call

---

[*] Tolhurst still maintains a relationship with Anderson. "Andy is a great musician and friend when he is well." Anderson and Tolhurst once undertook a short US tour, but the next time he was scheduled to return, Anderson simply didn't show. "It's not Syd Barrett, but he's unpredictable. I like him a lot but he can be something of a liability."

was to Mike Nocito, his RAK sidekick during the *Pornography* sessions, who had been playing the drums for as long as Thornalley had been a bassman. As tempted as he was to join a band that was about to play a selection of middling-sized venues in the USA (including the Beacon Theater in New York and the Hollywood Palladium), Nocito passed, mainly because his studio reputation had blossomed since *Pornography*. "Tempted?" Nocito laughed when I asked him about his near thing. "It would have been magnificent." Thornalley's next call was to Vince Ely, whom he'd met while working on The Psychedelic Furs' *Talk Talk Talk*. "Count me in," Ely replied.

But Ely, who was working on the West Coast at the time, was purely a fill-in, someone to keep the beat for the band's first six US shows. Boris Williams, another contact of Thornalley's, via his work with The Thompson Twins and Kim Wilde, shifted into the drummer's stool for their November 7 show in Minneapolis. Williams would stay in the chair for the best part of the next 10 years, even though he admitted to not being the band's biggest fan. "I like some of the stuff The Cure have done, but I've never bought their albums," he said not long after joining. What did endear The Cure to Williams was their fondness for booze; The Thompson Twins had been an alcohol-free zone. "The idea of a party with The Thompson Twins," Williams said, "was a cup of coffee and a cheese sandwich."

Though there were only 16 dates in their North American tour, there were already further signs of what would eventually become known as Curemania. An in-store at a Vancouver record shop provided hints of the hysteria that would burst out during subsequent tours. The band was scheduled for a 4pm signing session at Odyssey Records; when they finally arrived, almost two hours late, the store was packed. "What was an orderly line has now become an impatient mass halfway into the store," reported local journalist, Dean Pelkey. When Smith and band arrived, they were swamped. "They [were] instantly mobbed," he reported, "besieged for autographs, presented with banners, stuffed toys and smothered with kisses. It makes me wonder if the boys in Duran Duran had not better start worrying a bit." A little less than a year later, when The Cure returned to North America, Pelkey would learn how accurate his off-the-cuff prediction truly was.

Andy Anderson wasn't the only Cure reject from this period. Phil Thornalley knew his time was almost up once the band returned to the

UK at the end of November. Within a few weeks of the tour he'd realised that he just wasn't built for touring; the safety zone of the studio was much more his style. "It's not for the faint-hearted, touring, but it was worthwhile just to find out how flawed my character really is," Thornalley told me. "You're flying everywhere, you're not looking after yourself; it can take a toll very quickly. When anybody else would ask me to come back out on the road [after The Cure], I'd have to be particularly hungry."

Thornalley's exit was hustled along considerably when roadie Gary Biddles negotiated a reunion between Gallup and Smith. Gallup had been deeply scarred by his Brussels set-to with Smith; he admitted to feeling a deep sense of resentment whenever he saw The Cure on *Top Of The Pops*. Gallup also believed that Thornalley didn't belong in the band – he should be The Cure's bassist, not this studio cat. After all, Gallup figured, he and Smith were old mates, they should be playing together. Chris Parry realised this, too, and initiated a clever plan to squeeze Thornalley out of the band when the word came through that Gallup and Smith had got drunk and made up. Almost 20 years later, Thornalley was still impressed by Parry's machinations.

"It was very artful, the way it was done," he said to me. "Robert wasn't involved with it at all, it was Chris Parry, who's very politically expedient. He was clever. He said, 'With the next record, we want you to be the engineer. We don't want you to co-produce, we don't want you to play bass.' Of course if you've just come off being the bass player and producer, it makes you ask, 'What's going on?' I got into a flap. Looking back on it, it was very clever because it made me self-combust."

Once the dust had settled early in 1985, Simon Gallup was back in The Cure, as was Porl Thompson, the former greatest guitarist in Crawley. The Cure was about to enter their golden age.

Chapter Ten

"Everything I'd ever dreamed of doing was coming to fruition. I suddenly realised that there was an infinite amount of things I could do with the band."

— Robert Smith

SIMON GALLUP had kept himself busy enough during his 18 months as a Cure outsider. As part of Fools Dance, alongside erstwhile Cure keyboardist Matthieu Hartley, he'd released a mini-album called *Priesthole* and played some minor club dates in Europe. But it seemed as though every time Gallup headed up to the bar at his local at Horley, there'd be a Cure song playing or someone reminding him of his past. Gallup had two options: he could completely erase his days with The Cure from his memory, or he could reconcile with Smith and work out whether they could make new music together. Fortunately for Gallup, Biddles made that decision easier for him when he called Smith from the King's Head one night and got the pair back together.* As Biddles would recall in *Ten Imaginary Years*, "They both met round my house and said hello very quietly and it moved on from there. After a few pints, they were talking again." It was clear that Biddles' area of Cure responsibility extended beyond the usual driving, humping amps and throwing the occasional punch.

"The actual decision for me to go and meet Simon and ask him to rejoin the group was the most positive thing I'd done for ages with regards to The Cure," Smith said. "Once he'd agreed [to rejoin], I knew I could pick up where I left off with *Pornography*." But Smith's revised master plan for The Cure involved music that was far more positive in mood than what had gone before. "I could then use what

---

* Tolhurst told me that he tended to avoid the King's Head, even though it was also his local, because "Simon . . . was still quite angry about leaving the band and if he saw me it was a little like a red rag to a bull – especially if he'd had a few beers, which he usually had."

was in the group to uplift people," Smith continued, "rather than just moaning about things."

Come February 1985, and the new Cure – Smith, Tolhurst, Gallup, Boris Williams and Porl Thompson – convened at F2 Studios in Tottenham Court Road, where Smith premiered a tape of demos that would form the nucleus of their next album, *The Head On The Door*. Gallup, who clearly wasn't the most nimble-fingered bass player known to man, wasn't so sure that he could help hold down the rhythm section alongside a player as skilled as Williams. However, just like his reconciliation with Smith, Gallup found that a few beers helped ease his nervousness. (Which was ironic, really, given Gallup's later problems with drink and drugs.)

The Head On The Door's songs started to come together by spring, with the sessions moving between Angel, Townhouse and Genetic studios. Dave Allen, whose first major credit was that of co-engineer on The Human League's 1981 breakthrough album *Dare*, co-produced with Smith. The sessions progressed smoothly enough, although large cracks were starting to appear in the relationship between Tolhurst and the rest of the band. According to Smith, Tolhurst couldn't get through a single session without drinking himself to a shit-faced standstill. "I don't think Lol remembers much about it," Smith said afterwards. "He was off the planet every night and had to be sent home in a cab." Tolhurst knew he had a major drinking problem, but didn't quite know how to deal with it.

"I wasn't aware enough to decide what the problem was," he said in 2004. "I just thought, 'Well, I'll carry on drinking.' I'd sit in the studio getting very upset at myself for not being able to play something or think of a good idea, which I'd always been able to do before." Tolhurst's only solution was to keep drinking. To his credit, however, he did receive a more substantial musical credit for *The Head On The Door* than he did with *The Top* ("keyboards" as opposed to "other instruments"). But this time, unlike their previous five albums, there was no musical or lyrical input from Tolhurst; each song was a Smith original. The new Cure ground rules were in place: Robert Smith was bandleader, dictator and its creative force.

More so than any Cure album that came before, *The Head On The Door* is the sound of The Cure feeling more comfortable with its place in the world, denying neither their melodic nous nor Robert Smith's pessimistic world view. It opened with the runaway hit 'Inbetween Days', where Smith achieved the near impossible, somehow managing to make the dire pronouncement about his feeling so aged he could die sound like a celebration. It was one of the key musical achievements of his career, the perfect balance of melody and melancholy. Powered by skittish guitars and a wheezing, tubercolic organ, 'Inbetween Days' made it very clear what listeners were in for – a pop album with a dark core, a candy-coated treat with a poisonous centre. Even on a track as miserable as 'Kyoto Song', a song that had come to The Cure singer after another night on Severin's floor during his *Blue Sunshine* bender, Smith managed to fuse his sullen lyric to a playful, inventive melody, with a vocal that's both daring and experimental. (Smith's confidence was growing as much vocally as it was in front of Tim Pope's camera.) This was pop, but unlike much of anything else calling itself pop music in 1985.

'The Blood', with its faux-Flamenco guitars and stop-start rhythms, was actually a drinking song. It was written (or scrawled, more likely) after Smith had polished off a bottle of Portuguese plonk known to wary locals as 'The Tears of Christ'. When Smith moaned how he was paralysed by the blood of Christ, he wasn't tapping into some long-submerged spirituality. He was singing about getting tragically, completely pissed on this potent local brew, whose label featured an unholy image of the Virgin Mary with baby Jesus under one arm and a bottle cradled in the other. Steve Severin kept a stash of this and other equally potent liqueurs in his house.

A rolling, tumbling piano figure opens 'Six Different Ways', a song about multiple personalities and one of *The Head On The Door*'s many highs. It was another classic study of Smith's fast-developing popcraft and oft-neglected sense of humour – in a world dominated by the austere, no-fun sounds of Simple Minds, Echo & The Bunnymen and U2, The Cure sounded like aliens beamed in from some parallel pop universe. 'Push', however, seemed a backward step, its chiming rhythm guitars and cavernous drums moving way too close to the turgid "modern rock" of Big Country and their peers. If there was one song on The Cure's sixth album that was a compromise, a concession to the musical world around it, this was it. But it was a rare misstep on a record that offered up such small-scale masterpieces as the infectious minimalism of 'Close To Me'.

Robert Smith wasn't necessarily in a healthier state of mind for *The Head On The Door* – this was an album, after all, that stuck with such familiar subject matter as drugs, either as a theme ('Screw'), or as a source of inspiration (Smith would admit that 'New Day' was a "drug-induced improvisation"). Smith also let loose his frustration towards the unstoppable march of time (see 'Sinking'). And just as Smith had done way back with 'A Forest', he was also documenting his bleakest nightmares in such tracks as 'The Baby Screams' and 'Close To Me'. Robert Smith had tapped into this negativity many times before – in fact, he'd made a handsome living doing just that. But this time around, overriding these downbeat lyrics and themes was the type of musical free-thinking that would soon cement The Cure's position as accidental stars. They were one seriously fucked-up pop band who'd somehow managed to find a way to combine their leader's dark nights of the soul with such flights of musical fancy as 'Inbetween Days' and 'Close To Me'.

These were pure pop songs that operated on two levels. On the surface, they were very easy to sing along with, but they could also be scrutinised more closely for signs of Smith's ever-changing moods. As Smith explained, his goals with the album were very clear. "I wanted to write moody songs and pop songs and put them on the same record. I knew that there were people ready to accept the two things at the same time." Smith also fancied *The Head On The Door* as a rebirth of The Cure. That was a fair enough comment, too, given that it was recorded with yet another revised line-up. "There was a real sense of being in a band for the first time since *Seventeen Seconds*," Smith said. "It felt like being in The Beatles – and I wanted to make substantial, 'Strawberry Fields' style pop music. I wanted everything to be really catchy."

In reality, many Cure fans would be alienated by *The Head On The Door*, especially those who swore allegiance to the turbulent trilogy of *Faith*, *Seventeen Seconds* and *Pornography*. But for every browned-off member of the overcoat brigade, The Cure enticed a handful of cashed-up pop fans over to the dark side. It was an artful piece of manipulation on the part of Smith and The Cure, which was to prove particularly effective in North America, where their following had been increasing in both size and levels of fanaticism. And as Smith and Parry both knew, America was where they could make real money.

Smith had never made any secret of his ambition to create the best possible music with The Cure; now he wanted to sell that music to as many people as possible. "I was looking for a bigger audience," he admitted. "It wasn't to do with being well known; I wanted more people to hear us. I thought we were in danger of disappearing a bit."

To achieve that goal, another call was made to Tim Pope, who truly excelled himself with two benchmark Cure videos for 'Inbetween Days' and 'Close To Me'. The former marks the arrival of The Cure's full-blown, large-haired, baggy-clothed, lipstick-smeared phase. It's a performance video, of sorts, albeit one with a wildly surreal touch: the band seems to spend the entire clip being pursued by a battalion of flying fluorescent socks. Pope insisted that he was merely giving life to Smith's creative vision (all for the princely sum of £8,000). "Robert's brief was to make it look fresh and vivacious. They were supposed to be a kind of blurry colour effect, but when we got the video back, they looked exactly like socks. Robert was really pissed off." MTV didn't mind, however, because the clip quickly went into maximum rotation.

'Close To Me' was another performance video, but with a twist – the band was wedged into a cupboard that was slowly filling with water, which was teetering on the edge of Beachy Head.* The video worked on any number of levels – it was perversely entertaining, the images seemed to match the bare-boned electro-pop song beautifully, and, crucially, it stuck in the head of MTV viewers. Not only did it make global stars out of The Cure, but it also became a signature video for Tim Pope. "Wherever I go," he said in 2003, "someone mentions it." Pope's memories of the shoot aren't exactly nostalgic: they revolved around a tiny wardrobe, a massive studio and Lol Tolhurst's digestion. "Lol's bowels were a problem in a very confined space," Pope admitted.

"We were stuck in this horrid, tepid water for several hours at a time," Tolhurst recalled. "It was kind of bizarre. I like the little trick it played on people; it was fun. The only thing I would say is that Tim always picked me to do the most dangerous thing to do in videos. I'd always come back a few days later with bruises and mild concussion from things he made me do. But I trusted him."

Again, Pope had taken a very literal approach to a Smith concept.

---

* A million Cure fans sighed their disappointment when they learned that the majority of the clip was filmed in a studio.

They'd met a week before the shoot, when Smith mentioned that he had an image in mind for the sleeve of the single: the band jammed in a wardrobe about to take a tumble off Beachy Head. "I thought it'd look quite surreal," Smith said. Pope thought the image would be wasted on a record sleeve and stole the idea for the video. According to Smith, "Tim translated that as, 'How can I make it even more uncomfortable?' He stuck us in a wardrobe and dropped us in a tank of dirty water."

The Cure and the charts were now firm friends. 'Inbetween Days', backed with 'The Exploding Boy', a song that Smith felt perfectly expressed "the happiness I felt playing in the new line-up", fairly galloped to number 15 on its release in July 1985. Even the press was warming to Smith's weird pop ways, if somewhat reluctantly, as typified by Steve Sutherland's take on *The Head On The Door* in *Melody Maker*.

"Robert Smith has wormed himself into an enviable but precarious position over the past 18 months," he wrote. "We don't know what to expect any more. He's slipped the straitjacket of brooding depression that shaped *Faith*, cleaved through the claustrophobia of *Pornography* . . . and now roams among us, a harmless eccentric." Sutherland could spot *The Head On The Door*'s obvious appeal, noting that 'Close To Me' was a seductive pop song and admitting that the entire album was "perfection of sorts", even if it was merely "a collection of pop songs". *Rolling Stone*, however, weren't quite so sold on the album. While acknowledging that this was the LP that would make them much more than contenders Stateside, they still felt that the album hung "on the engagingly sweet single 'Inbetween Days' and not much more".

It didn't really matter. By the time the new Cure hit the road, playing their first show in Barcelona on June 20, their star status was confirmed. So much so, in fact, that after a show in Athens, where they shared the bill with Nina Hagen, Talk Talk and Boy George, Tolhurst was mistaken for the Boy himself. Many free champagnes later, he crooned 'Do You Really Want To Hurt Me' as if he really was the artist sometimes known as George O'Dowd. Mary Poole, who'd commandeered the hotel bar, laughed along. By September 12, they were filling the 11,000 capacity Wembley Arena, followed by full houses at the Manchester Apollo and the 12,500 capacity Birmingham NEC. When 'Close To Me' dropped in September, the band was readying itself for yet another US tour – 14 shows in a month, culminating with a sold-out show at New York's Radio City Music Hall. The Cure was an unstoppable force, with a hit album and two high-rotation MTV videos.

So why The Cure? Nothing radical had occurred in the charts; in August 1985, when *The Head On The Door* was released, Huey Lewis was celebrating 'The Power Of Love', Bryan Adams was daydreaming about the 'Summer Of 69', and Dire Straits was cranking out 'Money For Nothing'. It was mediocre business as usual. With the odd exception, such as Kate Bush's Fairlight extravaganza 'Running Up That Hill', the Top 40 was still a very safe house, a place for respectable acts to preach to the converted and then count their cash. But with their winning blend of eccentric pop tunes and wonderfully weird videos – and a look that fell just on the acceptable side of dangerous – The Cure had found their place amongst the Tinas, Phils and Whitneys of the world. It was a major achievement: five wild-haired Brits, one an alcoholic and several drunks-under-development, had managed to become pop stars.

Robert Smith's year in the spotlight was made complete with a December appearance on the BBC TV Oracle service, mixing a cocktail of his creation. He'd become a celebrity, of sorts: teen magazine *Just 17* wanted to know his star sign, *Smash Hits* made him a cover star. Smith's premature mid-life crisis seemed to be in remission as he flirted with the press, even starting a rumour that he was contemplating an EP of Sinatra tunes. The press, who'd dubbed him variously Mad Bob, in light of his "chemical vacation" with Severin, and Fat Bob, due to his expanding waistline, lapped it up.

In many ways, Smith was the perfect star. He didn't bullshit when asked reasonable questions, yet at the same time he fully appreciated the power of spin – his ever-changing responses to the "secret" behind the title of *The Head On The Door* alone were enough to fill a chapter of this book. He even managed to convince a gullible writer that Mary Poole was at various times a nun and a stripper. And The Cure now had an instantly identifiable look, courtesy of Tim Pope, with a back catalogue large enough to satisfy both long-termers and recent converts who, prior to 'Let's Go To Bed', didn't know The Cure from The Cutting Crew. Their live sets, which now ran to 20 or more songs, could easily accommodate the many sides of The Cure, encompassing everything from '10.15 Saturday Night' and 'Boys Don't Cry' to 'Inbetween Days', 'The Walk' and 'One Hundred Years'. The compromises were small, the rewards were large.

As The Cure took a breather over the early months of 1986, Smith had the chance to review the 18 months that had slipped by since he had left the Banshees. If facts and figures counted for anything, Smith had made a shrewd move: over the course of two albums and a handful of hit singles – 'Close To Me', 'Inbetween days', 'The Caterpillar' – his band had become bona fide pop stars on the continent and were edging ever closer to mainstream success in the US. It hardly mattered that the UK press was still writing off The Cure.* Smith, however, was having the last laugh, as MTV continued to spin Pope's videos and *The Head On The Door* clung to the charts like a fluoro-coloured barnacle.

Smith's next move was typically unexpected. The band's record deal was up for renewal and Polydor had plans for the obligatory best of. Smith was wary of career backtracks; they were usually a clear sign that an act was past its sell-by date. Aware that he couldn't stop Polydor from issuing a compilation, he decided to become actively involved in the process. "If we were not to re-sign," Smith realised, "they would immediately put out what they would call a greatest hits album and package it very badly. So that made me think we should do it now rather than wait for them to do it."

Smith not only helped with the selection of tracks, but also re-remixed and re-recorded the vocal for 'Boys Don't Cry'. Alongside Tim Pope, Smith also helped compile a set of Cure videos. As no clip had been made for 'Boys Don't Cry', the pair opted to shoot a performance video with a twist. Smith and Tolhurst hand-picked three pre-teens from a local drama school, who could convincingly lip-synch the song, while the original Three Imaginary Boys – Smith, Tolhurst and Michael Dempsey – strummed along from behind a screen. Sure, Smith was treading water by revisiting the band's back catalogue, but at least he was finding a way to put a new spin on an old favourite.

Tolhurst recalled the reunion as "kind of strange". The three had met beforehand for lunch in a London club; then just prior to the shoot

---

* After their September show at the Brighton Centre, *NME* got very personal. "I wouldn't like to be washed up on a desert island with this boring old sod," it declared.

they shared a very gentlemanly game of three-man racquetball. Times had definitely changed.

Dempsey had been a Cure outsider since his departure in 1979. Not surprisingly, he was taken aback when Smith called and informed him of the planned video. But he was unsure if it was an act of generosity on Smith's part "or whether it just fitted in with the general scheme". Regardless, he turned up and plugged in one more time. The clip worked brilliantly, even if Smith's new vocal seemed strangely hysterical in parts.

The band's worth on the continent was building to the stage where 'Close To Me' was actually heading for the top spot on the French chart. With that very much in mind, in April 1986, The Cure returned from their brief exile for an appearance on a TV show, *Champs Elysee* ("*Wogan* and *Top Of The Pops* rolled into one," according to Tolhurst). With Thompson and Williams still on vacation, Tolhurst made a brief return to the drums while Martin Judd, a flatmate of his, mimed keyboards. *Record Mirror* looked on and couldn't help but notice just how big the band had become, even without their full line-up available. They reported that "The Cure are the biggest thing to happen in France since Joan of Arc's heart refused to burn at Rouen."

Just like Pink Floyd before them, and Jeff Buckley afterwards, The Cure had tapped into the part of the French psyche that was drawn to moody, melancholic music. "The rock press loved the band, they toured France, their music is very emotional and 'romantic' – and the French love that," explained Claude Duvivier, a Paris-based music industry professional. The French press, meanwhile, were convinced that Judd was the latest addition to The Cure. Lol Tolhurst has fond memories of Chris Parry "frantically running around trying to tell everybody he wasn't the new band member, much to my and Robert's amusement."[*]

The band celebrated in very Cure style on May 22, when they rode the Orient Express to Venice for a proposed *Old Grey Whistle Test* live shoot. (Their show at Verona was scuppered by the local fire chiefs, so the *Whistle Test* filmed their on-board antics instead.) Freed of any immediate commitments, the band and their partners ran up a record Orient Express bar tab. Depending on which report you take as gospel, it ran to somewhere between £1,500 and £2,000. They'd come a long

---

[*] French Cure collectors can still buy a postcard of the band featuring Judd.

way from pushing Smith's green Maxi van from show to show and singing for petrol money.

When *Standing On A Beach*, their 13-singles-strong compilation, was released in May, along with the video compilation *Staring At The Sea*, the band decided against the usual all-stops UK jaunt. Instead they played selected European festival dates, topped off with a celebratory headlining spot at Glastonbury on June 21, where a virtual greatest hits set ended in a blaze of lasers and retina-burning lights. The Cure mightn't have been the most lively band on stage – Gallup's low-slung bass playing being the only real rock move on display – but they now had the budget, and the audience, to turn on their very own rock'n' roll spectacular. Smith was on such a high at Glastonbury that when he wished the masses a "happy tomorrow", the persistent rain actually stopped falling. Only a star could do that.

Success in Europe was all well and good, but Smith and Parry still had their eyes turned Stateside. The Cure returned to America in early July for three weeks of shows to coincide with the release of *Standing On A Beach*. The standard question asked by the press was this: who's the old codger on the album cover? It turned out to be one John Button, a fisherman living in quiet retirement in the harbour town of Rye. His wizened, leathery mug was perfect for the cover. Button was also the only person to appear in the newly shot clip for 'Killing An Arab'. For a moment in time, Button became the sixth face of The Cure. ("If I can help these youngsters break through, after all, why not?" he said, when asked.)

The Cure was now onto its fourth US label, Elektra. (Sire had issued *Japanese Whispers*, but passed on *The Top*.) As always, there was more than a little backroom argy-bargy at work. In their very literal way, American radio programmers had begun to use 'Killing An Arab' as some sort of propaganda tool; its release came just after the US air and sea raids in the Gulf of Sirte in Libya on March 24, 1986. Quickly, the American Arab League petitioned Elektra to have the track withdrawn from *Standing On A Beach*. Smith responded by advising Elektra that they could delete the entire album, but the song stayed. They reached a compromise when Smith agreed to pen an explanation of the song, which appeared on a sticker affixed to the album's cover. It read: "The song 'Killing An Arab' has absolutely no racist overtones whatsoever. It is a song which decries the existence of all prejudice and consequent violence. The Cure condemn its use in furthering anti-Arab feeling." 'Killing An Arab' was quietly withdrawn from US radio airplay, but that didn't stop the album from selling.

"I just despaired, really, that I had to step in and explain," Smith said, "and I got very annoyed at Elektra's initial suggestion that they delete the song but keep selling the album, which I refused to do. The song was written . . . when I was 16. It seemed ludicrous to me that it suddenly became an issue."

Against Smith's wishes, Elektra re-released 'Let's Go To Bed' to help flog the best of, rather than Smith's choice, 'Boys Don't Cry'. Smith felt that The Cure sold more singles than albums in the States, anyway, and was uncharacteristically mellow about the disagreement. "I've given up fighting with the record company in America," he commented, as their US tour wound from the East to the West Coast, where the band would have their unfortunate meeting with suicidal self-mutilator Jonathan Moreland. "As long as they release the album and don't mess about, I don't really care."

Smith was both right and wrong. *Standing On A Beach* was fast becoming their biggest seller in the US, but it was selling on the strength of the band's singles, especially those with an accompanying Tim Pope video (as seen on MTV, of course), such as 'Close To Me' and 'Inbetween Days'. Smith's public image didn't hurt their value either. The *East Village Eye* captured the zeitgeist perfectly when they described Smith as a "prophet of gloom [who] is the cuddliest thing since the Qantas koala bear; he is cute in a Pillsbury doughboy sort of way".

By February 1987, *Standing On A Beach* was The Cure's first gold record in North America, shifting more than 600,000 copies. Their video collection, *Staring At The Sea*, would also go gold, in September 1987. (*The Head On The Door* had shifted around 250,000 copies after 38 weeks on the US album chart; everything that came before had averaged sales of 40–50,000.) "*Standing On A Beach* was a huge commercial success," Smith stated. "Everything I'd ever dreamt of doing was coming to fruition. I suddenly realised that there was an infinite amount of things I could do with the band."

Smith was as good as his word. After the LA tragedy, their greatest hits tour ended at a Roman amphitheatre in Provence on August 9, where the band had several thousand Cure-crazy French fans and Tim

Pope's cameras for company. Pope had snagged a reasonable £150,000 to shoot what would be known as *The Cure In Orange*, which had a low-key theatrical release in October 1987. When asked why the band was so big in France, Smith was stumped. "They like us because we're odd," was all he could offer.

Live film in the can, The Cure was now ready to begin piecing together an album that would reflect the band at their most prolific. They might as well have named their seventh album *The Many Sides Of The Cure* — it was truly all over the shop.

The recording of *Kiss Me Kiss Me Kiss Me* was also an indication of The Cure's new, gold-plated status. The various London studios in which they'd recorded — RAK and Townhouse, amongst others — might have featured all the production mod cons a band on an upward spiral (with a budget to match) could desire, with production staff who could make sense of the music ringing in Robert Smith's ears. But Miraval, where the band set up camp for 10 weeks, had that extra special something. For one thing, the studio was the perfect escape: it was deep in the south of France, situated roughly halfway between Marseille and Nice and about a 40-minute drive from Cannes and St Tropez. Miraval also had enough beds to house the band and their many guests (most Cure partners moved in halfway through the sessions). The studio also had a certain history; since opening in 1977, its occupants had included Pink Floyd, who brought their almost career-ending monster, *The Wall*, to Miraval. David Sylvian would also record here, as would Stevie Winwood, Yes, Sade and Belinda Carlisle. And Miraval, which was set in the grounds of an imposing 17th century Provençal chateau, offered all the usual indulgences, such as a swimming pool and games room, plus a grand dining room that was just right for the type of bacchanalia to which The Cure had become accustomed.

"Miraval was great," said Tolhurst, "because by that time we had enough money to record anywhere we wanted to. We realised the best place for us was somewhere far away from all the distractions." There was also some local history to the site, as Tolhurst explained. "[The owner] Jacques Loussier,[*] I think, had vied with the local Mafia for the

---

[*] A classically trained pianist, Loussier was famous for performing Bach's music with a jazz trio. His version of 'Air On A G String' became the soundtrack for the celebrated Hamlet cigar TV advert.

house. They wanted it for a safe house."

Crucially for The Cure, Miraval was surrounded by 300 acres of rolling hills, pine woods – and lush Provence vineyards. The Cure weren't averse to the occasional tipple, so Miraval must have felt just like home, even if it wasn't exactly the perfect location for Lol Tolhurst and his worsening alcoholism. By this time, according to Smith, "Lol became a pitiful figure."

"I wasn't well for some of the time," Tolhurst recalled. "Some of it was very good, some very sad."

The band's boozing during the sessions was so pronounced, in fact, that Tolhurst felt that the studio's owners missed a great opportunity. The usual deal was that by hiring the site, the residents were supplied with all the Chateau de Miraval they could drink. "[But] I think with us they would have preferred it the other way around. With all drinking stories there's an element of myth-making," Tolhurst added, "but without a shadow of a doubt, Robert, Simon and myself were the hardcore crew. By that time it had become *de rigueur*, we just had to do it."

"It was a very unreal situation," Smith commented. "Ten weeks of being completely cut off from the world. It was a very incestuous, very secretive kind of thing – because we were having so much fun we didn't want anyone to come and break the spell."

Miraval was also very nearly the end of the band – or at least most of its members. After yet another boozy night, Smith, Tolhurst and Boris Williams decided to try to pay a visit in Smith's jeep to racing car driver Alain de Cadenet, who lived nearby. The plan was to challenge him to a race. They didn't get very far, as Tolhurst reported. "We were racing around, with no lights on, of course. There were all these ledges coming down the side of the hill of the vineyard, with a drop of about 15 feet on either side. We got stuck and Robert burned out the clutch trying to get it off this incline. All we could see was darkness all around us. We managed to get out and walk back, but the next morning we saw how precariously it was balanced. The car was written off. And we never got to see Alain de Cadenet."

Despite all the band's wild nocturnal wanderings, *Kiss Me Kiss Me Kiss Me* was the most sprawling, musically adventurous outing of The Cure's career. The mixing took Smith and co-producer Dave Allen even further off-shore, to Compass Point in Nassau, plus New York and Brussels. It was one strange trip, especially in light of the album's more humble beginnings: the early demos had been recorded in Beethoven Studios in chilly London during downtime in summer 1986.

As the album would show, this truly was a team effort. It was also the first time that Smith would introduce a "scoring" system for each song offered by band members for inclusion. This relatively democratic system ran along simple lines: each Cure-ist would adjourn to their home studios, record demos on a cassette and then hand them to Smith, who would play each and make various notes in exercise books. As Boris Williams would relate, Smith then graded the songs. "He draws a little face, a frown, smile or blank face beside each song and out of all those we pick out the right sort of songs." Smith's more inclusive attitude might explain why there's plenty of flab on the bones of *Kiss Me Kiss Me Kiss Me*. It would also explain how Porl Thompson and Boris Williams came to score their first Cure songwriting credits.

To Smith, it was further evidence that this truly was the best Cure line-up he'd ever worked with – everyone was willing to chip in. Lol Tolhurst agreed. "That was the accomplished version [of The Cure]," he said to me. "Porl was a wonderful musician, Boris was a great drummer. It was a band that had real empathy with each other. Put us all together and it was like the best gang in town. That's what kept it going – we had this loyalty to each other and whatever we were doing, it worked."

This was very unlike the previous pair of albums, where Smith had strongly exercised what he called his "negative dictatorship". (This was redefined by drummer Williams as a "democratic dictatorship . . . when it comes down to final decisions, it's Robert's decision what songs are going to work on the album.")

"Among the five of us there is a genuine excitement about doing things," Smith said. "With this album, I insisted that the others gave me a cassette of music and I got six or seven songs from each one. It just showed that everyone really wanted to be involved in it." Smith would even liken the process to the Eurovision Song Contest.

Before hiding themselves away at Miraval, the band spent a fortnight demoing two cassettes' worth of band-approved tracks in Provence. Smith remembered these sessions almost as fondly as the band's leisurely months at Miraval. "It was really good fun," he stated. "They had a football pitch and we played the locals every day." As for the finished record, in spite of Tolhurst's battles with the bottle, Smith felt "it was a delight to record, a joy".

Looking back on that time, Tolhurst now realises how his chronic drinking problems were killing his creativity and poisoning his mind – he wanted to contribute to The Cure, but he found that the more he drank, the less he wrote. "I was there because I wanted to be there and contribute something," he said. "But having this broken psyche meant that I was living inside my head for a lot of the time; my mind wouldn't allow me to do it. It just wouldn't come out by that time."

If *The Top* was Robert Smith solo in all but name, and *The Head On The Door* was Smith backed by his favourite Cure line-up of all time, then *Kiss Me Kiss Me Kiss Me* truly was The Cure as an egalitarian enterprise, even if it could have used an iron-willed editor. It was a fine single album posing as an 18-track sprawl. Every track carried the Smith/Gallup/Thompson/Williams/Tolhurst credit line, which said as much about The Cure's one-in-all-in spirit as the diverse songs contained within. *Rolling Stone* got it exactly right when they stated that, "Under Smith's guiding presence, The Cure ploughs through wah-wah encrusted garage band rave-ups, suicidally bummed-out set pieces and thumping rock-disco grooves with equal assurance." In short, *Kiss Me Kiss Me Kiss Me* offered something for everyone – possibly even too much. To Smith, it was both a document of the band's patchy musical history and a blueprint for the next stage of their career. "Half of it's looking forward," he said, "and half of it's trying to sum up what the group's done in the past."

Kiss Me was not an album going anywhere in a hurry: it took almost four minutes of guitar squall during the opener, 'The Kiss', before Smith's voice emerged from the gloom with a signature wail. And then it was only to mutter some of the most gruesome lines of his lyrical life which invoked the f-word in a now typical abusive put-down aimed at his long-suffering tormentor. But then came a reminder that The Cure was a pop band deep down inside: 'Catch' was up next, a gentle valentine flavoured by a plucked acoustic guitar and keyboards posing as strings. It was a low-key charmer that, along with 'Just Like Heaven' and 'Why Can't I Be You?', was one of the trio of singles to emerge from this hugely successful long-player.

From then on in it was a musical tug of war between the band's MTV-ready, college-radio-friendly side, and their sullen nature, well represented by such urgent, insistent soundscapes as 'Torture' and 'Fight'. Darkest of all was the epic 'If Only Tonight We Could Sleep', which was based around a faux-Eastern riff – shades of Led Zeppelin – and a forlorn Smith vocal that may well have been recorded from somewhere deep inside a wind tunnel.*

The flipside of these unholy guitar-and-keyboards powered odes to nothingness were such sweet confections as the manic 'Why Can't I Be You?' and 'Hot Hot Hot!!!' It was here that The Cure came on like a funk revivalist act: the Sussex Soul Train, with Smith quoting directly from Charles Aznavour's 'She' at the opening of 'Hot Hot Hot!!!' Powered by some drunken funk guitar, Smith likened this raver to a "Louis Armstrong record". This pair of tracks was as freewheeling, raucous and irresistible as anything the band had previously unleashed on their slightly bemused, but no less loving public. More than anything on *Kiss Me Kiss Me Kiss Me*, these follies typified the band's anything-goes approach.

"We were trying to be lots of different bands that we liked at the time," Tolhurst explained.

'Just Like Heaven', of course, was another pristine few moments of Robert Smith the tunesmith; it was right up there with 'Inbetween Days' and 'The Lovecats' as a near-perfect pop song. The melody for 'Heaven' came to Smith at Maida Vale during another heavy boozing phase in his life. Smith admitted that in 1987 he needed to set himself a regimen of writing every other day, 15 days a month. "Otherwise I'd have just got up in mid-afternoon and watched TV until the pubs opened, then gone out drinking." As soon as Smith finished 'Just Like Heaven', he realised it was a good pop song, possibly a great one – even if the structure was not unlike that of The Only Ones' minor 1979 hit, 'Another Girl, Another Planet'. This similarity wasn't lost on Smith.

"I can still vividly recall hearing ['Another Girl'] on the radio late at night in the mid-Seventies. I introduced some different chord changes, which give it that slightly melancholic feeling."

---

* Years later it was given a wildly effective reawakening by dedicated Cure lovers, nu-metal moodists The Deftones, on an *MTV Icons* episode dedicated to Smith's not-so-merry band of men.

But Smith had no lyrics for the song, whose original tempo was much slower than the finished version. While still word-less, Smith gave the tune to French TV show *Les Enfants du Rock*, who used it as their theme tune. There was, of course, a method in Smith's munificence.

"I already felt it was the most obvious single," he realised, "and it meant that the music would be familiar to millions of Europeans even before it was released."

Not only a hit in Europe, the song even reached the fringes of the US Top 40 and has been recorded by various players in Spanish, German and French – there's even a version performed by LA's Section String Quartet. And 'Heaven', most famously, was given a hard, grungy makeover by Dinosaur Jr in 1989. Of all the many takes on Cure songs, this has become one of Smith's favourites, almost as soon as Dinosaur Jr's J. Mascis sent him a cassette. "I've never had such a visceral reaction to a cover version before or since," Smith said in 2003.

Smith was also smart enough to realise that placement was everything with an album as lengthy as *Kiss Me Kiss Me Kiss Me*. He wisely positioned such lightweight romps as 'Why Can't I Be You?' directly after the bummed-out sprawl that was 'If Only Tonight We Could Sleep'. Smith kept that balance pretty much constant throughout the 18 tracks. Given that there were two distinctly different Cure-lovers – the pop kids mad for Smith the Lovecat, and the doomed children of the night hoping for *Seventeen Seconds Revisited* – he was refusing to alienate anyone. The album was another savvy each-way bet on the part of Smith and the band – and it connected at the cash register with even more ker-ching than *The Head On The Door*. *Kiss Me* would go gold in the USA in August 1987, three months after its release, and platinum three years later. It wouldn't leave the US album chart for a year.

Lyrically speaking, Robert Smith was drawing from the usual sources. There were the obligatory drug songs, including 'Hot Hot Hot!!!' and 'Icing Sugar' (which featured some swinging sax from Andrew Brennen, whom Smith spotted blowing in a Compass Point cabaret band). There were songs about death ('If Only Tonight We Could Sleep'), and escape ('Why Can't I Be You?'), songs about Tolhurst's slide ('Shiver And Shake'), fight songs ('Fight', of course), party songs ('Hey You!!!', a not-so-subtle steal of *The Man From*

U.N.C.L.E. theme), sex songs ('All I Want'), even love songs ('The Perfect Girl'). The obligatory literary allusion came with the album's most pedestrian track, 'How Beautiful You Are', which Smith adapted from a Baudelaire short story.

"It's about how you think you're really close to somebody," Smith explained, "that you think the same way and enjoy the same things, but suddenly an incident will happen which makes you realise that the person thinks a completely different way about things, yet you can still get on with them really well." Smith was clearly considering both his faltering relationship with Lol Tolhurst, and the immeasurable worth of his loyal allies, Mary Poole and Simon Gallup.

Then there were the clearly autobiographical moments, such as 'Just Like Heaven', which in its own subtle way revealed the details of a night that Smith, Poole and some friends spent at renowned lover's leap Beachy Head, the same site where The Cure tumbled to their watery demise at the end of Pope's video for 'Close To Me'. It was also the spot where Smith and Poole would move when they'd had enough of London.

"We'd been drinking and someone thought it would be cool to go for a walk," Smith reminisced when asked about the night on the tiles that inspired 'Just Like Heaven'. "But suddenly the fog came in and I lost sight of my friends and couldn't see my hand before my eyes. I thought I might fall down the cliff if I moved another foot so I had to sit down until dawn. Later I heard my friends didn't even look for me." Smith and band revisited the site for the Tim Pope video; look closely and you'll spot Mary Poole, spinning and dancing like a fallen angel, looking exactly as you'd expect Robert Smith's partner to look.

The Cure's transition from band to brand was made complete with the release of *Kiss Me Kiss Me Kiss Me* in May 1987. Not so much because of its worldwide success – in the wake of the hefty sales of *Standing On A Beach*, that was almost a given – but by the image lathered all over the album's cover. Those are Robert Smith's lipstick-smeared lips in microscopic detail; a close-up of his eye featured else-where on the inside sleeve. Many rock stars had been synonymous with their body parts before – Iggy Pop was fond of unsheathing his "biggy", likewise Jim "The Lizard King" Morrison – but not since the rub-bery-lipped Mick Jagger at his Glimmer Twins' prime had an artist been so directly linked to a body part. Smith admitted to an obsession with mouths and lips; it's no accident that references to them appear frequently in his lyrics. "I suppose it's because they're a public orifice," Smith said. "And they have so many purposes – eating, speaking, sex. Something must have happened to me when I was very young. A giant mouth must have tried to sit on my face when I was in my pram."

It was clear that The Cure was about to hit their commercial peak, because Elektra had big plans for the album. They strongly suggested to the band that they hire hit-machine Bob Clearmountain to mix the album; he'd added his signature sonic boom to records from The Rolling Stones (*Tattoo You*), David Bowie (*Let's Dance*) and Bruce Springsteen (*Born In The USA*). Smith smiled, continued spending Elektra's money, and went back to work with Allen.

"We've always heard that kind of thing from our American record companies," Smith said, "and we've never paid any attention to it. Everything we've ever done has been very selfishly motivated."

With *Kiss Me Kiss Me Kiss Me* wrapped, Smith and Poole decided to take a driving holiday in France, staying in small, out-of-the-way places and trying their best to be a normal couple. All the trip achieved, however, was a reminder of just how big The Cure had become, especially in France. "In the morning there'd always be like 30 people outside the hotel because they'd found out I was staying there," Smith revealed. "It was a fucking nightmare. I realised very quickly that I didn't like that level of success."

Robert Smith was now entering a new phase of his life, where he was struggling to find ways to deal with his rapidly rising star. One tactic was to drop big hints about The Cure's demise. Like the Goth who cried wolf, *Kiss Me* would be the latest of many Cure albums where Smith would suggest, strongly, that this was the band's swan-song. He even let that slip during a quick US promo trip in March 1987, two months prior to the LP's release. "When we made this record," said Smith, "I really thought, 'This has to be the best Cure record, because it's gonna be the last.'" Typically, Smith would then turn around and say that this kind of statement was purely designed as a Cure motivational tool: what better way to get the band fired up than to suggest they were finished?

But if Smith was serious, then he'd obviously decided to go out in the biggest way possible. The band had their first South American tour booked for March 1987, preceded by several weeks of rehearsals in Eire, where they squeezed in another madcap shoot with Pope, this time for 'Why Can't I Be You?' Pope flew out and joined the band at a studio in Bray, owned by no less a legend than small-screen star Mary Tyler Moore.

It may have taken two or three videos for the band to warm fully to Pope's wicked ways, but now they fully embraced his mad methodology. For 'Why Can't I Be You?', it was all about dressing up. Smith chose to sport a bear suit. Gallup played the role of a crow, in black cape, huge yellow beak and dangerously tight tights; then he was a Morris dancer. Williams wore basic schoolgirl, while Thompson played both a Scotsman and a woman (Smith also doubled as a cross-dresser). As for Tolhurst, his role as Cure jester was made very clear: he wore blackface – "Prince's ugly brother," laughed one band member – then doubled as a bumblebee, flapping about helplessly on wires attached by Pope's crew.*

Smith, of course, laughed it all off. "This is it," he shouted as the madness of the shoot happened around him, "the grand finale, the climax. 'Drunken Schoolgirl in Gay Sex Orgy'." Then he returned to perform some of the most poorly choreographed dancing ever seen on MTV. As for Tim Pope, he couldn't be happier. "This is . . . the video I've always wanted to make," he whooped. "The Cure dancing! I can't believe I'm seeing this. They're finished." That may have just about been true for Tolhurst, but The Cure was only getting bigger.

If Smith needed evidence of just how big The Cure had become, how far they'd outgrown their life as a post-punk trio from suburban Crawley, it was on full display during the first South American jaunt. The signs were there from the moment their Aerolineas jumbo hit the tarmac at Buenos Aires on March 15. Rather than the usual drag of clearing customs, waiting for their luggage and piling into a van to the hotel, the band and Parry were given the full Beatles treatment, being led out through a side door into a waiting car, followed all the way into the city by what Smith would describe as "a bizarre motorcade of horn-blowing-screaming-waving cars". There were already 500, maybe

---

* Off camera, during the subsequent 'Hot Hot Hot!!!' shoot, Smith actually spat on Tolhurst. His downward spiral was just about complete.

more, diehards camped on the pavement outside the Sheraton Towers when they arrived, including members of the "Bananafishbones Club", which was as close to an official fan club as these reluctant stars had.

The bedlam intensified with their first show on the Tuesday night. There was, as Smith euphemistically reported, some "confusion" regarding ticket sales: 19,000 had been sold for a 17,000 capacity venue. A full-scale riot ensued: police cars were trashed, several security dogs killed – even the local hot-dog vendor suffered a heart attack and died – and all before the band even made it to the stage. "For almost two hours we play[ed] amidst deafening bedlam, before rushing off, screaming, into the car and away," Smith reported. The next night, when the band began their set, the temperature was hitting the 100 degree mark. In spite of beefed-up security and higher barricades at stage front, another riot broke out. (Smith swore blind that he spotted "several uniformed men on fire".) The crowd let it all out by pelting the stage area with anything they could lay their hands on: coins, bottles, whatever. Thompson was first to be hit, but Smith lost it completely when he was hit full in the face with a Coke bottle during '10.15 Saturday Night'. The rest of their set was a punky thrash, played as quickly as humanly possible. "Outside the ground," Smith reported, as they raced away from the mayhem, "is not unlike downtown Beirut."

Then it was Brazil, for a pair of shows at Porto Alegro's 12,000 capacity Gigantinho Stadium, a venue described by Smith as "a strange hybrid of Brixton Academy and Wembley Arena", but with dodgier wiring (throughout their set, the band received frequent shocks). By their second night at Gigantinho, the band was so drained by the heat and the noise that they required hits of oxygen before attempting an encore. The crowd was less volatile than Buenos Aires, even helping Smith out when he forgot the words to 'The Blood'.

Three days later the band was in Belo Horizonte for a show in front of 20,000 Cure-aholics at the Mineirinho Olymnasium. The heat and the crowd were every bit as intense as the previous South American shows, Smith recounting that "bodies are carried out by the hundred, but the survivors are still chanting madly as we run away".

More so than any of the madness that had gone before, by the third week of their tour, The Cure knew they were in a strange new pop universe. They turned up for a football game between local sides

Voscow and Bangu, at the Maracanzinho Stadium. Once settled in their seats inside the Director's Box, the band almost fell over when the massive electronic scoreboard beamed out a simple message: BRAZIL WELCOMES THE CURE. It was official – The Cure were superstars.

By this high water mark in their commercial standing, The Cure had locked into the well-established route of recording/press/touring; much of the rest of 1987 was consumed by lengthy jaunts through North America (July 9 to August 11), and Europe, which kicked off with an Oslo show on October 22 and concluded with no less than three nights at Wembley Arena from December 7 to 9.

With success, naturally, comes turmoil. The Cure had been subject to inner-band strife even when they were the most cultish of cult bands; now it seemed as though their troubles intensified in proportion to their success. By late 1987, Lol Tolhurst was falling to pieces. During a more candid moment on their wild ride through South America, Smith mentioned that, upon rising relatively early one day, "seeing Lol over coffee cheers us all up". The message was clear: Tolhurst was a man in serious trouble. Former Psychedelic Fur and Thompson Twins keyboardist, Roger O'Donnell, a close friend of new drummer Williams, had been drafted into the band for the European tour and onwards. He was startled by Tolhurst's limited musical contribution.

"I couldn't see why he was in the band. He could have afforded to hire a tutor and have daily lessons, but he wasn't interested in practising. He just liked being in the group." Gallup, however, explained Tolhurst's role to the new recruit: "It is fun to have him around," he said, "even though he doesn't contribute much to the music. He is part of The Cure."* The simple fact that O'Donnell was hired said a lot about Tolhurst's ever-diminishing input.

"He was like a safety valve for all our frustrations," O'Donnell admitted. "Which was really sick. By the end [of the tour] it was horrible." Tolhurst simply drank his way through the 1987 world tour, to such a level, according to Robert Smith, "that he didn't bother retaliating [to the band's provocation]. It was like watching some kind of handicapped child being constantly poked with a stick."

---

* Gallup was clearly being polite. Smith insisted that if Tolhurst stayed in the band much longer, "Simon would have thrown him off a balcony."

But as Tolhurst told me, Smith was a practical man: Tolhurst clearly had something to offer The Cure or he would have been benched long before. "People would ask Robert, 'Why are you keeping Lol around when he's not doing anything?' But I did keep doing things. Robert's very pragmatic: he wouldn't keep someone in the band who wasn't doing anything. [And] because we were friends, Robert held on to me for a long, long time."

As the frontman and central figure of a band in the midst of a super-nova rise, Smith was also having to deal with his own demons throughout 1987. Against his better instincts, he was being sucked into the pop-star vacuum – as he learned, when you're surrounded by yes-people and sycophants, whose main role is to remind you of your brilliance, it's hard to resist the temptation to agree with them. This self-obsession, brought into sharp focus every night when many, many thousand people scream your name and your songs, wasn't helped by the cocoon-like life on the road. When cities become a blur, and you're rushed from press conference to hotel to gig by a fleet of limos and private jets, it's pretty easy to forget about the rest of the world. His fan's obsessiveness added to his alienation; while in Europe, Smith tried various disguises (flat hair, hats, etc.), none of which seemed to work – incredibly, his signature high-top trainers usually gave him away. After that, he could only travel as part of a hefty entourage.

To his credit, Smith was able to eventually detect the tell-tale signs of complete self-immersion, although by the end of the 1987 tour he was in deep. "It was like dropping coloured ink in water," he admitted. "I became public property and I wasn't prepared for the level that we'd reached. It was fanatical. Suddenly I was recognised everywhere I went in America, and when I got back to London, there would be 30 or 40 people camped outside my flat.

"By the end of that tour, my personality had changed a lot. I'd become really conceited, not just pretending to be a pop star, but living it. I realised that I couldn't go on like that."

As 1987 turned into 1988, Robert Smith began a self-enforced hibernation. The Cure wouldn't play live again for another 18 months.

Robert Smith didn't just feel that he was losing his grip on reality, but once again he felt that The Cure was being misunderstood. 'Just Like Heaven' and 'Catch' might have been sweet pop tunes, but they didn't pack anywhere near the same emotional potency as the songs on

Pornography or *Faith*, or something more recent such as 'If Only Tonight We Could Sleep'. And Smith wasn't so sure that it was the pop spotlight he was craving when he, Tolhurst and Dempsey formed the band more than a dozen years ago.

As he and Poole started to consider a new life outside of Maida Vale, Smith became seriously withdrawn. Unlike the lead-up to *Kiss Me Kiss Me Kiss Me*, where input was requested from everyone in The Cure, Smith now recorded alone. And for the first time since the *Blue Sunshine* sessions with Severin, he started taking acid again on a regular basis. But he wasn't in the mood for another non-stop party or a "chemical vacation"; this time he was using the drug to get inside his troubled thoughts. And Smith was about to reach a life milestone, because the big 3-0 was little more than a year away. Robert Smith was sinking deeper and deeper into a funk that would either have him finally, truly kill off The Cure – or lead him to *Disintegration*.

Chapter Eleven

"I was fighting against being a pop star, being expected to be larger than life all the time, and it really did my head in. I got really depressed, and I started doing drugs again – hallucinogenic drugs."

– Robert Smith

ROBERT SMITH's *annus horribilis*, 1988, didn't necessarily start out that way. Rumours of The Cure's demise after finishing *Kiss Me Kiss Me Kiss Me* were greatly exaggerated, because he had decided to make at least one more album. And with no deadline hanging over his head, and with money in the bank – he'd even made the pages of Debrett's Peerage – Smith wasn't a man in a hurry. There were no live dates scheduled for the year. *Kiss Me* gradually faded from the charts, its final offering being a radically reworked 'Hot Hot Hot!!!', remixed by Francois Kervorkian, which crept into the UK Top 50 in February. The airwaves returned to normal: the first few months of 1988 offered up some quality pop, such as INXS' 'Need You Tonight' or 'Fairytale Of New York', wherein Pogues' dipsomaniac Shane MacGowan swapped insults with Kirsty MacColl, alongside the usual fluff, such as Morris Minor & The Majors' Anglo take on The Beastie Boys, 'Stutter Rap' or M/A/R/R/S's dance anthem 'Pump Up The Volume'. And the usual suspects ruled at the Grammys, where U2, Sting and Paul Simon cleaned up.

But it wasn't the state of modern music that led to Robert Smith's latest existential funk: it was his Dorian Gray-like fear of growing old. In April, he celebrated his 29th birthday with the usual gusto, but then hit what he called a "bad patch", when he realised that in 12 months he'd be 30. Part of his concern was the simple fact that he felt that The Cure, despite their platinum-plus success, were yet to deliver a genuine masterwork. He knew that the true rock'n'roll legends – The Beatles, the Stones, The Who, The Kinks, Led Zeppelin, Hendrix, Bowie, even Alex bloody Harvey – had all reached the pinnacle of their craft well before hitting 30. Almost as soon as Smith had puffed out the 29 candles on his birthday cake, he set to work writing "the most intense thing The Cure has ever done". If *Kiss Me Kiss Me Kiss Me* was a summation of The Cure's music for the first 10 years of their life, and a celebration of all the music that they loved, Smith wanted the next album to be way more personal, a return to the introspection of *Pornography*.

"I had wanted to get it all done before I was 30. [Then] the day after I became 29 I realised that next birthday I was gonna be 30," stated Smith. "It's like a paradox. I think the younger you are the more you worry about getting old; in my case it's true. I think the darker side of that record [*Disintegration*] came from the fact I was gonna be 30."*

In fact, Smith was shocked that he'd made it this far: like a post-punk Pete Townshend, he'd always thought he'd be lucky not to die before he got old. Smith made a pact with himself that there'd be no way at 30 he'd still be fronting the band. And Smith had another, far more pressing issue to deal with, as he started writing new songs: were they right for The Cure? By early summer a Cure summit meeting took place at Boris Williams' home, where Smith introduced the band to the home demos he'd recorded. He also wrote some other *Disintegration* songs, such as 'Lullaby', while sitting outside Williams' house during rare afternoons of English summer sunshine. "The demos were really, really good fun, brilliant fun," Smith recalled, and most of the band agreed. That's all it took to convince Smith to shelve, yet again, his solo LP plans.

"I would have been quite happy to have made these songs on my own," said Smith. "If the group hadn't thought it was right, that would have been fine." But when the band started to play along with him, Smith knew that these were Cure songs after all. Smith had brought along a 16-track recorder to this summer jam and 32 songs were recorded at Williams' house. When the sessions ended, Smith retired to continue scratching out his lyrics.

At the time, Smith had also started work on a musical sketch called 'Lovesong', a song that had a noticeably different mood to the rest of his new material. It was a gentle strum in the midst of some genuine fire and brimstone. For Robert Smith it was a first – and the title said it all. "It's an open show of emotion," he admitted. "It's not trying to

---

* "It's a very apt title," Lol Tolhurst told me. "I was disintegrating at that point."

be clever. It's taken me 10 years to reach the point where I felt comfortable singing a very straightforward love song. In the past, I've always felt a last-minute need to disguise the sentiment."

What Smith was actually writing was a gift to Mary Poole – a wedding gift. "I couldn't think of what to give her," said Smith, "so I wrote her that song – cheap and cheerful. She would have preferred diamonds, I think, but she might look back and be glad that I gave her that." Finally, after 15 years together, they were married in Worth Abbey on August 13, with much of The Cure (including the increasingly unstable Lol Tolhurst) along for the party. Simon Gallup was best man, while Smith played DJ for much of the night-long party that followed their nuptials.

"We just got married to have a nice day," Smith said soon after, "so that Mary could walk down an aisle in a white dress and [so we could] just have all my uncles and aunties there. It's really dumb but I was sort of overcome." For Smith, the decision to get hitched boiled down to simple maths: he and Poole had known each other for more than half their lives, so it was time to make it official. Smith, however, wasn't quite ready for parenthood. When asked by a local reporter after the wedding, he simply replied: "No, I don't think I'm cut out for fatherhood at the moment – and I'm lucky in that Mary doesn't think she's cut out for motherhood at the moment, either." They did, however, "adopt" two children through a World Vision-type scheme – Smith, a Guatemalan girl; Poole, a Haitian boy. They also decided to get the hell out of London and return to Sussex.

"I was going to kill my [Maida Vale] neighbours," Smith explained. "In Sussex you can have a house and a garden for the same amount of money and be really boring and normal. But it saves me [from] going to prison; I hate the sound of people walking around on the top of my head."

Smith's mood, however, had soured considerably by the time he and the band reunited in Hook End Manor Studios in Reading, to begin recording *Disintegration*. While Smith insisted that the main cause of his meltdown was a desire to record the band's career-defining album, and the realisation that 30 was just around the corner, there was also the issue of Lol Tolhurst that Smith knew he couldn't avoid for much longer. The honeymoon was most definitely over.

But Smith's behaviour was still hard to understand. The band had just enjoyed a truly purple patch, with gold (*Standing On The Beach*) and platinum (*Kiss Me Kiss Me Kiss Me*) albums and full houses across Europe and North and South America. But when they knuckled down to fine-tune the demos they'd pieced together at Williams' house, Smith sank into what he would call "one of my non-talking modes", shutting himself off from the same bandmates he'd partied long and hard with a few months earlier at his wedding.

"The others thought I lost the plot," said Smith. "They were still caught up with the idea that we were becoming a really famous band, and they weren't grasping that the music I wanted to make was incredibly morose and downbeat."

Despite their runaway success at the cash register, Smith was convinced that their more successful albums lacked the kind of gravitas that was all over *Pornography*. That's what he was striving for with *Disintegration*.

"It sounds really big-headed, but everyone wanted a piece of me [at the time]," Smith said in 2004. "I was fighting against being a pop star, being expected to be larger than life all the time, and it really did my head in. I got really depressed, and I started doing drugs again – hallucinogenic drugs. When we were gonna make the album I decided I would be monk-like and not talk to anyone. It was a bit pretentious really, looking back, but I actually wanted an environment that was slightly unpleasant.

"Everyone expected me to be writing songs that were gonna follow up 'Just Like Heaven'. They thought that we were gonna keep things light and bouncy with an occasional bit of gloom, but we did the opposite." Once again, as he had during the time of 'Let's Go To Bed', or when he signed up as a touring Banshee, Smith was doing an about-turn, rejecting the audience that had made him one of the few chubby, bed-haired, smudged-lipstick-fancying millionaire pop stars on the planet. What Smith was hoping to do was resurrect the side of The Cure that he felt he'd neglected. He was seeking "more depth of emotion. It's inherent in the music," Smith felt, "the same way that a piece by Beethoven is more emotive than a Bros single."

Smith envisaged *Disintegration* as an extension of the band's darkest musings: *Faith*, *Seventeen Seconds* and *Pornography*. (He would later include it as the second instalment of 2002's quite painful *The Cure*

Trilogy, where *Pornography*, *Disintegration* and 2000's *Bloodflowers* were played live, from grim beginning to miserable close, before a stadium of equally dour Germans.) It was only now that Smith had the budget and the time to sink deeper into the emotional mire than he ever had before.

"I know why the songs are like this," Smith explained. "It's got a lot to do with turning 30, getting married . . . things that have nothing to do with anyone else, really." To his credit, Smith was being true to himself: he'd tried writing in a more upbeat frame of mind, now he was feeling blue, so the music reflected that. As self-flagellating and indulgent as that seemed, it was hardly a new move on Smith's part – much of The Cure's career (the less commercially successful part, of course) had been built around heavy emotions and bleak thoughts.

"It's how I felt when I wrote these songs," he figured. "I didn't feel particularly, um, good at the time. The same things bother me and they always will. They are intrinsically tied to my own deterioration and they get more acute as I get older. When I was young, I could think about things that bothered me in an abstract way. Now I don't. They're too real."

Smith even visualised prospective listeners; he'd picture them in his mind's eye while he was buried somewhere deep inside *Disintegration's* vocals, which took five long, hard nights to record. "I had various imaginary and non-imaginary people who listened to the record," he explained, "and I found out what they'd feel listening to the songs. They were all in different rooms in this hotel. No room service."

Smith had laughed off *Kiss Me* as "a party record", a reasonable analysis that conveniently overlooked the reason why that album connected with so many listeners: it was loads of fun. The band's whimsy during 'Hot Hot Hot!!!' and 'Why Can't I Be You?' was almost tangible. But with *Disintegration* he was trying to make the kind of album that would not only end parties, but also have revellers reaching for the razor blades. In fact, death was very much in the forefront of Smith's mind during the sessions at Hook End Manor. Two New Zealand teenagers had recently committed suicide in a bizarre death pact; the subsequent investigation revealed that The Cure had provided the soundtrack. Smith was fully aware of the story – so much so that he had a newspaper clipping reporting the double suicide stuck to the studio wall during the sessions.

"I know it's tragic," Smith said, "but at the same time it's grimly funny because it obviously had nothing to do with us. We were just singled out." Smith was frustrated with being stuck in a pigeonhole alongside such rock'n'roll ghouls as Southern Death Cult and The Fields Of The Nephilim. He was convinced, not surprisingly, that The Cure had more to offer than an easy exit and a graveside dress sense.

"Everyone was joking about it being suicidal music and how I upset people with the words," he said. "They're [his songs] certainly not uplifting, but there's a satisfaction that comes from listening to something that you know a lot's gone into. You can tell that there are people involved and that those people care. I care a lot."

But caring about the music The Cure was making at Reading wasn't especially high on Lol Tolhurst's checklist of priorities. His boozing was now right out of control. Allegedly he spent most of the *Disintegration* sessions glued to the small screen, watching MTV, although he would tell me that his input to *Disintegration* was more substantial than many other albums. "I remember Dave Allen saying to me on *Disintegration* that I'd played more on that album than the last couple, but I don't remember it."

His monotone mood dragged the sessions – which had been briefly interrupted by a fire in a bedroom attached to the studios in December 1988 – down even further. While Smith's studio perfectionism was exhausting Thompson, O'Donnell, Gallup and Williams, Tolhurst simply shrugged and kept drinking. "Up until my last couple of years in The Cure, The Cure was my whole life, my whole existence," Tolhurst admitted to me. "Towards the end I got kind of sick and that destroyed a lot of things. Before that I put in everything I had."

The rest of the band, unable to get to Smith, who was locked away in his world of *Disintegration*, would taunt Tolhurst, even to the point of physically abusing him, just to get some kind of reaction. According to Smith, "The only way we could communicate that he was turning into a complete parody of himself was by beating him up. I didn't know who he was any more and he didn't know who he was either."

"Making the *Disintegration* album, I used to despair and scream at the others because it was fucking insane the way we were treating him," Smith continued. "I kept him in the band because I felt a certain responsibility towards him."

But the band couldn't take it any more: they gave Smith an ultimatum that Tolhurst had to go or they'd walk. They'd come to the perfectly reasonable conclusion that there was simply no way they could tour an album as grim as *Disintegration* while also carrying an alcoholic. They also felt that it was unreasonable that Tolhurst actually received a greater royalty than everyone bar Smith, despite his limited input. Although Smith, too, knew that Tolhurst had to go, it was a much tougher move than squeezing out Phil Thornalley or having Andy Anderson escorted to Tokyo Airport. Smith and Tolhurst had been incredibly tight; Tolhurst had even given the band their name (albeit with an additional Easy). He'd toughed it out when The Cure seemed to be going absolutely nowhere, apart from up and down a seemingly endless procession of motorways in Smith's dodgy green Maxi van. Tolhurst had endured the arduous Hansa liaison and had, of course, been a key creative contributor. During the days of *The Top*, The Cure was just him and Smith.

But their relationship stretched back even further – they'd been schoolmates at the freethinking Notre Dame Middle School and the not so progressive St Wilfrid's. They had a lot of history. Yet Smith also knew that if Tolhurst stayed in the band, he'd most likely drink himself to a very public death.

On reflection, Tolhurst understands the reaction of his then Cure bandmates. But he also believes that history played a big part in the imbalance within The Cure. "Up until the new [1986] deal with Polydor it was 50/50, me and Robert. And along the way all these guys joined the band and were treated very well, but their percentage worked out less than mine. They'd see me living the life of Riley and being this crazy guy. I understand their frustration.

"[But] the other side of it is that once I was removed, the problems weren't necessarily removed. In a perverse way I kind of thought to myself, 'Maybe I have to accept that; my behaviour wasn't the best.' In the last year, there was a point where I'd wake up and not be able to tell what was going to happen that day. I was very afraid; I thought I was going insane. I didn't know where I was going to end up. Frequently that's what happened. It was very scary."

Porl Thompson saw that, too, because during the *Disintegration* sessions he approached Tolhurst and asked him whether he was ready for rehab. In fact, Tolhurst had actually been through the first stage of detox about a year before he left the band. With the help of his London neighbours, an Australian couple, Tolhurst had approached a Harley Street doctor by the name of Campbell, who agreed to help him through the process.

"He got the problem within about 10 minutes of meeting [me]," said Tolhurst. "[He realised that] I'm not like other people. I can't drink or do other things recreationally. I'm allergic to it and my whole psyche changes; my whole mind changes. It becomes an obsession.

"He told me, 'We need to take you to hospital for a week or so, and we need to go this afternoon.' I wasn't ready for it, but I agreed and after a week I felt much better. He'd told me about this other place that I should go, but I said that I felt much better and went home. Then I had the worst year of my life.

"After a week I felt semi-normal, which was a mistake. The problem was that I'm not able to drink like other people; I'm an alcoholic. You can't drink when you have what I have."

A couple of weeks after leaving hospital, Tolhurst figured that he was sufficiently straightened out to attend a party at a friend's pub. He was very wrong, as he told me. "I figured I could have a couple of beers. It was like being on top of the roller coaster and looking down. It was too late, the obsession was back in me."

Smith could handle the trauma of another sacking; he wasn't so sure he could deal with a tragedy. "It was much easier for him not to be in the band," he figured. Tolhurst helped speed up his own departure by arriving for the *Disintegration* mixing session at RAK drunker than a lord. He then slagged the album mercilessly and a shouting match ensued.

Tolhurst knew this was the end of the line. "By that time it had really gone too far," he admitted. "I went along and Robert was playing me different things and asking me what I thought. I said something like, 'Well, half of it's good and half of it's not a Cure record,' and I left. That was the last time we talked for about 10 years. That was my parting shot. Now I realise most of it was frustration on my side at my inability to do things."

Just after Christmas 1988, Smith wrote to Tolhurst explaining why he felt the band's co-founder didn't belong in The Cure any more.

"I got a letter from Robert," Tolhurst recalled. "As soon as I saw it, I thought, 'OK, that makes sense, that's what he would do.' There's the other English thing – no confrontation. I called him up as soon as I read the letter.

"On reflection, the letter was quite nice. It said, 'It's not just me, everyone feels the same and don't put up a wall but I think you should get well and I don't think you should go on the next tour.' That was like a red rag to a bull for me at that point. I called him and he made himself unavailable; I had Mary to talk to for a little while."

Tolhurst knew what he had to do if he wanted to stay alive. He had to complete the detox sessions that he'd half completed the year before. Again he reached out to Dr Campbell, but this time he stayed for the full programme.

"Yes, it was the same doctor," he told me, "but then I went on to a rehab in London at The Priory on the edge of Richmond Park. Strangely enough I met someone else from another band, whose name I won't mention, who was in for something similar. Which was cool, because I had someone to hang out with for lunch."

In February 1989, Tolhurst's sacking was made official and Smith made this needlessly cruel statement to the press: "I was friends with him, but I was never really, really close. Lol was just there. From 1985 onwards I never had a conversation with Lol because we disagreed about virtually everything."

Tolhurst eventually replied to this in 1991. "What had started off as a band where everyone had their influence was getting eroded," he said, "until it didn't feel like there was anything that you could contribute even if you wanted to."

He went deeper into the issue two years later, stating how Smith told him, after he received the letter, to call him and they'd talk it through. "I did, but he decided he didn't want to talk to me. And so that's the point when I thought I shouldn't be here [in The Cure] any more. I think it was on a completely personal level.

"It was halfway through *Disintegration* that things weren't working out so great," Tolhurst added. "I wasn't feeling that well in myself and I guess The Cure psychosis struck again, big time. For many years it was fairly democratic and it was a happy situation. And then it became undemocratic and a lot of people around the band, like the record company, found it better that way because they only had to deal with one person. And that was a bit upsetting, as over the years I'd put a lot of my life into it."

When I asked him about his departure and his alcoholism, Tolhurst was almost serene. "To be honest, it's like that old Edith Piaf thing, 'I have no regrets.' If I hadn't gone through that, I wouldn't be the person I am now.* My existence is much, much happier now. I was quite a wealthy guy [at the time] but I was desperately unhappy. I don't know if I have much more control, but I have a lot of peace.

"When we first started in the music business," he continued, "it was almost expected of us, to be these out of control people. There was always plenty to drink and whatever. We were three suburban boys who'd never seen anything like that go on. Eventually you become like that. I'm grateful to have been like that and come out the other end and survive. I'm alive."

But that was in the future. After his sacking, Tolhurst was still very bitter and sued the band for what he believed to be outstanding royalties. The court case would effectively put The Cure out of commission for a couple of years, and by the time they finally returned from their enforced hiatus, popular music had moved on.

This didn't matter in 1989, of course. With Tolhurst gone, keyboardist Roger O'Donnell had been made a full-time Cure-ist during the *Disintegration* sessions, fleshing out the well-established Smith/ Williams/Gallup/Thompson line-up. And his input on *Disintegration* was crucial.

Ever since *Seventeen Seconds*, way back in 1980, keyboards had played a part in The Cure's bleak wall of sound. But with O'Donnell in the band, they played an increasingly important role in *Disintegration*, the album that finally, precisely, fused Smith's thematic hang-ups (mortality, death, despair) with music that was both grand and highly hummable. O'Donnell crafted huge, monolithic slabs of sound, the Great Wall of keyboards. They added the necessary gravitas to Smith's latest life crisis, something that Tolhurst's two-fingered noodling could never do.

"The songs flow at their own leisurely speed," noted *Rolling Stone* in its four-star write-up of *Disintegration*, which dropped in May 1989, "carefully piling layer after intricate layer of synthesized demi-classical textures on top of Smith's now-familiar plaintive cries and troubled love songs. *Disintegration* can be heard as The Cure's career-summing

---

* As of August 2005, Tolhurst has been sober for 16 years.

peak or an epic, art-rock snooze-athon." (By October 20, 1989, five months after its release, a million North American converts had sided with the former point of view. Globally, it would go on to sell 2.6 million copies.)

'Plainsong', just like *Kiss Me*'s 'The Kiss', set the mood for *Disintegration* perfectly, unravelling ever so slowly in a shower of synths and guitars, before Smith steps up to the mic, uttering snatches of lyrics ("I'm so cold") as if he were reading from something as sacred as the Dead Sea Scrolls. If Smith and the good ship Cure were going to go down with *Disintegration*, as he'd threatened they would, they were going to go out in the largest possible way. This was symphonic rock, the kind of widescreen soundscapes that wouldn't have been lost on Smith's teenage hero David Bowie, especially in his *Station To Station* daze. Smith knew that 'Plainsong' was the perfect mood-setter. "I wanted something very lush, very orchestral."

Balance, of course, was something Smith came to understand more clearly with each Cure album. Accordingly, the more immediate and accessible 'Pictures Of You' followed 'Plainsong', a sort of synth-pop yin to 'Plainsong's pathos-heavy yang. That's not to say it was any less morose in tone, but it had a melody that would have been wasted if it were buried somewhere in the midst of *Disintegration*; it was the perfect song to follow such a funereal opener. And when Smith wails how he remembers when the object of his affection was curled up in his embrace or how he hoped to feel her deep within his heart, while synths ebb and flow behind him, it almost made sense that he'd become a pop idol, of sorts. This was a love song, albeit one viewed through the eyes of a guy having major trouble dealing with the big 3-0.

Rumbling drums opened the next track, 'Closedown', before another swirling, skyscraping keyboard texture swept into the picture, this time matched to a spindly guitar line. Here, Smith is in especially despondent form – and that's saying something – as he lists his shortcomings. As Smith bemoans the absence of love in his heart, a symphony of synths swells behind like a one-man orchestra. Then it's another about-face, this time with the far more upbeat 'Lovesong', which was about as honest and sincere a valentine to Mary Poole that Smith was ever likely to write. Touchingly, like many a more traditional songwriter before him, he sang of the contentment he felt in her company. For a man who preferred to sing about loathing rather than loving, it was a fearless confession. The soundscape was infectious, too, built around a sinewy keyboard riff and an uncomplicated rhythm from Williams, which was pushed way forward in the mix.

Smith felt that 'Lovesong' was a key track on *Disintegration*. Without it, the album would have been the ultimate bummer, the biggest come-down of all. "That one song, I think, makes many people think twice. If that song wasn't on the record, it would be very easy to dismiss the album as having a certain mood. But throwing that one in sort of upsets people a bit because they think, 'That doesn't fit.'"

'Lullaby' followed, a brilliantly constructed ode to one of Smith's many nightmares. "That's the sort of lullaby my Dad used to sing when I was younger," Smith explained. "He used to make them up. There was always a horrible ending. There would be something like, 'Sleep now, pretty baby' [followed by] 'Or you won't wake up at all.'" Clipped strings and sharp stabs of rhythm guitar formed the perfect foil for Smith's hushed, increasingly desperate vocal. While the Tim Pope video was so right for the song that it actually outweighed the single it was designed to promote, 'Lullaby' was another example of Smith finding the perfect balance of pop and pathos.

Disintegration then wound through the dense 'Fascination Street', 'Prayers For Rain', a bummed-out sprawl that seemed to be as low as Smith had ever sunk, 'The Same Deep Waters As You' and the title track, before eventually drawing to a sadly beautiful close with 'Untitled', a song that was all wheezing accordion and bleak Smith wordplay. When it was over, it came as no real shock that Smith wanted to kill off the band – the Lovecat was completely drained; he had absolutely nothing left to give.

Yet not even Smith's contrariness could stop the rise of *Disintegration* and The Cure; the album was a massive worldwide hit. "I realised at this time that, despite my best efforts, we had actually become every-thing that I didn't want us to become: a stadium rock band. Most of the relationships within the band and outside of the band fell apart. Calling it *Disintegration* was kind of tempting fate, and fate retaliated. The family idea of the group really fell apart too after *Disintegration*. It was the end of the golden period."

Their record company agreed, at least on first listen to *Disintegration*. A month before it was completed, an advance listening party was organised with Elektra execs. According to Smith, they walked in expecting *Kiss Me* the sequel, and walked out muttering something inaudible. It was very similar to Smith's clash with Tolhurst during the mixing of the album – this wasn't the reaction he'd anticipated. "There was just this look of absolute dismay on people's faces," Smith recalled. "I was informed about a week later that I was committing commercial suicide. They wanted to push the release date back – they thought I was being 'wilfully obscure', which was an actual quote from the letter [Smith received from Elektra]. I actually kept the letter and I cherish it because *Disintegration* went on to sell millions. Ever since then I realised that record companies don't have a fucking clue what The Cure does and what The Cure means. I thought it was my masterpiece and they thought it was shit."

Melody Maker's Chris Roberts was every bit as confused as the suits of Elektra. "*Disintegration* is about as much fun as losing a limb," he wrote in May 1989. "How can a group this disturbing and depressing be so popular?"

One false step Smith did take with *Disintegration*, however, was the cover image, a solo shot of the Cure leader, another Parched Art design. Given the recent sacking of Lol Tolhurst, and the increased prominence of Smith as the star of the band, it seemed a strangely self-serving move. Maybe *Disintegration* was closer to the solo album that Smith had been murmuring about for years.

Accordingly, Smith received flak from both the music press and bandmates, but defended the move, insisting that he and the rest of the band had approved the image. He would also go into some detail about the shared songwriting on *Disintegration*; half of the dozen tracks had substantial musical input from other members of the band. It wasn't just Robert Smith and band, even if it felt and sounded like that was the case.

As for the album's title, Smith knew it would be read as The Cure's obituary, but that wasn't really his intention. It was more about the Dorian Gray effect. "It wasn't really to do with the group," he said when the album appeared. "It's more like an interior disintegration, and it's something which I felt really keenly and which I'll feel even more keenly as I'm getting older. It's that sense of everything falling apart."

If this really was the end of the road for The Cure, then someone had forgotten to tell their black clad public. Sprung on listeners in April,

'Lullaby' became the band's highest-charting UK single, climbing to number five. By May 13, *Disintegration* had peaked at number three, another all-time high for the band. The Prayer Tour followed – Gallup, quite justifiably, given The Cure's status at the time, was a little wary of the name, thinking that it might be confused with Madonna's current Prayer tour.

Smith realised that it was best to sign off in high style. Since 1987, he and Gallup had become increasingly wary of flying. So after the European leg of the Prayer Tour, which had seen them play to 40,000 Parisians over two nights at Paris Omnisports, and also venture behind the Iron Curtain for the first time, they decided against flying to New York to start their next North American tour. I mean, why fly when you can afford to sail on the *QE2*?

The *QE2* was as much a ruse as anything else in the career of Smith and The Cure. He told the world at large that because of his fear of flying (which Gallup just so happened to share), Smith couldn't travel by 747 to North America. Sea travel was the only option. But the truth was this: by implying a fear of plane travel, Smith was hoping to reduce the number of shows the band had to play and increase the numbers of days free for travel. Maybe promoters would baulk at the expense and the band wouldn't have to tour at all. Of course, that didn't happen. And Smith didn't realise what was up for grabs on the most up-market of cruise liners – there were as many bars onboard as waiters, while there was also a casino for those idle after-after-hours.

"I arrived in America shattered," Smith said of his Atlantic crossing. "It was five days in a boat with, like, 47 bars and a casino. It was like a tour before a tour."[*]

The next shock in store for the band was their opening 1989 US show at the 54,000 capacity Giants Stadium in New Jersey. More than 44,000 fans turned up – 30,000 tickets had sold on the first day – proving that The Cure had progressed way beyond cult band status. They were genuine pop superstars. Roger O'Donnell, for one, was gobsmacked by the reception the band received at Giants Stadium. "We had been at sea for five days," he gasped. "The stadium was too

[*] Not that this prevented him and some of the band sailing the *QE2* prior to their next two American tours, of course. It made for one of the weirdest pre-tour demands in the history of rock'n'roll.

big for us to take it all in. We've decided that we don't like playing stadiums that large."

Meanwhile, on the continent, French President Mitterand had issued the band a personal invitation to Paris. When would this madness stop?

"It was never our intention to become as big as this," Smith declared, as the tour wound its way to the Spectrum in Philadelphia. "The whole point was to enjoy what we were doing at the time."

Kiss Me's worldwide sales were sitting at two million and still rising, *Standing On A Beach* had reached 2.3 million. 'Fascination Street', the first US single lifted from *Disintegration* – due to a tie-in with the film *Lost Angels* – had already grazed the Top 40, while 'Lovesong' was fast charming its way to number two, the closest that The Cure would come to making it to the top of the US charts. *Disintegration* peaked at number 12 on the *Billboard* album chart, shifting its first million by mid-October; it eventually outsold even *Kiss Me*. So much for the "commercial suicide" verdict that Elektra execs had given the album.

The band worked up more than 50 songs to flesh out their sets, which were now running well over two hours. And in order to give the masses what they truly wanted, they had a video cameraman roam the various stadiums beforehand, fielding requests. Smith and band would check out the tape before plugging in.

When the Prayer Tour reached the West Coast, with The Pixies, Shellyann Orphan and Love And Rockets in tow, they were packing the 50,000 capacity Dodger Stadium. They had reached a level of fame enjoyed by such UK legends as The Beatles, The Rolling Stones, The Who, Led Zeppelin and Pink Floyd, and – naturally enough – it inspired Smith to issue his latest in a long line of death warrants for The Cure.

"It's reached a stage where I personally can't cope with it," he said, "so I've decided this is the last time we're gonna tour."

Smith's entourage, naturally, had swollen in proportion to the band's new status as stadium fillers, which also made Smith feel uncomfortable. "It's weird to be at the centre of a group of 30 people all listening to what you're saying," Smith admitted. "[But] when that group turns into 300 people it goes on from weird. Some people revel in it, and I don't."

The Cure might have kept their tickets reasonably priced (somewhere between $18 and $20), but that didn't stop the cash from pouring in. The opening night in New Jersey grossed a handy $966,189; two nights later they drew a house-filling 16,500 to Landover, Maryland, which deposited a further $321,750 in The Cure coffers. A sell-out in Philadelphia at the 15,000-plus Spectrum grossed more than $250,000, while two shows in Chicago at the end of August brought in almost $500,000 more. Their September 9 show at the 13,000 capacity Oakland Coliseum was another sell-out; The Cure then filled the 20,000 seat Shoreline Amphitheater in Mountain View, California, the 12,000 capacity San Diego Sports Arena and The Summit in Houston, where they pulled 13,185 punters and a cheeky $250,000. The biggest money-spinner of the tour, however, was their September 8 gig at LA's Dodger Stadium. There wasn't an empty seat in the house – and the night grossed a useful $1.25 million, which no doubt helped to line the coffers of the Robert Smith retirement fund. Of the 14 shows of the Prayer Tour where box office figures are available, The Cure grossed almost $6 million, drawing upwards of 270,000 punters. It was a very good year.

Behind the scenes, however, the mood wasn't so flash. While the epic sprawls of *Disintegration* were ideal for the cavernous US stadiums and concrete bunkers they were filling, the band's mood fluctuated on stage. After the tour, the biggest of The Cure's life, Smith would play various bootlegs of the shows, amazed at the many faces of The Cure on stage.

"Some of the nights we played were kinda really emotional," he said. "I was hysterical. I was tearing my hair out at the end of the tour. It was just a difficult tour. There was a lot of shit going on backstage."

That shit included the requisite recreational drugs that go hand-in-nostril with a band playing at this platinum level. For Smith, this only added to his already rapidly growing sense of self-worth, which was an intriguing twist for a man who once sang "it doesn't matter if we all die" – and believed it. Smith was even starting to indulge in rock-star like purchases: while in New Orleans, he picked up what he would describe as a "Red Indian invisible shirt with herb pouches all over it". UK Customs held onto the shirt for seven months, trying to work out what was in the pouches, which hadn't been opened in 200 years. Smith wore it exactly once before retiring it to the back of the wardrobe.

"It didn't seem like me," Smith said afterwards, reflecting on his on-tour mindset, "but that was part of the drugs as well. I was living two really different lives on the Prayer Tour. I was like really nasty. [And] if one person decides to act in a certain way, [then] everyone else is kinda really fucked."

To put additional stress on an already fractured relationship with all those around him, Smith would remind any journalist who felt like asking that this was their final tour. There was no question about it, at least to Robert Smith. The Cure was never meant to get this famous. He'd had enough. He just wanted to disappear in his backyard at Bognor Regis with Mary and his telescope and his father's home brew (and, of course, his handsome bank balance). But there was also one unanswered question: just how big could The Cure go?

Smith knew that there were external influences dictating the future of The Cure, including Fiction and Chris Parry. "You've got people like Bill [Parry] saying, 'Oh, you're at your peak, you sell more records, you've got to play for more people, you can only get better and get bigger.' But all the bases are the same. It's like, 'You can make a lot of money.'"

What Smith needed, once the band returned to the UK after 24 sell-out North American dates, was a new sensation. He was sick of the recording/promo/touring grind; he was keen to break the cycle. The idea he came up with, which would be known as *Mixed Up*, was probably the most misunderstood and maligned of his life.

But even before *Mixed Up* appeared, The Cure had a lively 1990, especially so for a band that was supposedly in hibernation. In February, 'Lullaby' was given the gong for Best Music Video of 1989 at the annual Brits. The award was well justified: the clip, where a bedridden Smith is oh so slowly digested by a gargantuan arachnid, while his cobweb-covered bandmates looked (and played) on, was a full-blown Gothic nightmare, quite possibly Tim Pope's finest work with the band. The £80,000 clip – "they're getting a feature film production 'ere," Pope said from the set – was shot in a south London warehouse. The "spider" was actually a large, furry orifice that, according to a *Q* report, was "full of some sticky gunk that looks and smells like Airfix glue". A trussed-up Smith, once again suffering for his art, was suspended from the ceiling and repeatedly lowered into the sticky, stinky black hole.

Entreat was the next reminder that The Cure was only sleeping. Comprising live takes on 'Fascination Street', 'Pictures Of You', 'Prayers For Rain' and various other tracks, culled from their Wembley shows of the previous summer, it was offered as a limited-edition freebie by HMV, on the proviso that the dedicated Cure fan also bought two albums from their back catalogue. Smith had originally planned *Entreat* as a promo-only album for Cure diehards in France; he was understandably pissed off when fans started moaning about the need to buy older albums to grab a memento of their most recent shows. Smith eventually intervened, but it wasn't until 1991 that the album was readily available in the stores.

As Smith did his best to soothe the savage Cure fan, a third *Disintegration* single, 'Pictures Of You', started the climb to number 24 on the UK charts at the end of March, which said a lot about the staying power of an album released 10 months earlier. It was a sign that despite a barrage of Cure product over the past three or four years, for some it was simply never enough. Already Smith was having second thoughts about killing off the band. When they were asked to headline Glastonbury for a second time, he didn't need a lot of enticement to agree. Pushed for a comment, Smith insisted that he'd only said that the band would never tour again. Simon Gallup was more direct. "The old bastard just wanted to do it again," he told the press.

In a move that would foreshadow a lot of Cure activity over the next decade, Smith and band hired a country mansion, the one-time home of actor Dirk Bogarde, to knock a set into shape for this one-off show. But again there were rumblings in Camp Cure – Roger O'Donnell, whose soaring soundscapes had been so crucial to *Disintegration* – had quit for a solo career. The band's official line was that the recently recruited keyboardist had fallen out with Williams and Gallup to the point where "they couldn't work together" (not until 1993, anyway, when O'Donnell rejoined).

His replacement was loyal Cure roadie Perry ("Teddy") Bamonte, a move that had all the logic of shifting Lol Tolhurst from drums to keys eight years earlier, because Bamonte was a guitar tech. Bamonte, who'd attended St Nicholas School with future Depeche Mode mainman Martin Gore, had actually been discouraged from playing guitar at school, especially when he tried to play left-handed. "Consequently I never started playing guitar until I was 17," he told me via e-mail.

A big fan of Glam heroes Bowie and Bolan, and guitar wizard Jeff Beck, Bamonte served his musical apprenticeship in long-forgotten outfits such as Anorexic Dread, The School Bullies and Film Noir. There was a reason for their anonymity, he told me. "All these bands were rubbish. I played with them all so I could get on stage and make a noise. There was no direction, no real spark of potential." Anorexic Dread did actually get signed, but based "mainly on our looks," said Bamonte. "Think Virgin Prunes meets *The Lord Of The Flies.*"

Via his brother Daryl (then a Depeche Mode roadie, now The Cure's manager), Bamonte scored a roadie gig with The Cure in 1984, gladly leaving his latest band. "The pay was better," he said, "and I got to watch one of my favourite bands every night."

"I never saw a possibility to join The Cure," Bamonte continued, "there was never a shortlist, because nobody intended leaving." During the *Kiss Me* sessions at Miraval, Smith's sister Janet took the time to teach Bamonte keyboards, hence his recruitment. "With the patience of a saint, she spent a month teaching me the rudiments of playing piano. Before this, I knew nothing." But once again his recruitment was as much a recognition of his dedicated services as a long-term Cure insider as it was a nod to his musical brilliance. It was similar to the recruitment of Gallup back in 1980: Smith was as keen as ever to surround himself with loyal friends, even if Bamonte, as he admitted, was "not a serious drinker – and I don't support any football team."

"We could have hired a professional to take his place," figured Smith, "but why not use someone who knows all the songs?" Bamonte explained how his roadie role with The Cure extended way beyond broken strings and mid-gig tuning. "My transition to band member was easy, because I was friends with everyone already and spent all my time with them. It was pretty seamless."

The next few months didn't just typify the year of The Cure 1991, but pretty much their entire Nineties: for every highlight there were several backward steps. Bamonte made his debut in Paris, at The Cure's annual Bastille Day show.

"I spent the day watching them construct the stage," he recalled, when we spoke, "thinking how it must have looked the same for prisoners seeing the guillotine being built. It [the show] lasted about an hour and a half, but it felt to me like 20 minutes, a daze of noise and light and black and white keys."

The Cure's headlining set at Glastonbury, which was followed by eight European festival dates, was well received, but Smith felt that the event was badly organised. ("I thought, 'What am I doing here?' " as he looked out over the huge crowd.)

Just prior to Glastonbury, the new Cure had spent time recording a planned EP with producer/remixer Mark Saunders (whose CV would go on to include Erasure, Lisa Stansfield and Tricky). Although the sessions were a mess, the hiring of Saunders was a very clear statement by Smith and the band that they hadn't been totally shut off from the outside world. The acid house movement had broken out all over England, having been transplanted from Chicago by such ground-breakers as Throbbing Gristle's Genesis P. Orridge, who'd frequented Chicago's clubs in the late Eighties. Mixed with the relatively new drug MDMA (street name, Ecstasy), the movement attempted to find some common ground between guitars, psychedelia and groove, and had led to such era-defining records as A Guy Called Gerald's 'Voodoo Ray' and 808 State's *Newbuild*. The Happy Mondays' *Bummed* soon followed – Smith was a fan, calling their sound "brilliant" – as did The Stone Roses' self-titled debut from 1989 and the monumental *Screamadelica* from Primal Scream. The cultural shift even inspired Irvine (*Trainspotting*) Welsh to write a book, imaginatively titled *Acid House*. Acid house also spawned such derivatives as "baggy", which seemed to be as much about wearing embarrassingly flared strides as it was the loved-up, white-man's-funk that was being delivered by such bands as Happy Mondays and Inspiral Carpets.

Smith had acknowledged the new sound of the UK, the so-called Summer of Love, if only to denounce it. "It all seems dreadfully contrived, what goes on in London," he told the *Chicago Tribune*'s Tom Popson. "I think it's all to do with T-shirt sales more than music."

His mood soon changed, especially in the light of the sessions with Saunders, which were a mess. "We were actually doing a lot of electronic stuff," Smith said, "and I thought now would be the time for us to really get to grips with it, whether or not it worked."

The only song that survived the Saunders sessions, 'Never Enough', was a loose-limbed, positively filthy guitar workout with a funky undercurrent, and it became The Cure's first new piece of music for the Nineties, making it to number 13 in the UK chart by late September. The Pope video, where much of the band was squeezed into a box for the first time since 'Close To Me', featured Chris Parry in his first on-screen cameo since *The Great Rock & Roll Swindle*. He can be spotted at the opening of the clip, in the guise of a freak master. It was clearly a case of art almost imitating life.*

Intrigued by the possibilities of the dance remix, which could effectively breathe new life into old songs, Smith started commissioning old songs, with vague plans of a Cure remix album. DJ/remixer Paul Oakenfold, a veteran of the Ibiza rave scene, was offered 'Close To Me'. 'The Walk', which had to be re-recorded (the original tape had been accidentally scrubbed), was given to Mark Saunders, as was 'A Forest'. William Orbit worked on 'Inbetween Days', while Bryan "Chuck" New was handed 'Pictures Of You'. *Mixed Up* started to take some tangible shape in the last few months of 1990, as Smith rebooted The Cure for the final decade of the millennium.

Smith, reasonably enough, defended the expected accusation of bandwagon-jumping. "We've had dance stuff done since 1982, and it was really only Depeche Mode and New Order from that same period who were doing dance. We've never been perceived as very fashionable or contemporary or cool, which is fine with me because it means we can do stuff and disregard what we're supposed to be doing. [And] if there was a bandwagon to jump on, it left a long time ago."

If anything, Smith and The Cure were slightly ahead of the pack. By the end of the decade, remixes were as commonplace as big-budget videos and all-mod-cons tour buses for everyone from U2 to Linkin Park, while such hip-hoppers as Sean "Puffy" Combs would try to prop up their dodgy reputations by declaring that they invented the remix. Yet The Cure's *Mixed Up*, despite a Top 10 chart debut in mid-November, slipped quickly out of the charts, having left Cure fans more confused than chilled. Robert Smith realised that in order to stay gold, The Cure would have to think more about guitars and less about groove.

The Cure's 1991 started in an even more low-key manner than 1990. There were a few moments of action – a "secret" gig in January at London's Town And Country 2, where they were billed not-so-

---

* Director Pope also cameoed in 'Never Enough', playing Turban Tim, the fortune teller.

secretly as Five Imaginary Boys, and another Brit award in February, this time for Band of the Year.

Presenter Roger Daltrey was clearly thrilled that a "real band", rather than another cookie-cutter pop act, had won the gong, making a caustic aside that it was a relief to hand the Brit over to humans and "not a drum machine". Robert Smith, typically, wasn't so impressed by the night. "It's a bunch of idiots," he stated at the after-show party at the Grosvenor Hotel. "And also the votes are really corrupt. It's just a fucking travesty, because I thought we were the best band the year before as well." Smith was of the opinion that the Brits' organisers had roped in The Cure to add credibility to the awards. (Other winners on the night included the soon-to-be-maligned Betty Boo, plus MC Hammer and Lisa Stansfield, so it was hardly a banner year in music.) Clearly incensed, and without the help of a backing track, unlike most of the other performers on the night, The Cure ripped up 'Never Enough' and then got rip-roaring drunk.

But the Brits debacle was nothing compared with the foul wind that was starting to blow in Smith's direction by mid-1991. Lol Tolhurst may have moved on from The Cure, first marrying Lydia, his girlfriend of several years (his son Grey was born soon after), and then forming a new act, Presence, with erstwhile Cure roadie Gary Biddles. But he was still torn up about his dismissal from the band. He also felt that he hadn't been fully compensated for his 12 years with The Cure.

In August, it was reported in *Select* magazine that Tolhurst was suing the band, demanding money he felt he was owed. Although other reports hinted at any number of core reasons for Tolhurst's suit – even ownership of The Cure name was mentioned, as was the misuse of royalties owed to him which were redirected back into the band's touring fund – the key factor for his lawsuit was this: Tolhurst's lawyers believed that the band's renegotiated deal with Fiction and Polydor, signed in December 1986, gave both Smith and Chris Parry an un-reasonable slice of The Cure's recording profits. Tolhurst had signed the contract, but was now insisting that he had done so without receiv-ing proper advice and information about the new deal. He said that he'd relied on Smith to talk him through the contract – and now he very clearly regretted that. (Anybody who played on a Cure album post 1986 would receive songwriting credits and performance "points", rather than a wage or flat fee. Given that by the end of the Eighties The

Cure had sold eight million albums worldwide, if anything, it was an especially generous deal on Smith's part. Perry Bamonte, for one, confirmed this. "All band members receive what I consider to be a very generous cut of the musical royalties for every album," he told me. "Robert is both shrewd and fair in this regard.")

"The court case – I had a lot of resentment," Tolhurst explained to me. "At the time, I don't know, I felt ill-treated.

"I went to see [a lawyer] in London . . . [to] see if I was contractually free to sign a new contract for Presence. He said, 'You are, but did you notice that in your 1986 contract you went from being a partner to basically a shareholder – and the partnership may not have been properly dissolved? Perhaps we should write to them.' I agreed. Which we did and that started the next four years off.

"I felt that at least I could explain to people and be vindicated in what I felt. I was upset at Parry more than Robert or anybody else."

Tolhurst admitted [in court] his serious drinking problems and that it had affected his creative role within the band. He documented how his boozing had made him the lowest man on The Cure totem pole.

"I was drinking very heavily," Tolhurst said, "and was the butt of everyone's jokes and aggression. As a result of the continuous abuse and criticism, I became very ill and lost over a stone in weight."

He also disclosed, in very frank detail, the "vicious circle" of drinking, how he drank to gain confidence but then found himself losing the right stuff to perform. This, inevitably, led to Tolhurst being abused by the rest of The Cure. "The other members of the band would constantly play practical jokes on me," he revealed. "As the days wore on these jokes became more and more malicious." (A cursory glance at any of The Cure's videos from the *Kiss Me* LP onwards will show how Tolhurst had been reduced to band stooge. His situation was far worse away from Tim Pope's camera.)

Smith, understandably, was as much incensed as he was dismayed by Tolhurst's actions. "It's really stupid," he said at the time. "He'll lose and he'll have to pay costs and it'll cost him more than he can hope to win. And he's going to lose any credibility he had as regards what he did in The Cure, because it'll all come out."

Smith was very clearly referring to the way Tolhurst's creative input had diminished record by record. Allegedly, when Smith dropped several thousand pounds buying Tolhurst an Emulator keyboard during his shift from drums to keys post *Pornography*, he hadn't even turned the machine on three months later. Instead he'd spent the time working on a coke habit. Tolhurst denies this. "I did try and learn it," he told me. "Back then you needed a physics degree to work out things; it had all sorts of hexadecimals and all that.

"At that point [circa *The Top*] I was the only person willing to investigate that kind of stuff. The band was kind of Luddite: if you couldn't hit it or bang it, you didn't want to play it. I wanted to try to understand that new technology. We were all interested in it but I was the only one willing to learn it." Justin Jones, of And Also The Trees, backed this up. "I recall Lol being much more interested in keyboards than drums [when] he was switching from one to another in The Cure," he said.

Tired of a court case that he considered completely pointless, Smith decided to retreat to the studio. By September, he and the band had finally started sessions for their next album, *Wish*. So taken by their pre-Glastonbury experience in Dirk Bogarde's old digs, the band set up Camp Cure in Shipton Manor, a rambling Tudor mansion-cum-studio in the Oxfordshire countryside, owned by Virgin entrepreneur Richard Branson. If the band needed a retreat from the bad vibes being stirred up by the Tolhurst court case, this was the perfect place – it was both spacious and secluded. As one writer reported from the site, "They're surrounded by advanced plushness: mammoth antique mirrors reflect heavy velvet curtains and sumptuous Persian rugs [and there's] a fireplace you could live in and a wooden table the size of Lord's."

Branson's spread was pure olde worlde, except for one very gaudy, very modern touch: a huge *trompe l'oeil* mural that decorated the Manor's atrium. This was Branson's own Sistine Chapel of Eighties Britpop, a daily reminder to The Cure of pretty much everything they reviled in music. Whenever they walked through the atrium they'd look towards the roof and be subjected to the larger-than-life images of Boy George, Mike Oldfield, Bono, Feargal Sharkey, Jim Kerr (a particular target of Smith's scorn over the years) and Phil Collins looking down on them. Oddly, Branson's children also featured in the mural.

The band was holed up in the manor that Virgin built for several months, but it didn't take that long for them to become involved in a little creative redecorating. Perry Bamonte, in particular, proved to be quite the artist-in-waiting. By the end of their stay, Phil Collins' smug grin remained, but his flowing locks had been replaced by a shiny pink pate, a way more accurate representation of the early Nineties version of Mr Sussudio. Bamonte had pulled off this piece of artistic sabotage during a late-night raid on the Branson mural.

Bamonte's artwork also extended to brutal caricatures of the group and their partners. These drawings were scattered throughout the studio, alongside Smith's dog-eared collections of Emily Dickinson poems, pictures of Tank Girl and favourite headlines clipped, poison-pen-style, from *The Sport* and the *News Of The World*. Bamonte's sketches also appeared on "The Merry Mad Manor Chart", which documented the advancing mania of each of the residents of Shipton Manor during the *Wish* sessions. (Louise, the manor's housekeeper, won in a canter, followed by Gallup, Bamonte, Smith, Thompson and Williams.) It was almost a repeat of the band's high times at Miraval during the making of *Kiss Me Kiss Me Kiss Me*, only with a few line-up changes and no vineyard at their disposal.

The band, along with regular producer Dave Allen, had also taken up pyromania while camped at Branson Manor. In fact, there were more fireworks on display outside the studio than inside: while the London demo sessions for the album had been relatively smooth, translating those to tape proved extremely difficult. Bamonte, who recalled the *Wish* sessions as "a wonderful time in a beautiful place", became The Cure's very own rocket man. He tapped into a pyrotechnic mother lode and the skies would light up night after night.

"What I actually did during our stay at the Manor," Bamonte said, "was build relaunchable rockets – first in kit form, then building my own, increasingly larger, designs. The best ones were the night launches, where I installed lights into the nose cones that would illuminate the parachutes as The Rocket descended. OK, I'm a geek, but it was really good fun."

And though the band didn't surpass their wine-guzzling feats from the Miraval sessions for *Kiss Me* (Cure legend has it that the band polished off 150 bottles and upwards per week), there was enough booze at Shipton to inspire the band to try their hand at the secret art of fire-eating. The sessions might have been a hard slog, but the nightlife was a blast.

When not lighting up the sky (or themselves), Smith and the band was finding it hard to re-establish themselves musically. While *Mixed Up* had been a failed attempt at experimentation, a sideways step into the world of remixing and Acid House, The Cure was now adjusting to a more guitar-heavy line-up. Bamonte had shifted across to his more familiar role as riff man, making for a triple-guitared assault. At the same time, the so-called "shoegazing" movement had gradually eroded the impact of "baggy". Many of the bands who'd stumbled out of Madchester in the late Eighties, including Happy Mondays and The Stone Roses, weren't making any new music – they were too busy falling apart in an orgy of dollars and drugs. Now hogging the music-press-generated spotlight were such bands as Slowdive, Ride, Lush and My Bloody Valentine, all peddling an effects-heavy, humour-less (and sometimes tuneless) take on rock'n'roll.

When asked if shoegazing had any impact on *Wish*, Smith simply said this: "I definitely think it would have been a totally different record if we'd had the same songs but recorded them at the time of *Disintegration*."

What is clear is that *Wish* was the last gasp of The Cure at their com-mercial peak. The album would debut at number one in the UK and number two in the USA, selling a million copies Stateside a month after its release. Released on Smith's 33rd birthday, the album is leaner than *Kiss Me Kiss Me Kiss Me* – it ran six songs less than their breakthrough hit of 1987 – and lacked much of the psychodrama of *Disintegration*. Instead, *Wish* was the sound of The Cure stripping back a few layers. With Roger O'Donnell out of the band, The Cure went easy on the towering synthscapes that had so dominated *Disintegration*. *Wish*'s arrangements were leaner, more guitar-reliant, even if its predominant mood was just as dark and foreboding as what had gone before.

Smith was clearly in a very literal mood because *Wish* opens with, erm, 'Open' (and ends with 'End'). 'Open' was a signature Smith out-pouring of mixed emotions and surly guitars that he simply described as being about "parties". But it's pretty easy to read the song as Smith's reaction to The Cure's five whirlwind years in the spotlight, especially when he sings of his despair at the PR pressure to gladhand those who might benefit his career – and the company's record sales – when he'd clearly much rather be in bed. It was virtually an assault on the syco-phants and yes-men he'd been surrounded by since *Standing On The*

Beach went supernova in 1986. It was also a big gamble on Smith's part, daring to taunt the very people who made him a star. But it was hardly out of character for one of the most contrary men in pop.

But Smith still understood the power of expectation – why else would he include such breezy pop gems as 'High'? Built around a Gallup melody, it was a very traditional few minutes of love and regret, set to a near-ethereal guitar line from Porl Thompson. But there was something not quite right, not entirely convincing about the track – it was as if the Lovecat was merely staying in character, seduced by the possibility of just one more hit. (*Wish*, while hardly a flop, didn't generate a single with quite the across-all-formats potency of 'Lullaby' or 'Just Like Heaven', even though 'Friday I'm In Love' was quite possibly the cheeriest Smith would ever sound on record.)

Wish then took a much deeper, darker turn with 'Apart' and the album's centrepiece, the windswept 'From The Edge Of The Deep Green Sea', a deceptively simple yet no less epic song built around an insistent guitar riff and Smith's six-verse-long emotional purge. When asked about the song's subject matter, Smith would simply reply: "Drugs". If 'Deep Green Sea's motivation was truly something that direct, then Smith had been taking some top-shelf intoxicants – what else would explain such terminally depressing lyrics that describe the prelude to love-making in a matter of fact, disheartening fashion that climaxes with dutiful surrender and not satisfaction.

Wish was a deceptive album: the return of guitars to the core of The Cure's sound might have made for a simpler, more direct soundscape, but Smith was actually opening up even more lyrically. Unlike *Disintegration*, he didn't have a dense sonic hedge to lose himself in this time around.

Of course *Wish* couldn't get any bleaker – Smith may have wanted to shed a few come-lately fans with the album but he didn't want to completely alienate everyone. Powered by the most funked-up Cure guitar sound since 'Hot Hot Hot!!!', 'Wendy Time' was breezier and cheesier and probably the album's weakest link, not quite sure if it was a pop song or some kind of funk-rock experiment.

'Doing The Unstuck' – with its "let's get happy" chant – was the most vibrant Smith had sounded for years. It was the first song that the band had written while at the Manor. Smith was so taken by 'Doing The Unstuck', in fact, that he pinned the lyrics to the inside of the control room door, "so everyone would feel like they had to make the most of that day". But the following track, 'Friday I'm In Love', would top even that for sheer good-natured exuberance. With a crisply strummed acoustic guitar and Smith in full Lovecat mode – made complete by a typically chaotic, whimsical Tim Pope video – 'Friday' was a sure-fire hit, even if a closer examination of the lyric hinted that its author was in the doldrums for at least six days of the week, until Friday lifted him out of his funk. (As it transpired, 'Unstuck' and 'Friday' were the two most recently completed Smith tunes on the album. Everything else had been written during the preceding two years when his mood was a little grimmer.)

'A Letter To Elise', one of the most darkly romantic and emotionally effective tracks Smith and the band had ever recorded, carried the obligatory literary reference, with inspiration courtesy of both Jean Cocteau's *Les Enfants terribles* (which Smith had almost scored for the Royal Ballet nearly a decade earlier) and Franz Kafka's *A Letter To Felice*. Smith characterised it simply as a song about "resignation".

'Cut' and 'To Wish Impossible Things' kept the bad times rolling. The latter was another of Smith's "relationship" songs. "In all relationships," he said, "there's always aching holes and that's where the impossible wishes come into it." Smith brought the album's solemn mood to a new low with 'End'. His insistent plea to fans that they'd misunderstood him was a shout-out to the band's over-zealous followers, the acolytes who had forced Smith into an almost hermit-like existence, to simply back off. Almost 30 years earlier Smith had tuned in while his sister spun 'Help!', The Beatles' very own cry of pain. Now Smith understood the downside of celebrity and fame almost as powerfully as the Fab Four.

"In one sense," he said, "it's me addressing myself; it's about the persona I sometimes fall into. On another level, it's addressed to people who expect me to know things and have answers – fans and certain individuals. It goes beyond my circumstances as a star."

In 2004, during yet another *Rolling Stone* conversation, Smith admitted that he felt very isolated during the making of *Wish*. There were some parallels with the dark days spent recording vocals for *Disintegration*, with the rest of the band long gone. "[It was] like I was making the album on my own, and the others were just playing," he said of *Wish*. "Some days it would be really, really great, and other days it would be really, really horrible. I felt we weren't really doing anything different with it; I just felt we were making an album. I suppose that's what was wrong with it. It was almost like consolidating where we were.

"We were gonna go back out and we were gonna get more fans and we were gonna play bigger places, and somehow I lost my enthusiasm. There were elements lyrically and the way I was singing that I was almost going through the motions."

It was hardly a vote of confidence, given that yet another stint of globetrotting lay ahead for Smith, Gallup, Williams, Thompson and Bamonte. Stardom had delivered some major creature comforts for Smith and all the band, but it also meant that their lives – for at least six months of the year – didn't really belong to them. It was no great surprise that Smith was writing songs such as 'Open', with its overbearing sense of entrapment, or 'End', where he simply requested that anyone too close should just fuck right off.

But what Smith didn't know was that another Cure member was headed for a meltdown. Robert Smith was about to lose, at least for the short term, his closest Cure ally.

Smith and the band decided, wisely, to ease themselves gently into another year-long promotional slog for *Wish*. After an acoustic session with the BBC's Mark Goodier in March, they then set out on the cringingly titled 'Cure Party Night', a run of 10 UK club previews (with giveaways) of *Wish*. Next was an 11-date club and theatre tour, which kicked off on April 21 in Bradford. By mid-May they were back on board the increasingly familiar *QE2* and heading in the direction of the city that never sleeps. Whereas with their Prayer Tour they stepped off the boat in New York and virtually onto the stage of Giant's Stadium, this time Smith and band were confronted by an MTV welcoming breakfast, followed by a meet-the-press session at the Lone Star Roadhouse. Smith grimaced, tried his best to keep his food down and his head together, and faced the media.

While 'Friday I'm In Love' continued its chart rise on the other side of the Atlantic, peaking at number six in June, The Cure joined forces with British moodists Cranes for the Wish Tour, which ran virtually non-stop from mid-April to early December. Both Gallup and Smith had been devotees of Cranes' *Wings Of Joy* album; so much so that they opted for the band over such other contenders as My Bloody

Valentine, Curve and PJ Harvey. "We were as surprised as anyone," former Cranes' guitarist Mark Francombe told me. Their first show together was in Pittsburgh on May 23.

Francombe has vivid memories of the tour; he found The Cure an especially welcoming headliner. After their first date at Pittsburgh, The Cure even toasted The Cranes with champagne. It turned out, surprisingly, that the big-name headliners were somewhat apprehensive about approaching their support band.

"We were summoned backstage to say hi," Francombe recalled, "and it was very scary and awkward – and I remember Simon coming over and stammering, 'It's just as scary for us to meet you.'"

Ice well and truly broken, the two English groups underwent some righteous bonding during the tour, sometimes opting for a game of backstage football instead of laborious soundchecks. There was even a running battle with water pistols. "It got a bit out of hand," Francombe said, "and was stopped by the tour manager because we were making the corridors of the venues too wet for the roadies to load out."

During a quiet moment, Smith told Francombe that The Cure often hand-picked their support acts simply to "have some friends on the tour – they needed other musicians to hang out with." Hang out they did – when the roadshow had a pit-stop in Universal Studios they even filmed a Cure-created episode of *Star Trek*, with Perry Bamonte in the role of Captain Kirk and Cure security man Brian Adset playing a Vulcan. Cranes' singer Alison Shaw also featured. Smith's largesse was legendary: while in Florida, when the hotel bar closed for the night, he ordered a selection of booze and invited everyone back to Chez Lovecat, where the party continued.

And Cure creature comforts were not neglected backstage during the Wish Tour. The Cure entourage had continued to grow, despite their partners not being with them on the road for the entire tour, although they did turn up quite frequently. ("It must have been quite often," recalled Francombe, "because I do know them all.") And despite the hundreds of devotees that would camp in front of hotels and await The Cure's every movement, the one thing the headliners didn't have was groupies – Francombe insists they were "not that kind of band".

Francombe remembers the backstage set-up as "very cosy, with candles and curtains and so on". Smith also had a stereo, TV and mini-bar set up. On most nights, tapes of UK football games were couriered over and Smith would slump in front of the TV, keeping up with QPR's every game. Unlike the Prayer Tour, drugs weren't that common. "I don't believe that drugs played an important part at all [in the tour]," said Francombe. "But they liked a drink. Oh yes, a drink or three."

As the tour progressed, Gallup's typically fragile physical state started to deteriorate dangerously. He was still separated from his wife Carol and his two children, and spent most of his time in the company of his then girlfriend (and now wife) Sarah. Gallup was depressed; he was also boozing way too much and barely bothering to eat. A total physical collapse was imminent. As Robert Smith would recall, "It was obvious that Simon was getting really ill, right from the first concert. I couldn't believe how bad he looked when we started. I thought something was going to happen, because we had a lot of long journeys."

Francombe witnessed the moment where Gallup suffered his breakdown. "I can see the show," he told me, "but I can't remember which [city]. He was suddenly screaming, and then crying, and Brian Adset was comforting him. I don't think he cared about the feeling ill side of things; he just wanted to go home."

Suffering from a severe vitamin deficiency, Gallup was given a Vitamin C shot before playing a show in Milano on October 31, "and did the show in a bad mood", as Francombe told me. And that was it – Gallup was flown home the next day. His departure changed the entire mood of the tour. "It was pretty crap until Simon came back," said Francombe.

Smith saw Gallup's breakdown coming, but felt powerless to stop his long-time friend and tightest Cure ally from falling apart. "It's really difficult," he said, "when there is someone that you love a lot and you try to make them do something, you try to make them see what they're doing is wrong, and they pay no attention to you. [But] I shouldn't have waited for Simon to be so bad that he had to be flown home to hospital."

Stand-in bassist Robert Suave was brought in for Gallup, but by then the steam had gone out of the Wish Tour. By November, as the roadshow finally started to wind down, Smith was looking forward to another extended break. "[The tour] seems much longer than six or seven months," he admitted. "It seems like about 20." What Smith couldn't have predicted is that it'd be another four years before The Cure went out on a full-blown, coast-to-coast tour again, and by that time, the Britpop revolution – aka Cool Britannia – had rendered them pretty much obsolete.

Despite his own wariness about fatherhood – Smith was convinced, and probably with some justification, that he wasn't the most responsible man on the planet – by the early Nineties he was a devoted uncle, with many of his 20-plus nephews and nieces frequently staying with him and Mary in Bognor Regis. Smith, a man for whom money was not in any great shortage, would even grab a random selection of younger Smiths and whisk them off to Euro Disney for the weekend, on a whim. This surrogate parent role would consume increasingly large chunks of his time during the Nineties, as would such grounding, not-very-rock'n'roll chores as gardening. Upon returning from the final *Wish* show, in Dublin on December 3, that's exactly what Smith did: he got a little dirt on his hands.

"I went into the garden and pulled out two years' worth of weeds," he reported. "I really enjoyed it." Smith was even slowly adjusting to The Cure nuts who'd set up camp just outside his home. Occasionally he'd step outside to speak to them, but usually he just let them be. Fanaticism took on a different perspective in England; Smith knew it was unlikely that any of the nutters in his front garden was likely to do him or Mary serious harm. This wasn't Hollywood.

Smith's plans for the next couple of years – the band would play one show in 1993 and none at all in 1994 – were very straightforward: he wanted to continue tinkering with his never-ending solo record. And he also planned to guide the recently filmed *Show* to completion. This consumed most of his time between January and April 1993, but he wasn't thrilled by what he saw on the screen.

"When the director's cut came back it was awful," said Smith. "I was really disappointed and I couldn't believe someone could make us look that boring and bad on stage." By the time the film was ready for its premiere, Smith was happier with the celluloid Cure, so much so that he showed up at the screening. "I think it's good," he finally admitted, before adding, "but I would say that anyway."

The Cure's latest large-screen indulgence was really only a diversion for their leader. The Tolhurst court case cast a large, dark shadow over almost everything The Cure did in the mid-Nineties. Smith's mood towards his former Cure comrade and school friend fluctuated: Smith had actually checked out Tolhurst's new band, Presence, in 1991, several months after Tolhurst had written to him threatening legal action. Smith felt Presence were "dull, boring. Lol's at the front pretending to play keyboards and he didn't play anything all night. Nothing's changed." But Smith's mere presence at the gig suggested he was up for a little peacemaking. Things changed quickly enough, though. By the time of the Wish Tour, Smith and band were taking aim at a Lol Tolhurst dartboard, the gift of a Cure associate. When asked about the pending lawsuit, Smith was blunt: "I can't fucking wait for the court case," he whooped.

According to Perry Bamonte, the band's attitude towards the Tolhurst case was to laugh it off. "We spoke about Lol a lot during the case, lots of silly jokes. I guess we were really pissed off about the whole deal so joking was a good safety valve. It was a pretty surreal and stupid affair and with hindsight I feel sorry for Lol." Bamonte, along with the rest of the band, were asked to testify. "But I didn't have a lot to offer."

Smith, however, was a slightly rattled man, especially as more and more correspondence bounced between their lawyers. "At the time," said Smith, "I tried to ignore it, but I was getting letters on a regular basis, because I didn't really want to go to court because I knew it would be a waste of time and money. [It] distracted me quite a lot. I got really fed up with them." For the first time since The Cure formed in the Seventies, Smith had thoughts of killing off the band for reasons other than road weariness or fatigue. If this is what success reduced you to, he'd had a gutful.

Smith was spending more and more time in London in heavy discussions with his legal crew; the case was due to be heard in the High Court by early 1994. Songwriting was the last thing on his mind. Instead, he was poring over old Cure contracts and thousands of other documents. Smith knew that if he lost – which was unlikely – he might even lose the rights to The Cure's name. "Had Lol won," Smith realised, "it would have meant a lot."

The case of Tolhurst v. Smith was finally dragged through the courts in February and March, 1994. Just before the trial began, Chris Parry called Tolhurst and asked him to reconsider. This only made Tolhurst more determined to proceed. "The way I was thinking was that if they're willing to do that there must be something they're hiding – and we're going to go on with it," Tolhurst said.

On September 16, 1994 a decision was handed down, and Tolhurst had lost. Mr Justice Chadwick ruled that the latest Fiction deal was not unfair, which left Tolhurst to deal with a legal bill estimated at more than one million dollars, a figure he confirmed when I spoke with him.

The judge rejected claims that the band's 1986 deal, which gave Tolhurst some 2 per cent of gross sales, was signed under undue influence, and said Tolhurst was lucky to get that much because he was only being kept on because he was a founding member of the group.

Tolhurst was by that time wealthy enough to handle the financial blow, but only just. "Up to that point I was pretty wealthy, I had a nice house, money in the bank," he said to me. "But I got divorced at the same time, because it's not easy to have a relationship with someone who's been on that self-destructive bent. The judge told me that 75 per cent of my income would go directly to court costs and that I would receive 25 per cent of my royalties, which was my only source of income. I was also paying tax on that. It took me to last year [2003] to clear everything and be a normal person again. Financially it was gigantic.

"My honest take on it now is that none of the good things that have happened since may not have happened. I may have ended up as the sad figure in the local pub at Devon; I would have become everything I didn't want to be in the first place. But out of the pain has come forth joy.

"I could have done without losing a million dollars, but it's only money. Sixteen years ago I was quite wealthy and very miserable, now I'm not so wealthy and very happy."

When the decision was handed down, Tolhurst had had enough of England. In late 1994 he shifted base to Los Angeles and hasn't returned since. As for Smith, it took him some time to recover fully from the drawn-out ordeal. "Lol . . . had taken away more than a year of my time," said Smith. "Our argument puts a shadow over my life." Gradually, hostilities would cease between the pair – they even exchanged letters not too long after the court case was finally settled. "Ultimately, he's the person I've known the longest in my life," Tolhurst said soon afterwards. "Things between us are never going to be the way they were before, but our friendship is still there, though it has evolved."

When Smith and Tolhurst did eventually reconcile, Tolhurst had a confession to make. "I told him that my motivation for the case was my resentment and that wasn't right. I know now that it wasn't right. It was a Catch 22 – there was no way Robert could have told me, 'I love you but get right and come back, or whatever' – it couldn't have worked. I realise that now."

Robert Smith found the time to revisit Giants Stadium in New Jersey during 1994, but it wasn't to headline a show in front of screaming Cure fans. Not quite. Along with Perry Bamonte's brother Daryl, producer Alan Wilder, and Depeche Mode's Martin Gore and Dave Gahan, Smith had far more pressing concerns on June 18. He was in town to check out the Ireland versus Italy first-round clash of the 1994 FIFA World Cup.* It was in this very Smith-friendly environment – beer and football being Cure staples – that the *Wild Mood Swings* album started to take shape. During their far-ranging conversation, as the East Coast heat beat down on these big-haired, pale-faced football fans, Smith mentioned that he was on the lookout for a new producer for their next record. His relationship with Dave Allen, which spanned such huge successes as *Kiss Me* and *Disintegration*, had run its natural course. The uncomfortable, somewhat unfulfilling sessions for *Wish* were proof of that. When the name Steve Lyon was raised, everyone there agreed that he could be the guy to solve The Cure production conundrum.

Up to that point, Steve Lyon had been very much Depeche Mode's man. As much an engineer as a record producer – exactly the kind of sonic sidekick Smith preferred – Lyon had worked on several Mode albums: 1981's *Speak And Spell*, 1982's *A Broken Frame*, *Construction Time Again* (1983) and *People Are People* from 1984. Just like Phil Thornalley before him, Lyon was not a dedicated Cure fan, as he told me when we spoke in late 2004. "I wasn't an avid follower of everything they'd done. I'd seen Robert play with the Banshees and The Cure, at the end of the punk time. I think I owned a couple of records."

Via Ita Martin, the long-time Fiction Records staffer, a meeting was organised between Smith and Lyon in a London pub. They spoke for a

---

* Ireland won, 1–0.

couple of hours. Several pints in, Lyon mentioned his indifferent take on the band, but Smith didn't see that as a potential problem. "Completely the opposite," Lyon related to me. "He said, 'I want a fresh approach and someone who's not intimidated by my past.'" Initially, Lyon was offered the gig of engineering the album, because Smith was adamant that he was going to produce. "He was fed up with the way the last record, *Wish*, had gone," Lyon said, "even though it had done very well. He had a lot of frustrations."

Smith's frustrations extended beyond the million-selling success of *Wish*. Though he was about to reclaim the name of The Cure – the Tolhurst decision was still a few months away – he'd lost much of the band in the process. During this extended break, which had engulfed 1993 and half of 1994, The Cure had fallen apart. Smith's brother-in-law, Porl Thompson (who, by now, had four children with Smith's sister Janet), had been made an offer he couldn't refuse by no lesser personages than Jimmy Page and Robert Plant who needed an extra guitarist for their touring band. A serious Led Zeppelin devotee, Thompson knew he couldn't pass up the offer.[*] Drummer Boris Williams had also moved on, principally to work in The Piggle, a group formed by his girlfriend Caroline Crawley. What had started out as a temporary spot for the unstable Andy Anderson had become an almost decade-long residency for Williams in The Cure.

Also missing from The Cure fold circa 1994 was Simon Gallup. Even though the bassman had returned, post-meltdown, to complete the Wish Tour, he was still in a bad way when Smith tried to reassemble the band for this new LP. According to Lyon, "Simon had been in and out of the band; he had a lot of personal problems at the time." Lyon declined to comment further, but it was relatively well known that Gallup's drinking problems added to his dodgy emotional and physical state.[†] So when serious discussions began about their next album, The Cure was a gang of two: Smith and relatively new recruit Perry Bamonte. Smith may have been a dab hand at doubling up on his much-loved six-string bass, but The Cure was shy of a drummer, a

---

[*] A Cure insider told me that due to their strong family connection, it was much easier for Thompson to move in and out of The Cure over the band's lifespan.

[†] Lol Tolhurst would tell me that he and Smith discussed Gallup's toxic troubles when they finally resumed their friendship.

keyboardist and a lead guitarist. Exactly what kind of an album could they make?

As Lyon related to me, "There were long discussions about how we were going to do this – because they didn't have a band." What Smith did have was some songs, or at least the fragments of roughly 20 tunes-under-development. During one of their pre-recording meetings, Smith played these demos to Lyon, but he found them very sketchy. "The demos didn't have structure, really," said Lyon, "no vocals, no top melody line – and I had no idea where the chorus, bridge and middle eight would go. I kind of guessed."

Smith had obviously taken a liking to working in stately country manors, because he was insistent about revisiting the idea for *Wild Mood Swings*. *Kiss Me, Wish* and *Disintegration* had been recorded outside of the usual studio environment, and now Smith was intent on getting the mix of location and mood just right. It helped that Steve Lyon had already recorded with Depeche Mode in a rural setting. "He [Smith] was interested in my experience with that," Lyon said to me.

By late 1994, Simon Gallup had recovered sufficiently to rejoin. Smith now told Lyon that he and Bamonte would handle the guitar parts, Gallup would play bass and they'd hire some session drummers to keep time. The band was as ready as it could ever be, although Bamonte realised how tough it would be replacing the best player in The Cure's long history. "Moving from keyboards to guitar was actually quite hard," he confessed, "because although guitar was my first instrument, I found it far more personal and expressive to play than, say, a synthesizer. I felt more exposed, naked. And remember, I was filling Porl Thompson's shoes – quite a challenge for an accomplished musician, let alone an amateur like myself."

As far as locations go, The Cure couldn't have found a better hideaway than St Catherine's Court, which was located near Bath. Just like Branson Manor, it was the kind of house to get lost in – quite literally. With its nine bedrooms, six bathrooms, six reception rooms, ballroom and Elizabethan dining room, the home was owned by no less a star than Jane Seymour, aka Dr Quinn, Medicine Woman. And this was a spread with some history; its Benedictine origins dated back to somewhere around AD 950. As the lady of the house proudly proclaims in the St Catherine's Court website, "This is a house where you can be very grand for dinner or muck about in jeans and take hikes." The men of The Cure weren't exactly the hiking types, but they did find the pool and the tennis court (and their scalextric set) very much to their liking. But St Catherine's, unlike Hook End or the Branson Manor, wasn't a working studio, so Smith, Bamonte and the band's crew spent a week setting up in early November, Smith bringing in a lot of his home equipment, which included mics, a small sound desk, preamps and computer gear. They were soon joined by Lyon and Gallup.

As Lyon told me, there wasn't a great deal of renovation required to turn Seymour's stately home into a recording studio, apart from setting up the main desk in the library. As for the ballroom, it was tailor-made for a rock'n'roll band. "It was a massive ballroom," Lyon said, "at least 100 square metres, which was fantastic – and very conducive to late-night jams." (Lyon recorded many of these all-nighters; some even made it to *Wild Mood Swings*.) Smith and his wife Mary, who drifted in and out of the sessions, chose the bedroom directly above the library as their HQ.

Unlike most Cure albums – *Pornography* and *Disintegration*, especially – this was a record without a precise outline. This made it difficult for Lyon to approach *Mood Swings* like a typical production. "There wasn't a grand plan," he said, "it was just, 'Well, we have these songs, let's work on them and see what comes out.' [Whereas] I'm more of a straight-ahead, practical person. It became evident in its infancy – they didn't have a band, Robert didn't know what the record should sound like and I think that those elements led to the fact that it was a very diverse record.

"There were moments I found incredibly frustrating but those were vastly outnumbered by the pleasurable moments I had being around the guys, working on songs and living in the house. I learned a lot; I've never worked with someone who works in the way Robert does. Everything flows around him, and that's the way it is. Anyone who joined the band would be naïve to think that's not the way it is."

Smith was every bit the tinkerer – Lyon would mistakenly think that a song was finished only to find Smith spending hours rearranging it. And it didn't help their forward progress, in those pre-Protools days, that much of their recording time was devoted to backing up their finished work. This, of course, didn't stop machines from either breaking down or chewing up tapes (they did both during the *Wild Mood Swings* sessions).

Towards the end of 1994, Roger O'Donnell was asked to return to The Cure. He came back to a very new line-up, not just in members, but in the band's more relaxed attitude towards the use of computers. ("There were now computers everywhere," marvelled O'Donnell.) At the same time, Smith was trying out drummers, who would be put through two separate auditions. During the initial try-out, the tub-thumping hopefuls would play and be filmed by the band; those invited back would actually jam with the band. Smith was still planning to use a variety of drummers on the album (which he ultimately did), but he also knew that some lucrative European summer festival dates were in the offing. What The Cure really needed was a permanent sticks man.

Some well-regarded players put up their hand, including Mark Price from Goth popsters All About Eve, Louis Pavlou from The Cure's Fiction labelmates God Machine, as well as Bob Thompson, Malcolm Scott, Martin Gilkes and Ronald Austin (Pavlou, Austin and Price would all get credits on the finished record). Another contender was Jason Cooper, who'd responded to a drummer wanted ad that The Cure placed, anonymously, in the *NME*. ("I bought the *NME* that week, fortunately," Cooper told me via e-mail.)

Of all the hopefuls, the London-born, Bath-raised Cooper was the least seasoned. Apart from some session work, he'd played with Strangler Jean Jacques Burnell, as well as Billie Ray Martin, and had also composed music for TV and films. But what he did have going for him was this: he was a dedicated Cure fan. Cooper's father, who worked for Virgin Records, had handed his teenage son a copy of *Seventeen Seconds*, "which I played extensively", Cooper told me. Cooper had seen The Cure at Glastonbury in June 1990, but his strongest connection to the band was much more intimate. "My favourite memories are listening to *Faith* drinking cider," he admitted.

At Cooper's first audition, he played along to the demo of 'Jupiter Crash'. When he was invited back to jam with the band they played 'Disintegration' and 'From The Edge Of The Deep Green Sea'. Smith was impressed, as was Steve Lyon. "Mark [Price] was a very, very good drummer but I thought that Jason would fit better into the odd marriage of people in the band at the time," Lyon said. "Jason was a very big Cure fan. I said to Robert that I thought he would fit. I think I had a slight influence on him joining the band." Cooper's youthfulness didn't do his claims any harm, either, as the rest of The Cure weren't getting any younger.

Now that a permanent drummer was on board, Smith was about to make Lyon an offer that he would have some trouble refusing. *Mood Swings*' engineer was about to be promoted to co-producer. "I was flattered," Lyons said, "but I had to ask, 'How long is this going to take?'" Smith requested that Lyon not take on any more work until the album was finished. In exchange, Smith would compensate him (handsomely) for any jobs he had to pass up. "Little did I know that it would take about 18 months," Lyon said.

The album sessions were first put on hold during March; Smith then devoted the next couple of months to rehearsals for their European summer dates, which ran from June 6 until July 18. Not only was the money useful (these sessions weren't cheap) but it was also a chance to road test some of their new songs.

When work finally resumed on *Wild Mood Swings* (a title that had actually been the proposed moniker for Smith's solo record), the focus of the first four months had gone slightly askew. More recording was done at Haremere Hall in Sussex, while strings for several tracks, heard to best effect on 'Numb', were recorded at Peter Gabriel's Real World Studio. A cover of David Bowie's 'Young Americans' that ended up on a 104.9 XFM compilation was pieced together at another roomy country home just outside Bath that was owned by a model railway nut. When Cooper walked into the garden, where the owner's treasured railway set looped in and out of his rose bushes, he realised he'd visited the house as a child.

Then Smith told Lyon that he also wanted to mix the album away from the studio, which presented a whole new series of challenges. A few early mixes were attempted at St Catherine's, but while the house that Dr Quinn built may have been ideal for late-night jams, it wasn't conducive to fine-tuning songs. Band and gear was bumped out and re-established in Haremere Hall. It was there that co-producer Lyon got a very clear picture of Robert Smith's wealth.

They'd been renting a Neve V-series console, a mother of a mixing desk that was roughly four metres long, two metres deep and two metres high. "It's a massive thing," Lyon said to me. It was also valued at £100,000. Frustrated by having to rent the desk week by week, Smith went away, did some sums, and then told Lyon that he was going to buy the monster. "He said it was cheaper than renting," Lyon stated.*

Wild Mood Swings broke down, yet again, when The Cure was asked to join Page & Plant, The Black Crowes and The Smashing Pumpkins for a three-week-long South American jaunt during January 1996. As Lyon recalled, "That put the kibosh on that for the moment." He did, however, get to work on the band's live sound. "I had a fantastic time, but got no work done on the record."

For a record that had such a leisurely, stop-start evolution, things changed when Cure and crew returned to the UK in early February. Up to now, Smith had been avoiding Chris Parry's calls to the studio, leaving Lyon to invent excuses for his absence. "I had to say things like, 'He's asleep,' or 'He's not here right now'; I think Robert took advantage of that situation sometimes."†

But this time Parry did get through, and he told the band that the album's scheduled release date was two months away. Not one track had been mixed.

According to Lyon, the haste to finish the album led to the most disappointing part of his lengthy sojourn with the band. He and Smith knew they had no option but to outsource the mixes, which wasn't going to help an album that was already madly eclectic in nature.

"I found it difficult to say to him, 'No, this is not the right thing to do,' because Robert is his own man, he's been doing it long enough, and at the end of the day it's his record. But I do think that some of the material lost its edge because we'd worked on it for too long and then it had been farmed out to people who hadn't been part of the history of the song."

Those people included Mike "Spike" Drake, who mixed 'The 13th' and 'Numb' ("No good at all," according to Lyon), as well as Flood, whose mix was "really good" to Lyon's ears, but didn't make the album's final cut. Tim Palmer was also hired (Lyon: "I thought his mix of 'Jupiter Crash' was also very good"), as was Paul Corkett, who

---

* Lyon, like many others I spoke to, had no problems with Smith's largesse. "Robert's a very generous person, both financially and socially."
† Lol Tolhurst told me that within a few years, Smith and Parry barely spoke at all. "Robert told me in 2000 that he hadn't spoken to Chris in six months. He'd send missives from his yacht. He said he'd gone crazy and doesn't talk to him any more."

worked on 'Mint Car' and would go on to produce the next Cure long-player. Smith and Lyon co-mixed five *Mood Swings*' cuts, including 'Jupiter Crash' and 'Gone!'

"For me," Lyon continued, "that was the only disappointing element of the whole thing. I think we needed to mix in the studio — that would have been a better option. But I didn't have the power to do that; Robert was so set in the way that he wanted to do it." This led to the one true showdown between Smith and Lyon, who was becoming increasingly frustrated as the sessions leaked into their third calendar year. "The band was getting ready to go on tour; they hadn't decided on a single; there were all these mixes flying around — it was kind of a confusing situation.

"I said to Robert, 'Look, I don't agree with everything that's going on and I don't think that you're necessarily making all the right decisions.' I don't think that he liked that very much."

These differences of opinion extended into the choice of first single, which only contributed to *Mood Swings*' indifferent results (if you can call million-plus sales disappointing). Lyon was keen on the more upbeat 'Mint Car', which Smith had tried out on his mother, who allegedly loved it. But Smith, whose vote was final and non-negotiable, opted instead for 'The 13th'. As Lyon recalled, "There were long, long — overly long — discussions about that. By that time, however, some of the edges were a bit blurred; I'd been working on the record too long." Lyon also felt that the record ran over time at 14 tracks; he felt 11 tunes would have been just right.

Single selection and album length weren't the only problems faced by Smith and The Cure. During their lengthy absence, as they tried to piece together *Wild Mood Swings*, put the band back together and deal with the drawn-out Tolhurst vs The Cure court case, the orbit of the musical world had shifted. Acid house and Madchester had blazed briefly then burned out, likewise grunge and the British shoegazers. But Britpop, with Blur, Suede and Oasis as its main banner-wavers, was now in the midst of its second coming. Even the US market was tuning in to such breakthrough records as Oasis' *Definitely Maybe*, something that hadn't happened to Happy Mondays or The Stone Roses. Lyon was convinced that The Cure could have slotted comfortably into the movement — after all, they had opened up America unlike any British band this side of The Beatles or the Stones — if only they'd had *Mood*

Swings ready earlier. "But with the first single chosen, and the time that elapsed, I think it suffered a little because of that."

Robert Smith, however, would defend this patchy, unpredictable batch of tracks, insisting it was the moment where he rediscovered his smile. "There are some pretty demented songs on there," he reflected in 2004. But you wouldn't think so on the evidence of the opener, 'Want', which was very much Cure angst-by-numbers, propped up by the usual dense guitarscapes. But the album took its first odd turn with 'Club America', where Smith tried a new voice, much raspier and lower than his Lovecat moneymaker. For the first time on record, Smith sounded as if he's singing from somewhere deep in his boots, as he growls like a predatory sex machine, hoping to score with a creepy come-on about how the object of his desire's eyes have been burning a hole in his head since the moment he caught sight of her. It was hardly Julio Iglesias (or Charles Aznavour for that matter, whom Smith had mimicked back in the days of 'Hot Hot Hot!!!'), but if you wanted a clear sign that *Wild Mood Swings* wasn't completely Cure by-the-book, here was Exhibit A.

The following track, 'This Is A Lie', was Smith in darkly beautiful form, virtually reciting his lyrics while real, live strings ebbed and flowed behind him. This was the nearest that Smith had come to replicating the autumnal blues of Nick Drake, a perennial favourite. Then, suddenly, the band slipped into what Smith would describe as a "sort of crackpot salsa vibe" for 'The 13th', a failed but brave experiment in redefining The Cure's musical future. Such unexpected right-turns would lead to some of the worst press The Cure would ever cop when *Wild Mood Swings* finally appeared in mid-1996.

"It was a shame, because it got slagged when it came out," said Smith. "Fans hated it as well. It's the only time I've been hugely disappointed. I suppose it was because ['The 13th'] was the first thing that they'd heard from the band in years, and I don't think they gave it a chance after that."

'Strange Attraction' is another breezier moment of *Wild Mood Swings*, an ever-so-cheesy song of seduction underscored by frothy keyboards and a repetitive, hollow drum sound. The Cure wouldn't come any closer accidentally to replicating the sound of The Thompson Twins, one of Smith's most despised pop peers (who, admittedly, had driven both Boris Williams and Roger O'Donnell to the more hedonistic Cure). Then came the mysteriously titled 'Mint Car', another light-hearted effort from a band who'd been missing a funny bone for years. When Smith exploded with fizziness at the sunrise, it was the most upbeat he'd been since declaring that 'Friday I'm In Love'. It made for a peculiar flipside to the champers-and-pills celebrations of Oasis, even if the Britpop kings currently lorded it over The Cure in the charts.

Wild Mood Swings may have still sold a million copies in the USA, but that was a big commercial comedown from *Wish* and *Disintegration*. The writing was very clearly on the (Elektra) wall: The Cure's salad days were just about over.

It's unfair to completely write off *Wild Mood Swings* as a brave failure, as little more than Robert Smith's folly. 'Jupiter Crash', a contender for the album title at one point (ditto 'Bare'), is a stylish ballad-of-sorts, an insider's portrait of Robert Smith the Bognor Regis stargazer, looking into the sky through his telescope and inquiring about what happens when a star falls. During 'Round & Round & Round' Smith seems positively jolly as he hints at his own legendary indecisiveness. I mean, what else could he be getting at when he shrugs and admits – characteristically obliquely – that he'll never overcome his own uncertainty. The album then bounces between moods either delirious ('Return'), solemn (the string-sodden and quite haunting 'Numb' and the equally stirring closer, 'Bare', where Smith comes clean on "what I've really become") or somewhere in between ('Trap').

Robert Smith had some very clear-cut explanations as to why exactly the 14-track-long *Wild Mood Swings* failed. "The album suffers from being too long," he explained. "And it's disjointed. I was trying to write in different styles, and wanted us to sound like different bands, almost going after the *Kiss Me* idea. But, because we'd lost Boris, and before Jason [Cooper] settled in, we had a different drummer every week. I would often forget the name of the person who was drumming."

Smith took aim at the usual target: his record company. "Every album up to that point had sold more than the last one, and suddenly the record company was confronted with this horrifying drop in sales, and they didn't have a fuckin' clue as to why we'd ever sold records in the first place," Smith figured. "They didn't really know what they were promoting or who to."

275

And for the first time since the very early days of *Three Imaginary Boys*, The Cure seemed like the wrong band at the wrong time: a bird's nest of hair and a slash of smudged lippy didn't quite fit with the *Loaded* sensibilities of such middle-class bands as Blur, or the thuggish swagger of Oasis' Gallagher brothers.

In 1996, The Cure was old and in the way.

Chapter Twelve

"I can even imagine doing this at 60; I don't care what others think."

– Robert Smith

LIKE the shark and the Abominable Snowman, sightings of The Cure in the late Nineties were mainly seasonal and not all that common. They toured *Wild Mood Swings* heavily, bringing it all home with shows at Wembley, Sheffield, Manchester and Birmingham in December 1996. They'd followed that with an abbreviated US tour in late 1997, where they played little more than a dozen shows, as opposed to their usual 70 or 80. In 1998 they did another lap of European festivals during July and August, while in 1999 they played exactly one date, and even then it was a special promo gig at Sony Studios in New York.

In the wake of *Wild Mood Swings*, Smith was reluctant to start planning another album, as he was still smarting from the subdued response it had received. "In the UK, Britpop did kill us," he said, somewhat reluctantly. "For the first time, *NME* and *Melody Maker* were right in their view of how the public perceived us. It was the first album in The Cure's history that didn't do better than the last one." (*Melody Maker*'s take on *Wild Mood Swings* basically amounted to this: "Smith looks exactly the same as ever, and his Cure haven't exactly engaged in fearless pursuit of innovation either." The *New York Times* was equally disparaging. "For all the torments of heartbreak, the anguish doesn't seem so earthshaking as it was the last time, and all the times before.")

Smith – rather than The Cure – made a low-key return to public life in early 1997, after he returned home one night to find a message on his answering machine. "Hello, Robert, this is David Bowie. I'm hosting my 50th birthday party at Madison Square Garden and want you to come along and play. It'll be a blast." Almost 25 years had passed since Smith first laid eyes upon Ziggy Stardust on *Top Of The Pops* and experienced one of his first musical revelations – now he had the chance to sing alongside the Thin White Duke himself. But Smith was a natural-born sceptic: "How is it," he asked Mary, "that Bowie could have my unlisted number?" At first, Smith was convinced it was a Cure buddy taking the piss. Cautiously, he called Bowie's number, leaving a wary message. "I'll call you back," he said, "I'm not sure." Deep down inside, though, Smith was euphoric – especially when Bowie phoned again and confirmed that the request was legit.

The show was staged on January 9, 1997. Also there to help Bowie blow out his 50 candles were Lou Reed, The Smashing Pumpkins' Billy Corgan, The Foo Fighters and Sonic Youth. Smith and Bowie duetted on two songs: 'The Last Thing You Should Do', from Bowie's most recent album, *Earthling*, and *Hunky Dory*'s 'Quicksand'. To most, it was the highlight of the night. Backstage, the co-producer of *Earthling*, Mark Plati, looked on in amazement. Two of his life-long musical heroes were sharing a mic, only a few yards away.

"They were both stellar," Plati said to me, "genuine highlights of the gig." Plati, who was soon to play a key role in the next chapter of The Cure, didn't have such a shabby musical history himself. New York-based, he'd been engineer to production king Arthur Baker, and had worked with revered DJ Junior Vasquez, tweaking remixes for Janet Jackson, Talking Heads and Prince (he'd worked on his Purpleness' *Graffiti Bridge* album), before signing on to produce *Earthling* with Bowie.

Plati's relationship with the cult of The Cure had started in a fairly unusual place. "I lived for a time with an all-female band in Dallas, Texas," he said to me. "I was an intern at a local studio and I exchanged free studio time for a space on their couch for a few months. On one occasion, one of them listened to 'Boys Don't Cry' for around 36 hours straight. That struck me as being rather serious." Plati was a fan of the band's more "commercial" side – or at least their heaviest selling records – including *Kiss Me Kiss Me Kiss Me*, *Disintegration* and *Wish*. "On the production side, I really loved the records they did with Dave Allen. I felt that they didn't sound like anyone else out there, which is always something I find attractive."

The after-show party for Bowie's 50th was held at the downtown loft of artist Julian Schnabel. Plati was making the rounds with long-time Bowie guitarist Reeves Gabrels (who was also soon to work with Smith). As befitting such an A-list party, Plati revealed, there were "various libations on offer". Having been actively involved in the production of the birthday show, Plati was exhausted and needed to let off some steam.

"By the time I got to Robert's end of the room, where he was camped out at a table with director Tim Pope, I was out-and-out shit-faced. In all honesty, if I hadn't been in that state I probably wouldn't have found the nerve to approach him." Plati chose the subject of the 'Lullaby' video as an icebreaker; he asked Smith how it felt to be eaten alive. "I tried to get him to tell me what made him think up such a thing, and what it was like to have all those legs and whatnot, all the while trying to keep my composure in the face of overwhelming drunken giddiness. He and Tim probably thought I was bonkers. They probably still do."*

Bonkers or not, Smith commissioned Plati to work on a mix of a new Cure track, 'Wrong Number', that was to be added to the upcoming retrospective, *Galore*. Studio time was scheduled in London for early in the northern summer, at around the same time that Bowie's *Earthling* tour was doing its UK run. Plati called Gabrels and suggested he come down to the studio. "I'm pretty sure that was Robert's intention all along. He was a big fan of Reeves', as it turned out. [And] I might have mentioned [to Gabrels] that bringing a guitar wouldn't be a bad idea."

By this stage, Smith and the band had recorded 'Wrong Number' and handed it out to Adrian Sherwood and Mark Saunders for mixing. "At first, Robert was just looking for a remix," Plati said. "At the same time, he really liked the previous attempts of the song, but didn't think he'd cracked the definitive version yet." Plati and Smith pulled the track apart and rebuilt it around a new beat, based upon a sampled Jason Cooper drum loop. They also added a few new keyboard parts and effects.

It was around this time that Gabrels walked into the control room; within a few hours he'd laid down a "gazillion guitar tracks", according to Plati. Then Smith realised he needed to re-cut his vocal, because the

---

* Smith didn't hold back at the after-show party either, as it turns out. He even argued with Bowie about floating himself on the stock market, which had produced a handy $50-plus million pay-off. "We disagreed on almost every point," Smith said afterwards. "I had drunk too much and I was quite aggressive."

song was now so radically different to the original. For a fan such as Plati, it was almost impossible to conceal his joy when Smith took his place at the mic.

"When Robert began to sing, I was really blown away – it's always amazing to hear somebody's voice, but when a voice like Robert's comes out of the speakers, it's a whole other ball game." At one stage, Plati couldn't control his glee – he began jumping up and down, shouting, "It's Robert Smith! It's Robert Smith!" to no one in particular. Smith stopped singing and asked Plati whether he had a problem. "I had to tell him how fantastic the whole thing was for me. His reply was something along the lines of, 'Really? Nobody ever gets excited when I sing.' I thought it was sweet."

With Smith's vocal and Gabrels' guitar in place, all that was needed was one final touch: Smith needed someone to state "You've got the wrong number," which would give the song an added hook. "It sounds easy," Plati recalled, "but it took forever." They eventually settled on the number of a high school friend of Plati's. Smith called, the wife of Plati's friend answered appropriately, and the track was complete.

"I think it turned out much better than we hoped," Plati added. "It became the single. It was much, much different from either of the versions he'd recorded up to that point. The Adrian Sherwood version was fairly 'dubby', with horns and female backing vocals – and this was miles from where we landed. We were a lot more rock in the end."* Smith preferred the Plati mix, too; he felt it was a handy companion piece to 'Never Enough', the one new track from their *Mixed Up* set.

Once released in late October 1997, the initial response to 'Wrong Number' was positive, and it reached the number nine spot on *Billboard*'s Modern Rock Tracks chart. (*Galore* featured four tracks that had topped that *Billboard* chart: 'Fascination Street', 'High', 'Friday I'm In Love' and 'Never Enough'.) But even though The Cure upped their American profile considerably in the latter months of the year, *Galore* failed to connect in the same way as their first best-of collection, *Standing On A Beach*. "No radio station played ['Wrong Number'] in the UK," Smith said. "I even wondered if it wasn't a conspiracy."

Mark Plati, for one, had no real idea why the song and the album

---

* The Mark Saunders mix found a home on *Join The Dots*.

didn't become heavy sellers. "There are a hundred explanations for why something is or isn't a hit," he told me. "In the end it's down to luck, timing, the moon, whatever. I still think 'Wrong Number' is a great track – Robert's vocal is outstanding, the guitars are twisted and the song takes chances. It's an awesome miniature event."

As good as it was, the failure of the single and *Galore* had a powerful impact on Smith. "I think that's what killed The Cure as a pop band," he said. And Smith wasn't feeling much love for his US label Elektra, accusing them of indifference towards *Wild Mood Swings*. "They were thinking, 'Well, they'll sell a couple of million records and we don't have to do anything.' We owe them a certain amount of money and it goes in their budget on fucking idiot bands that are never going to go out and sell a record in their lives. Because we're older and unfashionable, there isn't anyone who will go out on a limb for us." He was livid.

The Cure had one more album to run on their contract. Convinced that the band was a spent force commercially, Smith decided that The Cure should bow out with a record that reflected their deeply serious character, rather than their 'Friday I'm In Love' side. He was going to write and record the third and final part of his accidental trilogy of despair and heartbreak, which had begun with *Pornography* and continued with *Disintegration*. But first he had to save the world.

During the early Nineties, the litmus test of a rock'n'roll band's coolness was gauged by one simple fact: had they cameod on *The Simpsons*? The Matt Groening-created cartoon had long been the edgiest thing on the small screen, drawing guest appearances from former Beatles (George Harrison, Ringo Starr and Paul McCartney), arena rockers (Aerosmith, U2) and the headliners of the Lollapalooza Generation (The Smashing Pumpkins, Sonic Youth, *et al*). But things changed in the mid-Nineties, thanks to Trey Parker and Matt Stone, two bratty film students from the University of Colorado. In 1991 they pieced together an animated short going by the name of *Jesus vs Frosty* (also known as *The Spirit Of Christmas*). Crudely made and packed with expletives and random acts of violence, the short made its way into the hands of execs at the Fox network. In 1995 Fox's Brian Graden commissioned the pair to make another seasonal short, which would be distributed amongst fellow suits. This one was formally titled *The Spirit Of Christmas* and featured a lively martial arts battle between Jesus Christ and Santa Claus. A hit on the fast growing internet (an information network that The Cure had also started to exploit with some success), *The Spirit Of Christmas* led Parker and Stone into serious discussions with Fox, and then Comedy Central. The iconoclastic and seriously fucking irreverent *South Park* premiered to an unsuspecting public on August 13, 1997.

If Bart Simpson had been the cause of renewed interest in juvenile delinquency (as many wowsers wanted the world to believe), then the kids of snowy, remote South Park – Stan, Kyle, toilet-mouthed Cartman and Kenny, doomed to die a bloody death in each episode – were clearly the devil's spawn. No subject was too puerile, no taboo was safe from Parker and Stone (the show actually copped a TV-MA rating for its predilection towards swearing and gore). The 1998 film, *South Park: Bigger, Longer & Uncut*, featuring the sensitive ballads 'Blame Canada' and 'Uncle Fucka', even received an Oscar nomination. In true *Simpsons*-style, the show had drawn some A-list cameos, including an ex-president (Bill Clinton), a murder suspect (O.J. Simpson), an escape artist (David Blaine) and various rock acts either cool (Korn, Radiohead) or cold (Stevie Nicks, Toto).

The February 18, 1998 episode of *South Park* began in typical fashion: Cartman discovered an ancient triangle, which he passed along to Kyle. When Kyle was interviewed on TV, it drew the attention of film critic Leonard Maltin and fading diva Barbra Streisand. It turned out that there were two triangles – Streisand had the other. If she recovered the second she would have the power to rule the world (as she has always hoped to, clearly). Only three people could stop her – Matlin, legendary actor Sidney Poitier and, erm, Cure mainman Robert Smith. When Smith reached South Park, old Babs had morphed into the murderous Mecha-Streisand, which meant that Smith had to adopt his own superhero persona, Smithra. An epic battle of Godzilla vs Mothra scale ensued, during which Smithra grabbed Mecha-Streisand's tail and tossed her deep into space.

The world now saved from the evil that is Babs, Smith prepared to leave, but first had to recover a walkie-talkie that he'd left with Cartman. When the fat kid with the foul mouth refused to hand it over, Smith kicked him in the balls. As a triumphant Smith walked into the sunset, cowboy-style, Kyle yelled out: "*Disintegration* is the best album ever." Cartman then added, "Robert Smith kicks ass." A bigger rap simply didn't exist in Parker and Stone's twisted comic universe. (It was such a big rap, in fact, that "Robert Smith Kicks Ass" T-shirts would soon be doing a healthy trade amongst Cure fans.)

Smith couldn't have found a better gauge to determine if he still featured on the pop culture radar. But at first he was somewhat hesitant about doing the *South Park* voice-over. Stone and Parker, both major Cure fans, had sent him a tape of an episode that featured a gay dog called Sparky (voiced by Hollywood hunk George Clooney). "I really laughed," Smith said, "but at the same time I found it ignoble." Eventually Smith grew to trust Parker and Stone – but he couldn't have imagined the favourable response to his cameo, especially within the Smith clan.

Smith's 20-plus nieces and nephews now realised that their strange Uncle Robert with the big hair was one very cool dude. "Being in *South Park* has made a huge difference to their lives," he said. "When my nephews saw that, they worshipped me, but kept asking, 'What is a disintegration, Uncle Bob?' Now that I'm a cartoon character I'm fully accepted into their world. Everything I do – travel, experiencing so many things, making good-selling records – means nothing to them [but] since my appearance in *South Park* I'm immortal. Bastards."

During the obligatory globetrotting in the wake of *Wild Mood Swings*, Robert Smith had begun to learn about a side of his nature that he didn't realise existed: he was yearning to spend more time at home. Twenty-odd years of endless recording and touring can have that effect, as he discovered. According to Smith, "I have found out that I was feeling comfortable staying at home." His many nephews and nieces played a key role in the life of the new Robert Smith. He was often spotted kicking a football with them or collecting a bunch of younger Smiths from school. "In the past," he admitted, "there was no chance: I preferred touring and recording with The Cure [to anything else] and my whole life was going on inside the group. Drugs, drinking and the inevitable tensions – it's not for me any more. I'd rather stay at home."

Smith now had a well-established home studio in place and when the band completed their meagre 1998 commitments – 14 European festival dates in all – he began working on songs for another Cure album. This new-found domesticity and reflection would be a key creative spark for these songs, encapsulated, most obviously, in one song, '39'. As literal as ever, Smith had written the song as a birthday present for himself, in much the same way that 'Lovesong' had been his belated wedding gift to Mary Poole.

Bloodflowers was originally planned for a spring 1998 release, but demand for The Cure wasn't running at its highest at the time. When it did eventually appear in February 2000, Smith blamed the delay on numerous things: the ever-changing moods of the album itself, the record company's wariness about a pre-Christmas release date, as well as a sense within himself that this just could indeed be The Cure's much ballyhooed finale. Smith might actually live up to his ongoing threat of killing off The Cure. There was a certain logic at work here: the sales of the band's two most recent releases, *Wild Mood Swings* and the best-of *Galore*, had tapered off considerably from what had gone before; Smith was soon to turn 40 (a pensionable age in rock'n'roll); their record deal was about to expire – and there seemed to be a symmetry to shutting down the band at the end of the millennium. Smith was also starting to field other offers, such as filmmaker Tim Burton's proposal that he score his film *Sleepy Hollow* (which didn't eventuate).

"It definitely will be the last album we're doing for our record company," was all Smith would say at the time, "so it would certainly be easy to stop there. Whether or not it's the last album . . . it's a good way to stop."

Bloodflowers was an album of two key sessions, the first lasting about a month prior to Christmas 1998 and the second for a few months in spring of the following year. Paul Corkett co-produced the album with Smith, which was mixed in the English countryside at Fisher Lane Farm in Surrey.

As the recording progressed, a very familiar sensation overtook Smith: these sessions were very similar to those for the band's massive 1989 set, *Disintegration*. Cure long-termers Simon Gallup and Roger O'Donnell recognised that, too – and not with any fondness. Two weeks in, they told Smith just that. By mixing time, the whole band had disappeared, leaving Smith alone with Corkett. Increasingly convinced that this was going to be The Cure's grand farewell, Smith was burying himself in the project, alienating his bandmates in the process. It was hardly the freewheeling, several-months-in-the-country affair that was *Wild Mood Swings* or *Kiss Me Kiss Me Kiss Me*'s French connection. This was almost method record-making; to get right into the mood, on the night before recording officially began, Coach Smith had played the band both *Disintegration* and *Pornography*, insisting that he was after a similar intensity for *Bloodflowers*.

"In order to have any chance at being the best Cure line-up," he told Gallup, O'Donnell, Bamonte and Cooper, "you have to come out with an album that's got this kind of emotional impact. What [The Cure] is remembered for is albums like these.

"When we made *Wild Mood Swings*," he continued, "the house was full of friends and family and people laughing, 26 people at dinner, that sort of vibe. With *Bloodflowers*, absolutely no one was allowed in the studio that wasn't recording. Everyone thought I was being really horrible, and I guess I was because I wanted everyone to really focus on the album.

"For about three months, the rest of the world just took a back seat and I didn't worry about anything except making the album. It's been 10 years since I've done that." (Smith would cheerfully report that the band was "all good friends" again once the sessions ended and the album was finally released.)

Of all The Cure's dozen studio albums, *Bloodflowers* is probably the most overlooked, the most unreasonably neglected. Yet as a sustained piece of work, a lengthy meditation on melancholy, it works almost perfectly. It's clear why Smith would include it as the final act of the Berlin Trilogy shows in November 2002 – just like *Pornography* and *Disintegration* before it, *Bloodflowers* clung to a single mood with the persistence of a leech. Not since *Disintegration* had Smith sounded more solemn; each song seemed like a eulogy for the rapidly fading flower of his youth. His inclusion in the liner notes of a quote from Alfred, Lord Tennyson's 'The Princess' – "tears from the depth of some divine despair . . . and thinking of the days that are no more" – wasn't done on a whim, it was a perfect summation of *Bloodflowers*. The album's title was actually an amalgam of two similar works of art – a reference to a book of letters from the painter Edvard Munch, and a line of poetry from a book Smith had read that reflected on World War I.

"He [Munch] had said that he was sure that he had done a good artwork when he felt that a blood flower popped out from his heart," said Smith. "[And] one of the poems described how a wound in one of the soldiers, hit by a bullet, opened a blood flower in his body. I liked this analogy, between pain and art."

Yet Smith somehow managed to steer clear of the melodramatic claptrap that *Bloodflowers* could well have become. His emotions here seem convincingly real, unlike, say, *Faith*, where he was simply a coked-up Crawley 20-something with a chip on his slouched shoulders. *Bloodflowers* truly does sound like The Cure's farewell (little was the world to know, of course, that yet another Cure resurrection lay a few years down the line). Throughout the record, Smith sounds exhausted, physically, mentally and creatively drained. When he bemoans his lack of feeling and inability to articulate during 'There Is No If . . .', it's clearly not the same guy who petulantly snapped "it doesn't matter if we all die today" back in 1984. This was a guy whose wisdom and worldly insight have been hard earned. Sure, it isn't 'Just Like Heaven' or 'Inbetween Days', but much of the album's heavy-heartedness sounded truly authentic.

Smith couldn't have written a better mood-setter than the opening track, 'Out Of This World'. It's a song where Smith sounds so down, so lost in the twilight world, that it's a shock that he actually found the energy to sing. And when he does move towards the mic, he delivers a lyric that proved just how intent he was on capturing a singular mindset throughout *Bloodflowers*. When he sings about the inevitability of nostalgia it's as if he was channelling some sad-eyed nightclub crooner, necktie loosened, large brandy in hand, half-empty pack of cigs nearby.

And throughout *Bloodflowers*, Smith tapped into the more reflective side of his nature, which was quite different from the chronic self-flagellator at the centre of *Seventeen Seconds* and *Faith*. During 'Watching Me Fall' he even appeared to be floating outside his body, looking back at his life. Smith sees himself falling eternally through space, growing smaller until he disappears completely. The band, meanwhile, cooked up a tempestuous guitar storm behind him, creating the perfect soundtrack for Smith's heavy heart.

Like the surlier moments of *Kiss Me* (especially 'From The Edge Of The Deep Green Sea') and *Disintegration*, nothing is rushed on *Bloodflowers*. ("The intros to *Disintegration* were even longer," insisted Smith.) These nine slow-burning tracks unfold slowly, gradually growing in atmosphere and tension as guitars are piled up like sonic building blocks, while Gallup and Cooper anchor the sound with a succession of hard-rock grooves (Cooper's playing is especially steady-handed). Only one track, 'There Is No If . . .' clocks in under four minutes; 'Watching Me Fall' runs to a tad over 11. It was clear that when Smith confessed to a love of The Smashing Pumpkins and Scottish noise-makers Mogwai, he wasn't merely jumping on the nearest bandwagon. (Mind you, he was also tuning in to opera at the time, his father's music of choice, "a sure sign I'm getting old".)

Even if The Cure was back in commercial favour in 2000 – which they weren't – finding a song for radio amidst *Bloodflower*'s sonic and autobiographical blood-letting would have been as tough a task as trying to run a comb through Robert Smith's bird-nest hair. Only 'Maybe Someday' had something resembling a trademark Cure melody, but even then the track ran to a very radio-unfriendly five-minutes-plus. Elektra knew this. Smith told the press that the label's response to The Cure's final album for their US master was about as positive as their first take on *Disintegration*. Smith sprinkled their words "commercial suicide" quite liberally throughout interviews upon the album's release.

"Before we did *Bloodflowers* I actually wanted it to be a short album, because I find that 70 minutes of one artist is, almost without exception, too much," Smith admitted a few years after its release, an observation that was as much a comment on the CD age as it was on the band's tendency to overcook their songs. So with *Bloodflowers*, Smith had set himself and the band an album target of 45 minutes, but editing was never one of The Cure's strongest suits, as the overly long *Kiss Me* had proved back in 1987; likewise the 14-track *Wild Mood Swings* much more recently. "I realise, in hindsight, that it's the songs themselves that probably need trimming back, but I think that they benefit from their length," Smith believed.

Smith had actually performed a home edit on the 11-minute opus 'Watching Me Fall', which trimmed five minutes from the track, but felt that it just wasn't the same song. And even after cutting more than 90 seconds from 'Out Of This World', having been advised it needed an edit for radio, he was told that the intro was still too long. "But I like that slow development," Smith said, "and I didn't want to impose the three-and-a-half-minute structure on anything I was writing, because it just felt stupid. We did a couple of what we'd consider to be pop songs at the demo stage and they just sounded so shallow." Such highlights from *Bloodflowers* as 'The Last Day Of Summer' and the title track would have been ruined if their languorous, sprawling soundscapes had gone under the knife; they set the tone perfectly for the sad songs that followed.

As it turned out, of all The Cure LPs, of all the millions of records they've shifted over the past 25-plus years, *Bloodflowers* remains very close to the top of Robert Smith's list of favourite Cure albums. "Recording *Bloodflowers* was the best experience I've had since doing the *Kiss Me* album. I achieved my goals, which were to make an album, enjoy making it, and end up with something that has real intense, emotional content. And I didn't kill myself in the process."

Bloodflowers wasn't quite the failure that Elektra suspected it would be. It was released in the midst of *Supernatural* mania, in which Woodstock veteran and cosmically inclined blues guitarist, Carlos Santana, had reinvented himself with a lot of help from such new kids as Matchbox Twenty's Rob Thomas. In the same week that *Supernatural* shifted a cheeky 219,000 units in the USA, *Bloodflowers* debuted at number 16, which was the best performance that week (mid-February) from a new release. (The Cure sold 71,000 albums.)

As ever, The Cure found themselves amidst some unlikely chart buddies, including wailing popster Christina Aguilera, Eurotrash Eiffel 65, Kid Rock, Backstreet Boys and R&B lady-killer, Sisqo (who was casting his seductive spell with a little charmer called 'Thong Song'). 'Maybe Someday', the song that was eventually lifted from *Bloodflowers* for radio, also charted surprisingly well, reaching number 12 on *Billboard*'s R&R Alternative chart. 'Watching Me Fall', meanwhile, had been included on the *American Psycho* soundtrack, keeping The Cure very much in the spotlight.

Their subsequent US tour was a scaled down version of their late Eighties, early Nineties heyday: it was a five-week stretch, where the band mainly played amphitheatres rather than the corporate-sponsored super stadiums of a few years earlier.

Buoyed by the reasonable sales of an album that he knew was not designed for Cure fans reared on 'Just Like Heaven', and the solid ticket sales from their Dream Tour 2000, Smith started to revise his plans for laying The Cure to rest. But that was hardly out of character – by now

Smith must have realised that he shouldn't do interviews at the end of a physically and mentally draining stretch. He had a tendency to make bold statements that he'd live to regret.

"If it's going to be the last album with The Cure – [as] I thought – I have to be sincere," said Smith. "Now everyone around me is saying that the record has had a positive impact on me towards the band, and I have to admit it's true, because I have changed my mind during the last six months thanks to *Bloodflowers*. I found new enthusiasm in the group. I have found out that The Cure are a great band again, an important one – to me, at least. I don't give a fuck what the rest of the world thinks about us."

But rather than disappear back into the studio, Smith decided that he'd prepare two career backtracks for Polydor: yet another "traditional" greatest-hits set and a four-disc journey through The Cure's back pages. And if it happened that The Cure didn't get around to making another studio album, at least Smith could boast that he was actively involved in compiling what he thought would be the definitive Cure collection.*

Smith also had some personal history to reconsider. He and estranged Cure co-founder Lol Tolhurst had exchanged letters around the time of *Bloodflowers*. It seemed to both that enough time had passed for them to be able to resume their lifelong friendship. As Tolhurst told me, "I wrote to Robert and said this is what I did, this is what I'm sorry for, and I'd still like to be friends, because that's what we were in the very beginning. He wrote back, we met in LA and sat up all night talking about things." Smith had some very frank admissions to make: Tolhurst wasn't the only member of The Cure to fly a little too close to the sun.

"He told me that three or four years ago Simon hit a brick wall with all this stuff [drugs and alcohol]," said Tolhurst. "Robert's constitution is such that as soon as he gets too near the brink, the abyss, he'll pull back and stop. He's been close a few times. I got to the abyss, looked over and jumped in.

"I think it's part and parcel of being in a band like The Cure. I also

---

* In 1997 he predicted this, stating: "The final thing that will come out will be my version of the greatest hits. It will be my personal selection of what I think our best work is."

think of bands like Nirvana and Joy Division – people expect you to look into the abyss for them, that's part of the experience. It goes with the territory. I've been close enough and fallen in, so has Robert and Simon."

Despite the guiding hand of Robert Smith, the differences between *The Cure Greatest Hits*, which appeared in 2003, and 1997's *Galore*, weren't that vast. There were 18 "hits" on each and although the song selection was markedly different, there was still a strong focus on the commercial side of the band. Both of these collections effectively compiled The Cure's best-known songs, the singles and the radio standards. While 'Wrong Number' had been the bonus new track on *Galore*, Greatest Hits featured 'Just Say Yes', a good-natured vocal trade-off between Smith and Republica shouter Saffron, and 'Cut Here', another Plati/Smith co-production. The key difference, however, was an extra bonus disc for *Greatest Hits*, which added acoustic renditions of 'Lovesong', 'Lullaby', et al, plus two discs of mainly Tim Pope-directed videos.

Join The Dots, of course, was a vastly different baby. Subtitled 'B–Sides & Rarities 1978–2001 The Fiction Years', it was an authoritative and exhaustive backtrack, a 70-track, four-disc journey into Cureworld, which ranged from the little-heard 'Do The Hansa' to Mark Plati's reworking of 'A Forest'. And it was squeezed tight with curiosities, such as 'Harold And Joe', Simon Gallup's tribute to the pair from Aussie soap *Neighbours* (a Gallup small-screen fave), which had previously been buried on the B-side of 'Never Enough'. There were also alternate mixes (Mark Saunders' take on 'Wrong Number', the Dizzy Mix of 'Just Like Heaven' and others) and one-offs, including covers of Bowie's 'Young Americans', The Doors' 'Hello I Love You' (in three different flavours) and Hendrix's 'Purple Haze'. These were served up with hard-to-find soundtrack cuts from the films *Judge Dredd* and *The Crow*, plus 'More Than This', a track recorded for TV's *X-Files*. (Like Fox Mulder, sky-watcher Smith, a devoted viewer, also wanted to believe.)

Join The Dots was purely for Cure completists, but unlike most releases that Smith had intimated would be the band's farewell, this smartly packaged backtrack actually had all the trappings of finality. What better way to sign off than to trawl through the archives and

return with 70 tracks of obscurities and ephemera?* Whispers about
The Cure's demise grew stronger and louder when it was announced
that Chris Parry had sold Fiction to Universal Music – much to Smith's
chagrin. Smith made it known, every chance he had, that Parry had
sold him out. But as one member of The Cure inner circle told me, the
truth is slightly different.

"The whole story about Chris selling to Universal without Robert's
knowledge is complete bullshit," I was told. "Chris has been on
Robert's case for many years, asking him to buy him out of Fiction.
Problems with Robert's attitude and him refusing to look into options
for Fiction led to the sale to Universal. Robert knew about all this." By
this stage of a relationship that lasted longer than many marriages,
Smith and Parry communicated mainly by fax – and even then Parry
spent most of his time at sea on his boat.†

So all indications were that The Cure was ready for the knackery,
leaving Robert Smith to get back to a solo album with one of the
longest gestation periods in the history of rock'n'roll. But Smith and
the band were about to meet Ross Robinson.

Of all the people least likely to help mount The Cure's 2004 resurrection, American Robinson would had to have been near the top of the
list. Robinson started out in the late Eighties as a tearaway guitarist in a
long-forgotten thrash metal outfit alongside future Machine Head
drummer Dave McClain. His first studio credit – assistant engineer –
was for his work on WASP's 1993 LP, *The Crimson Idol*. Not long after,
Robinson made a crucial connection (for both his reputation and bank
balance) with angst-ridden nu-metallers Korn, possibly one of the most
miserable bands this side of, well, The Cure. Robinson produced their
first two albums, 1994's self-titled debut and their multi-platinum hit
from 1996, *Life Is Peachy*.

Robinson's place as the Phil Spector of nu-metal was well and truly
confirmed when he worked the desk for Limp Bizkit's 1997

---

* Mind you, the same could be said for *The Cure Trilogy* DVD, which captured their
November 2002 one-off in Berlin where the band played *Pornography*, *Disintegration* and
Bloodflowers, back to back.
† No figures are publicly available regarding the sale, but Parry – who then retired to his
native New Zealand and rejoined Fourmyula – clearly pocketed many millions of
pounds.

breakthrough, *Three Dollar Bill Y'All*. The Bizkit, with an oversized shit-stirrer with undeniable ambition by the name of Fred Durst out front, and Korn, led by the pimp-like Jonathan Davis, fronted the rap-metal vanguard that would dominate MTV and airwaves throughout the late Nineties. When Robinson went on to produce albums for art-rockers At The Drive-In and anarchic clowns Slipknot, he'd done his bit to start a revolution.

Not that Robert Smith was a huge fan of nu-metal. Smith said just that back in 2001, while in conversation with misty-eyed acolyte, Brian Molko of Placebo. "I like some part of the guitars," he said, "[but] the problem is that, with these kind of bands, I don't like the voices, [the way they] scream the same way. And I've got the feeling that nu-metal is horribly cynical; they must be too dumb to understand they're victims of a huge marketing plan." One of Smith's nephews was a nu-metal diehard – he'd played his Uncle Robert his Slipknot albums, but Smith remained unimpressed.

"Slipknot?" he said. "They look like Alice Cooper, but they can't hold a candle to him."

Ross Robinson had met Smith backstage in California at the annual Coachella Festival in 2004. While still no great fan of his work, Smith was charmed by the man – how could he not be when Robinson confessed to being a huge Cure lover? "We got along immediately," said Smith. "He has more zest for life than anyone else [I know]. [But] some things Ross did, like At The Drive-In, I really like. Limp Bizkit, however, does nothing for me.

"I'd read things about how he said he'd die to make the [next] Cure album," Smith continued. "I didn't expect we'd get on."

Ross Robinson was a man of admirable commitment and focus. He was so determined to make a record with Smith that after their first meeting he almost drowned the Lovecat in letters and faxes, spelling out why they should work together and how they'd create sonic magic in the studio. Finally, Smith relented and signed a three-album deal with Robinson's I Am Recordings, having just knocked back an offer from Virgin Records. By 2004, as unlikely as it seemed, The Cure found themselves labelmates with Glassjaw, Slipknot and Amen. Smith even promised to cede all studio responsibility to Robinson; he hadn't been so acquiescent since *Three Imaginary Boys*, and he only did it then because he didn't know any better.

Smith's original plan was that Robinson would produce the now almost mythical Robert Smith solo LP. "But he didn't agree," Smith said. "He said, 'The time is right for a new Cure album. I have a gut feeling.'"

Robinson's commercial instincts were pretty damned sound. Having spent years on the fringes of the land of cool, especially in the UK, The Cure was suddenly being namechecked all over the music press. There was a revivalist spirit sweeping rock'n'roll. While the glacial grooves of *Pornography* could be heard in the sound of New Yorkers Interpol, you could be mistaken for thinking that Steve Bays, the vocalist for Canadians Hot Hot Heat (a Cure steal in itself), was actually channeling Smith. If it wasn't such a compliment, Smith should have been talking to his lawyers about some kind of copyright infringement.

Other breakout acts, including The Rapture, Razorlight and Smith's much-fancied Mogwai, all paid dues to Smith and The Cure, both in conversation and on record. The White Stripes' Jack White even stated that he wouldn't be a musician without Smith's influence, while such other bands as AFI and Black Rebel Motorcycle Club emulated the various stages of The Cure's career in their breakthrough records *Sing The Silence* and *Take Them On, On Your Own* respectively. For a band that had seemed dead only a few years ago, The Cure was suddenly very much alive. Smith was also popping up in the strangest of places, putting in musical cameos with punk-popsters Blink-182, Dutch cut-and-pasters Junkie XL and elsewhere. He even joined forces, once again, with guitarchitect Reeves Gabrels for the excellent 'Yesterday's Gone'. Tickets for their one-off show during March at Barfly in London were fetching a neat £2,000 apiece.

By spring 2004, Robinson and The Cure convened at London's Olympic Studios for six weeks of recording. The band brought 37 demos into the sessions, which would eventually be culled to a dozen tracks. The original plan had been to record in LA, but Smith had the final say and insisted on working closer to home. ("We convinced him that the doom and gloom of London is more conducive to making our music than sunny California," Smith chuckled.) Robinson, just like Mark Plati before him, was lucky to make it through the first day, because he found it so hard to keep a lid on the sheer thrill of working with one of his all-time favourite bands. His first move was to simply let them play for an hour – much of the resulting album, *The Cure*, was cut live in the studio – and then talk through his plans with the band. At the end of that first hour, however, Robinson was jumping out of his skin.

"He just went absolutely mental," said Smith. "He kept saying, 'Don't you know who you are? You're The Cure. What the fuck are you doing?' Everyone in the room thought, 'Oh my God, he's really saying obvious things.' " The Cure was not a band comfortable with confrontation or over-exuberance, and now a bespectacled American rap-metal geek was dancing in front of them like a madman. According to Smith, "Suddenly we had this bloke kicking things over, going, 'Do you realise who you are?' "

Smith, however, was overjoyed with Robinson's attention and zealousness. "I was almost crying with happiness," Smith admitted. "I knew at that moment it was going to work."

But the rest of the band wasn't so fond of Robinson's extreme working methods, his odd attraction to method record producing. Simon Gallup, for one, was quite willing to slam Robinson. "Don't tell me he's a great producer," said the bassman, who was still coming to grips with his problem boozing. "For me he's only been a nightmare. From my mouth will never come a positive word about him; he's just an idiot." When we spoke, guitarist Perry Bamonte was a tad more diplomatic. "It's been said that Ross's approach is a little contrived, but I think he had a very real passion for what he was doing. Not everyone shared his vision and it could well be argued that he'd not quite understood The Cure, but he believed completely in what he was doing and I think that's a very good thing."

Though not quite as sprawling or one-dimensional as *Bloodflowers*, *The Cure* was still an album drawn from the moodier, heavier side of The Cure: this clearly wasn't *Kiss Me* revisited. "I started writing really heavy songs, because, when you're working with Ross, he's bound to want dark and moody," Smith said when the album was released on June 29, 2004. "What became very apparent is that he liked all the kinds of things we did. He's really into the melodic side of the band and the pop side of the band." Again, just like the sessions for *Bloodflowers*, The Cure became hostages of the studio, not leaving for months. "We had no visitors. No one was allowed in. It was quite a surreal experience," Smith said.

"It was treated as almost a long live event. Every day it was a different song. We'd be facing the control booth so we could see Ross and we would figure out the technical stuff. He put us in a very confined space, right on top of each other, with eye-to-eye contact. At night, we'd face the other way, light the candles and suddenly it became very real. I would stand up and away we would go.

"Everything we'd done before was going to culminate on this record – that was the mindset that we had when we were in the studio. And I would say that more passion went into the making of this record than all the others combined."

While *The Cure* wasn't a runaway hit, it sold slightly better in its first week than *Bloodflowers*, shifting 90,000 copies and muscling its way to number seven in the US Top 10. It was a useful reminder that the American public hadn't completely moved on from the Lovecat and his crew.

But Smith had a new plan in mind for the band's latest US roadtrip. The Cure had been invited to headline the appropriately named Curiosa Festival, which also featured Smith's hand-picked favourites Mogwai, Interpol and The Rapture, along with other acts such as Muse and Auf Der Maur. Curiosa stopped in 22 cities, opening on July 24 at West Palm Beach and closing shop in Sacramento five weeks later. The attendances were lower than expected – in Atlanta a little over 7,000 turned up to a venue that could hold 15,000, while in Cincinnati only 5,700 fans were spread liberally throughout a site that was ready for more than 20,000. At the closing show in Sacramento, a paltry crowd of just under 5,000 filed into a stadium built for 17,000-plus. (Daily takings typically ran between $200,000 and $400,000, bottoming out at $159,000 in Cincinnati.) As for The Cure's headlining two-hour set, it was a case of something old, something very blue. They mixed the obligatory singalongs – 'Inbetween Days', 'Just Like Heaven', 'Lovesong' and even 'Boys Don't Cry' – with the heavy guitar work-outs of their two most recent long-players.

Despite its mixed box office, Curiosa was still amongst the more successful US summer festivals of 2004, a solid achievement in a holiday season most notable for failures, including the cancellation of the once peerless Lollapalooza extravaganza. (Morrissey was a Lollapalooza headliner, which must have made Smith chuckle quietly.) The reviews of the Curiosa shows were just as fawning as the other bands' attitude towards their veteran headliners. Melissa Auf Der Maur was one of many acts to thank The Cure from the stage, declaring Curiosa "the most romantic tour of the summer".

"Frontman Robert Smith kept to himself throughout much of the set," MTV noted of the New York show of July 31, "stepping away from the mic to rock gently with his head down. Luckily the props, light show and a large video screen . . . made up for the lack of visual allure."

If Smith was a subdued on-stage presence, then Simon Gallup was a man resurrected, wielding his low-slung bass like a jackhammer. "Compared to Smith and his other stiff bandmates, Gallup was a dance machine on par with the most fervent in the crowd," MTV declared. "Shuffling his feet and throttling the neck of his instrument, he energetically rode the songs' weaving basslines that are responsible for The Cure's grooviness . . . often overlooked in favour of Smith's gloomy lyrics, uppity hairdo and penchant for wearing black."

While Curiosa wasn't quite the cash cow promoters had hoped for, The Cure hit the jackpot with three Mexico City sell-outs on September 4 to 6. More than 50,000 fans turned up in total, earning The Cure a handy $696,622 each night.

Back in London, a buoyant (and flush) Cure was given the full *MTV Icons* treatment. Looking like the Gothic answer to the English royal family, the band watched on while AFI, Blink-182, Razorlight, The Deftones and the evening's host, the God of Fuck himself, Marilyn Manson, worshipped at the altar of The Cure. Backstage, past Cure-ists such as Porl Thompson mingled with the current line-up, which was fast approaching its first decade together. One Cure insider, with whom I spoke, was underwhelmed by the night. "The band looked bemused and bored at the same time," I was told. "The after-party for this 'event' was mostly uneventful, unlike other Cure after-parties. It was mostly drunken band members dealing with people asking them what brand of hair products they favour." But the simple fact that MTV anointed The Cure as icons almost 20 years after they first played the Tim Pope clip for 'Let's Go To Bed' said plenty about these suburban survivors.

Most people I spoke to for this book weren't that surprised by The Cure's reluctance to lie down and die. To Phil Thornalley, former

Cure producer and bassist, it simply comes down to Smith's ability to pen killer tunes. "To me, anybody who writes great pop songs, that's how you attain longevity in my arena. If somebody has a lot of hits, for me, that's why you remember them. I think Robert has written some cracking pop songs. Sure, the other artistic thing has come along the way as well, but frankly I'm not interested in that."

Cure co-founder Lol Tolhurst, quite reasonably, figures that the band's ongoing success is more than the work of one man. "The whole thing for Robert is that The Cure is his whole life; sometimes it's a bit of an albatross, as well. But I'd have to say that without other people's input, it wouldn't have happened. Simon's still there, but that's about it. It's not the way it was. I think it's telling that Robert is yet to embark on a solo career – The Cure is more than Robert and more than an idea. It's a whole set of circumstances and people, without whom it would never have happened. It's a big soap opera, pretty much.

"To me, sometimes it feels very strange to read stuff about myself that refers to me 16 or 17 years ago," added Tolhurst. "It's like I got frozen in time. I was that, but I'm not that any more. My part in The Cure was all encompassing, all involving. That's really what I want people to know: it really was my baby, too, for a long time. But I have no axe to grind, I would really, really hate to be seen as the Noel Redding to Robert's Jimi Hendrix. I'm not an old, bitter man – it's something I'm very proud of. There's always two sides to the story – the truth is that it's a little more involved than people might have thought."

The Cure's original bassist, Michael Dempsey, is convinced that their success is based upon Robert Smith's "unshakable" approach to his craft. "What motivated him then [when the band first formed] motivates him now," he said, when we spoke in 2005, "which is quite an achievement. He has the same kind of ethic now as he had then. Generally, he's unshakable in the way he's gone about it – he's hard working, solid. He has a sense of purpose that's gone through fashion and fad. It's quite rare to see a band do that and prosper."

"There are a lot of Cure fans out there now," figured Steve Lyon, the producer of *Wild Mood Swings*. "It's also cool to like the Banshees and The Creatures now, they have that rebellious nature." Fellow musicians, such as Mark Francombe of Cranes, credit some of The Cure's longevity to their deft ability to move in and out of the spotlight. "[They're still about] because they know how to rest," Francombe said. "Do an album, tour it and then take a few years off. And luckily there are 500 Goths in every town in the western world, so their albums still get bought." Yet the band continues to hover on the brink of a break-up: even current member Perry Bamonte has no idea what lies ahead. "It's really hard to call The Cure's next move," he told me in 2005. "The Cure are always on the verge of imploding, but have lasted 25 years. I never take a single day for granted."

Whatever his next move, Robert Smith – who, of course, now truly is The Cure – stands as one of rock's great survivors, fronting a band that simply refuses to die. His immediately recognisable appearance has transcended the world of rock'n'roll and multi-million sales – simply look at *Edward Scissorhands*, the Tim Burton creation given life on screen by Johnny Depp: that's Robert Smith, just with added hedge trimmers. It was one of the most iconic Hollywood looks of the Nineties and could be traced directly back to the man from Crawley.

As 2005 dawned, and Smith finally approved the reissues of early Cure albums, reports of The Cure's demise appear to have been greatly exaggerated. Smith has threatened that, just like Stone Mick Jagger, he might keep rolling for some time yet.

"I can even imagine doing this at 60; I don't care what others think," Smith said recently. "As long as I make music with people I like it's wonderful; it's something most people dream of. But if I work the next one or two years with The Cure thinking I'd rather be at home, then I wouldn't be honest with myself."

Whatever he decides to do, however, it's clear that wherever a black overcoat and eyeliner is to be found, there'll be a clutch of Cure fans, ever faithful, still arguing the merits of *Pornography* over *Faith* or *Disintegration*. And no one can lay claim to the same evangelical level of adulation from their devotees as The Cure. Irrespective of the band's future, however, Robert Smith has given one concrete assurance: "I will most certainly not be wearing black and lipstick in 2011. That's a guarantee."

Postscript

Of course, like any long-running soapie, there's always an unexpected twist lurking nearby in the story of The Cure, and early 2005 was no exception. On April 6, 2005, Craig Parker, the Webmaster of Cure fan site Chain of Flowers, heard a rumour that roadie-cum-guitarist Perry Bamonte and long-time keyboardist Roger O'Donnell were no longer in The Cure. And on April 18 it was officially announced that manager Daryl Bamonte was relieved of his duties, a report that Parker posted on his site.

Parker then heard from a reliable source that Robert Smith had actually started work on a new Cure album. He contacted O'Donnell, who denied knowing anything about the sessions. By May 20, however, as Parker told me, "things really went insane". An official release announced that The Cure had booked summer festival dates in France and Spain (plus an appearance at the Bob Geldof Live8 extravaganza in Paris on July 2). The unofficial word was that this would be a "new" three-piece Cure of Smith, drummer Jason Cooper and long-time Smith ally Simon Gallup. Again, Parker asked O'Donnell about the shows and the line-up changes and was told "it was probably just rumours".

Meanwhile, a fake email began circulating that the "new" Cure would comprise Smith, drummer Keith Airey and former Smith confidant (and toxic twin) Steve Severin. Given that Smith and Severin had fallen out almost 20 years earlier, without so much as a Christmas card in between, this reunion seemed unlikely. Although Parker subsequently began to doubt the authenticity of the email, he posted this "news" on his website, and a source close to the band wrote to him to confirm that The Cure was now indeed a trio, but denied the recruitment of Severin and Airey. ("It is true that we are talking again, but I haven't spoken to Robert since this story broke," Severin told www.billboard.com. "All I know is that we are working together on making the most exciting remaster of *Blue Sunshine* possible.") Meanwhile, on the band's official website, www.thecure.com, Smith began attacking Parker and disputing the credibility of the news section of Chain of Flowers.

Again, Parker emailed O'Donnell, and between them they dismissed the Severin rumours as "a bad joke". When Parker went back to his Cure "insider", he was informed that Team Cure 2005 had actually recorded five songs, having reunited with *Three Imaginary Boys'* producer Mike Hedges. It was like 1978 all over again.

And this news was true: Smith, Gallup and Cooper had re-recorded the tracks 'Three Imaginary Boys', 'Seventeen Seconds', 'Faith' and 'Pornography' for a planned iTunes special, along with a John Lennon cover for an upcoming Amnesty International CD.

Yet as late as May 23, neither O'Donnell nor Perry Bamonte had been contacted by Smith regarding their place in the band or any involvement with these new sessions. But a day later, on May 24, O'Donnell emailed Parker and advised him that both he and Bamonte were now officially out of The Cure. Finally, they'd been advised of their sacking.

Writing on www.rogerodonnell.com on May 27, O'Donnell couldn't conceal his disdain. "As of Tuesday this week [May 24] I am no longer a member of The Cure," he stated. "It was sad to find out after nearly 20 years the way I did but then I should have expected no less or more." He is currently completing work on his solo album, *The Truth In Me*. Whether the title is ironic or not is unclear. When I asked O'Donnell about his dismissal, he was equally abrupt. "I'm more interested in the future than the past now," he wrote via email, "and I think I can only do harm by talking about the past."

As for Perry Bamonte, he spelled out his reaction to the news, and the feedback he'd been receiving from Cure fans, on his website www.perrybamonte.de. "I never knew I had that much of an impact or how important a part of The Cure I was for so many people," he wrote. "I wish the band well and bear no grudge. I have no definite plans at this time but will inform you if I become involved in any other projects."

Whether all this unrest spells the end of The Cure is uncertain. Lol Tolhurst, for one, feels that the streamlining of the band is a good idea – and he told Smith just that when they spoke in June. "As much as I like the Bamonte brothers personally," Tolhurst subsequently admitted to me, "it really was time for some kind of change."

What is clear, however, is that as soap operas go, *Neighbours* has nothing on The Cure.

Source Notes/Bibliography

Prologue
Wyman, Bill, The Cure: The Popes Of Mope (*Creem*, 1992)

Chapter One
Anon, Caught In The Act (*Q*, May 1989)
Anon, Fifteen Minutes of Robert Smith (*Sassy*, October 1990)
Anon, High 5: Robert Smith, The Cure (Australian *Rolling Stone*, December 1993)
Anon, Musica (June 17, 2004)
Anon, Robert Smith And His Books (*Rock & Folk* magazine [France], August 2003)
Balfour, Brad, After 10 years, Robert Smith Is Still The Cure (*Spin*, March 1988)
Barbarian, Smith, Robert & Sutherland, Steve, *The Cure: Ten Imaginary Years* (Omnibus Press, 1988)
Black, Johnny, Curious Case Of The Cure (*London Times*, April 26, 1989)
Compo, Susan, The Cure's Robert Smith (*Spin*, November 1993)
Frost, Deborah, Taking The Cure With Robert (*Creem*, October 1, 1987)
Herpell, Gabriela, Interview With Robert Smith (*Sueddeutsche Zeitung*, July 3 2004)
Hodgkinson, Will, Pop Cure-alls (*The Guardian*, May 30, 2003)
Keeps, David, Dear Superstar: Robert Smith (*Blender*, August 2004)
Manrique, Diego A, Interview With Robert Smith (*El Pais Tentaciones*, January 28, 2000)
Miller, Kirk, Robert Smith Draws Blood (*Rolling Stone*, July 2004)
Simmons, Sylvie, Everything Falls Apart (*Revolution*, September 1989)
Sullivan, Jim, The Cure's Last Tour (*Boston Globe*, September 21, 1989)
Sutherland, Steve, A Suitable Case For Treatment (*Melody Maker*, October 1985)
Tellier, Emmanuel, Les Attrapes-Couers de Robert Smith, The Cure (*Les Inrockuptibles* magazine, October 22–28, 1997)
Thompson, Dave and Greene, Jo-Ann, *The Cure: A Visual Documentary* (Omnibus Press, 1988)

Chapter Two

Anon, High 5: Robert Smith, The Cure (Australian *Rolling Stone*, December 1993)

Azerrad, Michael, Searching For The Cure (*Rolling Stone*, 1989)

Black, Johnny, Curious Case Of The Cure (*The Times*, April 26, 1989)

Bogle, Vicky, Our Favourite Uncle (*Shake*, December 1984)

Comer, M Tye, Black Celebration: Robert Smith On The New Cure Album (*CMJ*, December 1999)

Considine, JD, What's The Big Idea? Robert Smith's Conception Of The Cure, (*Musician*, 1989)

Dery, Mark, A Dose Of Keyboard Fever (*Keyboard,* August 1987)

Frost, Deborah, Taking The Cure With Robert (*Creem*, October 1, 1987)

Keeps, David, Dear Superstar: Robert Smith (*Blender*, August 2004)

Oldham, James, The Gothfather (*Uncut*, August 2004)

Reynolds, Simon, Dr Robert Explains All (*Pulse*, June 1992)

Tellier, Emmanuel, Les Attrapes-Couers de Robert Smith, The Cure (*Les Inrockuptibles* magazine, October 22–28, 1997)

Thrills, Andrew, Ain't No Blues For The Summertime Cure (*New Musical Express*, December 16, 1978)

Witter, Simon, The Art Of Falling Apart (*The Face*, 1989)

Chapter Three

Anon, Black Celebration – Robert Smith On The New Cure Album (*CMJ*, December 1999)

Barbarian, Smith, Robert & Sutherland, Steve, *The Cure: Ten Imaginary Years*, (Omnibus Press, 1988)

De Curtis, Anthony, George-Warren, Holly & Henke, James (eds) (*The Rolling Stone Album Guide*, 1992)

McCullough, Dave, Kill Or Cure (*Sounds*, January 27, 1979)

Oldham, James, Bad Medicine (*Uncut*, February 2000)

Sutherland, Steve, A Suitable Case For Treatment (*Melody Maker*, October 1985)

Thrills, Adrian, Ain't No Blues For The Summertime Cure (*New Musical Express*, December 16, 1978)

Chapter Four

Anon, Live: Siouxsie & The Banshees (*Melody Maker*, October 2, 1976)

Barbarian, Smith, Robert & Sutherland, Steve, *The Cure: Ten Imaginary Years* (Omnibus Press, 1988)

Birch, Ian, Interview With The Cure (*Melody Maker*, March 24, 1979)

Crandall, Bill, The Cure; Album By Album: Robert Smith Recounts His Band's Many Wild Mood Swings (*Rolling Stone*, June 18, 2004)

Green, Jim (*Trouser Press*, 1981)

Kent, Nick, 'A Demonstration Of Household Appliances' (*NME*, May 19, 1979)

Morley, Paul, This Is Siouxsie & The Banshees. They Are Patient. They Will Win. In The End (*NME*, January 14, 1978)

Oldham, James, Bad Medicine (*Uncut*, February 2000)

Oldham, James, The Gothfather (*Uncut*, August 2004)

Sullivan, Jim, The Cure's Last Tour (*Boston Globe*, September 21, 1989)

Chapter Five

Anon, High 5: Robert Smith, The Cure (Australian *Rolling Stone*, December 1993)

Barbarian, Smith, Robert & Sutherland, Steve, *The Cure: Ten Imaginary Years* (Omnibus Press, 1988)

Crandall, Bill, The Cure: Album By Album: Robert Smith Recounts His Band's Many Wild Mood Swings (*Rolling Stone*, June 18, 2004)

DiMartino, Dave, The Head On The Cure (*Creem*, December 1986)

Kot, Greg, Smith's Picks (*Chicago Tribune*, July 12, 1992)

Oldham, James, Bad Medicine (*Uncut*, February 2000)

Oldham, James, The Gothfather (*Uncut*, August 2004)

Thompson, Dave & Greene, Jo-Ann, *The Cure: A Visual Documentary* (Omnibus Press, 1988)

Westwood, Chris (*Record Mirror*, November 16, 1979)

Young, Jon, Art For Pop's Sake (*Trouser Press*, July 1980)

Chapter Six

Barbarian, Smith, Robert & Sutherland, Steve, *The Cure: Ten Imaginary Years* (Omnibus Press, 1988)

Crandall, Bill, The Cure: Album By Album: Robert Smith Recounts His Band's Many Wild Mood Swings (*Rolling Stone*, June 18, 2004)

Oldham, James, Bad Medicine (*Uncut*, February 2000)

Swift, David, The Cure Paints An Intense Picture (*The Press*, Christchurch, August 8, 1981)

The Cure, Join The Dots, B-sides & Rarities Liner Notes (Fiction, 2004)

Thompson, Dave & Greene, Jo-Ann, *The Cure: A Visual Documentary* (Omnibus Press, 1988)

Chapter Seven

Azerrad, Michael, Searching For The Cure (*Rolling Stone*, 1989)

Cook, Richard, Savage Scream Of Birth (*NME*, April 1982)

Gore, Joe, The Cure: Confessions Of A Pop Mastermind (*Guitar Player* [US], September 1992)

Hodgkinson, Will, Pop Cure-alls (*The Guardian*, May 30, 2003)

Klemm, Elmar, The Kiss Of Spiderman (*Zillo*, July 2003)

Lindemann, Christoph (*Musikexpress*, July 2003)

Oldham, James, The Gothfather (*Uncut*, August 2004)

Petredis, Alexis, The Crack Up (*Mojo*, August 2003)

Sutherland, Steve, Still No Cure For The Cure (*Melody Maker*, May 1982)

Wilde, Jon, Lipstick Traces (*Melody Maker*, April 29, 1989)

Chapter Eight

Anon, MTV Italy, Interview (February 15, 2000)

Barbarian, Smith, Robert & Sutherland, Steve, *The Cure: Ten Imaginary Years* (Omnibus Press, 1988)

Cantin, Paul, Robert Smith Talks About New Cure Best-of (*Jam! Showbiz*, November 2001)

Gore, Joe, The Cure: Confessions Of A Pop Mastermind (*Guitar Player* [US], September 1992)

Newton, Ro, Robert Smith's Critical Guide To Robert Smith (*The Hit*, September 1985)

Petredis, Alexis, The Crack Up (*Mojo*, August 2003)

Roberts, Chris, A Momentary Collapse Of Reason (*Melody Maker*, June 5, 1989)

Sutherland, Steve, The Glove (*Melody Maker*, September 3, 1983)

Sutherland, Steve, The Incurables (*Melody Maker*, December 18, 1982)

Thompson, Dave & Greene, Jo-Ann, *The Cure: A Visual Documentary* (Omnibus Press, 1988)

Chapter Nine

Anon, Robert Smith – You Asked, He Answered (*Q*, 2000)

Barbarian, Smith, Robert & Sutherland, Steve, *The Cure: Ten Imaginary Years* (Omnibus Press, 1988)

Marie, Dawn, Interview With A Banshee

Pelkey, Dean, On The Trail Of Lovecats (*Discorder*, November 1984)

Petredis, Alexis, The Crack Up (*Mojo*, August 2003)

Thompson, Dave & Greene, Jo-Ann, *The Cure: A Visual Documentary* (Omnibus Press, 1988)

Chapter Ten

Anon, MTV Italy, Interview (February 15, 2000)

Azerrad, Michael, Searching For The Cure (*Rolling Stone*, 1989)

Azerrad, Michael, Something To Clap About (*East Village Eye*, July 1986)

Barbarian, Smith, Robert & Sutherland, Steve, *The Cure: Ten Imaginary Years* (Omnibus Press, 1988)

Black, Johnny, The Greatest Songs Ever Written – 'Just Like Heaven' (*Blender*, November 2003)

Considine, JD, What's The Big Idea? Robert Smith's Conception Of The Cure (*Musician*, 1989)

De Muir, Harold, An Interview With Robert Smith Of The Cure, *Eastcoast Rocket* (July 22, 1987)

Mitchell, Justin, Boris Williams' Steady Hand Adds To Cure's Disintegration (*Denver Rocky Mountain News*, September 3, 1989)

Oldham, James, Bad Medicine (*Uncut*, February 2000)

Petredis, Alexis, The Crack Up (*Mojo*, August 2003)

Simmons, Sylvie, There Is No Easy Cure (*Creem*, March 1986)

Simoncort, Serge, I Would Never Invite Myself To A Party (*Humo* magazine, July 24, 2003)

Smith, Robert, Three Imaginary Weeks – What We Did On Our Holidays – The Cure's South American Diary (*Melody Maker*, May 1987)

Sutherland, Steve, Fancy Dress Party (*Melody Maker*, April 11, 1987)

Thompson, Dave & Greene, Jo-Ann, *The Cure: A Visual Documentary* (Omnibus Press, 1988)

Chapter Eleven

Anon, Caught In The Act (*Q*, May 1989)

Anon, Putting The Boot In (*Vox*, December 1993)

Azerrad, Michael, Searching For The Cure (*Rolling Stone*, 1989)

Barbarian, Smith, Robert & Sutherland, Steve, *The Cure: Ten Imaginary Years* (Omnibus Press, 1988)

Comer, M Tye, Black Celebration: Robert Smith On The New Cure Album (*CMJ*, December 1999)

Considine, JD, What's The Big Idea? Robert Smith's Conception Of The Cure (*Musician*, 1989)

Cromelin, Richard, Robert Smith Decides To Pack It All In (*Los Angeles Times*, September 3, 1989)

Jean & Philippe, The Holy Hour (*Three Imaginary Boys* fanzine, July 1989)

Keeps, David, Dear Superstar (*Blender*, August 2004)

Kim, Jae-Ha, New CD Is The Cure For Common Fan (*Chicago Tribune*, December 7, 1997)

Kingsmill, Richard, Hello I Love You With The Cure's Robert Smith (Australian *Rolling Stone*, November 1993)

Mico, Ted, The Cure Melts Down (*Spin*, July 1989)

Moon, Tom, For The Cure, Adulation And Its Discontents (*Philadelphia Inquirer*, August 22, 1989)

Pearson, Roger, Former Cure Member Loses Royalty Fight (*Billboard*, October 8, 1994)

Popson, Tom, Cure Vocalist Nixes Planes, House Music (*Chicago Tribune*, August 25, 1989)

Popson, Tom, This Time Around, They Admit They're Big, Really (*Chicago Tribune*, August 27, 1989)

Reynolds, Simon, Dr Robert Explains It All (*Pulse*, June 1992)

Rioux, Rob, Cure Heads For The Top (*New Orleans Times-Picayune*, September 15, 1989)

Roberts, Chris, A Momentary Collapse Of Reason (*Melody Maker*, June 5, 1989)

Sawyer, Miranda, Strange Days (*Q*, May 1992)

Simmons, Sylvie, Everything Falls Apart (*Revolution*, September 1989)

Spencer, Lauren, Paint It Black (*Rolling Stone*, October 1990)

Taylor, Chuck, With Hits Galore And New Set Planned, The Never Fashionable Cure Endures (*Billboard*, December 6, 1997)

Thompson, Dave & Greene, Jo-Ann, *The Cure: A Visual Documentary* (Omnibus Press, 1988)

Ward, Christopher, Interview With Robert Smith (*Much Music*, 1989)

Chapter Twelve

Chang, Richard, Is This The Final Cure? (*Orange County Register*, May 26, 2000)

Chang, Richard, It's Not The End Of The Cure, But It's Close (*Orange County Register*, October 24, 1997)

Comer, M Tye, Black Celebration: Robert Smith On The New Cure Album (*CMJ*, December 1999)

Eggers, Dave, Intimate Portrait – Robert Smith (*Spin*, July 2004)

Gizicki, Steven, The Cure's Robert Smith Dials The Right Number (*Allstar*, October 28-30, 1997)

Molko, Brian, A Cure Ouvert (*Les Inrockuptibles*, November 2001)

Newman, Melinda, Hits "Galore" On The Way For Cure Fans (*Billboard*, October 4, 1997)

Roncato, Alessandra, Robert Smith Is Still Feeling Bad (*Tutto*, July/August 2004)

Acknowledgements

To all the following (and any whom I may have overlooked), this book would not have been possible without your guidance, input, mediation and insight:

To my wife, Diana, here's to our upcoming journey down Fascination Street; Chris Charlesworth, Andy Neill, Melissa Whitelaw and Norm Lurie at Omnibus Press, thanks for encouragement, support and belief above and beyond the call of duty; Johnny Rogan, for indexing; Phil Thornalley and Mike Nocito for sharing their *Pornography* with me, and much more besides; thanks also to Jason Cooper and Perry Bamonte for telling me how it is, Michael Dempsey and, especially, Lol Tolhurst, for speaking the whole truth and nothing but, in all its bloody detail; Steve Lyon for taking the mystery out of *Wild Mood Swings*; Mark Plati for all the backstage whispers from Bowie's 50th and proving how dialling a 'Wrong Number' can be a good thing; Lynn Hasty and Jay Frank for helping make the Lol Tolhurst connection; Father Patrick Fludder for the virtual tour of Worth Abbey; Teresa Browne at St Francis Junior School; Aaron Wilhelm, the man with both the names and the numbers; Justin Jones of And Also The Trees; Rick Gershon – thanks for the insider's tour of the LA Forum and much more besides; Laura & Sabine at Fools Dance: no one understands The Cure's world better than you guys; Michael Jay at Great Atlantic; Caroline Coon and Mat Snow; the backstage whispers of Mark Francombe of Cranes; Lydia Lunch and the tale of her "beautiful little funeral book" that she shared with Robert Smith during the 14 Explicit Moments Tour; Dan Kreeger for trying his best; ditto Gihan Salem at Elektra; Jen Dickert and curebloggers everywhere; and, finally, the lovely and incredibly helpful Barbera Jenner at St Wilfrid's, likewise Michael Georgeson (and, by extension, Rita and Alex Smith).

Team Cure –
Who Played What & When

Robert Smith
Co-founder/Singer/Songwriter/Guitarist
Played on: all albums

Michael Dempsey
Co-founder/Bass (1977–1979)
Played on: *Three Imaginary Boys*

Laurence "Lol" Tolhurst
Co-founder/Drums, Keyboards (1977–1992)
Played on: everything to *Disintegration*

Porl Thompson
Saxophone, Guitars and Keyboards (1977–1978 and 1984–1993)
Played on: *The Top*, *The Head On The Door*, *Kiss Me Kiss Me Kiss Me*, *Disintegration* and *Wish*

Simon Gallup
Bass (1979–1982 and 1985–now)
Played on: *Seventeen Seconds*, *Faith* and *Pornography* and then *The Head On The Door* onwards

Matthieu Hartley
Keyboards (1979–1980)
Played on: *Seventeen Seconds*

Andy Anderson
Drums (1983–1984)
Played on: *The Top*

Phil Thornalley
Bass (1984–1985)
Played on: 'The Lovecats' single; co-produced *Pornography*

Boris Williams
Drums (1984–1994)
Played on: *The Head On The Door, Kiss Me Kiss Me Kiss Me, Disintegration* and *Wish*

Roger O'Donnell
Keyboards (1987–1990 and 1995–now)
Played on: *Kiss Me Kiss Me Kiss Me, Disintegration, Wild Mood Swings, Bloodflowers, The Cure*

Perry Bamonte
Guitar, Keyboards (1990–now)
Played on: *Wish, Wild Mood Swings, Bloodflowers, The Cure*

Jason Cooper
Drums (1995–now)
Played on: *Wild Mood Swings, Bloodflowers, The Cure*

Note: This list only features those who have recorded and toured with The Cure.

Discography/Videography/Websites

Three Imaginary Boys

Fiction May 1979

10.15 Saturday Night / Accuracy / Grinding Halt / Another Day / Object / Subway Song / Foxy Lady / Meathook / So What / Fire In Cairo / It's Not You / Three Imaginary Boys / The Weedy Burton

Boys Don't Cry

Elektra February 1980 (USA)

Jumping Someone Else's Train / Boys Don't Cry / Plastic Passion / 10.15 Saturday Night / Accuracy / So What / Subway Song / Killing An Arab / Fire In Cairo / Another Day / Grinding Halt / World War / Three Imaginary Boys

Three Imaginary Boys (Deluxe Edition)

Fiction January 2005

10.15 Saturday Night / Accuracy / Grinding Halt / Another Day / Object / Subway Song / Foxy Lady / Meathook / So What / Fire In Cairo / It's Not You / Three Imaginary Boys / The Weedy Burton I Want To Be Old / I'm Cold / Heroin Face / I Just Need Myself / 10.15 Saturday Night / The Cocktail Party / Grinding Halt / Boys Don't Cry / It's Not You / 10.15 Saturday Night / Fire In Cairo / Winter / Faded Smiles (aka I Don't Know) / Play With Me / World War / Boys Don't Cry / Jumping Someone Else's Train / Subway Song / Accuracy / 10.15 Saturday Night

Seventeen Seconds

Fiction April 1980

A Reflection / Play For Today / Secrets / In Your House / Three / The Final Sound / A Forest / M / At Night / Seventeen Seconds

Faith

Fiction April 1981

The Holy Hour / Primary / Other Voices / All Cats Are Grey /
The Funeral Party / Doubt / The Drowning Man / Faith

Pornography

Fiction May 1982

One Hundred Years / A Short Term Effect / The Hanging Garden /
Siamese Twins / The Figurehead / A Strange Day / Cold / Pornography

Japanese Whispers

Fiction December 1983

Let's Go To Bed / The Dream / Just One Kiss / The Upstairs Room /
The Walk / Speak My Language / Lament / The Lovecats

The Top

Fiction May 1984

Shake Dog Shake / Birdmad Girl / Wailing Wall / Give Me It / Dressing
Up / The Caterpillar / Piggy In The Mirror / The Empty World /
Bananafishbones / The Top

Concert: The Cure Live

Fiction October 1984

Shake Dog Shake / Primary / Charlotte Sometimes / The Hanging
Garden / Give Me It / The Walk / One Hundred Years / A Forest /
10.15 Saturday Night / Killing An Arab

The Head On The Door

Fiction August 1985

Inbetween Days / Kyoto Song / The Blood / Six Different Ways / Push /
The Baby Screams / Close To Me / A Night Like This / Screw / Sinking

Standing On A Beach: The Singles

Fiction May 1986

Killing An Arab / Boys Don't Cry / Jumping Someone Else's Train /

A Forest / Primary / Charlotte Sometimes / The Hanging Garden /
Let's Go To Bed / The Walk / The Lovecats / The Caterpillar /
Inbetween Days / Close To Me

Kiss Me Kiss Me Kiss Me

Fiction May 1987

The Kiss / Catch / Torture / If Only Tonight We Could Sleep /
Why Can't I Be You? / How Beautiful You Are / Snakepit / Hey You /
Just Like Heaven / All I Want / Hot Hot Hot!!! / One More Time /
Like Cockatoos / Icing Sugar / The Perfect Girl / A Thousand Hours /
Shiver And Shake / Fight

Disintegration

Fiction May 1989

Plainsong / Pictures Of You / Closedown / Lovesong / Lullaby /
Fascination Street / Prayers For Rain / The Same Deep Water As You /
Disintegration / Untitled

Mixed Up

Fiction November 1990

Lullaby (extended mix) / Close To Me (closer mix) / Fascination Street
(extended mix) / The Walk (everything mix) / Lovesong (extended mix) /
A Forest (tree mix) / Pictures Of You (extended dub mix) / Hot Hot
Hot!!! (extended mix) / Why Can't I Be You? (extended mix) /
The Caterpillar (flicker mix) / Inbetween Days (shiver mix) / Never
Enough (big mix)

Entreat

Fiction March 1991

Pictures Of You / Closedown / Last Dance / Fascination Street /
Prayers For Rain / Disintegration / Homesick / Untitled

Wish

Fiction April 1992

Open / High / Apart / From The Edge Of The Deep Green Sea /
Wendy Time / Doing The Unstuck / Friday I'm In Love / Trust /
A Letter To Elise / Cut / To Wish Impossible Things / End

Show

Fiction September 1993

Tape / Open / High / Pictures Of You / Lullaby / Just Like Heaven /
Fascination Street / A Night Like This / Trust / Doing The Unstuck /
The Walk / Let's Go To Bed / Friday I'm In Love / Inbetween Days /
From The Edge Of The Deep Green Sea / Never Enough / Cut / End

Paris

Fiction October 1993

The Figurehead / One Hundred Years / At Night / Play For Today /
Apart / In Your House / Lovesong / Catch / A Letter To Elise /
Dressing Up / Charlotte Sometimes / Close To Me

Wild Mood Swings

Fiction May 1996

Want / Club America / This Is A Lie / The 13th / Strange Attraction /
Mint Car / Jupiter Crash / Round & Round & Round / Gone! /
Numb / Return / Trap / Treasure / Bare

Galore

Fiction September 1997

Why Can't I Be You? / Catch / Just Like Heaven / Hot Hot Hot!!! /
Lullaby / Fascination Street / Lovesong / Pictures Of You / Never
Enough / Close To Me / High / Friday I'm In Love / A Letter To Elise /
The 13th / Mint Car / Strange Attraction / Gone! / Wrong Number

Bloodflowers

Fiction February 2000

Out Of This World / Watching Me Fall / Where The Birds Always Sing /
Maybe Someday / The Last Day Of Summer / There Is No If . . . /
The Loudest Sound / 39 / Bloodflowers

Greatest Hits

Fiction November 2001 (some versions also included bonus CD Acoustic
Hits plus DVD Greatest Hits / Acoustic Hits)

Boys Don't Cry / A Forest / Let's Go To Bed / The Walk / The Lovecats /

Inbetween Days / Close To Me / Why Can't I Be You? / Just Like Heaven / Lullaby / Lovesong / Never Enough / High / Friday I'm In Love / Mint Car / Wrong Number / Cut Here / Just Say Yes

Join The Dots: B-Sides & Rarities 1978–2001

Fiction January 2004

10.15 Saturday Night / Plastic Passion / Pillbox Tales / Do The Hansa / I'm Cold / Another Journey By Train / Descent / Splintered In Her Head / Lament / Just One Kiss / The Dream / The Upstairs Room / Lament / Speak My Language / Mr Pink Eyes / Happy The Man / Throw Your Foot / New Day / The Exploding Boy / A Few Hours After This / A Man Inside My Mouth / Stop Dead / A Japanese Dream / Breathe / A Chain Of Flowers / Snow In Summer / Sugar Girl / Icing Sugar / Hey You!!! (Kervorkian 12-inch Remix) / To The Sky / Babble / Out Of Mind / 2 Late / Fear Of Ghosts / Hello I Love You (psychedelic version) / Hello I Love You / Hello I Love You (10 sec version) / Harold And Joe / Just Like Heaven ("Chuck" remix) / This Twilight Garden / Play / Halo / Scared As You / The Big Hand / A Foolish Arrangement / Doing The Unstuck (Saunders 12-inch remix) / Purple Haze (Virgin Radio Version) / Purple Haze / Burn / Young Americans / Dredd Song / It Used To Be Me / Ocean / Adonais / Home / Waiting / A Pink Dream / This Is A Lie (Palmer Remix) / Wrong Number (Smith Remix) / More Than This / World In My Eyes / Possession / Out Of This World (Oakenfold Remix) / Maybe Someday / Coming Up / Signal To Noise (Acoustic Version) / Signal To Noise / Just Say Yes (Curve Remix) / A Forest (Plati/Slick Version)

The Cure

Geffen June 2004

Lost / Labyrinth / Before Three / The End Of The World / Anniversary / Us Or Them / alt.end / (I Don't Know What's Going) On / Talking Off / Never / The Promise / Going Nowhere

Faith

Rhino April 2005

The Holy Hour / Primary / Other Voices / All Cats Are Grey / The Funeral Party / Doubt / The Drowning Man / Faith / *Carnage Visors:* The Soundtrack / Faith / Doubt / Drowning / The Holy Hour / Primary / Going Home Time / The Violin Song / A Normal Story /

All Cats Are Grey (live) / The Funeral Party (live) / Other Voices (live) / The Drowning Man (live) / Faith (live) / Forever (live) / Charlotte Sometimes

Seventeen Seconds

Rhino April 2005

A Reflection / Play For Today / Secrets / In Your House / Three / The Final Sound / A Forest / M / At Night / Seventeen Seconds / I'm A Cult Hero / I Dig You / Another Journey By Train / Secrets / Seventeen Seconds / In Your House (Live in Amsterdam) / Three /I Dig You / I'm A Cult Hero / M / The Final Sound / A Reflection / Play For Today / At Night (Live in France) / A Forest

Pornography

Rhino April 2005

One Hundred Years / A Short Term Effect / The Hanging Garden / Siamese Twins / The Figurehead / A Strange Day / Cold / Pornography / Break / Demise / Temptation / The Figurehead / The Hanging Garden / One Hundred Years / *Airlock:* The Soundtrack / Cold (live) / A Strange Day (live) / Pornography (live) / All Mine (live) / A Short Term Effect (live) / Siamese Twins (live) / Temptation Two (aka LGTB)

For complete discography up to March 1994 see: *The Cure On Record* by Daren Butler (Omnibus Press 1995) and www.allmusic.com

Videography

Staring At The Sea: The Images

Pvc May 1986

Killing An Arab / 10.15 Saturday Night / Boys Don't Cry / Jumping Someone Else's Train / A Forest / Play For Today / Primary / Other Voices / Charlotte Sometimes / The Hanging Garden / Let's Go To Bed / The Walk / The Lovecats / The Caterpillar / Inbetween Days / Close To Me / A Night Like This

In Orange

Elektra/Asylum 1988

Picture Show

Elektra/Asylum 1991

Why Can't I Be You? / Catch / Hot Hot Hot!!! / Just Like Heaven / Lullaby / Fascination Street / Lovesong / Pictures Of You / Never Enough / Close To Me (closer mix)

The Cure Play Out

Elektra 1992

Wendy Time / The Big Hand / Away / Let's Go To Bed / A Strange Day / Pictures Of You / Fascination Street / Lullaby / A Forest / The Blood / The Walk / A Letter To Elise / Boys Don't Cry / Never Enough

Side Show

Elektra/Asylum November 1993 (Australia and the USA only)

Show / Tape / Just Like Heaven / Fascination Street / The Walk / Let's Go To Bed

Galore

Elektra/Asylum November 1997

Why Can't I Be You? / Catch / Just Like Heaven / Hot Hot Hot!!! / Lullaby / Fascination Street / Lovesong / Pictures Of You / Never Enough / Close To Me / High / Friday I'm In Love / A Letter To Elise / The 13th / Mint Car / Strange Attraction / Gone! / Wrong Number

Websites

Bootleg list

www.musicfanclubs.org/cure/boots/bootindex.html

Official website

www.thecure.com

Other useful websites

www.musicfanclubs.org/cure/
www.curiosity.de/
www.thecure.netfirms.com/17seconds.html
www.plainsong.net/
ourworld.compuserve.com/homepages/ChainofFlowers/

Index

Singles are in roman type and albums in italics

1 2 3 4 5 6 7 8 9